GLENN J.
DORN

# PERONISTAS
# AND NEW DEALERS

U.S.-ARGENTINE RIVALRY

AND THE WESTERN HEMISPHERE

(1946-1950)

UNIVERSITY PRESS
OF
THE SOUTH

2024

Copyright 2024 by Glenn J. Dorn.

All rights reserved. No part of this publication may be reproduced, stored in a retrieval system, or transmitted, in any form or by any means, electronic, mechanical, photocopying, recording or otherwise, without the prior written permission of the Publisher.

Published in the United States by University Press of the South. Printed in the Netherlands by BookMundo.

E-mails: unprsouth@aol.com; punouveaumonde@gmail.com

Visit our award-winning web pages:   www.unprsouth.com

www.punouveaumonde.com

Glenn J. Dorn.

Peronistas and New Dealers. U.S.-Argentine Rivalry and the Western Hemisphere (1946-1950).

First Edition in English: ISBN: 978-1-931948-28-9 (2005) with University Press of the South, USA.

Second Edition in English.

Latin American Studies Series, 76.

338 Pages.

Front Cover Art: 'Juan and Eva Peron in Open Car,' by Bettmann. Reproduced with Permission.

1) History. 2) Twentieth Century. 3) International Relations. 4) Argentine.

5) Juan and Eva Peron. 6) Truman Administration. 7) U.S.-Argentine Relations.

8) Peronistas.  9) New Dealers.  10) Glenn J. Dorn.

ISBN: 978-1-952799-55-6

For Mary Dorn

# TABLE OF CONTENTS

Acknowledgements……………………………,……………......vii

1. Introduction……………………………………………………......1

2. "Public Enemy #1 of the Imperialistic Consortiums:"
   The Rise of Perón……………………………………………...…......25

3. Looking for a "Good Stick:" March-June 1946……………....…..59

4. "On the Wrong Road with Very Good Intentions:"
   Messersmith and Perón, June-September 1946………………….…..95

5. Consolidating Power: The Five-Year Plan and the
   Capture of Labor…………………...………………………………...127

6. "Into the Jaws of the Wolf:" Peronist Diplomacy and
   the Inter-American System……………………….....……………….161

7. The Changing of the Guard: January-July 1947……………….......203

8. The Beginning of the End of the Peronist Challenge
   August 1947-December 1948…………………………………….....235

9. Peronismo Penitent: January-December 1949……………….....265

10. Conclusion……………………………………………………..299

Bibliography………………………………………………………313

Index……………………………………………………………….329

First and foremost, I wish to thank Michael Hogan, my mentor at Ohio State, for giving me a chance at the start and providing excellent advice and guidance all along. I must also thank Carlos Escudé, Peter Hahn, Edward Ingram, Leonor Machinandiarena de Devoto, Alan McPherson, Lynette Porter, G. Micheal Riley, David Sheinin, David Steigerwald, William O. Walker III, and Randall B. Woods for their many invaluable insights, suggestions, and critiques. Any shortcomings of or errors in this volume are, of course, mine alone.

I will always be grateful to the staffs of the U.S. National Archives, the Truman Presidential Library, the Walter Reuther Center, the Clemson University Library, the M. P. Catherwood Center, the University of Delaware Library, the Lilly Library, and the University of Maryland Library. I also wish to thank Carlos Dellepiane of the Archivo del Ministerio de Relaciones Exteriores y Culto, Patricia Chomnalez of the Fundación Simon Rodríguez, and the staff of the Instituto Torcuato DiTella, INDEC, ISEN, and the Biblioteca Nacional. Finally, I must express my gratitude to Manuel Rojas and his staff at the Torre Tagle who operate the most efficient archive it has ever been my pleasure to visit. I would also like to thank Alain Saint-Saens and the staff at the University Press of the South for their efforts. The patience and expertise of these individuals made this project truly enjoyable.

I would be remiss if I did not express my gratitude to those who helped lighten my load in Springfield, Columbus, Delaware, Daytona Beach, Buenos Aires, Lima, and all points in between. These include Pablo Bustos, Beth Dold, Carol Doubiken, Richard Hallenbeck, Hector Maldonado, Sylvia Pounds, Richard Spall, Beverly Terry, Paul Wittekind, and many other great folks. As well, I must thank Bob Oxley and Nancy Parker, department chairs who supported this research, Jim Libbey and Steven Craft, exceptional colleagues, and the students, past and present, who have made every day an adventure.

I owe special thanks to Jeff, Kathy, Gary and Cassandra Dorn, who have supported me throughout. Finally, I must offer my eternal gratitude and deepest apologies to Mary for enduring this project over the years. Without her patience, love, and unwavering support throughout, nothing would have been possible.

# CHAPTER 1

## INTRODUCTION

> I have been witnessing one of the most dramatic and interesting social experiments in the history of the world—*"Peronismo"*—an effort to create changes in the economy of a country in four short years that should, under even a less ill-adroit government, take at least 20 years; a strange mixture of nationalism, dictatorship and paternalism which may produce a great social result—if the whole laboratory does not blow up.
>
> Stanton Griffis, 1 March 1950[1]

### I

Put simply, the election of Juan Domingo Perón to the Argentine presidency in February 1946 was nothing less than the beginning of a dramatic if ill-fated challenge to U.S. hegemony in the Western Hemisphere. Perón rose to power advocating a populist, yet authoritarian, path to economic development that relied upon state corporatist organizational controls; the elevation of the masses; bilateral, state-guided trade; and a determined foreign policy calculated to erode the power and influence of the United States. Every facet of this program was a direct threat to U.S. policymakers who sought to erect a global order based upon limited government intervention in the economy, liberal capitalism, privatist economic growth, multilateral trade, and their own dominance over the Western Hemisphere. In short, the emergence of Perón's alternative spawned a systemic clash between rival

---

1. Griffis to Truman, 1 March 1950, President's Secretary File, Foreign Affairs, Argentina, Harry S. Truman Presidential Library, Independence, Missouri (HST).

ideological models for national development in the Americas, just as European fascism and Soviet communism had done globally.

By viewing U.S. dealings with Perón as a multi-layered political, economic, and ideological struggle between two rival corporatist models, it becomes possible to better understand the battle that dominated U.S.-Latin American relations for five years. New Dealers in the United States, to use terminology employed by Guillermo O'Donnell, adhered to a unique brand of "privatist corporatism" featuring relatively weak but clear links between the public and private sector, a broker state capable of arbitrating disputes without the use of overwhelming coercive power, and the dominance of the capitalist class *vis-à-vis* labor.[2] Peronists, on the other hand, responded to the global crises of the 1930s and 1940s with a "statizing corporatism" that overturned the dominance of the capitalist class through a decidedly populist state apparatus and the implementation of far more rigid regulatory controls. Although both Peronists and New Dealers shared the desire to solve their nations' problems through corporatist organization, the variants they employed proved to be dramatically different.

Corporatism could be defined as a socio-political and economic system that organizes individuals and functional groups into a coherent, at least semi-formalized, structure to bring order and stability to the whole, or to borrow again from O'Donnell's definition, as "a set of structures which link society with the state." An outgrowth of medieval guilds and patron-client relationships, corporatism is nonetheless a modern phenomenon designed to deal with the problems faced by industrialized or industrializing nations. To control, regulate, or coordinate the activities of all sectors within the diverse modern nation-state, policymakers across the globe erected institutional links between the public and private sectors in the 1920s and 1930s. Peronists drew from a familiar Southern European and Latin American tradition of state corporatism, rooted in Roman Catholic thought, that permitted the imposition of the state into the private sphere on a grand scale,

---

2. Guillermo A. O'Donnell, "Corporatism and the Question of the State," *Authoritarianism and Corporatism in Latin America*, ed. James Malloy (Pittsburgh, 1977) 48-87.

whereas the corporatism that emerged in the United States during and after the New Deal reflected both the individualism and the deep-seated, reflexive fear of excessive state power that had long been U.S. hallmarks.

Not surprisingly, U.S. foreign policy evolved from the needs and principles of its corporate order, as diplomatic historians such as Michael J. Hogan, Joan Hoff, Charles Maier, and Carl Parrini have shown. Clearly, at least three generations of U.S. policymakers after World War I labored to "export the American Way" of free trade, corporate capitalism, and liberal democracy.[3] If Inter-American relations are examined with special attention to the role of the state in the domestic order of given nations, it is possible to see this connection and interplay between domestic and foreign policy clearly. The protracted campaign that U.S. leaders launched to unseat Perón must be seen as both an extension of their efforts during World War II to eradicate all vestiges of the rival socio-economic system developed by European fascists and as a regional manifestation of their drive to extend privatist corporatism globally. In this context, U.S. policy in Latin America can be understood as one facet of a global approach, firmly rooted in the domestic order adopted by the New Dealers in the 1930s, but heavily nuanced to fit local conditions.

On the other hand, Perón's efforts to implant state corporatism in Argentina must also be viewed as a direct and conscious repudiation of that same privatist approach, of U.S. efforts to disseminate that system and, not coincidentally, an outgrowth of the revolutionary domestic order he had built. For Perón, whose loyalty was primarily to a dual constituency of the Army and the working class, a powerful state apparatus was vital to promote national industrial development and the elevation of both

---

3. Joan Hoff, *American Business and Foreign Policy, 1920-1933* (Lexington, 1971); Michael J. Hogan, *The Marshall Plan: America, Britain, and the Reconstruction of Western Europe* (Cambridge, 1988) and *Informal Entente: The Private Structure of Cooperation in Anglo-American Diplomacy* (Columbia, 1977); Charles Maier, *Recasting Bourgeois Europe: Stabilization in France, Germany, and Italy in the Decade after World War I* (Princeton, 1975); Carl Parrini, *Heir to Empire: United States Economic Diplomacy, 1916-1923* (Pittsburgh, 1969).

the nation and its masses. There was no place for *laissez faire* economics or the U.S.-style privatism it often resembled, as decades of both had only promoted the interests of the agro-pastoral and commercial elite and its foreign allies.[4] Whereas the New Deal had to some extent been created to avert both communist revolution and fascist syndicalism, Perón was borrowing the rhetoric of the former and a number of the corporatist underpinnings of the latter.

Despite what the protagonists in North or South America may have believed, this was not a simple contest between the forces of democracy and dictatorship, oligarchy and democracy, totalitarianism and freedom, or imperialism and liberation. Rather, it was a clash between two corporatist variants, related yet quite distinct. Without understanding both the New Deal order in the United States and Perón's vision for Argentina, it is impossible to get beyond the rhetoric and propaganda and to understand the deeper implications of this conflict that shaped the next twenty years of inter-American relations.

## II

Although hardly a radical departure from the policies of the Republicans' New Era of the 1920s, the New Deal did bring to the fore new and important innovations that had lasting effects upon foreign policy. As scholars such as Thomas Ferguson, Ellis Hawley, Michael Hogan, and Kim McQuaid noted, the figures comprising Roosevelt's "Brains Trust" inherited many of their conceptual assumptions from the "associational" state forwarded by

---

4. Hugo Gambini, *La primera presidencia de Perón: testimonios y documentos* (Buenos Aires, 1983); Alejandro Horowicz, *Los cuatros peronismos* (Buenos Aires, 1985); Joel Horowitz, "Industrialists and the Rise of Perón," *The Americas* Volume XLVII (October 1990), 199-217; Paul Lewis, *The Crisis of Argentine Capitalism* (Chapel Hill, 1990); Peter Waldmann, *El peronismo, 1943-1955.* (Buenos Aires, 1986); Gary Wynia, *Argentina in the Post-War Period: Politics and Economic Policymaking in a Divided Society* (Albuquerque, 1978); Pablo Gerchunoff, "Peronist Economic Policies, 1946-1955" *The Political Economy of Argentina, 1946-1983*, ed. Guido DiTella and Rudiger Dornbusch (Pittsburgh, 1989) 58-85.

Herbert Hoover. Their faith in technocratic, scientific solutions to the traditionally political problems of society and their belief in limited, but positive, government intervention in a fundamentally liberal capitalist economy represents much more of an evolution than revolution.[5]

By accident or design, the New Deal order eventually brought stability, growth, a loose corporatist structure, and a new role for government to the United States. Arguing that the *laissez faire* of the nineteenth century and Hoover's weak voluntarist associationalism had been inadequate to prevent disastrous boom-bust cycles or provide stable growth that would undercut radicalism, the New Dealers strengthened the corporatist linkages between state and society. Although rejecting outright the corporatist language and centrality of the state that was increasingly associated with European fascism, New Dealers nonetheless found themselves using the federal government as a tool for organization, coordination, and positive intervention.

Indeed, the centerpiece of Roosevelt's first New Deal, the National Industrial Recovery Act (NIRA), explicitly drew upon corporatist assumptions by establishing industrial councils representing government, business, labor, and consumers. The NIRA may have gone farther toward state corporatism than most in the United States were willing to go, but the New Dealers persisted in their efforts to use the national government as a tool to preserve the essence of a capitalist system even after its failure.

With the "broker state" acting as arbiter, the private sphere could be influenced constructively without the control exerted by dictatorship, or a European-style corporatist regime dominated by an overweening, if not totalitarian, state. The coordination and organization of this minimalist privatist corporatism could, it was hoped, eliminate the economic dislocations, social discord, and

---

5. Thomas Ferguson, "From Normalcy to New Deal: Industrial Structure, Party Competition, and American Public Policy in the Great Depression," *International Organization* 38 (Winter 1984), 41-98; Ellis Hawley, *The New Deal and the Problem of Monopoly* (Cambridge, 1966), 3-52; Michael Hogan, *The Marshall Plan*, 1-25; Kim McQuaid, *Big Business and Corporate Power, from FDR to Reagan* (New York, 1982), 18-60.

class conflict that periodically emerged—putting to death any lingering romantic attachment to a mythical *laissez faire* economy in the process. Self-interest was to be redirected and ameliorated, but not eliminated as the "politics of productivity" expanded the economic pie for all sectors and defused radicalism through shared prosperity. Furthermore, the linkages between state and society were strengthened through new coordinating organizations and institutions but remained loose enough to retain the much-heralded freedom of liberal capitalism. The New Deal had the backing of a powerful bloc of "capital-intensive" firms, progressive businessmen, and organized labor, and although it did not create a fully corporatized state, neither did it allow a disorganized society once again to plunge itself into depression and chaos.[6]

Just as the New Deal had effected a lasting transformation in the domestic sphere, so it did with the nation's foreign policy. After defeating the protectionist visions of Raymond Moley and George Peek by 1934, Secretary of State Cordell Hull embarked upon a campaign to revolutionize world trade. Having drunk deeply from the Wilsonian well, Hull reasoned that "unhampered trade dovetailed with peace; high tariffs, trade barriers and unfair economic competition with war." Since his days as a Tennessee Senator, Hull had been an ardent advocate of full currency convertibility and relatively unfettered, multilateral commerce. Arguing that protectionism amounted to "economic suicide," Hull believed that the Great Depression could be ended only with the re-establishment of world trade—a cause to which he tirelessly devoted the State Department throughout the 1930s. The "capital-intensive" firms that had proved invaluable to the New Deal coalition echoed his sentiments, as did progressive labor

---

6. Charles Maier, "The Politics of Productivity: Foundations of American International Economic Policy after World War II" *International Organization* 31 (Autumn 1977), 607-633; Edward D. Berkowitz and Kim McQuaid, *Creating the Welfare State: The Political Economy of Twentieth Century Reform* (New York, 1980), 78-133; Robert M. Collins, *The Business Response to Keynes, 1929-1964* (New York, 1984); Ferguson, "From Normalcy," 41-98; McQuaid, *Big Business*, 18-60.

organizations who shared his hope that the expansion of foreign commerce might serve as a solution to underemployment.[7]

Hull's Wilsonian vision had even more important and far-reaching repercussions. "[It] must not be overlooked," he noted, "that the most moving and impelling influence supporting dictators' ambitions is unemployment and distress among the masses." Although he permitted exceptions, "it is a general rule that the single largest cause of riots, revolutions, and wars of aggression is a people in severe economic distress." Furthermore, dictatorships such as Hitler's Germany, which arose from the "distress of the masses," utilized "unfair" trading tactics and paralleled their domestic tyranny with "piracy" on the international markets. By diverting trade from private business and toward Dr. Hjalmar Schacht's Reichsbank and using the proceeds to prepare for a "war of aggression," Nazi Germany had been Hull's worst nightmare. Driven by the advantages that it gained from totalitarian domination of the national economy and trade, Germany's economic and military expansion had supplanted the investment and trade of the liberal capitalist powers throughout the 1930s. For Hull, the lesson was clear—depression led to dictatorship, which spawned "economic warfare" that degenerated all too readily into actual war. Dictatorship, oppression, autarchy, and war were inextricably linked, as were democracy, free trade, and peace. The "political line-up followed the economic line-up," as Hull put it.[8]

Although Hull left the State Department in 1944, his heirs shared his commitment to free, multilateral trade and the spread of U.S.-style democracy across the globe: a system compatible with the needs of the "capital-intensive" New Deal coalition. Indeed, all of these leaders had witnessed the Great Depression, the rise of

---

7. Cordell Hull, *Memoirs of Cordell Hull* (New York, 1948), 81, 352-368, 374-381; see also Lloyd Gardner, *Economic Aspects of New Deal Diplomacy* (Boston, 1968), 24-46; Ronald Radosh, *American Labor and United States Foreign Policy* (New York, 1969), 348-452.

8. Hull, *Memoirs*, 234-265; see also Gardner, *Economic Aspects*; Patrick Hearden, *Roosevelt Confronts Hitler: America's Entry into World War II* (DeKalb, 1987), 22-87, 155-189; Callum MacDonald, *The United States, Britain and Appeasement* (London, 1980).

fascism and nazism, and World War II. All had seen the horrors that totalitarianism and autarchy brought and sought to forge a postwar order based on multilateral trade and democratic capitalism. Assistant Secretary of State William Clayton, the foremost of Hull's successors, perhaps best typifies the ethos of free trade. Arising, ironically, from one of the most-protected industries in the United States, the Texas cotton magnate and vigorous free trader emerged as one of the dominant personalities in the administration of Harry S. Truman.

Like Hull, Clayton claimed that "there are only two economic courses open to the countries of the world." "They can continue on a nationalistic bilateral barter system, patterned along the lines developed so intensely by Nazi Germany," he asserted, or "they can go back to the multilateral basis where every country is free to trade with every other country with a minimum of restrictions and discriminations."[9] The first course would inevitably force the U.S. government to more tightly control the domestic economy to the point where it was "very doubtful" if liberal capitalism or "democracy would survive." It was therefore of vital importance that U.S. policymakers make use of their unrivaled position in the post-war world to impose a global order based on the second alternative as simple national self-interest dovetailed with an idealistic global vision of peace and prosperity.[10]

Whereas Hull's simple *laissez faire* approach had been somewhat out of step with the New Deal's focus upon the coordinating institutions of privatist corporatism, his successors determined to rectify this incongruity. For Clayton, Dean Acheson, and others in the Truman Administration, World War II had emphatically reinforced the lessons that the autarchic, zero-sum economics of the 1930s had driven the world to war. When given the chance to renovate the global economy, launch the *Pax*

---

9. Frederick J. Dobney ed., *Selected Papers of Will Clayton* (Baltimore, 1978), 160.

10. Dobney, *Selected Papers*, 53-55; see also Gregory Fossedal, *Our Finest Hour: Will Clayton, the Marshall Plan and the Triumph of Democracy* (Stanford, 1993).

*Americana*, and thereby create a world in which their own democratic institutions could flourish, these leaders naturally opted to use the same New Deal solutions that had ably undercut radicalism in the United States. Their efforts, revealed in the Marshall Plan to rebuild Europe and in financial innovations such as the General Agreement on Tariffs and Trade (GATT) and the International Trade Organization (ITO), demonstrate remarkable consistency in this regard. The principles they would use in this grand project were Hull's and Clayton's—multilateralism, free trade, and liberal capitalism bolstered by privatist corporatism. Their efforts unfolded differently in various regions, but these distinctions should not obscure the fundamental consistency that undergirded them all.[11]

In Western Europe, the Truman Administration was not content to merely rebuild war-devastated economies. The continent had to be reconstituted in a fashion that would prevent the re-emergence of dictatorship, cutthroat competition, and war. With these goals in mind, U.S. leaders placed at least as much emphasis upon the integration of a revitalized Germany into a harmonized continental economy that conformed roughly to U.S. values as they did on containing the menace of Soviet expansionism. The Marshall Plan attempted to create supranational bodies to organize this integration and to bring national policies into line with their concept of corporate liberalism, including the support for modest social welfare policies, labor-management partnerships, progressive fiscal policies, and liberalized trade. Rather predictably, Marshall Planners such as Acheson, Clayton, Paul Hoffman, and George Marshall chose to solve post-war dilemmas with a dual prescription of expanded trade and a "Europe made the American way."[12]

U.S. efforts in Asia also aimed to create a web of multilateralism and structures that could withstand inevitable economic fluctuations and deter radicalism. The occupying

---

11. Hogan, *The Marshall Plan*, 2-25; Maier, "The Politics of Productivity," 607-633; Thomas J. McCormick, *America's Half-Century: United States Foreign Policy and the Cold War* (Baltimore, 1991).

12. Hogan, *The Marshall Plan*.

authorities in Japan, for example, tried to recreate elements of the New Deal in Asia, sacrificing anti-monopolism and punitive measures against the Japanese to better fit Japan into the new global economy. They envisioned Japan, like Western Europe, as the center of a stable regional economy that would prevent the spread of communism, promote multilateral trade, and reduce the need for militaristic expansion. In essence, U.S. policymakers viewed Japan as the hub of an east Asian economy, just as did pre-war Japanese planners, but this time it would be based upon U.S. principles of democracy and open commerce.[13]

Just as Japan, England, and Western Europe were to stand as regional bastions of liberal capitalism and centers of the world economy, so too was the United States, as the self-appointed policeman, banker, and arbiter for the Western Hemisphere "Good Neighborhood." As the hemispheric manifestation of the New Deal, Roosevelt's Good Neighbor policy was, like the New Deal itself, hardly the dramatic reversal of prior policy its architects thought it to be. Put in its simplest terms, the Good Neighbor policy was a U.S. pledge not to intervene unilaterally south of the Rio Grande. Seeking to undo the damage done to hemispheric relations by Theodore Roosevelt's "big stick," Wilsonian interventionism, and the "dollar diplomats" of the 1920s, Franklin Roosevelt tried to put a pretty face upon U.S. hegemony over the region by renouncing its most obnoxious manifestation in the hope that Latin Americans would come to view the United States as a beneficent protector, rather than a feared juggernaut. The Good Neighbor policy seemed to be vindicated during the Second World War, when most of Latin America cooperated, more or less willingly, with the Allied war effort.

Through the rhetorical continuation of the Good Neighbor principle of non-intervention in the post-war period, U.S. officials hoped to assuage Latin American fears of *yanqui* imperialism, while

---

13. William S. Borden, *The Pacific Alliance: United States Foreign Economic Policy and Japanese Trade Recovery, 1947-1955* (Madison, 1984); Michael Schaller, *The American Occupation of Japan: The Origins of the Cold War in Asia* (New York, 1984); Howard Schonberger, *Aftermath of War: Americans and the Remaking of Japan, 1945-1952* (Kent, 1989).

private U.S. capital did the rest. In theory, progressive U.S. businessmen, tempered by New Deal wisdom, were to replace the exploitative "robber barons" that had plundered the south, provided a fertile field for revolution, and sullied the name of the United States. All that was needed was a safe and stable climate for U.S. investment, whereupon modernization along sound private lines could then proceed. If successful, revolutionary nationalists would no longer be able to call for the expropriation of foreign investment or rally the masses to their standards. Even if few Latin American nations possessed a U.S.-style democratic government, the extant oligarchic regimes could adequately serve as caretakers and generally be counted upon to cooperate with the United States.[14]

Consistent with their global vision of shared prosperity, the New Dealers argued that the United States would benefit from the economic development of Latin America. Indeed, they lamented that U.S. exports to Canada far outpaced those to Latin America and regularly noted that their best trading partners were industrialized, urbanized nations with the wealth and population to absorb massive amounts of U.S. exports. To paraphrase Roosevelt, if Jesus Fernandes in Rio de Janeiro earned higher wages, he could afford to buy more goods that Bob Jones produced in Chicago. Although critics argued that Latin American industrialization might cut into U.S. markets, New Dealers denounced such thinking as regressive and shortsighted. Just as some North American businesses and workers would be hurt by the restoration of the competitive European industry envisioned by the Marshall Planners,

---

14. Irwin F. Gellman, *Good Neighbor Diplomacy: United States Policies in Latin America, 1933-1945* (Baltimore, 1979); David Green, *The Containment of Latin America: Myths and Realities of the Good Neighbor Policy* (Chicago, 1971); and "The Cold War Comes to Latin America," *Politics and Policies of the Truman Administration*, ed. Barton Bernstein (Chicago, 1970) 149-195; Michael Grow, *The Good Neighbor Policy and Authoritarianism in Paraguay: United States Economic Expansion and Great-Power Rivalry in Latin America during World War II* (Lawrence, KS, 1981); Robert Potash, *Arms and Politics in Argentina: Perón to Frondizi* (Stanford, 1980), 46-89; Bryce Wood, *The Dismantling of the Good Neighbor Policy* (Austin, 1985); Gerald K. Haines, "Under the Eagle's Wing: The Franklin Roosevelt Administration Forges an American Hemisphere," *Diplomatic History* I (Fall 1977), 370-388.

so Latin American industrialization would temporarily cause dislocations and difficulties in the United States as small or relatively inefficient businesses paid the price of heightened competition. In the end, however, the benefits of the increased efficiency and productivity of a stable, industrialized Latin America would far outweigh these short-term obstacles, as the transnational ties developed by the increase in commerce would only cement hemispheric unity. By transforming the economic nationalism and competition of the 1930s into the search for shared prosperity in the post-war period, U.S. policymakers asserted that this "Inter-American system" was every bit as progressive as the ITO, the GATT, and the Marshall Plan.[15]

Still, U.S. efforts in Latin America differed from their European endeavors in one critical respect. While the Truman Administration dedicated itself to erecting an intricate web of supranational institutions to promote privatist corporatism in Europe, U.S. policies in Latin America appeared to be little more than efforts to spread primitive *laissez faire*. U.S. leaders were quite willing to grant a multi-billion-dollar loan to bring Great Britain around to the principles of multilateralism and to spend almost thirteen billion dollars to transplant the New Deal to Europe. However, as Elizabeth Anne Cobbs noted, they did not make good on their promise to "export corporatist ideology" to Latin America because it was "too expensive and too innovative." Because Latin America was neither on the front lines of the battle with communism nor as economically critical to the United States as Europe, she posits, the Truman Administration contented itself with *laissez faire* and the status quo in the south. The European status quo had twice been the forge of catastrophic world wars, providing an impetus for urgent, dramatic action that simply did not exist in Latin America.[16]

Unwilling to expend either the money or the effort necessary for a Marshall Plan in the south, U.S. policymakers

---

15. Green, *The Containment of Latin America*, 128

16. Elizabeth Anne Cobbs, *The Rich Neighbor Policy: Rockefeller and Kaiser in Brazil* (New Haven, 1992) 13, 236-248.

instead followed an expedient course of simply discouraging statist forms of corporatist organization for fear that it might easily mutate into economic nationalism. After all, Truman's administration was staffed by the same men who had watched the dynamic state-driven economic growth of Nazi Germany, Imperial Japan, and Fascist Italy catapult the world into war. If these men were unable or unwilling to effectively promote the creation of an ideal New Deal framework in Latin America, at least they could actively and efficiently discourage the "wrong path" of statism. In other words, the State Department was willing to countenance economic underdevelopment, negligible economic growth, or simple "man-on-a-horse" dictatorship in Latin America that ran counter to cherished democratic principles, so long as the hemisphere did not tread too far down the path of economic statism. To the men who had steered the nation through the disastrous years of the 1930s and early 1940s, it could hardly have been otherwise. The proponents of the Good Neighbor policy may well have been, as Michael Grow demonstrated, "liberal imperialists" dedicated to spreading U.S. influence deep into South America, but after World War II, they were also idealistically driven to leave a legacy of stability, peace and prosperity.[17]

U.S. leaders, unwilling to make a major commitment to reform in the south, therefore found themselves advocating narrow anti-statism and a purer capitalism than they themselves practiced. Latin America, they argued with characteristic paternalism, lacked both the political maturity and the economic infrastructure for its own New Deal, but foreign investment and U.S guidance would eventually bring both. Although distasteful, the often corrupt or repressive ruling oligarchies seemed capable of providing the stability necessary for economic growth that would profit U.S. investors and Latin Americans alike. Even though decades of relatively pure market capitalism had done little to advance Latin America, progressive businessmen such as Nelson Rockefeller and Henry Kaiser firmly believed that their "enlightened" practices would eventually do so. In effect, they and their proponents in Washington promised that the liberal capitalist status quo would

---

17. Grow, *The Good Neighbor and Authoritarianism in Paraguay,* 113-118.

eventually bring progress, if all involved simply had the patience to allow it to flower.[18]

From this perspective, it is both possible and profitable to examine U.S.-Latin American relations through the lens of corporatism. It would not be unfair to characterize the U.S. campaign against Perón as a disagreement over issues such as the degree of state intervention; the strength, formality, and nature of public-private ties; and the hierarchies of functional groups within society. These fundamentally corporatist concerns dominated—as they still dominate—political thought in every nation of the Western Hemisphere. Latin Americans, like their North American counterparts, were wrestling with these questions in their search for viable organizational techniques that would provide economic growth and social stability. That Latin Americans like Perón found alternatives very different from the New Deal is hardly surprising. Given the preoccupation of U.S. foreign policymakers with the role of the state and their arrogant, almost messianic impulse to aggressively disseminate their system, neither should it be remarkable that this approach led to friction. This goes some distance toward explaining how U.S. leaders who undeniably practiced a neocolonial dominance over the hemisphere did so with clean consciences, confident that they were ushering in a glorious new era of peace and prosperity.

It is, on the other hand, difficult to argue, as Cobbs did, that because U.S. policymakers did very little to encourage their own brand of corporatism in Latin America, corporatist analysis can not explain U.S. policies toward Latin America. On the contrary, the fundamental goal of the "Inter-American system" after World War II was to prevent the emergence of state corporatism, even if the New Dealers were unwilling to do much to sponsor their own variant. When Perón put forward his program, U.S. policymakers viewed it as at once a tragic legacy of the European fascism they knew all too well, a redistributive appeal vaguely reminiscent of communism, a dangerous mutation of classic Latin American nationalism, and the opening salvo of a new challenge to the hemispheric status quo.

---

18. Cobbs, *The Rich Neighbor Policy*.

### III

Like his New Deal counterparts, Perón advertised his corporatist variant, eventually labeled *justicialismo*, as a comprehensive social philosophy and economic program that could solve most of Latin America's problems. The guiding premise of *justicialismo* was that Argentina's traditional agro-pastoral and commercial oligarchs, in collusion with foreign accomplices, had through liberal capitalism monopolized wealth, inhibited national development, impoverished the great mass of citizens, and perpetuated itself in power through corrupt elections that allowed it to continue to loot the national patrimony under a democratic facade. The state, Perón asserted, had an obligation to guarantee "social justice" to all it represented in the short term and provide economic development to make it last in the long term. Because private capital and a weak national government had been able neither to sustain economic growth nor equitably distribute wealth, Perón argued, a powerful national government was necessary to guide the nation through the painful process of industrialization at the same time it meted out "social justice."[19]

In this, Perón consciously echoed the state corporatist solutions that the Catholic Church itself had advocated on more than one occasion. Trying to find an acceptable middle road between traditionalism and liberalism, late-19th and early-20th century Catholic thinkers had bought into corporatist organizational notions. With the Papal *Rerum Novarum* (1890) and *Quadragesimo Anno* (1931), Catholic intellectuals put forward an alternative pattern of development that could harness the forces unleashed by liberalism and modernization. Paternalism and organizational control seemed to be far more fitting to Latin

---

19. Perón, *La comunidad organizada* (Buenos Aires, 1949); Griffiths to Cabot, 6 December 1945, General Records of the Department of State, National Archives II, College Park, Maryland, Record Group 59 (RG 59), 835.00; see also Ray to Secretary of State, 31 July 1947, Record Group 84, Records of the Foreign Service Posts of the United States of America, Embassy in Buenos Aires, National Archives II, College Park, MD (RG 84, BA); Paul Lewis, *The Crisis of Argentine Capitalism*, 138-139.

American and Southern European traditions than Anglo-Saxon liberal parliamentary forms. When socialism emerged as a powerful force for change, altering old dialectics and shattering the traditional order, Catholic corporatist thought adapted to the new reality and remained a viable middle way for those who found Marxism repugnant, but acknowledged the need for social justice in the materialistic age of industrialization.[20]

The political polarization of Latin America further strengthened the drive toward a state corporatist solution. Privatist corporatism, as the New Deal demonstrated, was evolutionary, moderate, and relatively static. However, state corporatism, as Mussolini and Hitler had shown, could be harnessed to revolutionary rhetoric to mobilize mass support for dramatic changes, at the same time its authoritarian component blocked counterrevolution and placed limits upon the extent of revolutionary change. If Roman Catholicism had provided a buttress against atheistic communism, it had done little to ameliorate the basic maldistribution of wealth that spawned radicalism. Indeed, through state corporatism, it had provided an outlet for that radicalism into a socio-economic system capable of both dynamic change and iron-fisted control.

The Peronist coalition reflected this quite well. Melding nationalistic Army officers, an invigorated labor union movement, elements of the Church and middle classes, and the disenfranchised urban *descamisados* ("shirtless ones"), Perón steamrolled an alliance of the old Argentine political parties and the U.S. government in the 1946 election. Naturally, his regime served the interests of his constituencies, just as previous governments had operated for the benefit of the agro-pastoral elite. For Army officers, Peronism offered the means by which the military could hold power and spearhead the drive toward industrialization without resorting to martial law, while mass discontent was

---

20. See Howard J. Wiarda's excellent discussion of the evolution of corporatist thought, *Corporatism and National Development in Latin America* (Boulder, 1980), and Robert Crassweller's specific discussion of Peronism and Catholic thought in *Peron and the Enigmas of Argentina* (New York, 1987), esp. 194-195.

channeled and controlled by the state. For workers, the emergence of Peronism promised a government sympathetic to their cause and quite active in bettering their material lot. For the urban masses, Perón offered social welfare measures far beyond anything ever seen in Argentina. For members of Argentina's burgeoning middle classes, Peronism broke elites' stranglehold on power, and the Church could look to Perón as a counterweight to both revolutionary Marxism and secular liberalism.[21]

Although Perón's coalition, and the victory it delivered to him in March 1946, illustrated how corporatist nationalists bloodlessly could take control of a nation, the true test was whether the Peronist state could deliver the benefits it promised. *Peronistas* argued that the state could better perform the role that private capital traditionally played in society. To prove it, Perón placed his officials directly into business boardrooms and banks, nationalized foreign-owned enterprises, and established government monopolies to coordinate and centralize growth. Industrialization was to be financed, fittingly, by the same agro-pastoral elites that had inhibited it for decades. The profits of grain and meat exports were to be funneled through "economic czar" Miguel Miranda's state import-export monopoly, the *Instituto Argentino para la Promoción del Intercambio* (IAPI), directly into state-controlled industrial development projects.

With IAPI imposing government control over foreign commerce, Peronists were able to regiment exports and imports, making extensive use of bilateral barter—as had the European fascists of the 1930s. Perón determined that "Argentina cannot, in the long run, continue to export only raw materials," if the "Argentine working man should gradually arrive at a standard of living just one-quarter as high as that of the average American working man." Similarly, he presaged dependency theory as he noted that "raw materials leave the shores of Argentina with a value of, say, four pesos have already acquired a value of twenty-four

---

21. Alberto Ciria, *Política y cultura popular: la Argentina peronista, 1946-1955* (Buenos Aires, 1983; Carlos Fayt, *Naturaleza de peronismo* (Buenos Aires, 1967); Hugo Gambini, *Historia del peronismo: el poder total, 1943-1955* (Buenos Aires, 1999); Juan José Sebreli, *Los deseos imaginarios del peronismo* (Madrid, 1983).

pesos when they reach the port of destination;" hence, his nation was "practically exporting labor." IAPI, as the spearhead of his leviathan state, was to be the vehicle by which the entire Argentine economy would be irrevocably transformed in five years.[22]

Once in power, Perón paralleled his economic planning by launching a campaign to renovate and reorganize Argentine society along corporatist lines. By organizing functional groups into hierarchical entities clearly subordinate to the state, he sought to stabilize the political process and channel discontent through "proper" lines with a minimum of disruption. Consciously modeled, Paul Lewis argued, after Mussolini's labor legislation, Perón's Law of Professional Organizations granted the state significant power over private institutions. Workers were funneled into a single labor federation, the *Confederación General de Trabajadores* (CGT), maintaining a formidable union presence strong enough to bolster Perón against opponents, yet pliable enough to be dominated by his appointees. High school students were eventually organized into the UES, professionals into the CGP (*Confederación General de Profesiones*), and the college community into the CGU (*Confederación General de Universidades*). Although he was unable ever to gain enough business cooperation to find an effective industrial counterpart to the CGT, his efforts to do so merit notice. While politics would continue as usual, with democratic forms and geographic representation for the time being, Perón apparently envisioned a day when all of Argentine society could function through the formal syndicates he was working to create. Clearly, although his efforts to corporatize Argentine society proceeded by fits and starts, the depth and formalization of Perón's organizational state stood in stark contrast to those of his New Deal counterparts.[23]

---

22. Embassy Buenos Aires to Secretary of State, 15 December 1945, 835.00; see also Antonio Cafiero, *Cinco años despues* (Buenos Aires, 1961), 203-239; Jorge Fodor, "Perón's Policies for Agricultural Exports," in *Argentina in the Twentieth Century*, ed. David Rock (London, 1985), 66-87; Alejandro Horowicz, *Los cuatros peronismos*, 108-109; *Review of the River Plate*, 30 August 1946, 3-6.

23. Paul Lewis, *Crisis of Argentine Capitalism*, 134-171.

Still, in and of itself, the Peronist revolution was of little consequence to the United States. Geographically distant, historically linked to Great Britain, and the site of little direct U.S. investment, Peronist Argentina offered no obvious threat to any vital interest of the United States. However, Peronist diplomacy threatened nothing less than U.S. dominance in South America, and the Truman Administration understood this perfectly. Just as U.S. foreign policy in the postwar period was dictated by the needs and goals of the New Deal coalition, Perón's "Third Position" between capitalism and communism clearly reflected his ambitions and was very much the product of his domestic agenda. Committed to industrialization and economic growth, Perón had serious obstacles to overcome. First and foremost, Argentina lacked many mineral resources necessary for the development of heavy industry—most notably, petroleum, iron ore, and coal. Second, Argentina's population of fourteen million did not provide a domestic market large enough to encourage the development of economies of scale, even for those goods Argentines could produce. The solution to these difficulties rested, Peronists believed, in a bold diplomacy that stressed regional economic integration and recognized the failure of decades of *laissez faire*—or as U.S. policymakers put it, on the creation of a "southern bloc."

Although Perón repeatedly denied it, he and his followers clearly envisioned the creation of a relatively autarchic "southern bloc," industrializing independent of the United States and utilizing state corporatism to meld the economies of the Southern Cone into one. If neighboring states, individually suffering from resource deficiencies, could be brought together through economic integration, the entire region could be uplifted. Mineral-rich nations like Bolivia, Chile, and Peru could gain unfettered access to Argentine food and capital, and nascent industries in each would be given access to a nearly continental market, insulated from fierce competition of more efficient and well-established North American or European exports. In time, all nations of the Southern Cone might be able to do what Perón was doing—using the profits from one or two raw materials to develop alternatives that could strengthen each nation and the region as a whole. Perón prophesied that "the year 2000 will find South America united or dominated" and was determined to provide the leadership for that unity.[24]

To realize this dream, he did possess several key assets. At the end of World War II, Perón inherited large quantities of foreign currency and financial reserves—the result of wartime food sales to the Allies. Argentina was also one of the few nations capable of exporting large quantities of food at a time when widespread famine was a distinct possibility. Last and far from least, by standing defiantly against "Wall Street Imperialism" and proposing a populist reform program, Peronists had earned at least the attention, and in a number of cases, the respect of anti-U.S. nationalists across the hemisphere.

Although most of Perón's post-war financial reserves were to be allocated within Argentina for the promotion of industry, Miguel Miranda offered a portion of them to neighboring states in the form of developmental credits as an inducement to create economic linkages in the region. To some extent, Miranda and Perón were bowing to necessity by offering loans and credits, as their trading partners in Latin America and war-torn Europe rarely had the funds available to purchase Argentine food. Still, with the United States preoccupied by European reconstruction, Peronist Argentina sought to step in as South America's financier and guide the region toward independent economic development. The United States had long used loans and credits as a means to spread its own political and economic system, and Argentina appeared, however briefly, poised to do the same. But just as financial assistance could serve as a carrot, so too could control over the region's foodstuffs be utilized as a stick. Through government control over food exports, Peronists applied pressure to recalcitrant neighbors by threatening to withhold vital shipments. With the ability to reward cooperative nations and leaders with financial assistance and punish recalcitrant ones with informal food embargoes, Argentina's efforts to alter the hemispheric status quo promised to be formidable.

The third arrow in Perón's quiver, however, was for the United States, the most threatening. Put simply, Perón was in many respects the foremost representative of a large, disparate, unfocused

---

24. Siracusa to Secretary of State, 22 January 1954, RG 59, 635.00.

reservoir of anti-United States, anti-capitalist resentment that had once been characterized by the nationalism of the Mexican Revolution and would later be manifested as Castro-style Marxism. If it could fulfill its promises, Peronism offered a model for these discontents, and a formula for escaping the phenomenon of dependency by using the state to uplift the masses, industrialize, and implant populistic democracy.[25] The Peronist model threatened to give opponents of the status quo a rallying cry, inspire traditionalist regimes toward the Peronist brand of corporatist experimentation, and quite possibly polarize the hemisphere.

Indeed, Perón worked actively to export *justicialismo* and his "Third Position" between capitalism and communism. Peronists dispatched labor attaches who transformed Argentine embassies in Latin America into distribution points for propaganda that vilified "Wall Street imperialism," which it contrasted with the real benefits that Perón and his wife, Eva, were bringing to the Argentine masses. At the same time, they worked to encourage mass agitation or rebellion, Peronists established ties with existing revolutionary groups such as the Bolivian MNR, anti-U.S. nationalists like Fidel Castro, and ambitious military men such as Chile's Carlos Ibañez del Campo, Peru's Manuel Odría, and Venezuela's Manuel Perez Jimenez, hoping to draw them into Perón's camp. While Perón worked to woo or coerce existing governments through a blend of financial assistance, propaganda, and "economic blackmail," beneath the surface of this conventional diplomacy lay a revolutionary appeal that augmented the already formidable array of weapons that Perón lined up against the "Inter-American system."

## IV

---

25. Green, *The Containment of Latin America*; Grow, *The Good Neighbor Policy and Authoritarianism in Paraguay*, 15-41; Albert Vannucci, "The Influence of Latin American Governments on the Shaping of United States Policy: The Case of Argentina, 1943-1948," *Journal of Latin American Studies* 16, 355-365.

For five years, the conflict between these two rival socio-economic models dominated and threatened, from Washington's perspective, to tear apart the Western Hemisphere. Naturally, Perón's reliance upon state trade, bilateral barter, and protectionism to create industries that were, to U.S. eyes, "unnatural" stood in stark contrast to the New Dealers' vision of regional specialization and multilateralism. For U.S. policymakers, who had perhaps forgotten the role that protectionism had played in promoting their own nation's industrialization, the creation of industries that required protection for survival only perpetuated dangerous statism. Eventually, these businesses would fail, dragging down the governments that had sponsored them. However, Perón explicitly rejected the analysis that South American nations should rely solely upon their own limited resources to create unbalanced, small economic units as he worked to unite them into a larger, perhaps continental, body dedicated to his unique brand of state corporatist growth. The result was a determined Argentine foreign policy that aimed to integrate economically the Southern Cone and thereby divide the hemisphere. Ironically, the same U.S. policymakers who were obstructing Peronist integrative efforts in South America were devoting billions of dollars to integrate Western Europe. To defeat European autarchy, individual nations had to be drawn into a continental economic bloc, but in South America, the threat of autarchy came from a regional organization spearheaded by Perón and operating independently of the United States.

Therein lay the true threat Peronism posed for the heirs to the New Deal order. Perón's efforts to rectify what he believed to be the "incomprehensible error" by which the Southern Cone had been divided into separate nations was undergirded by an analysis that liberal capitalism of the sort advocated by U.S. statesmen had long retarded Latin American development.[26] Although U.S. leaders were not entirely unsympathetic to a limited government

---

26. Bowers to Secretary of State, 22 June 1948, RG 59, 625.3531; see also Alberto Ciria, *Política y cultura popular*, 24; Samuel Baily, *The United States and the Development of South America, 1945-1975* (New York, 1976), 62-63; Robert Alexander, *Prophets of the Revolution: Profiles of Latin American Leaders* (New York, 1962), 259-61.

role in the national economy and to the integration of regional markets—indeed, they were promoting these goals in Western Europe through the Marshall Plan—Perón's program relied far more heavily on statist intervention than U.S. officials deemed necessary or wise. Still, derailing Perón's state corporatist experiment proved to be a far more complex undertaking than some in the Roosevelt or Truman Administrations might have initially assumed. The tactics that U.S. leaders employed in this venture—both successful and not—illustrated well the nature of the challenge that Peronism posed for their hopes of a hemisphere united behind U.S. leadership.

This theme runs through the chapters that follow and ties together the disparate episodes. Chapter two traces the rise of Perón, culminating in the infamous *Blue Book* and his electoral triumph in early 1946; chapter three illustrates how U.S. statesmen regrouped as Perón consolidated his power. Ambassador George Messersmith's efforts to quietly divert Peronism into a direction more palatable for the State Department comprises chapter four, and chapter five discusses U.S. labor's efforts to do so on a more fundamental level as Peronism hit its zenith in 1947. Perón's formal efforts to forge a "southern bloc" and the U.S. counteroffensive follow. The subject of chapter seven is the bureaucratic struggle between Messersmith and Spruille Braden that ended in a rough consensus throughout the Truman Administration that Peronist Argentina should be destabilized and bankrupted without any evidence of overt interventionism. In chapter eight, this new approach bears fruit despite tension between State Department officers and Marshall Planners. Chapter nine examines Perón's capitulation, as he essentially traded his confrontational, revolutionary policies for mere political survival by submitting to increasingly onerous U.S. demands. The final chapter serves as a postscript by briefly examining the years that followed Perón's first presidency and the long-term ramifications of this struggle.

# CHAPTER 2

## "PUBLIC ENEMY #1 OF THE IMPERIALISTIC CONSORTIUMS:" THE RISE OF PERON

Argentina is a young and growing nation that is feeling its oats. . . Politically, Argentina occupies in many respects the same position in relation to the United States the United States occupied toward England. We must not forget that we opposed England when in the Napoleonic wars she was fighting the Hitler of her day and that for a century twisting the lion's tail was the favorite American political sport. . . and one of the favorite Argentine political sports is likely to be plucking the eagle's feathers.

John Moors Cabot, 8 January 1946[1]

## I

Born in Lobos, Argentina on 8 October 1895, to a ranching family, Juan Domingo Perón entered the Argentine Army in 1913 as a second lieutenant. Although he exhibited great skill at both boxing and fencing, his early career otherwise showed no unusual promise. In 1930, he joined General José Uriburu's effort to overthrow the civilian government of Hipólito Irigoyen. However, his support for Uriburu wavered, and he was consigned to teach military history at the *Colegio Militar*. The first inklings of Perón's abilities and the first public manifestations of his views started to appear in his academic work at this posting. His first major publication, *Apuntes de historia militar*, was a military textbook based upon the Prussian concept of the "nation in arms," constantly vigilant, organized, and prepared for the possibility of total war. In 1936, he was promoted to lieuChile andonel, transferred across the

---

1. Cabot to Secretary of State, 8 January 1946, RG 84, BA.

Andes to Chile, and charged with assessing Chilean military capabilities.[2]

Still, Perón seems to have been merely one of many Argentine junior officers without especially strong ideological views until he was dispatched to Italy in 1939 to study alpine warfare. During his time in Italy, he learned valuable lessons about Mussolini's brand of state corporatism and the alternative it offered to the oligarchic stagnation and exploitation he saw in Anglo-Saxon democracy. In Hitler's Germany and Mussolini's Italy, Perón saw the results of a dynamic state apparatus that had organized societal groups, focused class conflict into nationalist unity, and opened the door to national development and what he would later call "true democracy." He studied the role of industrial unions and seems to have been fascinated by Mussolini's ability to bring stability to Italian politics. In Perón's eyes, Mussolini had done what the Argentine aristocracy had apparently been unable to do—provide solid leadership, promote industrial growth, and transform the state and society.[3] When he returned to Argentina, his career went in an entirely new direction, as the world was thrust into war.

The outbreak of World War II in Europe had a significant impact upon Argentina. Like leaders of most nations of the hemisphere, President Roberto Ortiz responded with a declaration of neutrality. Although this was Argentina's traditional response to distant conflagrations, there were other good reasons for neutrality. Economically, links with the two key belligerents made choosing sides very difficult, because Argentina relied heavily upon exports to both England and Germany. Politically, Argentines were torn as well. Ardent nationalists, like Perón, who viewed Anglo-Saxon liberal democracy as a weak, ineffectual system naturally, looked upon the fascist nations of Europe as a model that Argentina might do well to emulate. A powerful clique of military men comprising perhaps a third of the officer corps, many of whom had also spent

---

2. Ciria, *Política y cultura popular*, 14-24; Fayt, *Naturaleza del peronismo*, 15-36; Joseph Page, *Perón: A Biography* (New York, 1983),19-40.

3. Uki Goñi, *Perón y los alemanes: la verdad sobre el espionaje nazi y los fugitives del Reich* (Buenos Aires, 1998), 27-29; Page, *Perón*, 35-50.

time in Germany or Italy, held some pro-Nazi beliefs and welcomed the Axis triumphs of the early phases of the war. In contrast, those elements that had profited from long and deep commercial ties with Britain and the democratic facade by which the Argentine oligarchs maintained their power naturally sympathized with the Allied powers. Nonetheless, as the *wehrmacht* rolled forward throughout 1940, few even among the pro-British elite seemed willing to risk an open rupture with Germany that might prove very embarrassing, if not dangerous, in the event of an Axis victory.[4]

Just as neutrality may have been inevitable for a nation as polarized as Argentina, so too were economic dislocations as Argentina's trading partners warred. As exports and imports dwindled and the economy approached collapse, Ortiz' presidency was the first casualty. Not long after campaigning in support of the Allies and cooperation with the United States, Ortiz, physically weakened and almost blind, "temporarily" turned over the reins of government to Vice President Ramón Castillo in mid-1941. Castillo's ascension was considered a victory for conservatives, isolationists, and nationalists, but despite his reputation as the most "reactionary man in the Buenos Aires Law School," Castillo's position could perhaps best be described as vacillating neutrality.

Despite U.S. fears that Castillo was a representative of the pro-Axis nationalists, he too tried to cement economic ties with Washington; his two foremost economic advisors, Federico Pinedo and Raúl Prebisch, envisioned "close and complete cooperation" with the United States as an alternative to warring, unstable Europe. Still, Castillo's government remained aloof from U.S. hemispheric defense planning and was therefore unable to partake of Lend-Lease arms shipments that started early in 1941. Although Castillo might have envisioned a turn toward Germany, even this option dissipated when Hitler's armies turned on the Soviet Union,

---

4. Michael J. Francis, *The Limits of Hegemony: United States Relations with Argentina and Chile During World War II* (Notre Dame, 1977), 46-57; Kelly, David, *The Ruling Few* (London, 1953), 287-288; Tulchin, *Argentina and the United States: A Conflicted Relationship*, 62-67; Randall Bennett Woods, *The Roosevelt Foreign Policy Establishment and the Good Neighbor*, (Lawrence, 1979) 11-20.

and it became clear that the Ukraine, not Argentina, was to become the new breadbasket for the Third Reich. In short, as the Castillo government vainly searched for a great power patron and markets for Argentine goods, the nation remained firmly wedded to neutrality when the Japanese struck Pearl Harbor at the end of 1941.[5]

For Washington, Pearl Harbor was the litmus test for the Good Neighbor policy, as it expected Latin American nations to declare war alongside the United States. To achieve this end, Hull dispatched Undersecretary of State Sumner Welles to a diplomatic conference in Rio de Janeiro to promote hemispheric unity and to see that Latin American nations severed their ties with the Axis. Welles arrived in Rio to discover that Castillo's Foreign Minister Enrique Ruiz-Guiñazú carried orders instructing him to stop short of a complete break in relations with the Axis. Therefore, the Argentine vetoed the initial U.S. proposal by which all signatories would agree to sever relations immediately. Welles was quickly faced with a troubling dilemma. If he insisted on the original draft, Argentina and Chile, which feared possible Japanese attacks on its undefended Pacific shores, would be isolated, but watering down the provisions to preserve a united front would not be well received in Washington.[6]

Welles opted to preserve what fragile unity existed in the New World. For the Latin American specialist, a schism within the hemisphere was intolerable and would thrust Argentina into the arms of the Nazis. So, when Ruiz-Guiñazú submitted a new declaration that merely recommended that nations break ties with the Axis, Welles grudgingly accepted it, hopeful that Castillo would eventually take that decisive step. Welles, who understood the Argentine sensitivity toward bowing to foreign pressure, believed that this was the best he could do to salvage the conference and

---

5. Antonio Angel Cirigliano, *Federico Pinedo: teoría y práctica de un liberal* (Buenos Aires, 1986), 129-134; David Rock, *Argentina, 1516-1987: From Spanish Colonization to Alfonsín* (Berkeley, 1987), 238-248.

6. Francis, *Limits of Hegemony*, 85-88; Woods, *The Roosevelt Foreign Policy Establishment*, 21-42.

present at least the veneer of a united hemisphere. Hull disagreed vehemently, arguing that Welles was treading the same appeasing path that had been followed at Munich, and dedicated himself to bringing both his subordinate and Argentina to their knees. For Hull, Argentina's neutrality in the grand crusade against fascism was nothing short of reprehensible; those who were not unabashedly on the side of good were not significantly different from the forces of evil.[7]

Whereas Hull, "who had endured a decade of irritation at hands of Argentina," viewed almost every Argentine stance and development as a response to the war, domestic political considerations seem to have been paramount in Argentina. Given the rise of nationalism and the pro-Axis bent of many in the Army, Castillo had little choice but to pursue neutrality. A turn toward the Allies would be perceived by the Army as caving in to U.S. pressure and a concession to British imperialism. On the other hand, the Castillo government, like Ortiz', was providing the British with vitally needed foodstuffs without immediate compensation. Although the British had pledged to pay for their purchases after the war, Argentines argued that they were already doing as much for the Allied war effort as they could reasonably be expected to do. Still, Hull's belief that every Argentine move was a response to the war should have been dispelled when the supposedly pro-Axis Castillo, approaching the end of his term, named his successor: Robustiano Patrón Costas, an extremely wealthy sugar planter from Tucumán described by one scholar as the "quintessential oligarch" and a likely "stooge for Anglo-American imperialism."[8]

---

7. Mario Rapoport, *Gran Bretaña, Estados Unidos y las clases dirigentes argentinos, 1940-1945* (Buenos Aires, 1980), 248-250; Woods, *The Roosevelt Foreign Policy Establishment*, 35-60; Albert Vannucci, "Elected by Providence: Spruille Braden in Argentina in 1945," *Ambassadors in Foreign Policy: The Influence of Individuals in U.S.-Latin American Foreign Policy*, ed. C. Neale Romning and Albert Vannucci (New York, 1987), 64-66; Wood, *Dismantling the Good Neighbor Policy*, 44-75.

8. Harold Peterson, *Argentina and the United States, 1810-1960* (New York, 1964), 427; Mark Falcoff and Robert H. Dolkart, "Political Developments," *Prologue to Perón: Argentina in Depression and War*, eds. Falcoff and Dolkart (Berkeley, 1975), 41; Rapoport, *Gran Bretaña*, 52-62.

The presidential election of 1943 showed all signs of being yet another in a string of corrupt, brokered elections. With the nomination of Patrón Costas, however, the Army weighed in. Weary of the corruption, the hollow politics, and the economic stagnation that had characterized the past decade of Argentine history, Generals Arturo Rawson and Pedro Ramírez spearheaded a coup on June 4, 1943. In the generals' minds, civilian rule had only weakened Argentina's position, while Brazil, Argentina's major rival, had enriched itself on Lend-Lease military aid from the United States. From the Army's perspective, the decay of Argentine society had become intolerable and was shifting the South American balance of power alarmingly. Many civilians, weary of the corruption and vapid conservatism of the oligarchy, backed Rawson, as did the United States, which somehow managed to see in the revolution a repudiation of Castillo's supposed pro-Axis position. However, Rawson did not last long. His cabinet, comprised mostly of civilians, looked far too much like Castillo's, and Ramírez unseated him days after their initial seizure of power.[9]

Initially, Washington hailed the emergence of Ramírez as a triumph because he promised to call elections at the earliest opportunity. More importantly, however, he seemed to be on the verge of breaking with the Axis, and this, at least, was not just wishful thinking from Hull's State Department. The German embassy staff in Buenos Aires also sensed a shift and started burning its records in anticipation of their expulsion. Obviously intent upon falling into line with U.S. policy and understanding that the war was turning against the Axis, Ramírez' Foreign Minister, Admiral Segundo Storni, wrote to Hull requesting that the United States lift its arms embargo against Argentina. If granted this face-saving gesture, Ramírez could make the break with the Axis freely and without fear of repercussions from nationalists. Although

---

9. Gary Frank, *Struggle for Hegemony in South America: Argentina, Brazil, and the United States during the Second World War* (Miami, 1979); Stanley E. Hilton, "The Argentine Factor in Twentieth-Century Brazilian Foreign Policy Strategy," *Political Science Quarterly* (Spring 1985): 27-51; Frank D. McCann, *The Brazilian-American Alliance, 1937-1945* (Princeton, 1973); Rapoport, *Gran Bretaña*, 52-62.

Ramírez' position was reasonably strong, he could not afford to let his actions appear to be the result of Yankee coercion.

Unfortunately, Hull, still unwilling to compromise, rebuffed Storni's overture coldly and publicly, demanding that the Argentines make the first move toward conciliation. Hull's response—a "masterpiece of sarcastic rejection"—unwittingly undermined Ramírez, Storni, and the Argentines who had fought for a break with the Axis by disgracing the government and essentially challenging Argentine national honor.[10] Ramírez had been willing to cooperate with the United States on some level, but Hull's actions would soon help to unleash forces that made that all but impossible. What Hull failed to recognize was that Ramírez was a moderate being challenged forcefully by a group of ultra-nationalistic officers who aimed to turn the June 4 barracks coup into a true revolution. At the heart of this nationalistic movement was a secretive cabal of junior officers calling themselves the GOU[11]

Under the leadership of Lieutenant Colonel Juan Perón, the GOU played a significant role in the June 4 revolution, and never stopped pressing for dramatic solutions to Argentina's problems. Stressing organization and national unity, the GOU's vague ideals all manifested themselves in a push for industrialization that would revitalize the nation economically and militarily. The Storni letter strengthened their hand immeasurably and gave them a weapon against the moderates. Soon thereafter, Storni and like-minded moderates in the Ramírez government stepped down to be replaced by nationalists. Most notably, General Edelmiro Farrell, patron of the GOU and soon to be revealed as Perón's puppet, was promoted to the vice presidency, heralding a major shift in Argentina's

---

10. Gary Frank, *Juan Perón vs Spruille Braden: The Story Behind the Blue Book* (Lanham, 1980), 24; see also Kelly, *The Ruling Few*, 297-298; Woods, *The Roosevelt Foreign Policy Establishment and the Good Neighbor*, 99-103.

11. Possibly "Grupo Obra de Unificación," or "Grupo Organizador y Unificador." Robert Potash, *Perón y el G.O.U.:Los documentos de una logia secreta* (Buenos Aires, 1984); Ernesto Lopez, "El peronismo en el gobierno y los militares," *Racionalidad del peronismo*, eds. José Enrique Miguens and Frederick C. Turner (Buenos Aires, 1988), 83-89.

posture. No longer would Argentina look to the established powers for guidance and support, but the nation would industrialize and move toward self-sufficiency on its own. The nationalists also had little compunction against the use of repression, as they brought their opposition into line through martial law—further proof for Hull that Argentina's new regime was taking on more fascist characteristics.[12]

Washington's distaste for the nationalist bent of Ramírez' regime only intensified throughout 1943 and early 1944, as two separate events seemed to bear out Hull's thesis that Argentina had become Hitler's Latin American proxy. The first of these was Lieutenant Colonel Gualberto Villarroel's coup in Bolivia in December 1943. Villarroel and a small lodge of officers had toppled the oligarchic ruling class, the *rosca*, with the support of Víctor Paz Estenssoro and his dissident *Movimiento Nacionalista Revolucionario* (MNR). Villarroel had used some Argentine weapons, which were probably supplied by GOU members, and the Nazis did laud his coup. Nonetheless, the Bolivian revolution seems to have been more a response to the *rosca*'s brutal suppression of strikes, and far more indicative of chronic Bolivian instability than any foreign intrigue. Because the tin barons who had run Bolivia were associated with the United States and had been supplying large quantities of tin and wolfram for the war effort, the natural assumption in Washington was that the revolution was part of a Nazi plot to foment dissent within the Allied camp and strike a blow at Allied war production. Hull and the State Department overlooked the domestic causes of the Bolivian coup and instead viewed it as the doing of perfidious nationalists in Argentina and their alleged masters in Berlin.[13]

The second turning point was an ill-conceived and ineptly planned effort by Argentina nationalists to procure arms from Germany. The GOU, as well as other members of the Argentine

---

12. Robert Potash, *The Army and Politics in Argentina: Irigoyen to Perón* (Stanford, 1969), 238-268.

13. Andrade, *My Missions for Revolutionary Bolivia*, 19-29; Woods, *The Roosevelt Foreign-Policy Establishment*, 117-121.

armed forces, seem to have genuinely feared for Argentine security and looked to Germany in desperation. Members of Ramírez' cabinet entrusted Oscar Hellmuth, a businessman and "amateur diplomat," to procure arms from the Third Reich. However, British agents captured Hellmuth before he left the hemisphere, interrogated him, and discovered the details of the plot. Ramírez did his best to save face and cut his losses. After making some of his own arrests, he informed Washington that he would be breaking relations with the Axis forthwith. When he did so on January 26, 1944, without the knowledge of either Perón or Farrell, he sealed his fate. Because Washington was threatening a full embargo unless the Argentines took this step, Ramírez had essentially caved in to *yanqui* pressure, and any assertions to the contrary rang hollow. Outraged by the capitulation, Perón, Farrell, and other nationalists moved immediately to unseat the hapless and vacillating Ramírez. Farrell took over the Casa Rosada, but most recognized that the man who would eventually hold the posts of Minister of Labor, Minister of War, and Vice President, Juan Perón, was the real power behind the throne.[14]

## II

Since Ramírez' ascension, Perón had distinguished himself from other GOU members and clearly had his own grand plans. Perón's first posting in the new government was, at his request, as the head of the National Labor Department. His choice of this post showed the impact of his trip to Italy and his vision of the future. A bureaucratic backwater, the Labor Department was a relatively impotent agency with little real power until Perón had the office elevated to cabinet level. Unbeknownst to his colleagues, it was the perfect position from which to assemble a mass base. Although the military's interest in labor had usually been confined to repressing its activities, Perón took a new approach calculated to win the favor of the unions. Creatively using his new powers and great charisma, he started to mediate strikes in favor of workers, grant wage

---

14. Wood, *The Dismantling of the Good Neighbor Policy*, 34-36; see also Goñi, *Perón y los alemanes*, 95-115.

increases, and institute social welfare reforms—ensuring that unionists understood that he was their benefactor. "The workers already know that Colonel Perón will attend to their demands," FBI chief J. Edgar Hoover reported. "It is only necessary for them to present their problems, and they will immediately, within a few hours, be attended to."[15] Perón took the title of "Argentina's Number One Worker" as he tried to establish himself as the one man in the government who would serve the working class.

Furthermore, he cultivated powerful union leaders such as Angel Borlenghi, Juan Bramulgia, Luis Gay, and Cipriano Reyes who would become his links with the rank and file. Early on, he seems to have decided that the powerful trade union association *Confederación General del Trabajo* (CGT) was to be his vehicle to power, and therefore focused his efforts on the unions comprising the federation. On the one hand, it secured for him a loyal mass and political base, but he also defended his actions to suspicious colleagues by insisting that he was seizing this opportunity to control shopfloor radicalism and stop the spread of communism. Because Argentina was industrializing rapidly, he argued, it was imperative that the revolutionary potential of the urban proletariat be redirected. Organization in accepted unions, dependent upon the state for their existence, promised to deflect revolutionary currents, and bring order and stability to the workforce, at the same time union backing would serve as a springboard for his presidential ambitions.

In this endeavor, he seems to have benefited from the expertise of one of the Labor Department's key functionaries, José Figuerola y Tressols. Figuerola, a staunch advocate of state corporatism who had worked with Miguel Primo de Rivera and the Falange in Spain, had been studying Argentine working conditions for years. In Perón he found a leader with a willingness to experiment and the ambition to implement a state corporatist revolution. If Perón's views on labor organization were not well developed before his association with Figuerola, they were soon

---

15. Hoover to Berle, 28 December 1943, RG 319, Records of the Investigative Records Department, Case Files, File AB667334, National Archives II, College Park, MD (IRR); Fayt, *Naturaleza del peronismo*, 86-113.

thereafter. Together, the two worked to bring unionism to fields where none had existed and to consolidate the existing unions into a united syndicalist federation. Although he referred to the Army as the "first Argentine syndicate," more and more, Perón's fate was linked to that of the unions that flourished under his patronage.[16]

Still, Perón also did try to gain the support of the Argentine industrialists. Since one of his foremost goals was to further the process of industrialization, he hoped to enlist the Argentine business community. Like the New Dealers in the United States, Perón tried to convince businessmen that labor organization was in their interest as it led workers away from truly radical alternatives, and that statism would be beneficial for subsidizing and coordinating the process of industrialization. Unlike the United States, however, few "progressive" Argentine capitalists could overlook his class-based demagoguery and state-mandated wage increases. Although Perón did enjoy some support from local capitalists when he acted against foreign firms, the great majority stonewalled. For the time being, Perón abandoned his dreams of assembling a truly universal corporatist movement—featuring business and labor wings—and contented himself with a working-class syndicalism that could eventually blossom into a functional "organized community." Although he never stopped making appeals to Argentine capitalists, the "twin pillars" of organized labor and the Army were to be his true base of power.[17]

As Ramírez discredited himself—first through the Storni episode and later through the rupture with the Axis—Perón adroitly capitalized on the situation. After Farrell was installed in the presidency, it was almost inevitable that Perón be given the

---

16. Hoover to Berle, 28 December 1943, RG 319, IRR; see also Hugo del Campo, *Sindicalismo y peronismo* (Buenos Aires, 1983), 151-169; Joel Horowitz, *Argentine Unions, the State and the Rise of Perón*, 180-215; Lewis, *The Crisis of Argentine Capitalism*, 140-142; Juan Carlos Torre, *La vieja guardia sindical y Perón* (Buenos Aires, 1990), 79-102.

17. Joe C. Ashby, "Labor and the Philosophy of the Argentine Revolution," *Inter-American Economic Affairs* V (Summer 1950), 71-93; Horowitz, "Industrialists and the Rise of Perón," 199-217; Lewis, *The Crisis of Argentine Capitalism*, 144-148; Waldmann, *El peronismo*, 78-82.

extremely powerful post of Minister of War in addition to his Labor Ministry posting. Still, Perón recognized the shortcomings of the military government he now dominated. "You must not tie yourself too closely with the Government," he warned his nationalist allies, for "this Government will make many mistakes and will be discredited, then we will rise and make the true revolution." The Revolution of June 4 had been, in Perón's mind, little more than a necessary step between the oligarchs' "false democracy" and the "true democracy" promised in his syndicalist state.[18]

For policymakers in the United States, the emergence of Perón signified the final shift of Argentina away from U.S. leadership and hemispheric cooperation and toward the Axis. Coming as it did, soon after the Bolivian coup, the Hellmuth fiasco, and the rupture with the Axis, the rise of an Italian-trained colonel who spouted syndicalist rhetoric and seemed to be assembling a fascistic alliance with labor was the final straw. Hull's State Department refused to recognize the Farrell regime, furious that even as fascism was dying in Europe, it somehow had been transplanted into the Western Hemisphere. It is easy to dismiss Hull's attitudes toward Argentina in general and Perón in particular as the "irrational" ravings of an elderly statesman who had outlived his usefulness and was about to be shelved. State Department functionary Merwin Bohan expressed this viewpoint best in 1974, calling Hull's campaign a "regular old Tennessee feud" and a "personal vendetta," opining that "Mr. Roosevelt more or less gave Argentina to Mr. Hull to play with, to keep him out of his hair."[19] Indeed, Hull's attacks upon Castillo and Ramírez do seem greatly out of proportion to whatever threat Argentina might have posed to the United States, the Allies, or the war effort.

---

18. Hoover to Berle, 28 December 1943, RG 319, IRR; Griffiths to Cabot, 6 December 1945, RG 59, 835.00.

19. Merwin Bohan, Oral History, HST; Ronald Newton, "Disorderly Succession: Great Britain, the United States and the 'Nazi Menace' in Argentina," *Argentina between the Great Powers, 1939-1946*, eds. Guido DiTella and D. Cameron Watt (Pittsburgh, 1990), 111; see also Vannucci, "Elected by Providence," 49-67.

Still, although Hull's actions may have been counterproductive and foolhardy at times, they were quite understandable from a passionate Wilsonian dedicated to liberal capitalism, free trade, and democracy. Historian Ronald Newton illustrated that the threat of a "Nazi menace" in Argentina was "nonsense," and an "obsession" with U.S. policymakers, but also explained that the Germans and British had worked hard to foster that myth for their own reasons. The rhetoric and reality of "fifth columns," the visible penetration of South America by Germany prior to the war, and the omnipresent U.S. attitude that Europeans or North Americans could easily have their way with Latin American states made this a natural conclusion. Newton also showed that the British played their own role in convincing Hull that the Nazis were engaged in great plots to subvert Argentina. Eager to convince Washington of the threat of Nazism and "lead their North American cousins around by the nose," British agents fabricated or exaggerated stories of Nazi penetration, such as the "Patagonia Plot," the "Great Nazi Bug-Out," and the "Myth of the Fourth Reich." It should have not come as a surprise to the English that the State Department took these hoaxes seriously and acted accordingly. Hull undoubtedly had been duped and acted unwisely, but his mistakes must be understood within the context of the unparalleled brutality and bloodshed of World War II.[20]

Hull's resignation at the end of 1944 did usher in a brief rapprochement, as Nelson Rockefeller, the first Assistant Secretary of State for Latin American Affairs, dedicated himself to reversing Hull's course. Rockefeller believed that Hull had deviated from the successful path laid down by the Good Neighbor policy and that the campaign against Argentina created tension, if not mistrust, within the hemisphere. Furthermore, it had been futile and counterproductive, as the rejection of the Storni note had shown quite clearly. Hull may have been bull-headed enough to persist in the face of this evidence, but Rockefeller and new Secretary of State Edward Stettinius believed that the crusade against Argentina

---

20. Ronald Newton, *The 'Nazi Menace' in Argentina, 1931-1947* (Stanford, 1992); see also Alton Frye, *Nazi Germany and the American Hemisphere, 1933-1941* (New Haven, 1967); Kelly, *The Ruling Few*, 303-304.

promised only to tear out the fragile foundations of inter-American harmony and unity.[21]

Rockefeller's efforts at conciliation bear this out well. The first of these was a favorable response to Perón's call for a hemispheric meeting. Rockefeller understood that such a meeting was needed for several reasons, believing that it was necessary to articulate U.S. economic policy and to convince Latin Americans that they should continue to trust in U.S. leadership. Furthermore, the United States had to provide a framework for the reintegration of Argentina into the "Inter-American system" and repair the festering schism. At the Chapultepec Conference in early March 1945, U.S. and Latin American delegations provided such a framework. The State Department agreed that if Argentine government declared war on the Axis, ceased its repression, made steps toward democratic elections, and eliminated Axis influences within its borders, Hull's embargoes would be lifted. Perón and Farrell responded quickly, making a belated and rather meaningless declaration of war on March 27, 1945, just weeks before the war in Europe ended. For their part, U.S. officials did press for Argentina's inclusion in the United Nations over strident Soviet objections.[22]

In April, however, Roosevelt perhaps unwittingly undid all that Rockefeller had worked to achieve when, with the final diplomatic appointment of his presidency, he named Spruille Braden as ambassador to Argentina. A lifelong Republican and old-style conservative who abhorred the New Deal, Braden nonetheless possessed excellent credentials for the job. The son of a copper miner who had done extensive business in South America, Braden had an expertise and background in Latin America that was

---

21. Woods, *The Roosevelt Foreign-Policy Establishment*, 169-172.

22. Carlos Escudé, *Gran Bretaña, Estados Unidos, y la declinacion argentina, 1942-1949*, (Buenos Aires, 1983), 163-174; Rapoport, *Gran Bretaña*, 267-272 and "Foreign and Domestic Policy in Argentina during the Second World War: The Traditional Political Parties and the Military Regime, 1943-1945," *Argentina Between the Great Powers*, 85-93; Peterson, *Argentina and the United States*, 440-446; Wood, *The Dismantling of the Good Neighbor Policy*, 81-85.

almost unequaled in the State Department. He had served the Roosevelt Administration for years throughout the hemisphere and had a well-earned reputation for aggressive, no-nonsense diplomacy. Although his heavy-handed approach and unyielding manner had made enemies in some of his postings, when he left the Department in 1947, he received dozens of commendations and awards from Latin American leaders who admired his character and respected his activities. When he left Argentina after less than a year, however, he won no medals for his efforts.[23]

Braden arrived in Buenos Aires and immediately but unwittingly exposed one of the fundamental problems that the United States was to have with Perón over the course of the next decade. Braden had a number of old friends among the Argentine elite opposed to both the military government in general and the demagogue Perón in particular. He had circulated among the oligarchy during the 1930s and associated with the interests, conservatism, and democratic sentiments of that particular class. When Braden arrived, he sought out his old friends of the *gente bien* who, in the words of one Perón supporter, "raised fat cows and thin peons."[24] Unfortunately for all involved, Braden never seems to have tried to understand the Peronist phenomenon more deeply, or to have spoken with any of the growing numbers of lower-class Argentines who were coming to view Perón as a savior. When he acted, he did so blind to the possibility that the Farrell-Perón government was anything more than a "'bush league' *de facto* fascist dictatorship" devoid of genuine popular backing.[25]

---

23. Braden, *Diplomats and Demagogues* (New Rochelle, New York, 1971); Frank, *Juan Perón vs. Spruille Braden*, 27-34.

24. Mann to Brown, 20 December 1945, RG 59, 835.00.

25. Gilmore to Warren, Butler, and Mann, 4 September 1945, RG 59, 835.00; see also Frank, *Juan Perón vs. Spruille Braden*, 58; Callum MacDonald, "The Braden Campaign and Anglo-American Relations in Argentina," *Argentina between the Great Powers, 1939-1946*, eds. DiTella and Watt (Pittsburgh, 1990), 139-143 and "The Politics of Intervention: The United States and Argentina, 1941-1946" *Journal of Latin American Studies* 12: 386-390; Embassy staff member Philip P. Williams toured the interior of Argentina conducting an extremely informal poll and survey in November and found

Within weeks Braden started to act with characteristic vigor, launching a campaign against the regime that made even Hull's pale by comparison. "Perón is too quick-thinking, effective in action, and firmly entrenched to be ousted," he argued, "except after a knockdown dragout by a much better organized and intelligent opposition" than "now appears to exist." Lamenting that "the opposition, ignoring its responsibilities, places its hopes on a foreign (USA) intervention which they themselves would be the first to resent," but hopeful that "Perón is on the ropes and could be dealt a finishing punch were there any leadership or initiative among the opposition," he attempted to provide both.[26] He delivered speeches that demanded that the military government fulfill the Chapultepec pledges and eliminate censorship, while his underlings established connections with both open and clandestine enemies of the regime. Perón, stung by U.S. news correspondents who almost daily published scathing attacks on the regime, sought a *quid pro quo* from the new ambassador. He would grant freedom of the press to Argentine journalists if Braden would work to muzzle U.S. reporters. The ambassador naturally refused, citing the principle of freedom of the press. When Perón unilaterally lifted some restrictions on the press, it seemed as if Braden had won the first round.

The end of the World War II, the triumph of democracy over totalitarianism, and the lifting of restrictions spurred the Argentine opposition, as Braden's attacks on the beleaguered Perón continued. Pushed into a corner, Perón struck out at the most obvious of his foes. After calling Braden to the Casa Rosada, he made a thinly veiled threat against U.S. journalists and the ambassador himself, asserting that there were "fanatics" within his camp who might take it upon themselves to murder the enemies of the regime. Braden demanded protection for all U.S. citizens, but

---

Perón to be extremely popular. This conclusion could not have been more different than those Braden had reached while traveling among the Buenos Aires elite. Williams to Cabot, 28 November 1945, RG 59, 835.00.

26. Braden to Secretary of State, 3 August 1945, RG 59, 835.00; Braden to Secretary of State, 17 July 1945, RG 59, 835.00; Braden to Secretary of State, 13 July 1945, RG 59, 835.00.

Perón retorted that he had no control over such vigilantes and instead warned the ambassador to curb his activities. Refusing to back down, Braden offered the U.S. embassy as a haven for journalists to guarantee their safety and the continuation of their anti-government reporting.[27]

Although some of his allies in both the United States and Argentina viewed his partisanship as at best, inappropriate, and at worst, a dangerous form of interventionism, Braden was soon rewarded with a promotion to the post of assistant secretary of state and given control over U.S. policy toward Latin America. This was a clear signal that Braden's policies and tactics were condoned by his superiors. Even Rockefeller, who was most sensitive to the Latin American fears of interventionism, gave Braden his stamp of approval, asserting that "he had at all times my full support and the full support of our Government" and that he was "in line with the policy of the State Department."[28] Interestingly, there was some opposition to Braden's promotion in the Senate Foreign Relations Committee. Senators Arthur Vandenberg and Tom Connally, two of the earliest Cold Warriors, doubted that U.S. interests were being served by repeated assaults on a non-communist regime. Others, influenced by Welles and likeminded proponents of a conciliatory interpretation of the Good Neighbor policy, challenged Braden's interventionism. The committee grilled the unrepentant ambassador at his confirmation hearing and deliberated for almost a month before approving his appointment.[29] Braden lamented that he would be leaving the battlefield in Buenos Aires but contented himself that he could

---

27. Frank, *Juan Perón vs. Spruille Braden*, 61-79.

28. Text of Rockefeller's speech, 31 January 1946, RG 59, 711.35.

29. Gary Frank related an episode that bears repeating. After Braden told of Perón's personal threats against him, Connally asked him, "Do you mean to say that he threatened you, the American Ambassador? Why didn't you take a gun and shoot him?" Braden responded, "If I had done that, I might have been accused of intervention." Afterwards, Braden called his rejoinder "one of the stupidest moves I ever made" and noted that Connally never forgave him for it. Frank, *Juan Perón vs. Spruille Braden*, 96-97.

better coordinate the attack on Perón from Washington. Furthermore, there would be no new ambassador to Argentina, suggesting that Braden would still be running the embassy, in spirit if not in body, and that relations were far from normalized.

Braden's best hope was that economic warfare might precipitate crises in Argentina and fuel a counterrevolution that would topple Farrell. In addition to the arms embargo, the State Department had frozen Argentine assets in U.S. banks and withheld deliveries of critical products such as oil, coal, and rubber throughout the war. Unfortunately for the State Department, the British were hesitant to cooperate with these measures, seeing no reason to needlessly antagonize Argentina, which was, after all, serving the British Isles quite well by continuing food deliveries. Whitehall resisted U.S. efforts to economically destabilize the various Argentine governments throughout the war, arguing that every dislocation precipitated by Washington's embargoes only reduced food exports and exacerbated Argentine nationalism. Although Acting Secretary of State Joseph Grew raged about this "Tory appeasement complex," the British position was firm.[30]

British standoffishness may have hindered what Carlos Escudé called the "moral imperialism" of U.S. efforts to destabilize Argentina, but Farrell and Perón waged their own campaign to thwart the State Department. In the process, they provided a taste of what the United States could expect from Argentina throughout the post-war period. The first embargo that the Farrell government tackled was that on rubber. Through the Rubber Development Corporation (RDC), U.S. officials purchased and distributed the hemisphere's rubber surplus for the duration of the war. Originally conceived to help fight the "warehouse war" against the Axis, the RDC nonetheless fit well into the State Department's embargo against Argentina.[31] The rubber quota RDC allocated to Argentina

---

30. Grew to Rockefeller and Warren, 26 May 1945, RG 59, 835.504; see also MacDonald, "Politics of Intervention," 381-382, and "The Braden Campaign and Anglo-American Relations, 1945-1946," 144-146; E. Louise Peffer, "Cordell Hull's Argentine Policy and Britain's Meat Supply," *Inter-American Economic Affairs* (Autumn 1956), 3-21.

31. Escudé, *Estados Unidos, Gran Bretaña*; Warren Dean, *Brazil and the Struggle for Rubber: a Study in Environmental History* (Cambridge, 1987), 85-

amounted to less than one-fifth of the nation's pre-war consumption. By 1943, Argentines were predictably suffering from a severe shortage that drove tire prices as high as $150 each. The situation worsened when, after Farrell's *golpe de estado*, Argentina was removed from the RDC framework altogether. These restrictions, in conjunction with the embargoes on oil, coal, capital goods, and arms, went a good distance toward crippling the Argentine economy, to Braden's delight.[32]

Despite the apparent successes of this approach, U.S. policymakers had to relent when Farrell made his belated declaration of war. Officially, the withholding of rubber had never been intended as a punitive measure, but merely as a reflection of Argentina's peripheral role in the war effort. However, Adolf Berle, the U.S. ambassador to Brazil, warned that "Argentina is far more interested in rubber than anything else," so "a rubber agreement should not be made until Argentina has agreed on all other matters which may be at issue," for "if Argentina gets her rubber, she probably can and will be pretty independent about other matters." Braden concurred, likening the rubber embargo to a "club" and a "lever" to be used "as a means to get rid of Perón."[33]

However, this strategy was doomed to failure. With the sudden Japanese capitulation in August, the RDC announced that 350,000 tons of Southeast Asian rubber would be available by the end of the year. Because the United States purchased nearly seventy percent of the world's rubber exports, it was essential that the price be kept low. The State Department would have liked very much to maintain its pressure on the Farrell-Perón regime, but the Argentines could simply bid on the open market if they were dissatisfied with their RDC quota. Therefore, Farrell had to be

---

90; Randolph Resor, "Rubber in Brazil: Dominance or Collapse?" *Business History Review* 51 (September 1977), 351-353.

32. Berle to Secretary of State, 23 August 1945, in *FRUS*, IX, 1945, 709; *India Rubber World* 111 (October 1945), 105; *Rubber Age* 65 (September 1945), 718.

33. Berle to Stettinius, 24 April 1945, in *FRUS*, 1945, IX, 706; Braden to Secretary of State, 3 September 1945, RG 59, 835.6176; Braden to Secretary of State, 30 August 1946, RG 59, 835.6176.

convinced to remain within the RDC framework because "his demands, although small, could easily result in forcing up the price at which we purchase rubber for our own needs." The only way to do this was to increase the Argentine quota to a more acceptable level. Braden conceded in August that "if [the] tire supply situation is easy and cannot serve as a club any longer, it is my recommendation that any objection by the U.S. be lifted."[34]

Still the RDC dragged its feet until Farrell found a cudgel of his own and took the Brazilian food supply hostage. In October, the Farrell government warned that unless tires were made immediately available, desperately needed wheat shipments to Brazil would stop. According to the Argentines, because of petroleum and rubber shortages, it was proving impossible to collect crops or deliver them to port. To punctuate the threat, the regime announced that two ships had already sailed out of port empty. The RDC was especially skeptical of the "transportation bottleneck" thesis, suggesting that "the correlation between tire imports into Argentina and wheat exports therefrom is highly debatable." Indeed, officers of the RDC noted that "the Argentines seem to be in the habit of using the wheat shortage as a lever for obtaining tires and are ready to link tires and wheat in any way that seems advantageous."[35]

Nonetheless, within a month, food riots in Brazilian cities forced the Truman Administration's hand. The State Department quickly rushed an emergency shipment of tires to Argentina, making it clear that this was but an acknowledgement of the desperate need for Argentine wheat.[36] The U.S. shipment alleviated

---

34. On the other hand, Clayton argued that Uruguay should receive tires, because of their interpretation of "non-intervention" which supported Braden's activities in Argentina. Kennedy to Thorp and Wilcox, 7 December 1946, RG 59, 835.61311; Braden to Secretary of State, 30 August 1946, RG 59, 835.6176; see also Memorandum of Conversation, Braddock and Celso Raul García, 27 March 1946, in *FRUS* 1946, 120; *India Rubber World* 112 (November 1945), 69.

35. McLaughlin Memorandum, 12 January 1946, RG 59, 835.24; see also Thorp to Braden, 14 December 1945, RG 59, 835.24.

36. Berle to Secretary of State, 20 November 1945, RG 59, 835.61311;

the immediate crisis in Argentina, but had the unwanted side effect of undercutting Brazilians' efforts to barter their rubber for more wheat. Perón and Farrell hardened their stance toward Brazil and saw little need to step up their deliveries when they could sell the wheat profitably in Europe and still obtain tires from the United States.[37] The Brazilians cried foul, arguing that the U.S. action had been a betrayal. Red-faced, the State Department admitted that there was "no good defense" to these "justified protests," and Dean Acheson resorted to issuing a thinly veiled threat to the Brazilians, suggesting that if they did not cease their complaints, they could expect no "further assistance" from the U.S. government.[38]

Although there was undeniably some truth to the Argentine "transportation bottleneck" argument, other evidence suggests that it was in many respects a pretext rather than a valid explanation for the lack of food deliveries. The Argentine Secretary of Commerce and Industry cited no transportation difficulties and shed all pretense when he threatened to cut off Bolivian food shipments in September. Claiming that Bolivia was "taking undue advantage of Argentina" by charging exorbitant prices for rubber and then "committing an absolute injustice" by not delivering it, the Argentines justified their own *quid pro quo* embargo. Although the State Department managed to circumvent this threat by arranging an emergency shipment of 10,000 tons of Australian wheat to Bolivia, once again the Argentines had proven their point. In the war-torn world, they were willing to use their precious food surpluses to the fullest advantage.[39]

---

Kennedy to Thorp and Wilcox, 7 December 1946, RG 59, 835.61311; Braddock to Chalmers, 16 January 1946, RG 59, Office of American Republics Affairs, Memoranda regarding Individual Countries, Argentina (MRIC).

37. Daniels to Secretary of State, 23 January 1946, RG 59, 835.24; Secretary of State to Embassy Rio de Janeiro, 25 January 1946, RG 59, 835.24; Berle to Secretary of State, 30 November 1946, RG 59, 835.61311.

38. McLaughlin Memorandum, 12 January 1946, RG 59, 835.24; Braddock to McDermott, 20 February 1946, RG 59, MRIC, Argentina; Acheson to Embassy Rio, 18 January 1946, RG 59, 835.24.

39. Tewksbury to Secretary of State, 4 September 1945, RG 59, 835.6176;

To overcome the oil and coal embargoes, the Argentines upped the ante. In late 1945, the Farrell-Perón government, claiming that transportation was now being paralyzed by a fuel shortage, announced that it would soon have to resort to burning grains and edible oils for fuel if it did not receive petroleum imports. Furthermore, Peronists asserted that this shortage was contributing to the "transportation bottleneck" and forcing the government to "drastically curtail" grain shipments to England and UNRRA. Millions of tons of grain sat in silos awaiting export, Farrell claimed, but the trucks to haul it to port lacked fuel. If the Argentines were forced to burn food vitally needed in Europe by an embargo considered by many to be petty, U.S. prestige might well suffer. Secretary of State James Byrnes, "under considerable pressure and criticism," responded by almost immediately lifting the embargo and allotting the Argentines a quota of 20,000 tons of coal per month. Soon thereafter, he lifted the oil restrictions, and by November, the State Department was bending over backward to supply great quantities of fuel oil and "as much coal as possible" to Argentina—decisions that were made "reluctantly" and "dictated solely by the compelling necessity of getting food to Europe."[40]

The lessons were learned both north and south. For Peronists, it was clear that economic blackmail worked, as it had driven U.S. leaders to betray their staunch allies in Brazil in order to accede to Argentine desires. For Brazil and other Latin American nations, it was made clear that the colossus of the north was far from invulnerable. Farrell and Perón had exposed serious weaknesses in the "Inter-American system" and shown that Argentine power, at carefully selected points, was a match for that of the United States. As a result, in the words of the U.S. ambassador to Chile, "neighboring nations will be loath to come out

---

DuBarry to Phillips, 18 December 1945, RG 59, 635.61311.

40. Byrnes to Embassy Rio, 16 May 1946, RG 59, 835.6176; Thorp to Braden, 14 December 1945, RG 59, 835.24; Braddock to Chalmers, 6 November 1946, RG 59, MRIC Argentina.

publicly and formally against" Perón for fear of inadequate U.S. protection.[41]

### III

While Argentine efforts to undercut Braden's embargoes proceeded, the political developments of October dwarfed the impact of these diplomatic conflicts. General Eduardo Avalos, one of Perón's chief rivals in the Farrell government, feared both the power Perón was accumulating and the ties he was making with the working classes. Along with a number of other prominent officers, Avalos also resented Perón's dalliance with Eva María Duarte, an actress and radio star from Junín. Although it was certainly not uncommon for Argentine officers to keep mistresses, Perón publicly flouted his relationship with Duarte and even gave her a role in the federal bureaucracy. When he tried to promote her friends and family members within the government, many viewed this as the same sort of nepotism that had brought the Army out of the barracks in 1943. Avalos managed to swing key members of the officer corps to his position and moved to arrest Perón. Having witnessed the carnage of the Spanish Civil War and unwilling to risk the bloody confrontation that would have resulted from resistance, Perón simply resigned from his posts and urged his followers not to resort to violence as they continued their heroic fight for social justice. When unionists started to gather in protest on October 12, Farrell and Avalos had Perón seized and sent to the island prison of Martín García.

As Braden and the State Department celebrated his fall from grace, Perón's allies rallied to his defense in one of the most critical moments in Argentine history. Union bosses joined Eva Duarte in the working-class neighborhoods around Buenos Aires proper, rallying and mobilizing workers' families as they organized a massive general strike. On October 17, groups of workers, *descamisados*, and other Peronists marched upon the Casa Rosada. Chanting "Free Perón," the expectant mob swelled to perhaps

---

41. Bowers to Braden, 13 March 1946, Claude Bowers MSS II, Lilly Library, University of Indiana, Bloomington, Indiana.

300,000, filling the Plaza de Mayo outside the president's office. Avalos, and what U.S. Chargé John Moors Cabot described as "the most insignificant cabinet that was ever chosen for office in any American republic," floundered in the face of this overwhelming show of support for Perón.[42]

Unwilling to open fire on the crowds, Avalos ultimately appealed to Perón to quell the crowd. Argentina's Number One Worker, who had been preparing for exile, played his cards well, and refused to address the assembled masses until Farrell and Avalos had met his conditions. Avalos had to retire from public life, while Farrell appointed a cabinet stacked with *peronistas*. Furthermore, Farrell was to call elections and accept Perón's resignation from the Army, which would pave the way for him to run for the Presidency as a civilian. When his demands had been met, Perón triumphantly stepped out onto the balcony of the Casa Rosada and dispersed the victorious crowd. The significance of October 17 cannot be overstated. The long-ignored working classes of Argentina had spoken forcefully, undoubtedly exceeding even Perón's expectations, as their spontaneous demonstration transformed Argentine politics forever and formally launched *peronismo*.[43]

While opponents of the regime clamored for the Supreme Court, the last bastion of the oligarchy, to preside over the elections, the Farrell government insisted that the Army was the only institution capable of holding a truly clean election. The Army promised Argentines a "guaranteed election" that would be as honest as recent ones had been corrupt, and Perón predictably threw his hat into the ring, theoretically independent of both the Army and the government.[44] Although he could, of course, count upon both the support of the Army and the unions, he also received

---

42. Cabot Oral History, 35.

43. The finest telling of the story of October 17 is Felix Luna's *El 45: Cronica de un año decisivo*, 273-298; see also Crassweller, *Perón and the Enigmas of Argentina*, 162-171; Hugo Gambini, *Historia del peronismo*, 51-63; Page, *Perón*, 112-137; Torre, *La vieja guardia sindical*, 116-140.

44. Potash, *The Army and Politics in Argentina: Perón to Frondizi*, 17.

backing from elements of the Radical Party, which tore itself apart over the issue of Perón's candidacy. Dissident radicals and several ultra-nationalist groups were the only established parties to endorse him, as the rest (including the Communists) united into the *Unión Demócratica*.

Hastily assembled and united only in their opposition to Perón, this seemingly powerful alliance of Radicals, Conservatives, and a number of smaller parties was much stronger on paper than in the streets. The Radicals and Conservatives had relied upon "skullduggery" and electoral fraud to win elections in the past, and were skilled enough in these practices, an ITT executive commented, to "almost be successful in Chicago or New Jersey." However, the pro-Perón Army and police forces would guarantee that the only "funny business" that occurred would be that employed against the *Unión Demócratica*'s nominee, José Tamborini, whom U.S. chargé John Cabot described as having "the general appearance, and rather less than the intelligence of a tame teddy bear."[45] Given Tamborini's weakness, the State Department was forced to consider the prospect that Perón might win the Casa Rosada.

For the British and some other witnesses, the events of October 17 had proven that Perón had the backing necessary to win the election. Ambassador Claude Bowers, observing from across the Andes, concurred. He explained that "a bad man cannot be defeated without an opponent" and suggested that most of the opposition was trying to keep a low profile to avoid retaliation in the event that Perón did win. Braden agreed with the prediction, if not the rationale, arguing that "it is an odds on bet that Perón will, through fraudulent elections, be elected."[46] Cabot reported to Washington that Farrell's government was indeed giving support to Perón, but conceded that this aid was "not wholly disproportionate to the aid which an administration candidate normally receives in

---

45. McKim to Page, 27 November 1945, RG 59, 835.00; Cabot to Secretary of State, 9 January 1946, RG 84, BA.

46. Bowers to Braden, 24 December 1945, Bowers MSS II; Braden to Bowers, 29 December 1945, Bowers MSS II.

the United States." On the other hand, the police force was waging a more effective intimidation and harassment campaign against the opposition, leading Cabot to wryly suggest that he might invest in the construction of a "tear gas factory in Buenos Aires," as "it ought to make piles of money." Whatever the reasons they gave, almost every outside observer seemed to believe that Perón would win and that the elections would be rigged in one way or another.[47]

Perón's domestic opponents seemed to agree, and in early February planned a last-ditch effort to overthrow the military regime and preempt the election. Although the coup attempt that came out of this plotting was an especially feeble one, unremarkable in the chaotic days leading up to the election, several aspects of it were intriguing. First and foremost, the State Department seemed to have possessed foreknowledge of it and had been in contact with a number of would-be revolutionaries. R. B. Smith, a U.S. businessman in Argentina, approached Braden in November 1945 at the behest of one such group. These Argentine rebels, Smith claimed, had "unlimited financial backing" and could easily smuggle "sub-machine guns and bazookas" across the Uruguayan border into Argentina if the State Department could supply them. Braden rebuffed Smith coldly, asserting that the United States government could not procure arms or even "suggest how or where they might be acquired." A Danish horse breeder associated with anti-Perón forces approached J. Edgar Hoover with a similar request in December. From his post in Lima, Ambassador William Pawley reported an even more "ridiculous" entreaty. Apparently, the naval attaché of the Argentine embassy had approached him, asking for "30 flying fortresses, 100 tanks, and 5,000 machine guns" to oust the government.[48]

---

47. Cabot to Secretary of State, 8 January 1946, RG 84, Argentina; Cabot to Neal, 7 February 1946, John Moors Cabot Papers (on microfilm), Argentina, HST; see also Frank, *Juan Perón vs Spruille Braden*, 99-100; Crassweller, *Peron and the Enigmas of Argentina*, 176-180.

48. Memorandum of Conversation, Smith, Braden, and Mann, 26 November 1945, RG 59, 835.00; Pawley to Braden, 29 January 1946, RG 59, 835.00; Hoover to Lyon, 4 December 1945, RG 59, 835.00.

Cabot himself suggested that it might be useful for the United States to break relations with Argentina in order to "free our hand to help the Argentine people free themselves, i.e., openly to furnish material help to revolutionaries who started anything with any chance of success." When his superiors, who still feared an open rift within the hemisphere, rejected this course of action, Cabot requested their assistance to enforce the official U.S. policy of non-intervention. Apparently, U.S. citizens in Argentina were persisting in their attempts to influence or stop the election, so Cabot asked that the Department publicize its hands-off approach, if only to deter them. These episodes are somewhat telling. Cabot's embassy, its military attachés, and the small horde of informants, operatives, and spies circulating in Buenos Aires all had close ties and strong informal contacts with the anti-Perón camp and a desire to be of assistance to it.[49]

More significantly, a "fairly good source" reported to the embassy in the middle of January that anti-Perón elements in the "Army and Navy are planning a revolution."[50] The U.S. military attaché in Buenos Aires, Major F. F. Gibbons, had much more concrete information about the measures that the "democratic forces" would put into effect "as soon as the revolution starts." He named three radio stations that would announce the start of fighting and then be silenced. The only stations that would continue to broadcast were Uruguayan and clandestine ones operated by the rebels that would "keep the public and world informed," as police and official communications would be sabotaged. "The proposed revolution, which is planned because the democratic forces are convinced that honest elections cannot possibly be held," Gibbons explained, "is expected to get underway within a matter of days and certainly before 24 February."[51] The plot had been in the works

---

49. Cabot to Secretary of State, 30 September 1945, RG 59, 835.00; Cabot to Secretary of State, 26 November 1946, RG 59, 835.00.

50. n.a., 22 January 1946, Naval Aide Files, HST. Hoover to Lyon, 11 February 1946, RG 59, 835.00.

51. Gibbons, "Revolutionists' Plan to Sabotage Argentine Radio Stations," 3 February 1946, RG 84, Argentina.

since at least September, when U.S. military and naval attaches assessed whether the Argentine Navy could succeed alone. Cabot had then recommended "against doing anything with direct purpose of encouraging Navy to rebel," but only because "we would be embarked on a perilous course with no end in sight." Still, the would-be revolutionaries carried on with their plotting as they sought to acquire their own broadcasting equipment. Although they had been unable to procure it "within the limits of necessary discretion," the plot had continued.[52]

Although it is hardly surprising that U.S. officials knew about the coup attempt, Perón claimed that U.S. involvement did not end there. Once the revolt was squelched, Perón made what seemed to be outlandish accusations, claiming that "the police constantly were picking up arms that had been smuggled across the River Plata," that the United States had provided $300,000 to "finance the campaign" against him, and that the "United States Embassy was involved in this counter-movement." Perón never did present this evidence—if it ever existed—and it seemed that this episode was little more than another of his infamous unsubstantiated accusations. Perón, like other Latin Americans, knew well that U.S. "military intervention in Argentina would have catastrophic repercussions throughout" the hemisphere and probably hoped to draw the State Department into a brawl.[53]

However, Cabot did make one cryptic remark to Jack Neal, chief of the State Department's Division of Foreign Activities Correlation, in early February that bears notice. "The next time you boys in the Department try to supply the revolutionaries here with bean bags to fight police tommy guns," he wrote, "you'd better be more careful. Just see how nearly you got caught (?)."[54] It is

---

52. Cabot to Secretary of State, 30 September 1945, RG 59, 835.00; Griffiths to Cabot, 24 November 1945, RG 59, 835.00.

53. Cabot to Secretary of State, 4 February 1946, Cabot Papers, Argentina, HST; Rada a Ministro, 1 Febrero 1946, Archivo del Ministerio de Relaciones Exteriores (AMRE), Lima, 5-1-Y/21; see also MacDonald, "The Politics of Intervention," 309.

54. Cabot to Neal, 7 February 1946, Cabot Papers, Argentina, HST.

impossible to know whether Cabot was sarcastically poking fun at his friend in Washington, if this was intended as a warning, or if he simply did not know whether the State Department was engaging in some covert activities without his knowledge. It is suggestive that Neal served as the liaison between the FBI and State Department, and the possibility does exist that U.S. citizens were funneling arms to the self-styled "democratic forces." Informers reported to the embassy that "the procurement of arms and ammunition has been extremely difficult," but that the revolutionaries had somehow obtained enough small arms "to meet the needs of what might be termed the 'shock troops.'"

Although there is no concrete evidence that U.S. officials assisted in this arms build-up, Braden had no aversion to bending rules when he felt the cause was just, and had on one occasion proudly and illegally procured arms for Ernest Hemingway during the war.[55] The British suspected that Braden had played a role in the abortive uprising, at the very least maintaining "back-stair connections" with anti-Peronists and continuing to "flirt with a cabal of Argentine Naval officers." For his part, Cabot believed that since Perón had tapped embassy phones during the war, he was "loaded with ammunition to prove charges against US." Therefore, the State Department should no longer meet any of his accusations, as "specific denials are therefore likely to be refuted or smeared."[56]

---

55. Griffiths to Cabot, 24 November 1945, RG 59, 835.00; see also Potash, *The Army and Politics in Argentina: Perón to Frondizi*, 35. When Braden was posted in Havana during World War II, Falangist Spaniards were operating a spy network for the Axis. While Braden awaited FBI agents to deal with the problem, he enlisted the aid of Hemingway and his many friends. As payment for his services, Hemingway requested "a bazooka to punch holes in the side of [German submarines he had spotted off the Cuban coast], machine guns to mow down the people on the deck, and hand grenades to lob down the conning tower." Grateful for the author's yeoman service, Braden "scrapped the regulations, got him what he wanted, and sent him on his way." Braden, *Diplomats and Demagogues*, 283-284.

56. Wood, *The Dismantling of the Good Neighbor Policy*, 105-6; MacDonald, "Politics of Intervention," 309; Cabot to Secretary of State, 16 February 1946, RG 59, 835.00.

Regardless of the veracity of the charges, Braden's attacks upon various Argentine governments undeniably toed the line of intervention until, despairing of Perón's imminent victory, he leapt across it. Lamenting that his promotion had taken him away from Buenos Aires, he nonetheless determined to make the most out what he considered to be a bad situation. His best hope rested in five tons of captured German archival material that might prove Peronist complicity with the Nazis during the war. If Braden could present concrete proof that Perón was a Nazi puppet, then Argentines, as well as the rest of the hemisphere, might repudiate him. Cabot ominously warned, however, that if Braden continued to proceed along this line, "our Argentine policy may collapse in a grand smash, burying its principal authors" and tearing the Good Neighbor Policy into "ribbons." But Cabot understood that he was sadly "out of step with everybody else" who was actively searching and compiling the German material.[57]

The result of Braden's labors was the infamous *Blue Book*, innocuously entitled *Consultation Among the American Republics with Respect to the Argentine Situation*. The title was deceptive, as no other American republics had been consulted in any meaningful way until after the fact. The *Blue Book* focused upon both Castillo's and Farrell's governments, and highlighted episodes such as the Hellmuth mission, the Bolivian coup, and the active but ineffectual German espionage network in Buenos Aires. Perón, of course, was featured prominently within the tome, which did show that the Nazis had not discouraged the GOU's ambition to form a "bloc of states pointed against the USA," even if it could not demonstrate that they had assisted in any meaningful way. Without the amazing revelations that Braden had promised, the other accusations also fell flat as the *Blue Book* did not present the evidence to back up its sensational claims about Argentine-German collaboration.

The second half of the *Blue Book*, focusing almost entirely upon the Farrell government, made almost no effort to incorporate

---

57. Cabot to Cochran, 14 December 1945, Cabot Papers, Argentina, HST; Cabot Oral History, 32; see also MacDonald, "The Braden Campaign," 147-151.

German evidence. Instead, Braden and the State Department simply editorialized about the conditions in Argentina, with chapters such as "Totalitarian Control of Labor" and "Perversion of Educational System." What emerged was a scathing denunciation of Perón, significantly devoid of even the few Nazi documents that had been used to bolster the earlier portion. In its tone and style, the *Blue Book* was not unlike many acidic polemics that always surrounded Perón, but this one, significantly, had been compiled and released by the United States government.[58]

Despite its numerous failings, Byrnes considered it to be adequate and released it to the press in February, just weeks before the Argentine election, with Tamborini's approval. Cabot had urged him not to release the *Blue Book*, as it surely would be "pounced on by Perón clique as [a] clumsy effort to influence [the] election." Moreover, "to throw [an] atomic bomb directly at [the] Argentine government in present supercharged atmosphere is to court incalculable results."[59] Regardless, Braden dropped his "atomic bomb," but it quickly became clear that Tamborini, not Perón, was the one struck by it.

Most Argentines, as well as Cabot, had to read about the *Blue Book* in newspapers, but it nonetheless made a profound impression. Cabot related Argentine reaction as one of "stunned surprise" and "stunned humiliation." Partisans on either side interpreted this "humiliation" quite differently. Peronist Juan Cooke viewed the *Blue Book* as an unusually fortuitous development, as nationalistic Argentines resented this obvious intervention and repudiated the *Unión Demócratica*. On the other hand, the opposition to Perón rallied to the publication as verification that Perón was indeed the Nazi-Fascist they had always claimed him to be.[60]

---

58. U.S. Department of State, *Consultation Among the American Republics with Regard to the Argentine Situation*. (Washington, 1946), 1-133.

59. Cabot to Secretary of State, 4 December 1945, RG 59, 835.00; Cabot to Secretary of State, 8 February 1946, RG 59, 835.00.

60. Cabot to Armour, 25 February 1946, Cabot Papers, Argentina, HST.

Never one to take a passive defensive posture, Perón counterattacked vigorously. In a series of speeches, he announced that the true leader of the *Unión Demócratica* was not Tamborini, but Braden, the incarnation of "Wall Street imperialism." Therefore, patriotic Argentines should realize that their choice on election day was not Tamborini or Perón, but "Braden or Perón." Virtually ignoring the content of the *Blue Book*, he focused instead upon the implications of the U.S. intervention. Did Argentines want to elect Tamborini, who was obviously a shill for Braden and the United States, or did they want to elect a patriotic Argentine who would steer their nation on an independent course? While Peronists chanted "argentinos sí, yankis no," Tamborini's followers retorted with "argentinos sí, nazis no" as the election degenerated, as Perón no doubt hoped it would, into a "personal fight between Mr. Braden and him." As one Peruvian diplomat noted, "many sectors" in Argentina admire the United States, but "in very few sectors is it loved." Unwittingly, Braden had given Perón an extremely potent slogan and an eleventh-hour boost, as even his most dedicated Latin American allies had to concede that "the Blue Book has failed."[61]

Perón won the election handily, defeating Tamborini's coalition and taking control of Congress. In the words of Albert Vannucci, "Braden may have acted like he was elected by Providence" to defeat Perón, "but Perón was actually elected by the Argentine people."[62] True to all predictions, Tamborini carried the rural elite and most of the business and middle classes, while Perón swept the working and lower classes. Although most voters had, of course, made up their minds much earlier in such a polarized struggle, the *Blue Book* may well have helped Perón bring out the vote. Voter turnout in the 1946 election was, not surprisingly, the highest in Argentine history. Regardless of whether Braden swung the election to Perón, he shouldered much of the blame. His later assertions to the contrary, he had tried to turn the election around

---

61. Rada a Ministro, 23 Febrero 1946, AMRE, Lima, 5-1-Y/42; Rada a Ministro, 15 Febrero 1946, AMRE, Lima, 5-1-A/46.

62. Vannucci, "Elected by Providence," 60.

for Tamborini and had failed. Although historians may argue over how decisive the *Blue Book* was, it quickly came to be regarded as a monumental blunder in both North and South America. Braden had misread the Argentine situation badly, it seemed, and played into Perón's hands.[63] Cabot had warned earlier that:

> . . . the bonfire under Perón is blazing merrily and there are few signs that it will go out of its own accord or that Perón can put it out though on the other hand there is little immediate evidence that Perón is about to be consumed by it. I conceive it to be our role to feed the flames with maximum efficiency but not to smother them with too much fuel.[64]

The *Blue Book* had done just that. As Paul Daniels, soon to become director of the State Department's Division of American Republics Affairs put it, Braden's efforts had made the voters choose "Argentina or the United States," and "that's pretty hard to lick," even if Perón "did a lot of nasty things."[65] Braden could argue that nothing had been lost because Perón would have won regardless, but this defense fell on deaf ears.

## IV

With the election of Perón, U.S. policymakers were forced to make a sweeping reevaluation of their policies toward Argentina and Latin America. They had initially perceived Perón to be an authoritarian demagogue, ideologically driven toward state corporatism as a developmental model and an alternative to free trade and liberal capitalism. In office, he proved this thesis to be, in many ways, correct. While Braden and others may have wanted to continue to pummel Perón and drive him from office, new realities made this approach impossible. Perón had been democratically elected and for the United States to attack him was to repudiate one of the central tenets of the Good Neighbor policy and the spirit

---

63. Frank, *Juan Perón vs. Spruille Braden*, 109-111.

64. Cabot to Braden, 6 October 1945, RG 59, 711.35.

65. Paul Daniels Oral History, HST, 29.

of the Four Freedoms. The Truman Administration was forced to accept his election or risk the precious, precarious amity that the Good Neighbor had built.[66]

For Argentina, the die had been decisively cast. Decades of oligarchic control over the nation had come to an abrupt end on June 4, 1943, and Perón's election finalized it. The masses of Argentina would have a voice in their government and a leader responsive to their appeals. Although Perón did employ a certain amount of authoritarianism as he implanted state corporatism over traditional structures, he kept a wary eye on the mood of the masses and his constituencies. How Washington chose to deal with the unleashed working class in Argentina and its new spokesman, who eventually labeled himself "public enemy #1 of the imperialistic consortiums," foreshadowed and laid the foundations for the next three decades of U.S. relations of Latin America.[67]

---

66. Vannucci, "The Influence of Latin American Governments," 371-382.

67. Pool to Secretary of State, 12 June 1951, RG 59, 735.00.

# CHAPTER 3

## LOOKING FOR A "GOOD STICK," MARCH-JUNE 1946

> The Argentine problem seems as insoluble as ever . . . In the meantime, we continue to put on as sour a face as possible to the Argentine, but when we look around for a good stick with which to beat a certain gent we never seem to be able to find one handy.
>
> John Moors Cabot, January 4, 1946[1]

### I

As Perón consolidated his victory and implemented his revolutionary agenda from March to June 1946, U.S. policymakers scrambled to formulate an adequate response in the wake of the *Blue Book* fiasco. Clearly, Spruille Braden's old hard-line policies were bankrupt, as Perón's victory validated his status as a legitimate, democratically elected head of state and forced an end to overt U.S. opposition. If leaders in the United States hoped to maintain the fragile "Good Neighbor" relationship with Latin America, they were compelled to accept Perón's victory or old suspicions of "Yankee imperialism" might again wrack the hemisphere. Even without this impetus, however, the *Blue Book* had already proven conclusively to sounder minds in the State Department that the demagogue Perón was far more likely to be strengthened by attacks from the north than weakened. To preserve the "Inter-American system" and deal with the not insignificant threat posed by Argentine nationalism, the U.S. response would need to display a subtlety and understanding that had heretofore been sadly lacking.

---

1. Cabot to Lockwood, 4 January 1946, Cabot Papers, Argentina, HST.

As the New Dealers adjusted to the new realities, Perón moved forward boldly to centralize and revitalize the Argentine economy. Any hopes that he might evolve into an apolitical *caudillo* quickly dissipated as he clearly intended to take Argentina far down a path reminiscent to that the world took in the 1930s and therefore quite unacceptable to his counterparts in Washington. So, although the Truman Administration bowed to necessity by aborting Braden's undeclared war on Argentine "fascism" and normalizing relations with Peronist Argentina, this shift was in many ways cosmetic. Few in the State Department actually sought genuine rapprochement with Perón, yet the pretense was vital. Other Latin American nations could rest easier that the Yankee colossus was not again taking up the "big stick," and Perón would no longer be able to rally nationalist sentiment by citing U.S. interference. This new strategy crystallized in April, and although the diplomats never implemented it as smoothly or comfortably as they would have liked, the lines drawn in these early months set the tempo for the next four years.

## II

Election results filtered in slowly. Initial estimates gave the edge to José Tamborini and the Democratic Union, but by March 4, "it now seems probable that Perón has won," chargé John Cabot reported, adding that "he will have a great majority in both houses of Congress." Furthermore, the Democratic Union, believing the initial estimates, had already conceded that the elections had been the "most honest...[Argentina] ever had," or at least, in Cabot's words, "reasonably fair by Argentine standards." Unable to raise the cry of electoral fraud, the State Department and the Democratic Union conceded defeat.[2]

The president-elect seized the reins immediately, as lame duck Edelmiro Farrell took full advantage of the almost dictatorial

---

2. Cabot to Secretary of State, 7 March 1946, RG 59, 835.50; Cabot to Lockwood, 4 January 1946, Cabot Papers, Argentina, HST; see also Potash, *The Army and Politics: Perón to Frondizi*, 45; Crassweller, *Perón and the Enigmas of Argentina*, 174.

powers he possessed until Congress could convene to issue a series of decrees on Perón's behalf. Drafted under the guidance of Perón's foremost economic advisor, Miguel Miranda, Farrell's eleventh-hour orders left little doubt of the course the *peronista* state was going to follow. Just days after the formal announcement of Perón's victory, Farrell dropped his first "bombshell" by announcing the nationalization of the Central Bank of Argentina. Created in 1935, the *Banco Central* had traditionally served as a semi-public institution, fusing private investors and bankers with government-appointed advisors. In the hands of the old elite, the Central Bank had been a vehicle for conservative, tight-money policies, but to carry through their program, Perón and Miranda required a far more powerful instrument.[3]

The bank quickly assumed new powers that transformed it fully into a *peronista* instrument and the "axis of the Argentine economic system." All financial institutions in Argentina were made accountable to the Central Bank and were required to register their deposits with the national authority. Furthermore, the Central Bank had to approve loans made from private institutions, ensuring that industrial growth and investment followed the dictates of the government. Perón took other steps on the twin assumptions that great amounts of capital "have been lying idle for extended periods" and that only the state could adequately perform as social arbiter for it. If private banks proved reluctant to make the loans Perón deemed necessary, Central Bank funds could be funneled through a specialized, state-controlled Industrial Credit Bank. On the other hand, if private banks did not comply with the dictates of the Central Bank, their assets could legally be seized—a nightmare scenario for Argentine and foreign bankers who understood all too well that this "far-reaching and profound" development might well be the harbinger of the eventual "elimination of private banks." At the very least, it was a major step in the establishment of a

---

3. *Review of the River Plate*, 29 March 1946, 7-8; *Review of the River Plate*, 2 January 1948, 7; Antonio Cafiero, *Cinco años después* (Buenos Aires, 1961), 244-246; Lewis, *The Crisis of Argentine Capitalism*, 159.

corporatism in which the balance of power was tilted decisively toward the state and away from traditional private interests.[4]

With a national financial authority firmly in place, Peronists revived and revitalized old protectionist practices of exchange control. By manipulating exchange rates, Perón and Miranda hoped further to "orient imports" and direct development toward their ends. The Central Bank could simply deny foreign exchange or mandate highly prejudicial exchange rates for imports competitive with the produce of nascent Argentine industries. Similarly, by mandating poor exchange rates for remittances, Perón's bankers could encourage foreign investors to reinvest their profits within Argentina. All of these steps aimed to shelter embryonic industries, as well as Perón's working class constituency from the heartless global economy. While Perón cited the nationalized banks in England and the U.S. Federal Reserve as his precedents, observers in the north naturally saw only "sinister implications." Moreover, this was, Farrell explained ominously, "no more than a beginning of the measures" to "promote the greatest possible expansion of private enterprise," by "assisting and encouraging it to follow the desired course."[5]

Perón was not content with fiscal control and quickly moved to extend the reach of his leviathan state directly into corporate boardrooms. Decree/Law 15,359 provided for the creation of *Sociedades de Economía Mixta* ("mixed companies") in which government and business shared management and ownership. Although the state could simply invest capital through the Central Bank to gain a voice in the management of existing companies, this law allowed for a more subtle penetration of the private sphere. "Mixed companies" were to be granted various benefits ranging from tax exemptions and financial assistance to "exclusive or monopolistic privileges" within a given industry, and the

---

4. *Review of the River Plate*, 31 May 1946, 3-4; *Review of the River Plate* 29 March 1946, 7-8; Cafiero, *Cinco años*, 246-263; see also Leonardo Paso, *Del golpe de Estado de 1943 al de 1955* (Buenos Aires, 1987), 93-94.

5. Cabot to Messersmith, 15 July 1946, Cabot Papers, Argentina, HST; *Review of the River Plate*, 29 March 1946, 13-17; see also Lewis, *Crisis of Argentine Capitalism*, 159.

government-appointed president of a "mixed company" had veto power over private officials in most matters. Intended to serve as vehicles for the retention of capitalistic innovation with the addition of *peronista* technocratic guidance, these entities promised to give Perón a vehicle to assume control of old German properties that had to be "denazified" as well as domestic ones over which he hoped to acquire influence.[6]

Of the *peronistas*' early activities, however, none had more profound and foreboding overtones than the creation of IAPI. Created explicitly as a "national autarchic entity," Perón granted the Argentine Trade Promotion Institute an almost monopolistic control over the sale and purchase of grains, edible oils, and "all kinds of goods," "natural or manufactured."[7] The significance of IAPI was not lost upon economists Celso Furtado, who considered it to be "the most comprehensive attempt made in Latin America to bring exports under the control of the state," and Pinedo, who asserted that it was nothing less than a throwback to old Spanish mercantilism.[8] Although there were precedents in Argentine history for state intervention in the agricultural economy, IAPI represented a dramatic populist turn. At the height of the Depression, the oligarchs had created the National Grain Board, which much like the U.S. Agricultural Adjustment Acts, had subsidized farmers to compensate for plunging global prices. Similar wine, meat, and milk boards had also purchased surpluses and buttressed the oligarchy against the uncertainty of the international market.[9]

---

6. Messersmith to Secretary of State, 30 May 1946, RG 59, 835.50; Tewksbury to Secretary of State, 7 June 1946, RG 59, 835.50.

7. Instituto Argentino para la Promoción del Intercambio, *Memoria Anual* (Buenos Aires, 1949), 1-23.

8. Page, *Perón*, 170; *Primera Plana*, 18 Julio 1966, 43; see also Tewksbury to Secretary of State, 12 June 1946, RG 59, 835.50; Cafiero, *Cinco años*, 216-239.

9. Prior to IAPI, forty firms had held almost exclusive control of grain exports. According to Cafiero, four of these had controlled 83.5% of the trade. Cafiero, *Cinco años*, 217; see also Crassweller, *Perón and the Enigmas of Argentina*, 225; R. Seipe, M. Monserrat Llairo and N. Gale, *Perón y las relaciones con el Este* (Buenos December, 1947, 7.

Agricultural protectionism and valorization of this sort had long been a staple of Latin American monocultural development, and a natural response to boom-bust international cycles, but IAPI turned the traditional formula on its head.

IAPI's stated goal was economic "development beneficial to all sectors, which is possible only through centralization and the direction of the State."[10] The fruits of the fertile soil of the *pampas*, which had flowed almost exclusively into the hands of the landed *estancieros*, *hacendados*, and exporting firms, were to be redirected to serve the elusive common good. IAPI was empowered to do so in several distinct fashions. First and foremost, farmers and ranchers were forced to sell their produce to IAPI at very low prices. The decreases in the cost of food were passed on to the urban working classes, lowering the cost of living and effecting some redistribution of wealth. In addition to siphoning wealth from his traditional enemies of the landed classes and benefiting his allies in the cities, Perón's "subsidization of consumption" fit nicely into his plans to push forward internally driven industrial growth. Just as higher wages for the working class, import substitution, and protectionism served the intensification and deepening of industrialization, lower food prices naturally gave Argentine consumers a larger disposable income to fuel growth. Perón tried to assuage landowners by claiming that if world food prices again fell, IAPI would be used to compensate them—a promise he did eventually keep—but this pledge rang hollow to those elites whose fortunes were to be diverted so crassly to the state and the working class.[11]

However, IAPI's participation in foreign trade made it the cornerstone of the Peronist economy, projecting the Argentine government into global commerce. As a unified seller representing one of the largest food exporting nations, IAPI exacted higher

---

10. IAPI, *Memoria Anual*, Anexos.

11. IAPI, *Memoria Anual*, Anexos; see also Guido DiTella and Manuel Zymelman, *Las etapas del desarrollo económico argentino* (Buenos Aires, 1967), 494-496; Jorge Fodor, "Perón's Policies for Agricultural Exports," 139-145; Paso, *Del golpe de Estado*, vol. 1, 95; *Review of the River Plate*, 30 August 1946, 3-6; *Review of the River Plate*, 20 December 1947, 7.

prices from other nations than any individual private exporter through bilateral negotiation. *Peronistas* calculated that during the past decade, low international food prices and exporters' willingness to accept them had cost Argentina billions of dollars. By negotiating bilaterally with war torn European states and traditionally dependent South American nations, IAPI would have far more leverage than any private seller, could drive hard bargains, and could barter for scarce industrial goods or raw materials. The difference between the low prices it paid to Argentine producers and the high price exacted from buyers abroad was to be funneled into machinery, capital goods, and raw materials, theoretically coordinating the drive for self-sufficiency and "economic independence."[12] While the world had become very familiar with the old German tactic of "dumping," charging high prices at home to allow inordinately cheap exports, IAPI inverted this formula to serve Perón's unique goals and coalition.

Although IAPI was clearly, on one level, an effective means by which to exploit the global food shortage of the post-war period and extort trading partners, Perón defended IAPI as a necessary response to the economic climate of the post-war world, and as a counterweight to the Combined Food Board and other international agencies charged with allocating and distributing food.[13] In the face of these buyers' monopolies, created to ensure the efficient conduct of the war and perpetuated to alleviate hunger in the war torn world, Perón and Miranda asserted the right to respond with a seller's monopoly. Argentines had witnessed firsthand the activities of the various product boards (most notably the RDC) and seen these supposedly impartial, apolitical organizations used as instruments of U.S. foreign policy and the "economic boycott" of Argentina.[14] Perón had no reason to believe that the food boards

---

12. IAPI, *Memoria Anual*, 9-12; Cafiero, *Cinco años*, 265-281; *Review of the River Plate*, 23 August 1946, 8.

13. IAPI, *Memoria Anual*, 9-10.

14. Escudé, "US Political Destabilization and the Economic Boycott of Argentina during the 1940s," *Argentina Between the Great Powers, 1939-1946*, eds. Watt and DiTella (Pittsburgh, 1990), 56.

would prove to be any more sympathetic to Argentine needs. Peronists further charged that as victims of "moral imperialism" and the global scarcity of capital goods, they were being forced to pay inflated "black market" prices for their imported manufactured wares. If Argentina was to be forced to pay exorbitantly for its industrial wares in the post-war period, IAPI merely redressed the balance.[15]

Nonetheless, IAPI's creation hardly seems to have been an entirely defensive measure or a simple reaction. Argentines had marveled during the 1930s as Schacht's Reichsbank in Germany had, through cutthroat economic pressure and bilateral barter, not only weathered the Depression, but built an economy capable of sustaining a massive arms build-up and war. Indeed, the Argentine reaction to the Depression and wartime shortages had been a strong adherence to the bilateral slogan of *"comprar los que nos compra"* ("buy from those who buy from us") and a strict import substitution regime that bordered on autarchy. These developments had been the spark for Argentine industrialization, and there seemed to be no reason why an even stronger application of the same principles should not be able to facilitate even more intensive industrial development. More importantly, however, Perón had witnessed the potential effectiveness of state trading and "economic blackmail" during the wheat-rubber crisis of 1945-1946. Given these early victories, *peronistas* had little reason to doubt that IAPI could secure even greater ones. So, although some observers simply wrote off IAPI as a clever, if sinister, scheme to capitalize on the global food shortage, it clearly constituted another solution to many problems facing Perón's constituencies.[16]

Together, the Central Bank and IAPI could manipulate and exploit the weaknesses of the global economy to further the cause of Argentine industrialization. Haste was essential, however.

---

15. Linville, "Problem of Obtaining Food Exports from Argentina," 22 May 1946, RG 353, Records of the Interdepartmental and Intradepartmental Committees, The Argentina Committee, National Archives II, College Park, MD (RIIC-ARG); Carlos Escudé, *Gran Bretaña, Estados Unidos*, 253-305.

16. Horowicz, *Los cuatros peronismos*, 108-109; *Review of the River Plate*, 7 February 1947, 3-4.

Resourceful Argentine industrialists had turned the wartime shortages and the U.S. embargoes to their advantage, using the enforced isolation to create new industries, and Perón hoped to build upon this foundation. But time was short, for within a few years, food prices would return to their normal low levels, as they had after World War I. Even worse, Perón fully expected the United States and the Soviet Union to go to war within five years, and when this happened, Argentine industrial imports would once again be shut off. For Perón, the task was to move as quickly as possible toward industrial self-sufficiency before this deadline arrived. In this context, IAPI and the Central Bank were vital lest this unprecedented opportunity pass, as only state coordination and organization could efficiently translate Argentina's agricultural wealth into industrial development.[17]

At the U.S. embassy, John Cabot took a dimmer view. He denounced the "ominous overtones" of the Peronist decrees which, taken together, were giving the government a "virtual stranglehold on practically every transaction."[18] Predictably, Argentine businessmen thought little better of these developments and attacked each until Perón effectively silenced them. He tried to woo the industrialists of the *Unión Industrial Argentina* (UIA) into becoming a wing of his corporativist state and a counterpart organization to the CGT, utilizing the same rhetoric that New Dealers had employed so effectively. "My dear capitalists, do not be afraid of my labor movement," he cajoled. "Capitalism has never been safer, because I too am a capitalist." "What I want," he claimed, "is to organize the workers so the state can control them, lay down guidelines for them, and neutralize in their hearts the ideological and revolutionary passion."[19]

Perón claimed to share with the industrialists and the Army the "*gran miedo*" ("great fear") of both the revolutionary potential

---

17. DiTella and Zymelman, *Las etapas del desarrollo económico argentino*, 494-496.

18. Cabot to Messersmith, 15 July 1946, Cabot Papers, Argentina, HST.

19. Quoted in Lewis, *Crisis of Argentine Capitalism*, 144-149 and Rock, *Argentina,* 257.

of the masses and the economic dislocations that would arise in the post-war period. Therefore, like Roosevelt, he tried to convince enlightened capitalists that his movement would become a buttress against Marxist upheaval. The UIA naturally ignored his rather hollow rhetoric of cooperation and instead focused upon his confrontational labor decrees, interventionism, and impassioned denunciations of the "*vendepatria*" elite. In June, he decreed a "Sixty-Day Campaign" that imposed price ceilings on many consumer goods, remarking that "those who cannot do business this way can close up shop." Clearly unsympathetic to corporate interests and bent upon inserting government officials into business boardrooms by any means necessary, Perón could hardly be considered an ally of the capitalist class. When the badly divided UIA resisted, he declared the organization to be without "juridical personality" and dissolved it. Ironically, Perón had been driven to discipline the same industrialists that he was more than willing to subsidize.[20]

Still, if any doubts remained about Perón's intention to create a truly "directed economy" and move decisively away from a privatist corporatism, these were all but eliminated by the selection of one man, Miguel Miranda, to head both IAPI and the Central Bank as "economic czar." A successful canned goods magnate and an "iconoclastic high-flyer," Miranda was one of the few industrialists who broke ranks to back Perón. For the new president, a man who was capable of managing his own financial empire using only a notebook in his breast pocket possessed the technocratic expertise required for the coordination of the national economy. Miranda claimed to be a staunch advocate of private enterprise, who once had "disagreed in principle with the present President," but said that during 1945, "I soon changed my mind" as he became the most ardent advocate of Perón's statist corporatism.[21] The British considered Miranda to be intelligent, if

---

20. *Review of the River Plate*, 21 June 1946, 6; Cristina Lucchini, *Apoyo empresarial en los orígenes del peronismo* (Buenos Aires, 1990), 44-47; Peter Waldmann, *El Peronismo*, 130-136; Paso, *Del golpe de Estado*, 106-107; Wynia, *Argentina in the Post-War Era*, 55-57.

21. *Review of the River Plate*, 28 March 1947, 12.

brutally candid. The U.S. embassy, however, did not take long to label him "utterly incompetent," "devoid of principle," and "of no character." His claim that "people will bring their dollars to us or they will become accustomed to living without food" epitomized for many in the United States and Great Britain the supposed ruthlessness of Perón's regime.[22]

While State Department officials could not yet know much of Miranda in 1946, they were well informed about José Figuerola, who Perón promoted to head his Technical Secretariat. The Spanish exile had been one of Perón's foremost advisors in the old Labor Secretariat, a mastermind in the "capture" of Argentine labor, and, in the eyes of Braden's aide, John Griffiths, the "least inept of [Perón's] cohorts." This "clever Catalan," Griffiths wrote, "has long been considered an enemy of democracy and an advocate of a single syndicate-corporativist type of totalitarianism." Griffiths conjectured that only Figuerola's academic theories that a corporatist state had to evolve slowly had restrained Perón from pushing forward even more quickly than he had. Although the State Department could take some solace from the fact that Figuerola held a sub-Cabinet post, it was not reassured to learn that most of his time was being spent drafting a Five-Year plan-the blueprint for the Peronist economy.[23]

Most of Perón's other appointees were virtually unknown outside of Argentina. As politicians, diplomats, and economists from the old political parties and the elite refused to serve in the government, the new president turned to political novices like

---

22. Bruce to Secretary of State, 26 September 1947, RG 59, 611.3531; Messersmith to Clayton, 3 September 1946, RG 59, 635.4131; Paz and Ferrari, *Política Exterior Argentina* 154; see also Hugo Gambini, *La primera presidencia de Perón*, 122; MacDonald, "The U.S., the Cold War and Perón," *Economic Imperialism and the State: The Political Economy of the External Connection from Independence to the Present*, eds. Christopher Abel and Colin Lewis (London, 1985), 407-409.

23. Griffiths, "A Resume of Labor Policies, Measures and Developments under the Argentine Secretariat of Labor and Social Planning during the Year 1944," 5 May 1945, RG 59, 835.5034; see also Gambini, *La primera presidencia*, 84-85; Page, *Perón*, 68-69; Wynia, *Argentina in the Post-War Era*, 55.

Miranda, old ideologues like Figuerola, and loyal labor leaders virtually unknown outside of South America. Juan Bramulgia, a socialist labor lawyer who would distinguish himself and eventually win international acclaim, was named Minister of Foreign Affairs and Worship. For the important post of Minister of the Interior, the president tapped Borlenghi, former president of the Argentine Federation of Commercial Employees. The AFL's primary troubleshooter in Latin America, Serafino Romualdi, erroneously deemed Borlenghi to be "the real strong man of the regime" and the leader of a "Secret Police along the lines of the Gestapo."[24] Heinrich Doerge, a German immigrant and a former associate of Schacht, became a financial advisor, while Rodolfo Freude, the son of suspected Nazi Ludwig Freude, headed Perón's personal secretariat, and Perón's mistress, Eva Duarte, "constantly up on a soapbox, intellectually scratching and biting at every form of wealth or special privilege," was given an office in the Labor Ministry. All in all, Washington knew little of Perón's retinue, but what they did know was hardly encouraging, as this cabinet certainly bore little resemblance to any that had ever been assembled in the Western Hemisphere.[25]

### III

If the initial stages of the *Peronato* hinted at radical developments, Peronist foreign policy seemed to confirm fears that the Argentines had not given up old dreams of assembling an autarchic "southern bloc." This implementation of the "Third Position" illustrated well that Perón's activism would not end at Argentina's borders. By capitalizing upon Argentina's privileged position at the end of the war, Peronists pressed forward, invigorated by victories over their domestic and foreign foes. The

---

24. Serafino Romualdi, *Presidents and Peons: Recollections of a Labor Ambassador* (New York, 1970), 151-152.

25. Stanton Griffis, *Lying in State* (Garden City, 1952), 253; see also Berger to Secretary of State, 26 May 1945, RG 59, 835.50; Nicholas Fraser and Marysa Navarro, *Eva Perón* (New York, 1980), 74-77 Gambini, *La primera presidencia*, 84-88; Page, *Perón*, 157.

South American balance of power provided excellent opportunities for mischief, and Perón overlooked few of them as he sought, or tried to create, allies across the continent.

Uruguay, traditionally overshadowed by its Argentine and Brazilian neighbors but closely allied with the United States, had the most to fear, as the Uruguayan press and government had been among the most vigorous of Perón's detractors for years. Uruguayan Foreign Minister Alberto Rodríguez Larreta had long been one of Braden's closest allies and had even proposed, at one point, that the American states should have the ability to intervene collectively in states where civil rights were abused—a clear call for U.S. action against Argentina. Throughout 1945, Perón had railed against other Uruguayan accusations that he was a "fascist," "totalitarian," and a "dictator." During his electoral campaign, he had urged Farrell to "adopt measures to counteract the violent and tendentious propaganda" coming out of Montevideo and find a "solution to this problem through diplomacy." He apparently found one for himself in April, as mildly anti-U.S. *Colorado* party candidate, Luis Alberto Herrera, and the avowedly pro-U.S. *Blanco*, Tomás Berreta, vied for the presidency.[26]

In what can only be construed as a crude attempt to manipulate the election, the Argentine government abruptly terminated wheat shipments to Uruguay and announced that they would resume only at Herrera's request. The Uruguayan government, controlled by the *Blancos*, urgently requested emergency shipments from Washington to compensate. The State Department supported the petition, and seventeen thousand tons of wheat originally destined for Europe was diverted to Uruguay, along with a promise of another seventeen thousand tons. When Berreta emerged victorious, members of his administration publicly thanked the United States for its assistance and privately vowed to "hold the line" against Argentina. Even the State Department's

---

26. Perón to Ameghino, 30 Abril 1945, Archivo del Ministerio de Relaciones Exteriores y Culto, Buenos Aires, Argentina (AMREC, BA), Uruguay 1945, Caja 12, Expediente 23; Santillán, "La Prensa in el Uruguay," 23 Enero 1947, AMREC, BA, Uruguay 1947, 13, 4; see also Peterson, *Argentina and the United States*, 451-2.

most levelheaded commentators noted that this intrigue represented a good reminder of the "continued danger Perón represents for us," as Perón's first efforts to create a more favorable atmosphere for himself in the Southern Cone failed miserably.[27]

The Bolivian situation looked far worse to Washington, as Major Gualberto Villarroel remained in power, and looked to be Perón's most natural ally. Still convinced of Nazi and Peronist connivance in the coup that brought Villarroel to power in 1943, Braden and his colleagues persisted in the belief that Villarroel was little more than a fascist puppet. Indeed, there were significant links between the two nationalist movements. Víctor Paz Estenssoro, once a powerful force in Villarroel's government and still a dominant political figure in the country, had maintained a long friendship with high *peronista* officials, and later conceded that Perón held a "certain sympathy" for the revolutionaries. Ties may have become even closer as Villarroel entered discussions with Peronists to have the iron fields of Mutún opened up to Argentine capital.[28] Bolivian Foreign Minister Ernesto Tamayo added fuel to U.S. fears by publicly proposing a "southern bloc" alliance to Chilean and Argentine leaders, while another revolutionary, "Comrade X," fanned the flames, lauding Argentina as "the only country which has succeeded in saving itself from the 'loving care

---

27. Braden to Acheson and Marshall, 13 February 1947, PSF, Foreign Affairs, Marshall File, HST; Cabot to Secretary of State, 12 April 1946, RG 59, 711.35; see also Dawson to Secretary of State, 2 April 1946, RG 59, 835.24; Fernando Lopez-Alves, "Why Not Corporatism?: Redemocratization and Regime Formation in Uruguay," in *Latin America in the 1940s: War and Postwar Transitions*, ed. David Rock (Berkeley, 1994), 187-209; Liborio Justo, *Argentina y Brasil en la integración continental* (Buenos Aires, 1983), 43-4. Peruvian diplomats believed that the Argentine embargo was not so much to assist Herrera as to punish the *Blancos* for their support of Braden. Rada a Ministro, 8 Abril 1946, AMRE, Lima, 5-1-Y/70; Rada a Ministro, 26 Abril 1946, AMRE, Lima, 5-1-Y/79.

28. Robert J. Alexander, *The Bolivaran Presidents*, 15-17; Carles, "Sobre infiltración brasileña en Santa Cruz de la Sierra," 9 November 1946, AMREC, BA, Bolivia 1946, 2, 11.

of the United States,' thus maintaining the rebellious and free spirit of South America."[29]

More substantially, the U.S. embassy in La Paz reported in late May that "Bolivia has probably joined the bloc allegedly being formed by Argentina." Elías Belmonte Pabón, a colleague of Villarroel and a suspected Nazi agent, was reputed to be returning to Bolivia from exile, where the embassy expected him "to play the role of a Junior Perón." The best evidence that U.S. diplomats could present for these assertions was Argentina's maintenance of food deliveries to Bolivia. According to Hector Adam, the U.S. ambassador in La Paz:

> In view of Argentina's blackmailing tactics toward Peru, Brazil, and Uruguay with regard to the shipping of wheat and meat which those countries need, it should be evident from the reported recent agreement by Argentina to provide 60,000 tons of wheat to Bolivia and the fact that ample meat supplies continue to be received here, that Bolivia must have come to terms which Argentina demanded before such concessions were made. Just what the Bolivian concessions have been cannot be determined with accuracy at this time.

In other words, Adam concluded that "there can no longer be any doubt that Bolivia, either through fear of reprisals or genuine willingness, has now signed up" in a "southern bloc."[30] Adam considered Villarroel "pathetic" when he "insisted for the dozenth time that he is no special friend of Argentina," but that "he had to treat Argentina with every courtesy because of Bolivia's dependence on it for food." Bolivia may well have been "at the continuous mercy of avaricious and more powerful neighbors," but Adam refused to believe that the regime was anything but Perón's willing partner. Although Adam badly overstated the case and ignored any evidence counter to his overblown thesis, any

---

29. Adam to Secretary of State, 1 May 1946, RG 59, 724.35; see also Andrade, *My Missions for Revolutionary Bolivia*, 22-24.

30. Adam to Secretary of State, 31 May 1946, RG 84, BA.

collaboration of these two nationalist governments boded ill for undisputed U.S. hegemony over a united hemisphere.[31]

In response to these accusations, the counselor of the Argentine embassy in Washington explained with some justification that Argentina was "damned if [we] do, damned if [we] don't." "If, because of difficulties in transportation, there is some delay in sending wheat or meat to Argentina's neighbors," he claimed, "they jump to the conclusion that we are trying to starve them in order to impose our will." On the other hand, if "we try to help them rebuild their industry and economy, we are accused of trying to form a 'southern bloc'" directed against the United States.[32] Although there was merit to this defense, the wheat-rubber scandal and the Uruguayan debacle illustrated clearly that Peronists were indeed using food as a weapon in the same fashion that Hull and Braden had utilized coal, rubber, and petroleum.

Other accounts of *peronista* activities continued to filter into U.S. embassies throughout South America, as Perón cultivated economic nationalists, critics of the United States, and potential allies across the continent. Cabot believed that he had a strong "desire to hunt in the same wolfpack" as Brazilian President Getulio Vargas and that Vargas might be responsive.[33] The U.S. ambassador to Brazil, Adolph Berle, had waged a Bradenesque campaign against Vargas in late 1945 despite his steadfast loyalty to the Allied cause during the war. For Berle and his superiors, Vargas' corporatist *Estado Novo* and authoritarian practices were far too similar to both Mussolini's and Perón's for comfort. Even though there was far more rivalry and mistrust between Argentina and Brazil than amity and goodwill, the State Department still

---

31. Adam to Secretary of State, 25 March 1946, RG 59, 711.24. Although Adam's accusations may appear to be extreme, they were endorsed strongly by at least one other diplomat in La Paz, Peruvian Ambassador Eduardo Garland, who believed that Bolivia was a "fertile field" for "Argentine political propaganda." Garland a Ministro, 7 June 1946, AMRE, Lima, 5-7-Y/35.

32. Ivanissevich to Bramulgia, 6 Enero 1947, AMREC, BA, Chile 1946, 10, Convenio, 4.

33. Cabot to Messersmith, 15 July 1946, Cabot Papers, Argentina, HST.

feared that the ideological common ground between Vargas and Perón might bridge these traditional impediments to Argentine-Brazilian cooperation.[34]

Also disquieting was Perón's apparent cultivation of Paraguayan President Higinio Morinigo. Although he had supported the Allied war effort, Morinigo nonetheless preached economic nationalism and practiced authoritarianism. Like Perón, Morinigo had emerged from a secret military lodge, the *Frente de guerra*, and was working to assert state power over the national economy to stimulate development. Some of Morinigo's chief lieutenants were even more suspect, especially Colonel Victoriano Benítez Vera, who held some *peronista* sympathies and had even exchanged gunfire with North Americans during the war. By May, Perón's envoys had formalized their overtures, offering a customs union with Paraguay. Even though Morinigo was clearly more interested in maintaining good relations with the United States than turning his nation into a vassal state of Argentina, Washington was continually reminded that Perón was a loose cannon with all of the power and influence of Latin America's wealthiest nation behind him.[35]

If Perón sought political and economic unity against the United States and the liberal capitalist order that had retarded Latin American development, his campaign also featured a creative appeal to religious, cultural, and ethnic solidarity. Perón could claim to have at least the nominal backing of the Catholic church, quite unlike either the Communists or the predominately Protestant

---

34. Berle to Secretary of State, 25 February 1946, in *FRUS* IX, 223-224; Wood, *The Dismantling of the Good Neighbor Policy*, 123-131; Justo, *Argentina y Brasil en la integración continental*, 42-48; Stanley Hilton, "Las relaciones Argentino-Brasileña: El punto de vista de Brasil," *Geopolitica y politica en el atlantico sur*, ed. Carlos Moneta (Buenos Aires, 1983), 29-39; Joseph Tulchin, "La relación Argentina-Brasileña: Punto de vista Argentina," *Geopolitica y politica*, 43-57.

35. Cabot to Messersmith, 15 July 1946, Cabot Papers, Argentina, HST; Cabot to Secretary of State, 3 May 1946, RG 59, 634.352; Goñi, *Perón y los alemanes*, 122-124; Grow, *The Good Neighbor Policy and Authoritarianism in Paraguay*.

United States. Perón, to be sure, had never received official papal approval, but important members of the clergy had backed him and his brand of state corporatism.[36] Furthermore, he also enjoyed close ties with Generalissimo Francisco Franco, which allowed him to capitalize on cultural ties based on much of Latin America's "blood relationship with Spain." When the Peronist ambassador arrived in Cuba, for example, he made a point of reminding the Cubans of the "common noble Hispanic origin" and of the "Catholic, Apostolic, and Roman religion" that they shared with the Argentines.[37] Ironically, the same Latin American Catholicism that had earlier provided a natural bulwark against atheistic communism was now being made into a wedge by Perón.

For U.S. officials who believed that Perón was "embarking on a career of fascist crime," a further disquieting sign was his apparent willingness to capitalize upon the global food shortage and refusal to cooperate fully with international relief agencies.[38] Former President Herbert Hoover and UNRRA officials had visited Buenos Aires and appealed to the Argentines, citing statistics that over ten thousand people worldwide were dying of starvation or malnutrition daily. Because *porteños* consumed more meat per capita than any other people in the world, relief officials urged Farrell and Perón to issue a decree instituting mandatory food rationing. They refused but did ask that households cut back on consumption. This voluntary rationing program was roundly belittled, as it amounted to little when Perón was lowering domestic food prices and thereby tacitly encouraging consumption.

Even worse, meatpacking workers launched a series of major strikes throughout 1946 that stalled desperately needed meat exports to England. British journalists lamented that "millions of Europe's inhabitants are facing starvation or acute hardship through lack of food," yet "10,000 tons of meat" were "approaching a state

---

36. *Primera Plana*, 18 Octubre 1966, 36-38; *Primera Plana*, 1 Noviembre 1966, 34-36; *Primera Plana*, 8 Noviembre 1966, 36-40.

37. Norweb to Secretary of State, 10 July 1947, RG 59, 735.37; see also Hoyt to Briggs, Wright, and Mann, 19 March 1947, RG 59, MRIC.

38. Cabot to Braden, 3 April 1946, Cabot Papers, Argentina, HST.

of putrefaction in Argentine packing plants."³⁹ Naturally, they concluded that this state of affairs was "no fault of the companies"—which happened to be U.S. and British owned. Because Perón could have ordered the strikers back to work, the *Review of the River Plate* held him to blame, although the Argentine press noted that the height of Truman's efforts to ration domestically involved little more than ordering that wheat not be used for beer production. Moreover, Peronists claimed that if they increased shipments to Europe, they would be unable to meet the "needs of the people of our continent." So even though Hoover, Fiorello LaGuardia, and Secretary of Agriculture Clinton Anderson admitted that Perón was doing his share to combat world hunger, the U.S. government's inter-departmental "Argentina Committee" succinctly concluded that "Argentina has done nothing to cooperate."⁴⁰

Other conciliatory gestures were similarly downplayed by his enemies. Perón and his followers repeatedly expressed their support for the "denazification" program to eliminate Axis influences as mandated by the Chapultepec Accords and did make some effort toward compliance. He sent messengers to the U.S. embassy to extend olive branches and otherwise make "friendly gestures" as Peronists were "falling all over themselves for cooperation," and being "just too nice for words." In light of the pattern that Peronists were establishing, however, these words rang hollow. Few in the State Department were at all convinced that Perón had "really had a change of heart," and some even questioned that he "has a heart to change."⁴¹ While Peronists clearly sought

---

39. *Review of the River Plate*, 1 March 1946, 18; see also *Review of the River Plate*, 1 March 1946, 6; *Review of the River Plate*, 5 April 1946, 3; *Review of the River Plate*, 12 April 1946, 3-4.

40. *Review of the River Plate*, 1 March 1947, 18; Rada a Ministro, 22 Marzo 1946, AMRE, Lima, 5-1-A/165; Baker Report, 18 September 1946, RG 353, RIIC-ARG; Anexo a la nota 463 de la Embajada en Washington, 8 Mayo 1946, AMREC, BA, Uruguay 1946, 14, 2.

41. Cabot to Secretary of State, 13 March 1946, Cabot Papers, Argentina, HST; Cabot to Deputy Director of the Office of American Republics Affairs, 26 March 1946, in *FRUS* IX, 238-239; Baldwin to Truman, 13 April 1946, HST,

some sort of superficial rapprochement with the Truman Administration, it was equally certain that their agenda was one destined to bring them into conflict with Washington.

## IV

Although these developments all seemed to confirm the State Department's worst fears, formulating a response proved difficult, and divided the Truman Administration into two camps. Aggressive champions of liberal democracy and market economics, led by Assistant Secretary of State Spruille Braden, advocated the continuation of the crusade to unseat Perón's "fascist" regime. More pragmatic defenders of self-determination such as Cabot countered that this sort of intervention had proven to be counterproductive, would leave Roosevelt's Good Neighbor Policy "torn to ribbons," "destroy confidence in our intentions," and cause damage that "may take decades for us to repair."[42]

For their part, Braden and Cabot's superiors largely remained aloof from the debate. While President Truman wrestled with domestic reconversion and Secretary of State James Byrnes tried his hand at atomic diplomacy in Europe, Undersecretary of State for Economic Affairs Will Clayton busied himself with the negotiation of the British loan. Assistant Secretary of State Dean Acheson's "almost complete lack of interest in [Latin America] and his generally superficial knowledge of it" left policymaking largely in the hands of Braden and the Department's second echelon for the time being.[43] This relative silence on the Argentine situation may have created an illusion of unconcern, but in truth, the broad strokes of policy had long since been painted, leaving functionaries like Braden and Cabot to quarrel over fine touches—the means to secure the hemispheric aspects of a global policy.

---

PSF, Foreign Affairs, Argentina, HST.

42. Cabot to Cochran, 14 December 1945, Cabot Papers, Argentina, HST.

43. Bohan to Bowen, 1 March 1973, Merwin Bohan Papers, Correspondence File, Argentina, HST; According to Bohan, Acheson "didn't pay attention to it, he didn't give a damn about Latin America." Merwin Bohan Oral History, HST, 46.

The Department's approach to Latin America in the postwar period had been spelled out quite clearly in March 1945 by Will Clayton at the Chapultepec Conference. The so-called "Clayton Plan" articulated at Chapultepec had been little more than a restatement of very familiar themes and principles. Arguing against the "establishment of enterprises which can only make their way through government subsidies or excessive tariffs," Clayton focused upon traditional New Deal notions of interdependence, constant economic growth, and the preservation of peace through multilateral commerce. Although Latin American development would by necessity take a back seat to European reconstruction in U.S. policy, this would eventually benefit Latin Americans, who needed the markets of the more developed countries. In the meantime, the "promotion of equal and reciprocal opportunity," "adherence to principles of free trade," and "development of competitive enterprise" were the best ways to avoid economic dislocations and the wars that inevitably followed. Clayton and George Messersmith had written these principles into the Economic Charter for the Americas at Chapultepec, over the objections of Latin American delegates. So although sorting out the nuances of the Good Neighbor policy fell to Braden and his colleagues, the ultimate global aim of U.S. policy, and its implications for Latin America, remained crystal clear.[44]

For Perón's self-appointed nemesis, Spruille Braden, the Argentine election "did not alter the fundamentals of the situation." Braden presented a number of convenient scapegoats—intransigent Argentine employers who had foolishly served as the perfect foil for Perón's demagoguery, the "old line politicos" like Tamborini who "blundered," and, of course, the U.S. Senate, which had delayed his own confirmation as assistant secretary. He naturally considered

---

44. Clayton Speech at Chapultepec, 4 March 1945, *Private Papers of Will Clayton*, ed. Dobney, 111-120; see also Thomas Bohlin, "United States-Latin American Relations and the Cold War, 1949-1953" (Unpublished Ph.D. dissertation, Notre Dame, 1985), 23-25; Paz and Ferrari, *Política Exterior Argentina*, 148-150; Vannucci, "U.S.-Argentine Relations, 1943-1948: A Case Study in Confused Policy Making" (Unpublished Ph.D. dissertation, New School for Social Research, 1979), 177-178; David Green, *The Containment of Latin America*, 171-208.

himself to be blameless and even agreed generously to "accept the verdict of the election." Nonetheless, he argued that "there is no room for middle ground," so long as "Argentina remains under the bare dictatorship of uniformed men who drink at the same fountain where drank Hitler, Mussolini and Franco."[45]

Braden rejected the argument that Perón was little more than a harmless relic of fascism, arguing forcefully that Argentina was destined to serve as the launch pad for a Fourth Reich. "The Germans in Argentina constitute a large, wealthy, unassimilated, politically-influential group which enjoys a virtual monopoly in various scientific fields," he wrote more than a year after the Nazi surrender, possessed of "extraordinary power" that would sooner or later "be used against the United States."[46] That Perón was employing suspected agents and German nationals in his government only seemed to confirm this thesis, for not only were *peronistas* pushing forward a fascistic program, but they were employing genuine fascists to do it.

With the defeat of the Axis and the inklings of a red menace in Josef Stalin's Soviet Union, Braden added communism to the list of charges he was piling up against Perón. Asserting that "Nazis and Commies are both authoritarian and often work together," he argued that they had forged a secret alliance for the post-war era. Naturally, he implicated Perón, Vargas, and several other Latin American leaders in this far-fetched conspiracy but conceded that "concrete proof of any such plan is lacking." Braden had even cabled Truman at the Potsdam Conference, urging him to force Stalin to quit "playing footsy" with Perón.[47] When Luis Prestes,

---

45. Braden to Messersmith, 8 March 1946, RG 59, 835.00; Jesse Stiller, *George S. Messersmith: Diplomat for Democracy* (Chapel Hill, 1987), 234; see also Wood, *The Dismantling of the Good Neighbor Policy*, 101-105; Vannucci, "Elected by Providence," 49-67. Braden claimed to have even "won three bets" that Perón would ultimately be declared the winner. Braden, *Diplomats and Demagogues*, 356.

46. Memorandum on the Argentine Situation, 12 July 1946, in *FRUS* IX, 273.

47. Braden to Secretary of State, 8 July 1946, RG 59, 711.35; Braden, *Diplomats and Demagogues*, 316-318; see also J. Edgar Hoover, "Red Fascism in the United States," AMREC, BA, EEUU 1948, 9, 3.

the powerful Brazilian communist chieftain came out in support of Perón as a fellow "crusader against capitalism" in "the last Latin American nation in which Yankee capital does not predominate" and criticized Argentine communists for opposing the "eminently democratic" Perón, Braden could not but see this as further confirmation of a Nazi-Communist conspiracy.[48]

Had Perón's election been openly fraudulent, Braden might have been able to restore the wartime sanctions against Argentina in the hope that deprivation of goods could fuel a counter-revolution against this "dangerous, uncontrollable megalomaniac" and restore the *gente bien* to power. Because even he conceded that it had been fair (despite "all the [Peronist] intimidation during the months preceding it"), Braden acknowledged Perón's victory.[49] This hardly implied that he had to permit the normalization of relations, however. To accept anything less than the restoration of traditional government dedicated to relatively free trade, economic liberty, and freedom of the press was nothing more than "muddleheaded" appeasement. Even if Perón purged Argentina of Axis agents and German influences, he argued, "it is obvious that Perón is following the Nazi technique" quite willingly and would persist in doing so.[50]

Braden's analysis, while extreme, had at its heart an emotional appeal that spoke very well to U.S. idealism in the post-war period. As Ambassador Claude Bowers argued, "with the millions dead and billions in treasure spent in a fight to end fascism, we emerge from the war with Franco and Perón keeping the old pirate flag afloat."[51] In this analysis, Peronist "fascism" was, like the brutality of the Soviet occupation of Eastern Europe, an insult

---

48. Mario Rapoport, *Política y diplomacia en Argentina: Las relaciones con Estados Unidos y Unión de Republica Sovietica* (Buenos Aires, 1986), 24-28; Davis to Flack, 15 March 1946, RG 59, MRIC.

49. Braden to Secretary of State, 30 June 1946, PSF, Subject Files, Argentina, HST; Braden to Messersmith, 8 March 1946, RG 59, 835.00.

50. Pepper to Cabot, 8 May 1946, Cabot Papers, Argentina, HST; see also Gary Frank, *Juan Perón vs Spruille Braden*, 98-107.

51. Bowers to Braden, 13 March 1946, Bowers MSS II.

to the martyred dead who had fallen to save democracy and avenge Pearl Harbor. Braden and his allies counted heavily upon this visceral anti-fascist sentiment to sway the public toward their position and stifle opposition. Braden himself conjectured that in the wake of the *Blue Book* debacle, only popular support for his crusade prevented Truman from firing him. There is some evidence to support this belief. A national poll revealed that thirty-nine percent of respondents considered Perón's Argentina to be a dictatorship (although fewer than twenty percent considered Rafael Trujillo's Dominican Republic to be), and forty-one percent believed Truman's policy was too soft on Perón.[52]

While Braden overestimated his importance to the U.S. public, Argentines made the same error. Peronists believed that Braden, a lifelong Republican, was the leader of the "leftist" forces in the United States. According to Martin Drago, counselor of the Argentine embassy in Washington, Braden virtually controlled what he considered to be the "extreme left-wing press," including newspapers such as the *Daily Worker*, *New Republic*, and the *Chicago Sun*. Through this propaganda network, Peronists argued, Braden had managed to turn the U.S. public against Argentina and its revolutionary government.[53]

Suggesting that Braden was a "leftist" seems ridiculous on the surface. However, the source of much of Braden's support lent some credence to the *peronista* argument. Ironically, Braden, who had little but contempt for organized labor, enjoyed the full backing of the Congress of Industrial Organizations (CIO), which was willing to cast its lot with him if it meant a chance to derail Peronism. Russian immigrants George Michanowski, labeled by

---

52. However, the same poll also revealed that only twenty-one percent actually believed that they had a clear idea just what that policy toward Argentina actually was, and a full one-third took no interest whatsoever in the matter. Foreign Activity Correlation to Braden, 5 March 1946, RG 59, 711.35; Memorandum on Public Opinion Polls, 28 October 1946, RG 59, 711.35.

53. Drago to Bramulgia, 6 Diciembre 1946, AMREC, BA, EEUU 1946, 8, 1; see also Luti to Ivanissevich, 11 Junio 1946, AMREC, BA, EEUU 1946, 8, 1; Primer Congreso Nacional de Periodistas, *La verdad periodismo y la prensa amarilla* (Buenos Aires, 1951).

one newspaper as "a CIOdious character whose Red sympathies are well known", and Jacob Potofsky of the CIO Latin American Affairs Committee repeatedly wrote to Truman and Byrnes, extolling Braden's virtues.[54] Soon, Romualdi, George Meany, and the American Federation of Labor (AFL) also joined his effort to unseat the "totalitarian" who had crushed independent unionism in Argentina and was threatening to spread his influence throughout Latin America. Finally, many of Braden's other backers, men such as Henry Wallace and Henry Morgenthau, came from the more liberal wing of the Democratic Party and argued that the Truman Administration was neglecting its obligation to exterminate the vestiges of fascism to pursue an unnecessary Cold War against communism.[55] Although the State Department was already shifting its focus to meet the communist threat, Braden still spoke for powerful constituencies, and his crusade against Perón, drawing upon the shared experience of the 1930s and World War II, still commanded respect.

    Braden's aggressive, uncompromising approach was not without critics, however. John Cabot, who had run the embassy since Braden's recall in October 1945, had never been especially fond of the ex-ambassador's "dogmatic and belligerent" stance. While prudently refraining from openly criticizing his superior, Cabot recognized that his approach was dangerously counterproductive, as each assault lent strength to Perón's appeal as an anti-*yanqui* nationalist. He had forecasted that the *Blue Book* could turn the election into a referendum on Yankee imperialism, and later claimed to have even begged Braden, "For Christ's sake, lay off." This plea predictably "went up like a lead balloon." When

---

54. *Times Herald*, 18 June 1946, 5.

55. Michanowski to Byrnes, 2 July 1945, James S. Byrnes, Folder 488(3), Special Collections, Clemson University Libraries, Clemson, South Carolina; Romualdi, "Peron's Anti-American Network," undated, Papers of Serafino Romualdi, 5459/11/11, Records of the International Ladies Garment Workers Union, M. C. Catherwood Center for Industrial Studies, Cornell University, Ithaca, New York (IGLWU); Romualdi, "Anti-Americanism in the Americas," Romualdi Papers, 5459/11/11, ILGWU; see also Drago to Ivanissevich, 6 Diciembre 1946, AMREC, BA, EEUU 1946, 8, 1.

Perón won the election, Cabot decided that he "was damn well going to see that the policy was changed, or I was thrown out."[56]

Although he shared Braden's view that Perón was an "excrescence on the Americas" that "looks disquietingly like some other ones which we have just finished performing operations on," he argued that the United States would have to learn to live with him. Continuing to oppose a constitutionally elected government risked nothing less than "wrecking the Inter-American system" and the goodwill brought by the Good Neighbor policy. Well aware that the mere mention of intervention "raised hackles on the back of every politician as far south as Cape Horn," he was nonetheless in no hurry to "shake the bloody hand that stabbed us in the back and may try to do so again." Cabot succinctly summed up the State Department's frustrations: "when we look for a good stick with which to beat [Perón] we never seem to be able to find one handy."[57]

Still, Cabot's view of Perón's success and domestic agenda stood in stark contrast to the picture of fascist tyranny that Braden had presented.

> With a disproportionately large part of the economic wealth of the country in the hands of foreigners and a selfish, Europeanized plutocracy which never did an honest lick of work in its life, this country has been over-ripe for reform. Perón has been practically the first man to do anything effective about it. To say that his means have been totalitarian does not impress the working masses. They contrast his acts with the empty words of his corrupt political predecessors.

He noted that "this does not mean we should endow him with gilded wings and a halo," but did argue that there were concrete

---

56. Cabot Oral History, HST, 1, 26-29; see also John Moors Cabot, *Toward Our Common American Destiny* (Medford, 1955).

57. Cabot to Lockwood, 4 January 1946, Cabot Papers, Argentina, HST; Cabot to Cochran, 4 January 1946, Cabot Papers, Argentina, HST; Cabot to Pepper, 1 April 1946, Cabot Papers, Argentina, HST; see also Sumner Welles, *Where are We Heading?* (New York, 1946), 198-201.

reasons why a majority of Argentines had opted to elect Perón. It followed that Braden's dreams of fueling a counterrevolution through sanctions were hopeless, Pollyannaish fantasies.[58]

Because the Department had made no definitive policy statement since the election, Cabot sent Byrnes his recommendations at the end of March. Dubious that Perón could be overthrown, he advised acceptance of the "will of the people" of Argentina, "however repugnant" Perón's "Fascist antecedents may be." The complete ostracism of Argentina only ensured that Peronist "subversive conspiracies against neighbors and international intrigues" would continue unabated, as Perón would have no incentive to aim for reconciliation with the United States. Furthermore, England and the Soviet Union would capitalize upon the blackballing of any American republic: the former to reestablish a commercial foothold in the New World, the latter for political and strategic advantage.

Therefore, Cabot explicitly rejected letting "bygones be bygones," but urged a public rapprochement with Argentina. He suggested that the Department take the position that Argentine wartime neutrality had done the United States a "grave injury." By holding out the lure that Perón could restore himself to Washington's good graces if he made reparations for the damages done to the war effort and fulfilled the Chapultepec commitments for "denazification," Cabot proposed to leave the "door cracked" for reconciliation. The State Department could lose little by pursuing a policy of patient "watchful waiting" and hoping that Perón's behavior became "less obnoxious." Moreover, if Perón failed to deliver on any of his promises to the Argentine people, he would be unable to blame U.S. subversion, a condition that could actually improve the chances of his ouster in the long run. As Congressman Joseph Baldwin succinctly noted, "the people of Argentina will take care of him if we don't make a national hero of him." In short, Cabot was "hopeful that we can reach reasonably

---

58. Cabot to Pepper, 1 April 1946, Cabot Papers, Argentina, HST; Cabot to Pepper, 3 June 1946, Cabot Papers, Argentina, HST.

satisfactory relations" with Argentina by employing a "combination of diplomatic toughness and conciliation, each at proper time."[59]

## V

Nonetheless, it fell to Secretary of State Byrnes to decide the U.S. response, and his preoccupation with European affairs weighed heavily upon his decision. With the "world food crisis continu[ing] to loom as one of the greatest, if not the greatest problem" confronting the State Department, Argentina, as one of the world's leading meat and grain-exporting nations, held a strong position.[60] In the wheat-rubber imbroglio, the Argentines had clearly shown a willingness to hold the European and South American food supply hostage, and Byrnes had felt it most acutely before he conceded to the "economic blackmail." For their part, Peronists were well aware that the global food crisis made U.S. "collaboration with Argentina invaluable" and therefore expected him to make a "change in the aggressive position."[61]

An Office of Research and Intelligence (ORI) assessment released in mid-April reached the same conclusion, arguing that there was little chance that "effective pressure" could "oblige Argentina to change the personnel and/or policies" to ones more "acceptable to the United States." The ORI suggested that whereas the Argentine dependence upon foreign commerce "might, at first

---

59. Cabot to Secretary of State, 22 March 1946, RG 59, 711.35; Cabot to Secretary of State, 13 March 1946, Cabot Papers, Argentina, HST; Baldwin to Truman, 13 April 1946, PSF, Foreign Affairs, Argentina, HST.

60. *Current Economic Developments* 40, 25 March 1946, HST.

61. Luti to Cooke, 25 Abril 1946, AMREC, BA, EEUU 1946, 8, 3; see also Luti to Cooke, 13 Febrero 1946, AMREC, BA, EEUU 1946, 8, 3; Famine Emergency Committee to Truman, 13 May 1946, Famine Emergency Committee Folder, James Carey Collection, Archive of Urban and Labor History, Wayne State University, Detroit, Michigan (AULH); Ernest May, "The Bureaucratic-Politics Approach: U.S.-Argentine Relations, 1942-1947," *Latin America and the United States: The Changing Political Relations*, ed. Julio Cotler and Patrick Fagen (Stanford, 1984), 130-164.

glance, convey the impression that Argentina would be highly vulnerable to sanctions," this was misleading. Argentina could easily, and was already predisposed to, resurrect import substitution schemes to alleviate import shortages and undercut sanctions. Furthermore, any sanctions applied to the Argentine industrialization scheme would adversely affect agriculture and critical food exports "in a fashion which cannot be formulated in statistical terms." Without Argentine beef and pork, British meat consumption would drop to forty percent of its pre-war levels, and the Low Countries would be even harder hit. The United States, which was struggling to meet its own commitments to Europe, could not hope to make up the shortfall, so any attempts to disrupt the Argentine economy could have far more serious repercussions in the all-important European arena than any potential benefits that might be gained in the Americas.[62]

Another authoritative report, a departmental memorandum entitled "Argentine Post-War Economic Policy" also suggested that punitive treatment of Perón worked against the aims of the Department's global agenda. Examining the possibilities that Argentina might return to a "bilateral trading regime," the memorandum argued that Argentine dreams of industrialization almost precluded immediate support for a free trade regimen. It warned that "Argentine cooperation is something less than a prerequisite for a successful system of international commercial liberalism, but if the cooperation of leading trading nations is something less than complete, Argentine cooperation would be a more important factor." Ominously, it also noted that if the economic nationalism being manifested by Argentina was typical of a widespread trend, it could "mean the breakdown of any efforts toward economic peace." The only feasible long-term option that might prevent Argentine reversion to narrow bilateralism was to foster goodwill and rapprochement. Unless Argentines could be convinced that the great powers intended to deal fairly and within a

---

62. Office of Research and Intelligence, "The Probable Effects of Sanctions Against Argentina," RG 59, Report 3717, 1-18.

multilateral framework, they would take the time-tested bilateral approach, and drag their trading partners into it with them.[63]

Byrnes also undoubtedly felt pressure from Vandenberg's and Connally's Senate Foreign Relations Committee, which had nearly succeeded in derailing Braden's appointment as assistant secretary of state. Vandenberg and Connally shared Cabot's fear that an isolated Argentina virtually invited further embarrassment, if not actual Soviet penetration. At a meeting with Byrnes on April 7, the senators, according to Cabot, told Byrnes that "you have damn well got to stop this business. There's to be no more interference in Argentine internal affairs."[64]

Although Byrnes' vague, public April 8 statement hardly reflected these influences, his April 12 directive to the embassy in Buenos Aires did. He argued that the "road will be open to inter-American unity only when and if [the] incoming Argentine regime complies with...the elimination of Axis influences." He was lifting all non-military sanctions, only because of the "dependence of Europe and some American republics on Argentina for essential foodstuffs" and the recognition that the United States lacked the ability "unilaterally to control Argentine imports." Byrnes further normalized relations by announcing the dispatch of George Messersmith as the new ambassador to Argentina. Byrnes summed up the new approach, echoing Cabot, as the adoption of an "attitude of watchful waiting."[65]

Although Cabot obviously had good reason to consider Byrnes' statement to be a victory, so too did Braden. So long as reconciliation hinged upon the removal of Axis influences, "denazification" could easily become a "well with no bottom."[66] No matter what Perón did to comply with Washington's dictates,

---

63. "Argentina's Post-War Economic Policies," 21 March 1946, RG 59, 835.50.

64. Cabot Oral History, 39.

65. Byrnes to Embassy Buenos Aires, 12 April 1946, RG 59, 711.35; see also Luti to Bramulgia, 6 Abril 1946, AMREC, BA, EEUU 1946, 8, 2.

66. Cabot Oral History, 49.

Braden could always find more demands, and the crusade could continue unchecked. In short, Byrnes had left his options open. If Perón proved to be a nationalistic authoritarian emulating fascist technique, the pretext for punitive sanctions aimed at encouraging a coup was already in place. In the meantime, Perón would be offered the lure of acceptance and the hope that the last vestiges of the "moral embargo" would be lifted.

Although Byrnes may have bent to necessity by lifting most economic restrictions, the arms embargo remained in force and served as a clear indication that Braden's position was not being entirely cast aside. The Truman Administration may have accepted the futility of economic sanctions, but military sanctions were an entirely different matter. Argentina's wartime neutrality had exempted it from the Lend-Lease program through which most other Latin American nations had, to some extent, modernized their militaries. Brazil, Argentina's traditional rival, had benefited enormously from the wartime aid, and Argentine desperation to restore the balance of power had already shown itself in 1944 with the disastrous Hellmuth mission. There was no reason to doubt it had abated. While Cabot claimed that the Argentines desperately sought to restore military parity with Brazil, Braden asserted that the desire for armaments was prelude to expansionism. Still others believed Perón needed weaponry to appease the professionalism of his Army backers. Regardless of why he wanted weapons, he did want them badly, and everyone associated with U.S. policy knew it.

Unlike commercial sanctions that jeopardized food shipments to European and South American nations, the arms embargo had tenuous international support. Although Great Britain had gone to some lengths to circumvent Hull's wartime economic campaign against Argentina, it had conceded to a "Gentleman's Agreement" withholding weaponry. Other nations, however, posed some difficulties and had to be brought into the fold. Over Acheson's objections, in April the Belgian government sold one thousand tons of TNT to the Argentine arms manufacturer, *Fabricaciones Militares*, in exchange for food. When State Department officials confronted "slightly embarrassed" Foreign Minister Paul-Henri Spaak, they were told that because the Argentines had already delivered half of the wheat, it was too late to cancel the agreement. The U.S. ambassador warned Spaak that "this deal might have repercussions in the Combined Food Board," a thinly veiled threat that illustrated all too well that the Peronists were correct to fear U.S. influence over "international" commodity boards and relief programs.[67]

Like the Belgians, Perón underestimated Washington's resolve. Despite the announced policy, Perón dispatched Gen. Carlos Von Der Becke to Washington to procure weapons in late May. While General Dwight Eisenhower proclaimed Von Der Becke to be "quite a guy," Braden found this "rabid nazi" to be "amazingly stupid."[68] Over the War Department's objections, Von Der Becke's requests for materiel were rebuffed coldly. As Braden's aide, Thomas Mann, explained, "Persons outside ARA simply do not understand that we do not have sufficient trust in the present government of Argentina to negotiate a treaty with it."[69]

Although Acheson denied it, Eisenhower and the U.S. Armed Forces could now be counted among Braden's growing list of relentless critics. It had long been a dream of the men leading the United States Army to unify and coordinate the defense of the hemisphere. Since the Germans had threatened U.S. security prior to the outbreak of World War II by using advisors and training missions to "subvert" Latin American militaries, inter-American defense had become a priority. These fears culminated in the proposed Western Hemisphere Defense Program (WHDP) by which Latin America's defense needs would be met by U.S. materiel. The benefits to the United States military establishment would be significant: all nations in the hemisphere would possess standardized, interchangeable weaponry; obsolete materiel could be disposed of readily within the hemisphere; and most importantly, the "military thought of Latin America" could be "reorient[ed] to the democratic lines of our military doctrine." Argentina was of

---

67. Kirk to Secretary of State, 27 May 1946, in *FRUS* IX, 248.

68. Braden, *Diplomats and Demagogues*, 366-367; see also *Primera Plana*, 7 Junio 1966, 43.

69. Mann to Braden, 21 March 1946, RG 59, 835.50.

particular importance, as its Army, in U.S. eyes, was clearly the one most in need of "reorientation."[70]

Braden spearheaded the opposition to WHDP on both practical and philosophical grounds. He opposed the introduction of large quantities of U.S. weaponry into Latin America, believing correctly that it would most likely be used to oppress domestic opposition or intimidate neighboring states. Furthermore, he feared that economic development in Latin America would be retarded by crippling arms races and increased militarism. "Argentina's neighbors are well aware, as we should be," he wrote to Truman, "that a modernized army, even though it is never employed in open aggression, would greatly strengthen Perón's hand in promoting a southern bloc through economic pressure and political penetration and modern techniques of aggression which, unfortunately, are not readily checked." Although he also worried that the War Department might replace the State Department as the dominant instrument of foreign policymaking in Latin America, the prospects of arms sales to Perón, and to a lesser extent Morinigo and Trujillo, appalled him most.[71]

Byrnes and Acheson, however, gradually warmed to the idea of inter-American arms standardization. Byrnes even testified before Congress in support of the WHDP's successor plan, the Inter-American Defense Act, at the same time he was backing Braden's postponement of the Rio de Janeiro Defense Conference

---

70. Quoted in Chester Pach, "The Containment of U.S. Military Aid to Latin America, 1944-1947," *Diplomatic History* 6 (Summer 1982), 230-243; see also Acheson, "Memorandum of the Press and Radio News Conference," 11 June 1946, #31, Folder 561, Byrnes Papers; Luti to Bramulgia, 24 Julio 1946, AMREC, BA, EEUU 1946, 8, 2; John Child, *Unequal Alliance: the Inter-American Military System, 1938-1978* (Boulder, 1980), 60-74; Roger Trask, "The Impact of the Cold War on United States-Latin American Relations, 1945-1949," *Diplomatic History* 1 (Summer 1977), 271-285.

71. Memorandum on the Argentine Situation by the Assistant Secretary of State to President Truman, 12 July 1946, in *FRUS* IX, 277. Braden considered U.S. military leaders to be "naive," especially when it came to Perón, but "what I regret about . . . reports from our Military Attaches is that they become a part of the record, and a part that is so hard to eradicate from the files." Braden to Messersmith, 6 February 1946, RG 59, 835.00.

that would put it into action. While the Army was pressuring Byrnes for rapprochement, its role should not be overstated. The secretary of state had been converted to the need for a hemispheric defense plan, and tacitly to eventual arms sales to Perón, but permitted Braden to block implementation. So as long as Byrnes retained Braden's services, the Department's message to Perón was clear: there would be no "appeasement" or military agreement.[72]

Although Braden's list of enemies continued to grow, and there was clearly little place for his "bull in a china shop" approach in a Department now committed to "watchful waiting," he had to remain in office, for as Messersmith noted, "it would do us infinite harm" and "injure our program infinitely if he were to retire."[73] Although historians of the "bureaucratic school" find Braden's retention to be anachronistic and inconsistent, it is not necessarily so. Ernest May suggested that Byrnes, suffering badly in his dealings with the Soviets, feared that Braden's removal, and the intendent perceptions of "appeasement," would cause an uproar that would only worsen his deteriorating position in the government. Braden had threatened that "if any attempt was made to shove me out, then I would fight with everything I had and they knew from my record that I could put up a pretty nasty fight—with no holds barred."[74]

In fact, the upper echelons of the State Department knew all too well that many of their policies had little or no public following and that any development in Latin America would be overshadowed by reconversion and the emerging Cold War. Still, Byrnes hardly needed additional difficulties, and Braden's presence did serve a valuable function as a foil to Perón. The sudden removal of Braden might easily have been interpreted as a symbolic capitulation and an indication that Washington had perhaps become too friendly with the Argentine regime. Indeed, at least one Latin

---

72. Child, *Unequal Alliance*, 90-94; Pach, "The Containment," 229-235; Braden, *Diplomats and Demagogues*, 364-5.

73. Cabot Oral History, 36; Messersmith to Secretary of State, 15 June 1946, in *FRUS* IX, 258-259.

74. Braden, *Diplomats and Demagogues*, 374.

American diplomat had already interpreted the appointment of Messersmith to be a "wise proceeding by the authorities in Washington, demonstrating that they are trying to forget the factors that caused the crisis between the two countries."[75] This was most assuredly not the message Byrnes sought to send. Because the new U.S. approach would be based upon the outward appearance of dispassionate neutrality and acceptance toward Argentina, Braden's continued presence illustrated that the State Department had not gone too far in its toleration of nationalism and remained a major asset in keeping Perón in line.[76]

## VI

It took less than two weeks in Argentina for Messersmith to ascertain that "one thing is very definite and that is that we will have to deal with President Perón for probably the full term of six years."[77] With this realization, any lingering hopes of unseating him disappeared. In their place emerged a more complex strategy calculated to garner better results. With a new ambassador on the ground to "advise" Perón and clarify a confused situation, the United States could implement a more informed and coherent policy. Cabot's ideal of the carrot balanced against prudent application of the "big stick" would be realized, if imperfectly executed. Perón would start to feel the push toward multilateral trade and liberal capitalist privatism, away from maverick nationalism, autarchy, bilateral barter, and statist corporatism as U.S. policy gradually became more refined, subtle, and far more effective.

Although there may be considerable debate about whether Perón was a "Nazi-fascist," there can be little doubt that he looked like one from Washington. Politically, Perón had long since made

---

75. Rada a Ministro, 5 Abril 1946, AMRE, Lima, 5-1-Y/65.

76. May, "The Bureaucratic Politics Approach: U.S.-Argentine Relations, 1942-1947," 130-164; Woods, *The Roosevelt Foreign Policy Establishment*.

77. Messersmith to Secretary of State, 15 June 1946, in *FRUS* IX, 258-259.

clear his intention to form a syndicalist state with "true democracy" closer to Mussolini than the "plutocracy" of Anglo-Saxon political systems. Economically, he appeared to be working toward a state-directed inversion of liberal capitalism with worker supremacy. In foreign affairs, Perón seemed to be fulfilling the prophecy that nations that practiced autarchy at home were expansionist abroad. In this context, Braden's retention and the formal normalization of relations were completely congruent, as the State Department prepared for a longer, more subtle, and more effective campaign against Perón. Even though Braden's tactics may have been repudiated, his analysis of Peronism was still by and large, that of the State Department. In the words of functionary Merwin Bohan, "We simply had to play the game with a rapier, not a meat axe."[78]

---

78. Bohan to Bowen, 2 February 1973, Bohan Papers, Correspondence File, Argentina, HST. The much-debated question of whether or not Perón was, by any meaningful definition, a true "fascist" appears to have been settled decisively by Cristián Buchrucker. Still, that the debate lasted for decades illustrates well how U.S. policymakers could, after World War II, have seen similarities between the two corporatist variants. Buchrucker, *Nacionalismo y peronismo: La Argentina en la crisis ideológico mundial*. (Buenos Aires, 1987); see also Ciria, *Política y cultura* popular, 41-47; Sebreli, *Los deseos imaginarios del peronismo*, 49-83.

# CHAPTER 4

## "ON THE WRONG ROAD WITH VERY GOOD INTENTIONS:" MESSERSMITH AND PERÓN, JUNE-SEPTEMBER 1946

> I do not mean that the Government here is not on the wrong road. It is in my opinion, definitely on the wrong road. To a very great extent I think it is on the wrong road with very good intentions, but you know the road to perdition is paved with the best intentions.
>
> George S. Messersmith, October 21, 1946[1]

## I

Ambassador George Messersmith arrived in Buenos Aires just days before Perón's inauguration with a mandate for rapprochement and an unexpected amount of Argentine goodwill. Although a number of State Department officers had come to consider Argentine industrialization inevitable, and even beneficial, none had by any means resigned themselves to acceptance of the Peronist path toward that goal. If Argentina's venture in state-dominated corporatism could not be derailed by eliminating Perón, then Perón had to be convinced to abandon it. Messersmith accepted the task of introducing him to the principles of U.S.-style liberal capitalism and leading him away from his statist experiments as the tone of U.S. policy changed. The fundamental goals had not.

From June to December 1946, U.S.-Argentine relations did improve substantially on one level. The Peronist Congress ratified the Chapultepec Accords, signifying tacit support for the principles of the "Inter-American system" and acceptance of the formula of

---

1. Messersmith to Clayton, 21 October 1946, RG 59, 835.50.

"denazification," at the same time that half-hearted Soviet attempts to exploit U.S.-Argentine differences were rebuffed. Just as significantly, Messersmith worked to supplant British influence in Argentina and secure United States hegemony while presenting a somewhat united front with Whitehall toward Perón. In spite of public affirmations of friendship for the United States and support of a liberal world order, however, Perón showed no signs of letting his revolution stray from the course he had set. In mid-1946, he completed the nationalization of the ITT properties in Argentina, and IAPI's activities continued unchecked throughout the year. Even though Perón understood that further industrial development would be next to impossible without at least the tacit support of the Yankee colossus, his program was fundamentally a challenge to U.S. hegemony. So long as Peronist economics appeared to be working, Messersmith and his superiors would have to content themselves with playing a waiting game.

    Messersmith had been instructed to oversee Argentine compliance with the Chapultepec Accords and the "denazification" campaign, facilitate rapprochement and undo the damage done by Braden's campaign. He had, as he argued, selflessly answered Byrnes and Truman's call to duty due to "the importance of getting the Argentine to collaborate fully in the inter-American picture," without "sacrificing any principle." With this ambiguous mandate, the strong-willed Messersmith immediately assumed personal responsibility for ensuring the establishment of harmonious relations.[2] As a true believer in the New Deal, and one who wished to extend it to Latin America in order to smooth modernization, Messersmith illustrated the inconsistencies, strengths, and weaknesses of the U.S. approach toward Perón and the hemisphere at large. He believed that Perón could be influenced through personal persuasion, failing to recognize that he was the product of decades of Argentine history, the representative of a

---

2. Messersmith to Byrnes, 30 October 1946, Messersmith Papers, 1813, University of Delaware Library, Newark, Delaware; see also Messersmith to Clayton, 31 October 1946, George S. Messersmith Papers, 1815; Messersmith to Clayton, 15 October 1946, RG 84, BA; Stiller, *George S. Messersmith*, 226-227.

powerful force for revision of the status quo, and to some extent, a hostage of the same nationalist movement that he led. Changing Perón's program would take much more than words, which was all Messersmith's superiors ultimately permitted him to offer.

## II

Given the State Department's analysis of Peronism as a sub-equatorial fascist variant, Messersmith appeared to be the perfect candidate for the Argentine posting. He had been attached to the U.S. embassy in Berlin during Hitler's rise and had been one of the *Fuhrer*'s earliest and most vocal critics. This, in conjunction with his term as ambassador to Austria during the *anschluss*, made Messersmith an expert on the excesses of fascism and an ideal choice to judge Perón's intentions. *Time* magazine, chortling that the new ambassador possessed an "uncanny nose that can smell a fascist s.o.b. as far as the wind can carry the scent," joined those who trumpeted his impeccable anti-totalitarian credentials.[3]

In addition to his expertise with European fascism, Messersmith had served with distinction in Latin America and was well in step with the tenets of the Good Neighbor Policy. He helped Clayton set the post-war agenda for Latin America at Chapultepec, unsuccessfully attempting to moderate the U.S. position by arguing that "if nothing further is offered by way of a program, it will cause the keenest disillusionment." He also served several years as ambassador to Mexico during the thorny years following the oil expropriations. Furthermore, he followed Braden's lead throughout 1945 and early 1946, and fully supported the release of the *Blue Book*, fearing that Peronism could easily become "infectious and spread rapidly" across the continent if left unchecked. As late as March, he counseled against recognition of

---

3. *Time*, 15 April 1946, quoted in Stiller, *George S. Messersmith*, 228-229; see also 26-95. Easily the most insightful assessment of Messersmith is Stiller's brilliant political biography, and this chapter relies heavily upon its analysis and conclusions.

the "perfect farce" of Perón's election, claiming that it would "be taking the heart out of sound elements in Argentina."[4]

In spite of the ill will that soon arose between the two men, Braden and Messersmith initially enjoyed a reasonably solid relationship. For his part, Braden was not entirely displeased with the selection of Messersmith. "I did not think Messersmith well suited to the post," he observed much later, but acknowledged that "on the other hand, he had always professed agreement with my Argentine policy." If Byrnes and Truman were shifting toward appeasement, as some critics suggested, the choice of Messersmith to be the point man was odd. Just as interesting was the selection of Joseph Flack, first secretary of the Berlin embassy with Messersmith, to head the mission in Bolivia. With Claude Bowers, a veteran foe of Generalissimo Francisco Franco in Spain, serving in the Chilean post, a good part of the team who had fought fascism in Europe during the 1930s was reassembled in the Southern Cone to deal with this new "fascist" threat.[5]

With considerable fanfare the new ambassador arrived in Buenos Aires to be the U.S. representative at Perón's inauguration. He was thrust into duty almost immediately, as Perón chose the occasion to re-establish diplomatic relations with the Soviet Union that had been severed since 1930. Although Perón claimed that this was a mere formality, a Soviet "special ambassador" and trade mission arrived on June 6, concurrent with the construction of a massive new Soviet embassy in Buenos Aires. The Peruvian ambassador in Buenos Aires saw "no other apparent object" to this venture "than to provoke a debate around Argentina's international policy," but U.S. officials initially leapt to other conclusions. Remarking on the Soviet "violent wooing of Perón," Cabot argued that "it is obvious that the Russians are trying to establish a political beachhead against us." The U.S. ambassador in Moscow

---

4. Stephen J. Rabe, "The Elusive Conference: United States Relations with Latin America, 1945-1952," *Diplomatic History* 2 (Summer 1978), 281; Messersmith to Braden, 25 January 1946, RG 59, 711.35; Messersmith to Braden, 16 March 1946, Messersmith Papers, 1775.

5. Braden, *Diplomats and Demagogues*, 358-360; see also Braden to Messersmith, 8 March 1946, in *FRUS* IX, 232-233.

ominously added that "any misstep on our part toward Argentina resulting in a feeling of grievance will be exploited to the full by the Soviet Union."[6]

To the uninformed, it appeared that the Soviets and Peronists, sharing a fundamental opposition to both liberal capitalism and U.S. hegemony, were on the verge of formalizing an anti-U.S. alliance and fulfilling Braden's predictions. The trade mission posed the greatest threat. With famine looming across the Soviet empire, Argentine food exports offered a ray of hope. On the surface, the Soviets appeared to have much to offer Perón as well. By offering captured German arms and dismantled munitions plants, the Soviet mission presumably hoped to lure Argentine Army officers away from their traditional anti-communist posture. In addition, the Soviets promised to deliver 10,000 trucks and 10,000 tractors, which could go a good distance toward modernizing Argentine agriculture. Messersmith warned that the Soviets were making "all sorts of illusory offers to both supply and buy goods" in order to "disturb established channels of trade" and stir up "disturbing political currents."[7]

Remarkably, after some reflection, the State Department opted to virtually ignore the possibility that Perón was considering seriously a closer relationship with the Soviets. An amused Messersmith considered the Soviet initiatives to be little more than a "nuisance" and cautioned against "naive," knee-jerk overreaction. Although there was "little doubt in my mind" that Argentine military men might be "interested in getting German war plant equipment," very few would "want to load themselves up with

---

6. Ledgard a Ministro, 6 Agosto 1946, AMRE, Lima, 5-1 A/354; Cabot to Pepper, 3 June 1946, Cabot Papers, Argentina, HST; Messersmith to Braden and Acheson, 22 July 1946, RG 59, 835.24; see also Paso, *Del golpe de Estado*, 101; Paz and Ferrari, *Política exterior argentina*, 138; Rapoport, *Política y diplomacia*; Seipe, et al., *Perón y las relaciones con el Este*.

7. Byrnes to Embassy Buenos Aires, 3 June 1946, RG 59, 835.24; Messersmith to Clayton, 16 July 1946, RG 84, BA; see also "Memorandum of the Press and Radio News Conference," 21 June 1946, Byrnes Papers, #33, Folder 561; "Memorandum of the Press and Radio News Conference," 10 July 1946, Byrnes Papers, #37, Folder 562; *Review of the River Plate*, 6 September 1946, 20.

second-rate" materiel when superior U.S. arms would soon become available through the hemispheric defense initiative. In short, "Soviet tactics are not deceiving many people," least of all Perón, who realized that the Soviet Union was an unreliable partner, and that the war-ravaged nation would be unable to meet the needs of his industrialization scheme. According to the president, the Soviets had come, so he had to talk with them, but he had "not the slightest intention of entering into any agreements with" them. Braden and Clayton concurred with the ambassador's analysis, and Byrnes concerned himself with the matter only to determine whether the Soviets were improperly offering to sell UNRRA-donated trucks or otherwise hampering relief efforts in Europe.[8]

Rather than viewing the Soviet challenge as a genuine threat, the State Department prudently chose to treat it as an attempt to draw concessions from the United States. Indeed, the State Department fully expected Perón to "play his Russian card" and threaten a move toward the Soviet bloc. Although other *peronistas* did mention to U.S. officials that they had an "ace in the hole, which was Russia," Perón bluntly and repeatedly reaffirmed his strident anti-communism.[9] In fact, he went so far as to make the astonishing proclamation that if a third world war erupted between the United States and U.S.S.R., he would abandon neutrality and bring Argentina in alongside the United States without hesitation. Thus, he cast himself as a diligent anti-communist who resisted enticing Soviet overtures—and should be rewarded for it. Even Braden agreed that "Perón is only using Russia as a lever, and he will continue to do so only as long as he thinks it expedient." For all intents and purposes, the Cold War had not reached South America yet, prompting Messersmith to state confidently that "if there is one thing" of "which we can be 100% sure, it is that the

---

8. Messersmith to Braden and Acheson, 22 July 1946, RG 59, 835.24; Braden to Messersmith, 13 June 1946, RG 59, 835.24; Braden, "Memorandum on the Argentine Situation," 12 July 1946, PSF, Foreign Affairs, Argentina, HST; Clayton to Messersmith, 23 July 1946, RG 353, RIIC-ARG.

9. Cabot to Secretary of State, 13 March 1946, Cabot Papers, Argentina, HST; see also Messersmith to Braden and Acheson, 22 July 1946, RG 59, 611.3531.

Government and people are anti-communist and have no interest in Soviet Russia."[10]

Just as Messersmith downplayed the significance of the Soviet efforts in Argentina, he also gave little credence to claims that Perón was attempting to assemble an autarchic "southern bloc." According to the ambassador, Perón and his followers did "not believe that either a "southern bloc" or a Latin American bloc is feasible or desirable." Although the new president may have had the idea of a "southern bloc" "in the back of his mind, just as many Argentines have," he was not acting upon it. Messersmith did not deny that many Argentines of all political persuasions envisioned a glorious restoration of the old colonial Viceroyalty of the Rio de la Plata with Buenos Aires at its center. He argued, however, that regardless of these dreams, "the present government in the Argentine has so many problems before it and so many of a difficult character, that they are not able to press the idea, even though they might wish to." In short, "whatever thoughts Mr. Perón and some of his followers might have in this direction, they will not have very much time to think about the formation of a bloc." Even if Perón did try, there was little chance of success, because "nationalism is the most striking characteristic of all of the proposed members," and the bloc would still be economically dependent upon the United States, "which could bring about its dissolution" if push ever came to shove.[11]

Events throughout Latin America seemed to reinforce Messersmith's claims. Of primary importance, Getulio Vargas had been unseated in Brazil, and conservative General Enrico Dutra had been securely emplaced. If the State Department still harbored its irrational fears of a Vargas-Perón ideological entente, the ascension

---

10. Braden to Messersmith, 13 June 1946, RG 59, 835.24; Messersmith to Clayton, 3 December 1946, RG 59, 625.3521; see also Cisernos a Ministro, 24 Junio 1946, AMRE, Lima, 5-2-Y/18; Rapoport, *Política y diplomacia*, 35-37.

11. Messersmith to Clayton, 3 December 1946, RG 59, 625.3531; Messersmith to Flack, 27 September 1946, RG 84, BA; Messersmith to Bowers, 10 June 1946, Bowers MSS II, Box 6; "Argentine Post-War Economic Policies," 2-19; see also Carlos Escudé, "Argentine Territorial Nationalism," *Journal of Latin American Studies* 20, 139-165.

of Dutra and his rollback of Vargas' corporatist *Estado Novo* quelled these fears to some extent. In Chile, Gabriel González Videla, a moderate leftist with ties to communists and the author of numerous denunciations of Perón, won the presidency, distancing Chile ideologically from the Argentine. Tomás Berreta and his successor, José Batlle Berres, in Uruguay maintained their steadfast opposition to Peronist "fascism" and their equally ardent support of most U.S. initiatives. Even though Higinio Morinigo remained in power in Paraguay, he had not showed any signs of responding to Perón's overtures. Still, for Washington, the most promising development occurred in late-July when a coup d'etat in Bolivia toppled Gualberto Villarroel's regime.

On July 21, just days after the arrival of Ambassador Joseph Flack in Bolivia, chaos erupted in the streets of La Paz. Protesting the government's austerity program, teachers and university students took to the streets. They quickly found support from the tin barons, the landed oligarchy, and dissident labor factions who joined in the effort to oust Villarroel. Víctor Andrade, the Bolivian ambassador to Washington and Víctor Paz Estenssoro, claimed that the Department of State and the "Bradenist plutocracy" had some hand in the affair as well, and the Argentines concurred.[12]

Peronists believed that the origins of the coup could be traced to Braden's office. In September 1945, they reported, Braden met with representatives of the tin barons and plotted the downfall of both Perón and Villarroel. "Kill the dog, and the fleas will die," Braden and the Bolivian oligarchs allegedly concluded, suggesting that the United States would engineer the defeat of Perón, and Villarroel would fall quickly once his puppet strings had been cut. *Peronistas* maintained that even though Braden's efforts in Argentina had failed, the State Department proceeded to bankrupt the Villarroel government, sponsor a provocative press campaign, and drive wedges between the military and civilian wings of the government. U.S. complicity was never proven, but the government nonetheless collapsed and "the bullet-riddled body of

---

12. Flack to Secretary of State, 15 November 1946, RG 84, BA; see also Flack, "Diary of a Successful Revolution," 25 July 1946, RG 84, BA.

Gualberto Villarroel was hung from a lamppost," as Estenssoro and much of his MNR sought refuge in Argentina.[13]

Still, while Brazil and other South American nations found the swift U.S. recognition of the new regime unseemly and "had asked that we go slow, mainly for the purpose of not encouraging revolutions and the spilling of so much blood," Flack was jubilant and proclaimed that "it appears that the problem [of Peronist influence in Bolivia] has been taken care of by the Bolivians themselves."[14] Newspaper correspondents warned him that at the time of the coup, "Villarroel had a mission in Buenos Aires prepared to give way to Perón's desires" and "assure '*anschluss*.'" Indeed, before his departure to La Paz, Flack had spoken to "two of the very highest officials" in the State Department who were "considerably perturbed" by the apparent Argentine penetration of Bolivia. He verified these fears, citing recently discovered evidence that Villarroel and the MNR were almost "ideologically along side of Argentina if not in its wake." Flack warned, however, that with the "*anschluss*" forestalled by the coup, Argentines would employ a new coercive approach. Perón was, he claimed, now attempting to apply pressure to the new regime by reducing desperately needed food shipments, as Argentine officials in La Paz belittled the authority of the new *junta* and assisted in the escape of MNR refugees.[15]

---

13. Memorandum sobre la situación de Bolivia," undated, AMREC, BA, Bolivia 1946, 1, 1, Anexo II, Parte 1; Andrade, *My Missions for Revolutionary Bolivia*, 115-123; see also "Movimiento Revolutionario de Bolivia," 21 July 1946, AMREC, BA, Bolivia 1946, 1, 1, Anexo 2, Parte 1; Luti to Bramulgia, 24 Julio 1946, AMREC, BA, Bolivia 1946, 1, 1, Anexo 2, Parte 1; James Malloy, *Bolivia: The Uncompleted Revolution* (New York, 1970), 125-130.

14. Messersmith to Braden, 23 August 1946, RG 84, BA; Flack to Messersmith, 20 August 1946, RG 84, BA; see also Torres Gigena to Bramulgia, 22 Junio 1946, AMREC, BA, Bolivia 1946, 1, 1.

15. Messersmith to Flack, 29 October 1946, RG 84, BA; Flack to Messersmith, 20 August 1946, RG 84, BA; Espy to Flack and Wells, 6 October 1946, RG 59, 624.3531; Flack to Secretary of State, 6 December 1946, RG 84, BA; see also Garland a Ministro, 7 June 1946, AMRE, Lima, 5-7-Y/35.

In the wake of these allegations, Messersmith took up Perón's defense. Although he admitted that U.S. officials were entitled to some "personal satisfaction" at Villarroel's ouster, he reassured his superiors that Perón was not applying pressure on the new government. According to Messersmith, the Peronists had learned "out of the Uruguayan experience that the holding up of foodstuffs did not pay" and "that it only causes inconveniences and difficulties." Even so, Perón could not be held completely responsible for the actions of his emissaries away from the capital who might indeed have stalled food shipments at the border. He explained that Argentine embassies and government offices were staffed by novices and nationalists who may have believed that their nation was being served by the pursuit of the "southern bloc" and had acted accordingly—without authorization from the Casa Rosada. Finally, Messersmith relayed the traditional Argentine excuse for delayed food shipments: shortages of rolling stock and transportation facilities. With regard to the MNR exiles, Argentina had only done what every embassy was entrusted to do by granting asylum for political refugees. In short, he concluded, Argentina had fulfilled its inter-American obligations. He did note, however, that some Peronists had been "unnerved" by the violent counterrevolution and its possible implications should Argentines ever opt to follow the Bolivian example.[16]

Messersmith's defense of Peronist behavior was consistent with his general attitude toward Perón and quite out of step with that of Braden and the hard-liners. Whereas Braden and other critics considered him to be an "Al Capone with Nazi tendencies" who "has shown no capacity to govern," Messersmith dissented.[17] Weeks of long, candid discussions with Perón convinced him of the Argentine's "sincerity and correctness of purpose." Writing furtively to Will Clayton, he expressed the opinion that Perón "is a much more sensible, intelligent, understanding and really right-

---

16. Messersmith to Braden, 23 August 1946, RG 84, BA; Messersmith to Flack, 27 August 1946, RG 84, BA.

17. Braden quoted in Bruce to Truman, 11 August 1949, Office Files, HST; Harriman to Secretary of State, 26 July 1946, RG 59, 635.4131.

minded person than he is given credit for." He posited that Perón was little more than a well-intentioned opportunist who had allied himself with labor and the Army not out of any grand fascist design, but because no one else would support him. For Messersmith, that opportunism could be translated into a strong U.S.-Argentine relationship, simply because no nation had as much to offer as the United States.[18]

Messersmith's assessments of Peronism were in many ways a reflection of his own general political beliefs. An ardent New Dealer who had learned firsthand from his experiences in Europe how easily revolutionary fervor could lead to totalitarian dictatorship, Messersmith heartily endorsed moderate alternatives. He accepted Perón's claims that his state corporatism served as a vehicle to undercut the revolutionary potential of the masses but believed that he was taking the "wrong path" toward this otherwise laudable goal. Just as the New Deal had repelled communism, socialism, and the radical populism of Huey Long, Perón could, if guided properly, become a bastion of orderly development.

Although some U.S. policymakers may have feared the implications of Latin American industrialization and economic diversification, and for want of a better alternative, hoped to see third world radicalism contained in a traditional repressive fashion, Messersmith encouraged Perón to undertake reform along the same lines Roosevelt had. Messersmith argued that the result of industrialization in Latin American nations "has been that their imports from us are on the increase" and that as "sound industry is developed," "their whole structure will become stronger and their buying power from us greater." Entirely comfortable with the creation of corporatist structures to encourage growth and contain radicalism, he could endorse a modified version of the Peronist program. He had enough experience in Latin America to recognize that the clock could not be turned back to the days of *laissez faire*, monocultural oligarchy. Even though he had helped set the U.S. agenda at Chapultepec—where Will Clayton did in many ways try to do just that—Messersmith had long been one of the strongest

---

18. Messersmith to Clayton, 31 October 1946, Messersmith Papers, 1815; see also Messersmith to Secretary of State, 14 August 1946, RG 59, 835.4131.

voices for a positive reform program for Latin America lest U.S. apathy spawn disillusionment.[19]

So while Braden, Byrnes, and others in Washington persisted in their belief that Perón was a blight upon the hemisphere, the new ambassador reported that there had never been an Argentine leader more willing to cooperate with the United States. Previous Argentine governments had looked to Europe for leadership, but Perón had good reasons for rapprochement with the United States. Years of wartime shortages and the "economic boycott" had taken their toll on the Argentine economy, and if industrialization was to proceed, capital goods, machinery, and technical expertise were badly needed. With Europe devastated by war and preoccupied with reconstruction, and with the Soviet Union impractical as either patron or partner, the United States was the only viable source for these commodities. In short, Argentina was "starved for goods of all types" and Perón had little choice but to try to get them from the United States.[20]

This pressing need, he argued, had already yielded concrete results in his first months in Argentina. Although isolationist Argentina had traditionally remained aloof from most foreign entanglements, Perón fully supported the Chapultepec Accords and pushed their ratification through the Argentine Senate. As Messersmith noted, opposition to ratification came primarily not from the *peronistas* but from Braden's friends, the old politicos who supported Argentina's traditional neutrality. When Perón pressed the issue, both houses of the Argentine Congress ended their bitter debates and voted to ratify. As one of the preconditions set down by Byrnes for the normalization of relations, the Argentine ratification of the Chapultepec Accords marked an important step.[21]

---

19. Messersmith to Clayton, 21 October 1946, RG 59, 835.50; see also Rabe, "The Elusive Conference," 280-281; Cobbs, *The Rich Neighbor Policy*.

20. Messersmith to Clayton, 16 July 1946, RG 353, RIIC-ARG; see also Messersmith to Clayton, 21 October 1946, RG 59, 835.50; Jorge Fodor, "Perón's Policies for Exports," 135-160; Stiller, *George S. Messersmith*, 238.

21. Messersmith Memoirs, Messersmith Papers, 2009, 1-9; Messersmith to Byrnes, 30 October 1946, Messersmith Papers, 1814.

Perón's government also pushed forward with "denazification" early in Messersmith's tenure. Throughout 1946, Peronists stepped up arrests and deportations of suspected Nazi agents. While there was consternation that Perón was expelling minor agents as "quota-fillers" and shielding more important, high-profile figures—notably Doerge, Ludwig Freude, and Ricardo Staudt—Messersmith was pleased with the progress. He understood and accepted Perón's reluctance to turn over men such as Freude, who had long been a personal friend; Doerge, who was working for the Central Bank; and Staudt, who had reportedly contributed more than one million pesos to his presidential campaign. Although these individuals had become a fixation for some in the State Department, Messersmith argued that they were insignificant in the grand scheme of things and could be ignored. Meanwhile, Perón's *Junta de Vigilancia* proceeded in its investigations and liquidations of Axis firms, leading the ambassador to report in October that Argentina "may now be said to have made a technical and fairly substantial compliance with regard to Axis firms."[22]

In light of such positive actions and Perón's oft-stated eagerness to cooperate within the "Inter-American system," Messersmith argued that the U.S. government was obliged to reciprocate. Believing firmly in the Wilsonian tenet that open trade and commerce were the keys to better political relations, he suggested that the Truman Administration should consider lifting an old sanitary ban on the importation of Argentine beef. Although Argentina had long been among the world's foremost beef exporters, no Argentine beef had entered the United States since 1929 due to endemic *fiebre aftosa* (hoof-and-mouth disease) in Argentina. Messersmith argued that this constituted a fundamental reason for historically weak U.S.-Argentine ties and dedicated himself to rectifying it.

---

22. Messersmith to Clayton, 21 October 1946, RG 59, 835.50; see also A. Kenneth Oakley to Messersmith, 12 December 1946, Messersmith Papers, 1832; Uki Goñi, *La auténtica Odessa: la fuga nazi a la Argentina de Perón* (Buenos Aires, 2002), 139-145; Ronald Newton, *The 'Nazi Menace'*, 361-372.

U.S. cattlemen had suffered periodic, crippling outbreaks of the disease in their own herds throughout the nineteenth and early twentieth centuries but had finally succeeded in eradicating it north of the Panama Canal by the late 1920s. To prevent fresh outbreaks, farmers and ranchers had furiously lobbied for the closing of U.S. borders to potentially infected animals. The cattlemen finally achieved total victory with the passage of the Smoot-Hawley Tariff, which enabled the Secretary of Agriculture to prohibit the importation of beef from any nation deemed "infected." Because *aftosa* was endemic in Argentina, Argentine meat imports were immediately banned. Cordell Hull, Sumner Welles, and even Roosevelt himself had fought a rearguard action to ease these onerous restrictions during the 1930s, but the cattle interests and their congressional allies had managed to stifle even a discussion of the issue.[23]

Messersmith had dealt with the explosive issue of *aftosa* as ambassador to Mexico and was among those who doubted that the ranchers' fears were entirely medical. Beef was an eleven-billion-dollar industry that had been helped immeasurably by the elimination of most imported competition. While Argentine cattle grazed freely on the *pampas*, often at little or no expense to the owner, U.S. ranchers utilized modern fattening techniques that doubled the cost of the meat they produced. As a result of this inefficiency, the sanitary embargo, and wartime shortages, U.S. meat prices had more than quadrupled since 1930. Cattlemen's associations apocalyptically predicted the collapse of the entire U.S. economy if hoof-and-mouth ever again hit U.S. shores, but Messersmith viewed their intransigence as little more than a pretense for selfish protectionism that was out of step with the tenets of free trade.[24] Argentines agreed, complaining that:

---

23. Manuel Machado, *Aftosa: A Historical Survey of Foot-and-Mouth Disease and Inter-American Relations* (Albany, 1969), 4-13; Bryce Wood, "The Department of State and the Non-National Interest," *Inter-American Economic Affairs* (Autumn 1961), 5-24; *Review of the River Plate*, 18 October 1947, 9-10.

24. Messersmith to Braden, 12 June 1946, RG 59, 611.355; Even though there is no real way to measure the benefits cattlemen received from this protection, a study done in 1947 is instructive. Economist Carl Wilken testified before

. . . if the domestic market is to be preserved for domestically produced meat (in spite of the fact that Argentine products are of superior quality), then North Americans should be honest enough to state such a fact and not hide their inability to compete profitably behind unreasonable sanitary regulations. A prohibitive tariff would at least save the United States from the possible charge of hypocrisy, remove the label of inferiority from Argentine meat, and clear the way for the frank discussion of diplomatic differences.[25]

This closing of the U.S. market bothered Messersmith for similar reasons. With such protectionism in place, U.S. policymakers could hardly portray themselves as selfless advocates of multilateral global trade. By its very language, the sanitary embargo, with its implication that Argentine meat was unsanitary, rankled Argentines, but more importantly, without the meat trade, Argentines had little way to obtain U.S. dollars.[26] If Argentina was to be pried from its traditional attachment to the British and made to truly look upon itself as a member of the "Inter-American system," meaningful commercial ties with the United States had to

---

Congress that a Mexican outbreak of *aftosa* had been a "blessing in disguise." With the enforcement of the sanitary ban against Mexico, American farmers' incomes would increase by two billion dollars per year. Furthermore, when Canada suffered a minor outbreak in 1952 and the embargo was enforced, Canadian ranchers lost $560 million in sales for one year. U.S. Congress, "Hearings Before the Committee of Agriculture," House of Representatives, 80th Congress, 1st Session, February 10, 1947, 81-84; J. J. Callis, "Foot-and-Mouth Disease," *Gustav Stern Conference on Foot-and-Mouth Disease*, ed Fred Rapp (New York, 1969), 15-16; *Review of the River Plate*, 2 January 1947, 20-21.

25. Thomas Mann, "Foot-and-Mouth Disease in Argentine-American Relations," 10 June 1946, RG 353, RIIC-ARG.

26. Characteristic of this attitude was the remark made by B. L. Simms, chief of the Bureau of Animal Industry, trying to convince the Agriculture Committee that once infected with *aftosa*, cattle were inedible. "We don't consider it to be edible. Some people in the world will eat anything." U.S. Congress, "Hearings Before the Appropriations Committee," House of Representatives, 80th Congress, 1st Session, February 24, 1947, 9; Ivanissevich to Bramulgia, 11 Octubre 1946, AMREC, BA, EEUU 1946, 8, 3.

be established. In October, Messersmith was approached by representatives of the Argentine meat industry, who sought a relaxation of the sanitary restrictions and permission to export beef and mutton to the United States from Patagonia—a region that all observers agreed was disease free. Messersmith forwarded the request to his superiors.[27]

However, even Will Clayton, the Department's most determined free trader, shied away from stirring up this "hornet's nest." Although he supported Messersmith's arguments and had worked in the past for the easing of the "sanitary embargo," he knew a lost cause when he saw one. Clayton's superiors went even further, warning off Vandenberg and Congressman Emmanuel Cellar, two legislators who had taken up Messersmith's cause. While Vandenberg sought rapprochement with Argentina as part of his anti-communist efforts, Cellar urged Truman to use Argentine beef imports to end meat rationing in the United States. Truman did not pick up the gauntlet. Ironically, the drive to lower trade barriers was foundering not only in Buenos Aires, but in Washington as well.[28]

Messersmith may have been justifiably tentative with regard to the sanitary embargo but had no reservations about encouraging other forms of U.S.-Argentine commerce. To alleviate the Argentine "starvation for goods of all types," he urged Clayton to "give a certain preferential treatment to industrial equipment for the Argentine." Realizing that diverting resources from loyal, wartorn allies to supposedly "fascist" Argentina would not go over well, Messersmith hoped that Clayton and Henry Wallace could "discreetly" influence U.S. manufacturers and exporters to make Argentina a higher priority. As a potential market for U.S. goods, Argentina had few rivals in Latin America, and Messersmith feared that while the Truman Administration ostracized Argentina, other

---

27. Messersmith to Braden, 12 June 1946, RG 59, 611.355; Messersmith to Clayton, 22 October 1946, RG 59, 611.355.

28. Clayton to Messersmith 22 October 1946, RG 59, 611.355; see also Ivanissevich to Bramulgia, 11 Octubre 1946, AMREC, BA, EEUU 1946, 8, 3; Kopplemann to Mullins, 3 October 1946, RG 59, 611.355.

nations would be willing and able to supply Perón. Once Europeans re-established their pre-war economic footholds in Argentina, political ties would follow the commercial ones, and Argentina would remain outside the inter-American framework. In essence, Perón's industrialization program offered an opportunity for U.S. corporations to get in on the ground floor and put Argentina economically and politically on the correct path.[29]

Not surprisingly, Clayton again found himself rejecting the overzealous ambassador's propositions. Although sympathetic, Clayton vetoed the idea that the U.S. government should quietly divert scarce materials to Argentina. Unwilling to encourage a government currently engaged in overtly statist behavior, he reminded Messersmith that "commercial and economic favoritism to Argentina could not be divorced from political favoritism."[30] Clayton's responses had the tone of a friendly rebuff, but others were not as polite. Robert Schaetzel, executive secretary of the "Argentina Committee," was "shocked" by Messersmith's request, and suggested that the "starvation" in Argentina hardly compared to that in wartorn areas. In spite of the lure of the Argentine market, the State Department could not give preferential treatment to a nation that had been considered a Nazi puppet at a time when loyal allies and war victims were still suffering.[31]

Failing in his attempts to induce his own government to make concrete concessions that might help to wean Argentina from state corporatism, Messersmith concentrated upon Perón. The ambassador's ill-fated pleas for concessions from the State Department, however futile, did endear him to the president. This was not accidental. "If Perón cannot have good friends" to push him toward liberal capitalism, Messersmith pragmatically noted, "he will have bad ones" that encouraged nationalist statism and a

---

29. Messersmith to Clayton, 16 July 1946, RG 353, RIIC-ARG; see also Messersmith to Acheson, 24 October 1946, Messersmith Papers, 1811; Messersmith to Byrnes, 30 October 1946, Messersmith Papers, 1813.

30. Clayton to Messersmith, 23 July 1946, RG 353, RIIC-ARG.

31. Schaetzel to Wilcox, 11 July 1946, RG 59, 611.3531; see also Stiller, *George S. Messersmith*, 247-248.

directed economy.[32] The ambassador desperately hoped that "being in a position to talk with the Argentine as a friend" would help bring Perón into the fold. Not only were IAPI's practices making enemies around the globe, but the extension of government into business on a grand scale was warping the Argentine economy with disastrous long-term consequences. Perón was using his state apparatus to create "unsound" industries and undertake projects that could only survive with continued government protection. As "such interventions in business can only be destructive in the end," they had to be ceased. If they were not voluntarily eliminated, they would eventually collapse, spawning economic dislocations and wild, unpredictable results. The United States, he believed, had astutely recognized and avoided this perilous path, but Perón lacked the experience to do so. Having Perón's ear, he hoped to put Argentine policy back on the right path to the benefit of the U.S., Argentina, and the liberal capitalist order.[33] Nowhere was Messersmith's somewhat idealistic approach more apparent than in his intervention in the Anglo-Argentine negotiations in September.

### III

The British found themselves drawn to the bargaining table with Perón in mid-1946 as the Malbran-Eden treaty was on the verge of expiration. Signed in 1936 as an extension of the more famous Roca-Runciman treaty, Malbran-Eden had granted a preferential exchange rate and tariff concessions to British exporters and guaranteed "benevolent treatment" of British investors in exchange for guaranteed purchases of Argentine meat. As bilateral arrangements typical of the 1930s, Malbran-Eden and Roca-Runciman had strengthened ties between the nations, but Argentine nationalists in the 1940s found them highly offensive since they fixed Argentine meat export prices at extremely low prices that hardly reflected world demand. Therefore, *peronistas* hinted that they were ready to allow the agreement to expire.

---

32. Stiller, *George S. Messersmith*, 239.

33. Messersmith to Clayton, 21 October 1946, RG 59, 835.50.

Compounding this threat was the impending expiration of the 1907 Mitre Law that had granted British investors tax exemptions and other special privileges in Argentina. The *Ley Mitre* had been tremendously successful in encouraging railroad growth in the past but was a sitting duck in a nation that considered itself to be a victim of imperialism. Whitehall feared that Perón might allow the Mitre Law to expire in 1947, tax the railroad companies, and expropriate them once their value had dropped, at the same time IAPI, liberated from the strictures of Malbran-Eden, raised the price of vital Argentine meat exports to the British Isles.[34]

Perón and Miranda undoubtedly encouraged this fear to draw the English into negotiations when their power was at its peak. In spite of Hull and Braden's claims to the contrary, Argentina's contribution to the Allied war effort had not been insubstantial, and the bill was coming due for the British. Various Argentine governments during the war had continued to supply Britain with desperately-needed supplies of meat at regular prices— approximately one third of the Chicago price—on credit. By 1946, Argentina's sterling balances had grown to almost 150 million pounds. For Perón, it was a mixed blessing. Although this sum was potentially invaluable for his industrialization scheme, he was unable to spend it due to British inconvertibility and export control policies. In essence, the sterling balances represented an interest-free loan to Britain with no date set for repayment. While Perón pressed for a resolution to this unhappy state of affairs, the British stalled and urged Perón simply to renew the Malbran-Eden contract and the *Ley Mitre*.

For Whitehall, the ideal solution would have been a continuation of the trade concessions and meat contract and the sale of the British-owned railroads in Argentina to Perón. Estimating the value of the railroad facilities to be almost equal to that of the sterling balances, Whitehall hoped to eliminate with one

---

34. Gilmore to Braden, 3 October 1946, RG 59, 635.4131; Nicholas Bowen, "The End of British Economic Hegemony in Argentina," 3-9; Jorge Fodor, "Argentina's Nationalism: Myth or Reality?" *The Political Economy of Argentina, 1946-1983* eds. Guido DiTella and Rudiger Dornbusch (Pittsburgh, 1989), 33-37.

stroke of a pen no small part of its wartime debts. As an additional benefit, the British would be able finally to unload the dilapidated railroads. Although the facilities had once been among the best in the Western Hemisphere, they were already showing signs of decay. Depression and war had prevented replacement equipment from reaching Argentina, portending the day when their ownership would become more of a liability than an asset. Fully cognizant of this, Argentine governments had for years resisted British efforts to peddle them. But Whitehall desperately presented its case once again, hoping that two birds could be killed with one stone if the sterling balances and the railroad albatross could both be eliminated.[35]

Perón appeared to be amenable to this solution and just prior his inauguration, informed the new British Ambassador, Sir Reginald Leeper, of his intention to purchase the railways as part of his call for "economic independence." The British leapt at the prospect and dispatched Sir Wilfred Eady to make the deal. Eady quickly learned that he had been duped.[36] Miguel Miranda met the British negotiators in July and immediately made it clear that he had no intention of purchasing the railroads after all. Described by Messersmith as "a very difficult man who has no knowledge of either finance or broad economic problems," Miranda set the tone for the meetings when he announced that no other issues would even be discussed until an agreement on the sterling balances had been reached. The balances, Miranda argued, should earn interest at 2.5 percent, the same rate that the U.S. loan to Britain was earning, and convertibility should be restored. Eady stonewalled, refusing to consider convertibility, as other nations would demand the same treatment.[37]

---

35. Harriman to Secretary of State, 14 June 1946, RG 59, 635.4131; Burrows Memorandum, 20 June 1946, RG 59, MRIC; Raul Garcia Heras, "World War II and the Frustrated Nationalization of the British-Owned Railroads in Argentina," *Journal of Latin American Studies* 17, 135-155; see also Fodor, "Argentina's Nationalism," 35-39.

36. Messersmith to Clayton, 3 September 1946, RG 59, 635.4131; *Review of the River Plate*, 26 July 1946, 3-4.

37. Messersmith to Secretary of State, 26 July 1946, RG 59, 635.4131; see also

Perón, frustrated by the deadlock, announced that he would unilaterally resolve the issues by simply tripling the prices of Argentine beef, allowing the *Ley Mitre* to expire, and leaving the railroads as they stood. If his speech was intended to cow the English into a more flexible attitude, however, it failed completely. Eady called the bluff and dug in his heels. In early August, the British rattled their own sabre, announcing that they had recently signed a new wheat agreement with Canada. Nearly all of Britain's wheat needs would be fulfilled by the arrangement, at less than half the cost of Argentine grain. The *Review of the River Plate* warned that Argentine intransigence might lead England also to search for alternative sources of meat and praised the Canadian willingness to be "reasonable." Like Perón's earlier bluster, however, this was an empty threat, and the stalemate persisted through August.[38]

By early September, Eady gave up hope and was making arrangements to return to England when Leeper made a last-ditch appeal to Messersmith. "Leeper said to me that if I could see my way clear to mention the matter to Perón," the ambassador reported, "a new basis could be found for the negotiations and an agreement arrived at."[39] Messersmith agreed to discuss the matter "in a purely informal and unofficial way" with Perón and Foreign Minister Bramulgia.

> I said that the responsibilities of Britain and the United States today were very great because they were the two countries which stood for certain trading principles as well as certain political ideas and these economic ideas and political principles had to control in the world or there could be no peace in any country, including the Argentine.

---

Bowen, "End of British Economic Hegemony," 11-15.

38. Fodor, "Argentine Nationalism," 37-38; *Review of the River Plate*, 2 August 1946, 3-4.

39. Messersmith Memoirs, "British-Argentine Agreement for the Purchase of Meat," n.d., Messersmith Papers, 1947; see also *Review of the River Plate*, 24 May 1946, 10; MacDonald, "The U.S., Britain, and Argentina in the Post-War Period," 183-193.

He pointed out that the United States had also "furnished great quantities of material to Britain during the war" and "that we had practically wiped the slate clean." To preserve the British position, the United States had even granted a $3.5 billion loan that would be used to aid recovery and help "Britain to become a competitor with us in many markets, but that we recognized that this was a healthy thing in the long run." Messersmith urged the same sort of restraint upon Perón, lecturing that a prompt British recovery was as vital to Argentina in the long run as it was for the United States.[40]

Perón replied that he understood, and that Miranda simply had been too intransigent. This of course only echoed British reports to Messersmith that the economic czar's "rough" and "discourteous" manner was the reason for the impending breakdown. Indeed, Messersmith believed that Perón had selected Miranda to head the mission for the very reason that he was "difficult." Perón nonetheless informed him that, henceforth, the more conciliatory Bramulgia would "play a more important part" in the negotiations. After the president thanked him for "help[ing] him in his task," the meeting broke up, but Messersmith remained dubious that any real solution could be reached.[41]

He need not have worried, as the Miranda-Eady Treaty was signed just two weeks after the pivotal intervention. Miranda was given new instructions the day after the conversation, and the deadlock broke almost immediately. The Argentines gave ground on all fronts. The sterling balances remained inconvertible, but all sterling earned by the Argentine exports in the future would be freely convertible. Furthermore, 30 million pounds of the balances were to be utilized to repatriate Argentina's national and provincial debts, while the remainder was to draw interest at only .5 percent. Finally, in the unlikely event that Argentina should run a trade

---

40. Messersmith to Clayton, 3 September 1946, RG 59, 635.4131.

41. Messersmith to Clayton, 3 September 1946, RG 59, 635.4131; Messersmith to Secretary of State, 19 September 1946, RG 59, 635.3531; see also Messersmith to Secretary of State, 14 August 1946, RG 59, 835.4131; Messersmith Memoirs, "British-Argentine," Messersmith Papers, 1947.

deficit with the sterling area, up to 10 million pounds of blocked sterling per year could be released to cover the shortfall.

Eady also managed to avert a drastic increase in the price of meat—agreeing to purchase the entire Argentine meat surplus for four years at prices only 12.5 percent higher than pre-war levels. While Argentina would be entitled to hold back seventeen percent of their surplus the first year and twenty-two percent the second, Britain retained the right to resell a portion of their purchases—allowing it to continue as Western Europe's unified meat distributor. Even though the English had been unable to sell the railroads, they nonetheless provided for the eventual salvation of the network. The Argentine government agreed to form a mixed company "for the purpose of acquiring and operating the assets" of the railways. The *Ley Mitre* exemptions would remain in force, and the Argentines further pledged to guarantee British owners of a four percent profit per year for two years. Any profits above six percent per year were to be used for the extension or repatriation of the network, and Perón was obligated to provide an additional 500 million pesos to further modernize it.[42] By any estimation, the British negotiators had scored a major victory, as the sterling question had been deferred, the meat contract had been renewed with a minimal price increase, and the Argentines were well on the way toward purchasing the railroads.

There can be little doubt that Messersmith's timely intercession had been pivotal. Bramulgia, Perón and the British all credited him with breaking the impasse, but journalists who were unaware of his action were mystified by the "amazing fruitfulness" of the last week of negotiations.[43] But if the British had managed to get the better of Perón, they also appear to have stolen a march on Messersmith, who had acted at Leeper's behest without instructions from Washington. Messersmith failed to mention Leeper's appeal in his explanations to Clayton, probably as historian Nicholas Bowen suggested, to "avoid even the hint that he might

---

42. Gilmore to Mann, Briggs and Braden, 1 October 1946, RG 59, 635.4131.

43. *Review of the River Plate*, 27 September 1947, 12; Fodor, "Argentine Nationalism," 50-51.

have acted at the instigation of another government" since "he was likely to be in sufficient trouble for having taken action, albeit successfully, without instructions."[44] Although there is no record of Messersmith receiving reprimand, he nevertheless was threatened with considerable embarrassment. He had asked Leeper to "be good enough to not to tell Sir Wilfred Eady or any of his associates that I had mentioned these matters to the President." Messersmith "was able to talk over these matters with the President because he knew that I did not talk them over with other persons." If it became known "that I discussed my conversations with other persons, I would lose the opportunity of having these conversations which have been so helpful so far."[45]

Messersmith was undoubtedly surprised when he was informed that both Sir Stanford Cripps and the Prime Minister were publicly sending their thanks. As Callum MacDonald has artfully shown, Whitehall and Washington had been cooperating in their efforts to ameliorate Argentine nationalism, at the same time they competed fiercely but quietly for the Argentine market. Messersmith's position was naturally stronger, but Leeper showed how this advantage could be used for English benefit through skillful diplomacy. Although his intervention does not appear to have become public knowledge, Messersmith was defending his action on other grounds soon enough when State Department analysts discovered that the Miranda-Eady treaty violated the terms of the Anglo-American Loan Agreement.[46]

Miranda-Eady stipulated that if Argentina ran an unfavorable trade balance with the sterling area, sterling would be released to cover the shortfall. Article 10 of the Anglo-American agreement stated that any unblocked sterling should be freely disposable, without restrictions. As a violation of the letter of this

---

44. Nicholas Bowen, "The End of British Economic Hegemony," 17-18.

45. Messersmith to Clayton, 3 September 1946, RG 59, 635.4131.

46. MacDonald, "The U.S., Britain, and Argentina in the Post-War Period," *The Political Economy of Argentina, 1880-1946*, eds. Guido DiTella and D. C. M. Platt, (New York, 1986) 190-194; see also Messersmith to Clayton, 25 September 1946, RG 59, 635.4131; Stiller, *George S. Messersmith*, 254-255.

agreement and the spirit of multilateralism, the provision evoked consternation from both the State and Treasury Departments. Messersmith claimed that he knew nothing of this provision, even though he had stated earlier that Leeper had kept him "fully informed."[47] When pressed, he admitted that the Englishman had not mentioned the matter to him. Although the provision was a minor one that was unlikely ever to go into effect, Secretary of the Treasury John Snyder reprimanded the British and led a futile effort to block implementation of the treaty. Ironically, Messersmith had helped the British negotiate a bilateral agreement with Argentina by lecturing Perón on the need for open, multilateral trade and opened himself up to criticism in the process.[48]

Messersmith justified his intervention by asserting that no good could have come out of a breakdown of the negotiations. Inasmuch as an Anglo-Argentine rift might have left the door open for U.S. business interests, he predicted more dire consequences. The British would have lost their guaranteed meat supply, and probably even more. Messersmith assumed that "tremendous resentments would arise" on both sides of the Atlantic and that the British would have no reason to continue to use their refrigerator ships to transport Argentine meat. Unable to sell their meat surplus, Argentina would be plunged into economic chaos that might be "easily translated into some violent acts of expropriation" of foreign properties. Once unleashed, indiscriminate outrage would not distinguish between U.S. and British capital. While Messersmith later bemoaned the fact that the deal had strengthened the British economic position in Argentina—presumably filling a gap that should have been occupied by U.S. investors and traders—he realized that U.S. interests could hardly be served if anything exacerbated the nationalism inherent in *peronismo*.[49]

---

47. Messersmith to Clayton, 3 September 1946, RG 59, 635.4131.

48. Gilmore to Briggs, Mann and Braden, RG 59, 635.4131; Snyder to Dalton, 31 October 1946, John Snyder Papers, Secretary of the Treasury, Box 2, Argentina File, HST; Messersmith to Clayton, 27 September 1946, RG 59, 611.3531.

49. Messersmith to Clayton, 25 September 1946, RG 59, 635.4131; see also Messersmith to Acheson, 24 October 1946, Messersmith Papers, 1811.

Although it is telling that the British were now forced to use Messersmith's good offices to accomplish their goals in Argentina, so too was Perón's reluctance to nationalize the railroads. Although Braden considered Perón to be a rabid nationalist bent upon wide-scale expropriation, again Messersmith saw him as a political novice, reluctantly at the head of a nationalistic movement he could not fully control. According to Messersmith, Perón the candidate "had advocated the self-sufficiency of the country and so far as possible the getting rid of foreign investments in the Argentine." While this "was a broad program to which he had not given very much thought," it was also "a part of the demagogic approach which he took" that nonetheless "represented certainly the feeling of a good part of the Argentine people."[50] In contrast to the restraint they had illustrated in their negotiations with the British, Peronists showed no reluctance as they nationalized the ITT subsidiary, *Unión Telefónica*, in August. By purchasing the telephone companies and turning their operations over to a "mixed company," he was in the eyes of some, setting the stage for a wave of nationalization that might well end with the elimination of foreign capital in Argentina. Messersmith, however, argued that this initial impression was an erroneous interpretation of both Perón and his program.[51]

In truth, Messersmith cabled Washington, the purchase was actually a good omen, as it demonstrated that Perón understood the value of U.S. investment, respected property rights, and stood as a bulwark against radical nationalism. Perón negotiated in good faith with ITT's Bill Arnold and Sosthenes Behn. He was willing to pay $95 million for the facilities—less than executives wanted, but enough to "completely satisf[y]" them, once he awarded ITT a ten-year contract for technical service and advice, that would more than compensate for the lower sale price. Messersmith noted that the deal was struck without the "duress and without the violence" which so frequently accompanied economic nationalism, and even Clayton, who was fundamentally opposed to any form of statism,

---

50. Messersmith Memoirs, "Argentine-British," Messersmith Papers, 1947, 3.

51. Braden to Messersmith, 5 July 1946, RG 59, 835.75.

conceded that it was "just as well. I imagine the I.T. and T. have not done so badly in the matter."[52]

Messersmith viewed the trend toward nationalization of utilities and vital industries to be unfortunate but understandable as moderate governments around the globe were moving toward gradual state control of vital utilities. He argued that Perón fit into this mold, rather than that of Mussolini, Hitler, or Stalin.[53] According to Messersmith, Perón only undertook the ITT purchase to prevent other Argentine nationalists from expropriating them in a more radical fashion. Perón had explained that the Argentine constitution gave provincial governors and local officials the right to "do things which caused great inconvenience"—one of which was expropriation of properties within their jurisdiction. He further claimed that he had spent weeks trying to dissuade the governor of Córdoba from exercising this right with the electrical company, but "could not eventually prevent the Governor from expropriating if he became bullheaded."[54] If the national government had not gone ahead with reasonable nationalization, Radical or *peronista* officials might easily have done so in a more provocative fashion and jeopardized the budding U.S.-Argentine rapprochement. Although it is unlikely that Perón, who had pledged himself to just this sort of nationalism during his run for the presidency, was being entirely candid, his explanation made a certain amount of sense.

Messersmith believed the justification at any rate, and the Argentine unwillingness to purchase the British railways supported his thesis that Perón's nationalism was considerably exaggerated. If the ITT purchase made little financial sense, it did have immense political value. Peronists publicized the move as a bold extension of their "recuperation" program, and the low sale price gave

---

52. Messersmith to Braden, 14 August 1946, RG 59, 835.75; Clayton to Messersmith, 4 September 1946, RG 59, 835.602; see also Messersmith to Braden, 20 August 1946, RG 59, 835.75; Arnold to Messersmith, 15 October 1946, RG 59, 835.75.

53. Messersmith to Clayton, 3 September 1946, RG 59, 635.4131; Messersmith to Secretary of State, 19 December 1946, RG 59, 835.50 Five Year Plan.

54. Messersmith to Byrnes, 30 October 1946, Messersmith Papers, 1814.

"sufficient material to certain highly nationalistic elements here to boast that they have got the better of a foreign company." So long as Perón continued to play the notes of the nationalist song, he had no reason to question his mass appeal or his popular base. As Messersmith wryly reminded the Department, if Perón was the dictator Braden believed him to be, he would not have to rely upon populist demagoguery and periodically "giving a kick in the pants to the foreigner."[55] As it was, however, Perón pushed forward with the popular "recuperation" campaign, even if he was unwilling to expend his sterling balances on the derelict railroads.

Although Perón did purchase the small French-owned rail network, the harbor facilities at Rosario, and several other minor enterprises, to the surprise of many, he made no effort to acquire the U.S. and British-owned *frigorificos*. As one of the most valuable and visible foreign investments in Argentina, the meat-packing plants made an almost ideal target for "recuperation." Argentine cattlemen, beef fatteners, exporters, and nationalists in general had long resented the stranglehold that foreigners had achieved in this critical industry. While Perón never made a direct move for nationalization, he was pressing the companies with what U.S. officials called "expropriation by attrition." The Miranda-Eady treaty essentially placed a price ceiling upon exported meat, whereas IAPI price controls kept domestic prices low. At the same time, Perón's government mandated wage hikes for meatpacking workers, catching the *frigorificos* in an "economic squeeze play" that might well have forced them to sell out eventually.[56]

Messersmith argued that the "squeeze play" was little more than a sad but incidental side effect of Perón's reliance upon a working-class constituency. He had given the president numerous lectures on the familiar theme of private capital's inherent superiority over state ownership of industry. A number of these

---

55. Messersmith to Braden, 20 August 1946, RG 59, 835.75; Messersmith Memoirs, n.d., Messersmith Papers, 2010; Gambini, *Historia del peronismo*, 128-129.

56. Hanson to Daniels, 13 December 1948, RG 59, 835.5034; Daniels to Bruce, 13 December 1948, RG 59, 835.5034.

discourses had focused explicitly upon the *frigorificos*. Although the Argentine government could feasibly take over the packing and distribution aspects of the trade, other considerations, Messersmith lectured, militated against such action. After three days, Perón assured him that there would be no expropriation, even though the "movement toward nationalization had taken so much hold in some quarters." As late as 1955, Messersmith continued to take considerable pride in the fact that Perón kept his word.[57]

Still, Messersmith probably gave himself more credit than he deserved, as there were several other explanations for Perón's unwillingness to nationalize the *frigorificos*. As a general rule, the meatpackers' unions were among the most militant and effective in Argentina. So long as the *frigorificos* remained in foreign hands, Perón could win double victories by arbitrating strikes in favor of Argentine workers—striking popular blows against the *extrañeros* in the process. Similarly, Perón and Miranda had little reason to support the complaints of the beef producers and ranchers. As Miranda put it in his inimitably blunt style, "the cattlebreeders are always a menace, and I hope that as long as I live I shall never see them again become the ruling class of Argentina." Because these groups would presumably be primary beneficiaries of expropriation, there was simply no good reason to expropriate the *frigorificos* and further ostracize the United States.[58]

It is possible to assert, as Jorge Fodor did, that Perón's nationalism was, in some respects, almost entirely a "myth." Fodor, like Messersmith, argued that Perón essentially stood as a bastion against more ardent nationalists and illustrated that U.S. and British commentators portrayed the Argentine to be far more xenophobic and aggressive than he was. Certainly, his willingness to accept low prices for his meat sales to Britain and cooperate on certain issues with Messersmith do not support the view of Perón as an irrational

---

57. Messersmith Memoirs, "Argentine-British," Messersmith Papers, 1947, 17-19; see also Fodor, "Argentina's Nationalism" 48.

58. *Review of the River Plate*, 10 January 1947, 20; see also Peter H. Smith, *Politics and Beef in Argentina: Patterns of Conflict* (New York, 1960), 234-241; *Review of the River Plate*, 28 March 1947, 12-13.

ultranationalist.[59] Nonetheless, he headed a nationalistic coalition in a nationalistic country at a nationalistic moment. So long as Perón could strengthen his domestic position through measures like expropriation or rhetorically "plucking the eagle's feathers," the climate for foreign investment would never be as good as U.S. leaders hoped. Any investment would be vulnerable to expropriation, target of his labor and social welfare decrees, and subject to his growing state control of the economy. Still, nationalism was a Pandora's Box that could not be closed by Perón or the United States, however much either might have wished to do so. With every gesture of conciliation and move toward rapprochement, Perón's hold on the tiger's tail became more tenuous, but at the same time, his every nationalistic pronouncement or gesture antagonized Washington. Messersmith was among the few observers who understood the tightrope that Perón was obliged to walk in 1946.

## IV

Therein lays the fundamental flaw in Messersmith's approach. He had determined early on that Perón was a relatively apolitical figure who could be quietly directed toward the right "path" to economic development. Perón gave him reason to believe this by not "playing his Russian card," ratifying the Chapultepec Accords, and cooperating with the British mission. Still, there was only so much that he could—or would have wanted to—do to collaborate within the "Inter-American system." He had come to power amid revolutionary fervor, was the vanguard of a movement that had been assembled to redress a half century of wrongs and was not about to renege upon the lavish promises he had made during his election campaign. He would do what he could to cooperate with the United States, as he required at least tacit U.S. acceptance, but could not deviate too far from the course he had set without alienating his constituencies.

At times, Messersmith seemed to appreciate this and urged Washington to give Perón incentives in order to facilitate the

---

59. Fodor, "Argentine Nationalism: Myth or Reality?" 31-56.

transformation of his statism toward a privatist approach. His superiors were, however, unyielding. Not only was Braden still in a position to veto any overture to Argentina, but even Clayton rejected several compromises, as the State Department hoped that Perón might be brought into line with minimal effort. At this point, Byrnes, Clayton, and other U.S. policymakers were still thinking of Perón as an autocratic dictator, believing that if they could simply redirect him, his nation and people would follow. They sought a quick fix to the Peronist problem and did not yet appreciate fully the implications of the Peronist revolution. Their new approach toward Perón was taking shape but had not yet blossomed into full maturity. Although the first months of Messersmith's tenure may have given the impression that he was making headway in his fight to redirect Perón, subsequent events proved otherwise. The differences between *peronista* and New Deal corporatist variants ran too deep to be smoothed over by Messersmith's peacemaking, as an examination of labor union diplomacy illustrates well.

# CHAPTER 5

## CONSOLIDATING POWER: THE FIVE-YEAR PLAN AND THE CAPTURE OF LABOR

The English-speaking unionists of the United States evidently cannot, as the minority they are, take the initiative to establish any system of hemispheric union cooperation.

*Periodico Seminal de la C.G.T*, 1 Julio 1946[1]

### I

Whereas the railroad negotiations had illustrated clearly that Messersmith could be effective in heading off the more nationalist *peronistas* from time to time, by the end of 1946 and the beginning of 1947, it was equally clear that the gaps between Peronist and New Deal democracy were still widening. Any hope that Messersmith might dissuade Perón from undertaking a corporatist centralization through conversations alone all but perished at the end of 1946 when the president announced his Five-Year Plan blueprint for Argentine national development. Although the plan was nowhere near as radical as some commentators may have believed, it nonetheless established that Perón fully intended to stay the course he had set during the opening days of his presidency. Using a combination of selective repression, demagoguery, a "whirlwind" of social welfare measures and labor reforms, and skillful political maneuvering, Perón entrenched *peronismo* throughout 1946 and early 1947.[2]

Still, Braden and his allies in the labor movement had not placed all of their hopes in Messersmith. In January 1947, the American Federation of Labor (AFL) cast its stamp on U.S.-

---

1. *Periodico Seminal de la C.G.T*, 1 Julio 1946, Rollo 5, FSR.

2. Watrous to Secretary of State, 7 August 1946, RG 59, 835.504.

Argentine relations by dispatching Serafino Romualdi and a team of delegates to study Perón's labor policies and the state of unionism in Argentina. Initially contemplating an alliance with the CGT, the AFL hoped that Peronist unions might be able to contribute to the battles against communism and Perón. Instead, its leaders quickly recognized that Peronism was as dangerous a threat to U.S. principles and interests in the hemisphere as communism itself. With this in mind, Romualdi launched an ill-fated but State Department-supported campaign to weaken Perón by eroding one of the "two pillars" or Peronism—his labor union support. While Romualdi's efforts resembled Braden's earlier ones in both tone and style, and failed just as miserably, they nonetheless illustrate that U.S. leaders were gaining a better appreciation of the nature of Peronism and at least beginning to understand how to undermine it effectively.

Despite their failure, these efforts are instructive. As both Perón and his New Deal counterparts spent the post-war period reining in the labor movements in their respective nations, these same unionists became ardent advocates for the very governments that were in the process of restricting their freedom. The AFL and CIO emerged as key spokesmen for a tame unionism that recognized the primacy of business in a privatist corporatism, as Perón's CGT argued forcefully that the statist Peronist alternative, with its dedication to the redistribution of wealth, offered far more. So although Romualdi's mission to Buenos Aires marked a flamboyant climax, it must be understood as a unique conjuncture in Argentine, U.S., and labor histories.

## II

**B**y adopting José Figuerola's Five-Year Plan in late 1946, Perón essentially declared his intent to proceed with his industrialization program and to keep the state at the center of the national economy. Although its name connoted centralized blueprints for development and long-term planning, the twenty-seven proposals of the Five-Year Plan were far more typical of Perón's scattergun approach to running a national economy. One opposition cartoonist even portrayed the plan as a headless, footless mannequin throwing money into the air as it strode through a minefield. Nonetheless, Perón portrayed the plan as a model of technocratic policymaking whereby "statesmen will give the objectives, and the technicians must indicate the road by which they will be accomplished."[3] By giving the president the power to reorganize cabinet posts, ministries, federal courts, the foreign service and the Buenos Aires municipal government, the plan strengthened the executive branch considerably. It also called for the chief executive to control Federal Court appointments, enabling Perón to complete his capture of the judicial branch—the last bastion of the old oligarchy. Although still reliant upon a rubber-stamp Congress for the passage of the various bills that comprised the plan, these efforts to consolidate power in the executive branch illustrated that Messersmith's appeals for moderation had gone almost entirely unheeded.[4]

Still, the Five-Year Plan went even further, as the president called for extension of the franchise and educational reform. Whereas the 1912 Sáenz Peña Law had established universal, compulsory suffrage for males over age 18, it ignored women and excluded non-commissioned officers in the armed forces. Perón predictably sought to rectify these omissions. Just as he could expect electoral rewards for enfranchising these groups, his educational proposals could do little but enhance his personal power. Greater educational opportunities would be granted to lower classes with a predictable emphasis on vocational training to fit the industrialization scheme. Furthermore, the entire educational system would be centralized under a national council, appointed by and responsible to, the president. With control over education, Peronists could effectively spread propaganda to the youth of the nation. Although the State Department did not pay much attention to this aspect of the Five-Year Plan, it ultimately became among the

---

3. Messersmith to Secretary of State, 19 December 1946, RG 59, 835.50 Five Year Plan; *Primera Plana*, 12 Julio 1947, 39.

4. Messersmith to Secretary of State, 19 December 1946, RG 59, 835.50 Five Year Plan; Gilmore to Mann, Lyon, Briggs and Braden, 14 November 1946, RG 59, 835.50.

most important factors in keeping Peronism alive in the decades to come.[5]

Perón's eclectic proposals in the area of "National Economy" ranged from cautious New Deal-style welfare statism to fairly radical socialism. Easily the most controversial of these measures was his program for employee ownership of business. Firms that voluntarily joined the program would limit their profits to five percent. Excess profits would be used to transfer stock to the workers gradually until they ultimately became full partners or owners. Since businesses that opted not to participate could expect to be penalized in one way or another, businessmen understood that "it doesn't require too much imagination to see how it could become compulsory."[6] Perón showed his enthusiasm for the program by quickly putting it into effect in the *Empresa Mixta Telefónica Argentina*, the former ITT properties.

In a vein reminiscent of the New Deal, the Five-Year Plan called for a series of social welfare reforms such as low-income housing, unemployment insurance, pensions, and public works. Also envisioning semi-socialized medicine, Perón aimed to ultimately have the health care of eighty-five percent of the nation paid for by the state, at the same time a national board controlled the manufacture of pharmaceuticals. Echoing Roosevelt and Hull's Reciprocal Trade Agreements, Perón also pushed forward customs reform, proposing that the president should be empowered to increase or decrease existing tariffs by fifty percent or levy a twenty-five percent tariff in areas where none previously existed.[7]

---

5. Gilmore to Mann, Lyon, Briggs and Braden, 14 November 1946, RG 59, 835.50; Hoyt to Braden, Wright, Mann, and Lyon, 11 February 1947, ARA, Argentina; Mariano Plotkin, *Mañana es San Perón: Propaganda, rituales políticos, y educación en el régimen peronista, 1946-1955* (Buenos Aires, 1994), 298-307. Perhaps their most impressive feat, Peronists increased the number of students in college from 63,319 to 201,437 in six years. Hugo Chumbita, *El enigma peronista* (Buenos Aires, 1989), 22.

6. Granger to Mann, 26 October 1946, RG 59, 835.50 Five Year Plan.

7. *Review of the River Plate*, 25 October 1946, 8-9; see also Gilmore to Lyons, Mann, Briggs, and Braden, 14 November 1946, RG 59, 835.50; Messersmith to Secretary of State, 27 November 1946, RG 59, 835.50 Five Year Plan;

Finally, Perón reaffirmed his commitment to state-sponsored industrial development by allocating almost 200 million pesos for the development of power resources, recognizing that Argentine industrialization would require far more energy than was currently available. Petroleum development was naturally the highest priority. Peronists hoped that oil production could be increased by more than a third by tapping newfound reserves in Mendoza, Patagonia, and elsewhere. The hydroelectric program was also ambitious; it called for nearly seventy new plants and dams, which in addition to supplying power, would irrigate more than 900,000 hectares of land and bring development to the oft-ignored interior of the nation. Naturally, these developments were to occur under the control of the government which was, of course, granted the right to nationalize any power facilities developed under the auspices of the Five-Year Plan.[8]

Perón concluded that this ambitious hodge-podge would cost close to $1.27 billion, but in the heady days of 1946, this hardly appeared to be a major stumbling block. Not only did he possess the massive sterling, gold, and dollar holdings from the war, but IAPI seemed to be flourishing, bringing in top dollar for agricultural exports from a desperate world. Although IAPI never disclosed its records, the CIA later estimated that the organization had brought in as much revenue to the government in one year as five years of wartime exports had. Few doubted that it was bringing in "fabulous" or "immense" profits, and some foreign observers estimated that IAPI's activities made the plan feasible.[9] The Peronist banking system appeared to be in a position to coordinate investment, and Miranda seemed to be an able "economic czar," arguing that the Five-Year Plan would not cost,

---

Gambini, *La primera presidencia*, 115-117.

8. Burrows to Secretary of State, 11 April 1947, RG 59, 835.61; Lewis, *The Crisis of Argentine Capitalism*, 158-9.

9. Central Intelligence Agency, "Probable Argentine Policy toward the U.S. through 1952 and its Effects on U.S. Interests," 15 February 1949, PSF, Intelligence File, CIA Reports 1948, HST; *Review of the River Plate*, 14 February 1947, 10; *Review of the River Plate*, 21 February 1947, 8.

but actually make, money. For example, the proposed gas pipeline from Comodoro Rivadavia to Buenos Aires might cost $90 million to construct, but once in operation, the pipeline would earn $16 million per year, swiftly paying off the initial outlay.[10] Still, even Perón acknowledged that the plan was too ambitious, but added that if *peronistas* "achieved 50 percent of it, they would be most fortunate, and if they achieved 25 percent, it would still be a great step forward." Reiterating his belief that Argentina had in the past suffered from chronic disorganization, Perón argued that the plan was necessary to achieve anything at all, even if modifications had to be made later.[11]

His critics hoped none of it would go through, as the very concept of a Five-Year Plan conjured up images of totalitarianism. Indeed, State Department officials understood that "the keynote of Russian internal domestic propaganda has for years been the dramatization by all available means of successive five-year plans." Stalin utilized five-year plans, Hitler employed four-year plans, and now Perón was apparently engaging in a "conscious imitation" of their tactics. Even the English business community in Argentina, which was in many respects the most even-handed of Perón's critics, labeled the plan to be the "vehicle of some vaguely threatened New Order," obviously inspired by the Soviets. The expansion of presidential power contained in the plan would, one U.S. businessman noted, give Perón "the power of Adolph and Benny the Bricklayer." One of Braden's supporters even surmised that the plan was nothing more than European fascism, modified only to fit local conditions.[12] Perón's defense to this charge was not entirely reassuring. Because totalitarians had war as their ultimate goal, he claimed, and "our goal is peace," he could not be

---

10. *Review of the River Plate*, 28 March 1947, 12.

11. Messersmith to Byrnes, 30 October 1946, Messersmith Papers, 1814; see also Potash, *Army and Politics*, 60-61.

12. Gilmore to Mann, 2 December 1946, RG 59, MRIC; *Review of the River Plate*, 4 October 1946, 8-9; Granger to Mann, 26 October 1946, RG 59, 835.50 Five-Year Plan; see also Gilmore to Lyon, Mann, Briggs, and Braden, 14 November 1946, RG 59, 835.50.

a totalitarian by definition. More lightheartedly, he poked fun at the accusations by congratulating the British, whose "King announced a similar plan, which signifies that the English are as totalitarian as we are." Therefore, "we are not in bad company." Although Perón often likened his Five-Year Plan to the New Deal—and even went so far as to claim that the British Labour government was emulating his model—few in the United States were convinced that it was so innocuous.[13]

Some U.S. businessmen, however, did rise to the bait that the Five-Year Plan offered. Two in particular, General Royal Lord and Admiral Henry Flannigan, journeyed to Argentina and took offices in the Casa Rosada as a sort of "advance guard" for U.S. business.[14] They expressed no serious qualms about cooperating with the Argentine government, and Lord was so enthusiastic that he returned to the United States in mid-1947 promising to recruit "hundreds" of engineers and technicians to help implement the plan. He argued that Argentina was, like the United States in 1880, on the verge of an economic takeoff and predicted that within seventy years, Argentina "may be a dominant power."[15]

Lord and Flannigan were not alone. Bethlehem Steel and other steel firms followed, negotiating for the construction of a mill with a productive capacity of 600,000 tons per year. Baldwin Locomotive Company and General Electric bid for contracts to sell diesel locomotives to the Argentine government, which appeared to be making good on its pledges to reinvigorate the rail network. Westinghouse and General Foods also expressed interest in becoming involved with the plan. Although the British lamented that U.S. businessmen were now "pursuing Perón with all of their usual energy," Messersmith was jubilant that these industrialists were taking the necessary steps both to supplant English rivals and show the Argentines the "proper" path to economic development.

---

13. Messersmith to Secretary of State, 11 December 1946, RG 59, 835.50 Five Year Plan; see also Prewett to Truman, 14 October 1946, PSF, Foreign Affairs, Argentina, HST.

14. *Review of the River Plate*, 7 February 1947, 11.

15. *Review of the River Plate*, 26 March 1948, 9.

Still, the response of U.S. corporations must not be overstated. Even though some were lured by the Five-Year Plan, Perón did not attract nearly as much interest as he wanted.[16]

While Perón's consolidation of executive power was viewed with displeasure in Washington, it was of more concern that he was unabashedly creating a "directed economy." If there was any aspect that all the varied bills in the Five-Year Plan had in common, it was the increased role of the national government. Not only would the state be spearheading the drive toward industrialization, but Perón was obviously planning to expand IAPI's operations to finance it. Although he did invite foreign capital to participate and constantly maintained that his government was defending private initiative by repressing harmful oligopolies, these vague reassurances carried little weight when he was busily constructing state monopolies. Few foreign investors were ever going to be comfortable operating under a statist corporatism in which a populist, authoritarian government owed its loyalty first and foremost to labor.[17]

## III

Although the Five-Year Plan caused a stir at the end of 1946, of greater consequence than these vague ambitions were developments in Argentine labor that reshaped the nation for decades. In January 1947, an AFL delegation traveled to Buenos Aires, and in the process, touched off a firestorm of controversy. This interaction between U.S. and *peronista* unionists serves better than any other single episode to highlight the fundamental corporatist differences that lay at the heart of U.S.-Argentine tensions. It is therefore important to understand the positions that

---

16. *Review of the River Plate*, 28 March 1947, 9-10; see also Messersmith to Secretary of State, 4 November 1946, RG 59, 835.50 Five-Year Plan; Memorandum of Conversation, Lord, Flanigan, Braden, and Lyon, 18 November 1946, MRIC; *Review of the River Plate*, 21 March 1947; MacDonald, "The Cold War and Perón," 189-190.

17. Gilmore to Lyon, Mann, Briggs and Braden, 14 November 1946, RG 59, 835.50.

both U.S. and Argentine labor unions occupied within the New Deal and Peronist frameworks to understand the crisis that emerged in January 1947.

The development of the New Deal order had important repercussions for labor, as it did for all of U.S. society. With the passage of Section 7a of the NIRA, the Wagner Act, and the creation of the National Labor Relations Board (NLRB), the New Deal essentially recognized labor's right to play a significant role in organizing and regulating the new economic order. While this did of course rankle much of the business community, key businessmen, especially those associated with "capital-intensive" firms, also shared the New Deal vision of a "corporative commonwealth" in which social harmony accompanied constant economic growth. Gone would be the bitter redistributive battles, unpredictable "wildcat" or "sitdown" disruptions, and the air of class conflict that had so often marred U.S. society. In their place would emerge a more efficient order in which labor and business could cooperate with the mediating "broker state" for the betterment of all.[18]

In exchange for its renunciation of militancy, organized labor was granted the role of a junior partner in the New Deal order. That role brought substantial gains to the trade union movement, especially to the fledgling CIO, which was able to unionize the steel, rubber, automobile, and other key industries. Nevertheless, labor remained subordinate. Roosevelt's famous "curse on both your houses" during the "Little Steel" strikes of 1937 and the "Little Steel Formula" of 1942 (which froze wages for the duration of the war while war industries reaped record profits) were telling indications of labor's ancillary position. Although the National War Labor Board's "Maintenance of Membership" policies buttressed the unions' position, even staunch supporters of

---

18. Irving Bernstein, *The Turbulent Years: A History of the American Worker, 1931-1941* (New York, 1970); David Brody, *Workers in Industrial America: Essays on the Twentieth Century Struggle* (New York, 1980), 173-214; Robert Collins, *The Business Response*; Melvin Dubofsky and Warren Van Tine, "John L. Lewis and the Triumph of Mass Production Unionism," in *Labor Leaders in America* eds. Dubofsky and Van Tine, (Urbana, 1987), 185-207; McQuaid, *Big Business*, 145-150; Robert H. Zeigler, *American Workers, American Unions* (Baltimore, 1986), 26-61.

Roosevelt like Phillip Murray grew disenchanted with the New Deal order throughout the war. War had brought financial gains to the workforce, they admitted, but union power had been substantially restrained.[19]

The defeat of Phillip Murray's and Walter Reuther's campaigns for worker co-determination demonstrated the limits under which labor operated in the New Deal order. Murray's 1941 Industrial Council Plan called for a restoration of NIRA-type councils through which labor and management would guide the nation's rearmament. The "Reuther plan" also envisioned industrial councils in which labor, management, and government would smooth the post-war reconversion of the economy through comprehensive planning and labor-oriented Keynesian spending. Labor's role, Reuther argued, should include a greater voice in both the workplace and national policy—reshaping the New Deal order to grant equity to the partners. His attempts to "link union power with government authority" went largely unheard by corporate executives whose belief in the sanctity of investment and managerial control precluded such a shop floor "revolution." Even though Murray and Reuther's dreams went unfulfilled, both men nonetheless retained government favor, unlike United Mine Workers chief John L. Lewis, who refused to renounce union militancy and rejected New Deal assistance in favor of independence. The New Dealers would tolerate a certain amount of dissent from their labor clients but had no more use for those who did not know their place in the order (like Lewis) than they did for communists.[20]

---

19. David Brody, "The New Deal and World War II," in *The New Deal: The National Level* eds. John Braeman, Robert Bremner, and David Brody, (New York, 1975), 267-309; Paul Koistenen, "Mobilizing the World War II Economy: Labor and the Industrial-Military Alliance," *Pacific History Review* 42 (1973), 443-478; Zeigler, *American Workers*, 41-100.

20. Brody, *Workers*, 174-188; Dubofsky and Van Tine, "John L. Lewis," 198-205; Nelson Lichtenstein, "Walter Reuther and the Rise of Labor-Liberalism," in *Labor Leaders*, eds. Dubofsky and Van Tine 280-300; Ronald W. Schatz, "Phillip Murray and the Subordination of the Industrial Unions to the U.S. Government," in *Labor Leaders*, eds. Dubofsky and Van Tine, 234-256.

If few fully perceived this hierarchical orientation of the New Deal Order before 1947, the passage of the Taft-Hartley legislation made it abundantly clear. Although Taft-Hartley was essentially a Republican creation, conservative Democrats hastened to affix their names to it, and President Truman only rose to fight it at the last moment, when his re-election seemed to be in doubt. Denounced as "slave labor" legislation by both the AFL and the CIO, Taft-Hartley is better seen as a largely successful effort to entrench the New Deal order. Under Taft-Hartley, the National Labor Relations Board could be turned against the unions, the threat of militant activity largely disappeared, and the government would clearly be able to dictate the course of future labor-management relations. While the unions remained as organized voices for the working class, their most militant members and organizers were isolated and ostracized by the act.

The CIO was forced to choose between supporting its own radical members or the red-baiting Truman, and by 1949, it had chosen to stick with the New Deal order. Even though renegades such as Lewis remained wedded to traditional notions of class conflict and workplace activism, Sidney Hillman, Reuther, and most other labor leaders accommodated themselves to labor's place in the new order. They proved reluctant to rock the boat and actively worked to reduce wildcat activity by the rank and file on behalf of a government seeking order and businessmen seeking profit. They also supported New Deal and post-war foreign policy initiatives to an extent that would have surprised even Samuel Gompers, as any semblance of independent unionism faded away.[21]

Like Roosevelt, Perón also embraced the unions to secure their political support. Using his powers as the Secretary of Labor and Welfare after 1943, Perón worked diligently to strengthen Argentine unions that were willing to hitch their carts to his rising star. By arbitrating strikes in favor of select unions and otherwise distributing largesse, he made it clear to unionists that they owed

---

21. Brody, "Workers," 121-133; Ronald Radosh, *American Labor and United States Foreign Policy* (New York, 1969), 1-29; Van Tine, *The Making of the Labor Bureaucrat: Union Leadership in the United States, 1870-1920* (Amherst, 1973).

their victories and gains to him alone. Building up the CGT and cementing its loyalty to his person paid great dividends in October 1945 when the workers of Buenos Aires rallied to save their patron from imprisonment and thereby paved his road to the presidency.

Although the unions were but one of the factions within the New Deal coalition, they were clearly Perón's primary concern as he strove continuously to support labor's demands for higher wages and greater benefits. IAPI punished landowners and redistributed wealth directly to the benefit of industry and its workers. The employee-ownership provisions in the Five-Year Plan only reinforced the nature of the very real gains that workers made and hoped to make under Peronism. Matching these shop floor gains with unprecedented ones in the political realm, dozens of union officials took seats in Congress and in the cabinet. In short, nearly every aspect of Perón's domestic and foreign policy in one way or another served his working-class constituency.

Still, the power of the unions was a double-edged sword. As organized labor grew more formidable and vital, so too did the need for Perón to establish his direct authority over the unions, eliminate their independence of action, and purge potential rivals from the movement. Until he did so, he could not count upon labor's unequivocal support. Moreover, like his New Deal counterparts, once in power he had little use for labor militancy that could cause economic dislocation or international embarrassment—as the meatpacking strike of 1946 had done. Clearly, while he was more than willing to reward the working class for its fealty, as president, he required greater control over the unions.

Acquiring it, however, presented him with difficult challenges as Argentina possessed a long tradition of independent unionism. Luis Gay, for example, had skillfully helped to steer his *Federación Obreros y Empleados Telefónicos* (FOET) through the repression of the "Infamous Decade" of the 1930s before allying himself with *peronismo*. Gay believed in independent, apolitical unionism, citing Gompers' old AFL as his model, but had thrown his weight behind Perón during the critical period at the end of the war. While Perón might be hailed as "Argentina's Number One Worker," union bosses such as Gay had a better claim upon the long-term loyalty of the rank-and-file. Although many newer union members fresh from the countryside might have seen Perón as an unequivocal savior, leaders such as Gay took a more pragmatic attitude and were determined to retain their independence. So long as strong intermediaries well accustomed to resisting government depredations existed, Perón could never achieve full control over the invigorated labor movement.[22]

Almost immediately after the election, union chiefs started to understand that their own goals were to be subordinated. As the members of the victorious *peronista* coalition prepared to divide the spoils and name their selections to the Senate, *Laboristas* naturally tried to nominate Gay, but the politically inexperienced unionists were outmaneuvered, and Admiral Alberto Teisaire was given the position. Angry *Laboristas* responded to this slight by passing over Perón's nominee to head the CGT, Secretary of the Interior Angel Borlenghi, in favor of Gay, whom it also named to head the *Laborista* party for good measure.[23] Still, throughout 1946, Perón lacked the security to move directly against this potential rival and instead worked to hinder him indirectly. The president offered to lend him the services of *peronista* loyalists to lighten his workload within the CGT and write his speeches. Gay politely declined the offer, undoubtedly seeing the trap, but when Perón offered him additional responsibilities in government, he accepted. He later recognized that these honors were intended primarily to keep him overburdened with work, but if Perón hoped that Gay would be brought around or distracted by these efforts, he was disappointed as the union chief steadfastly guarded CGT autonomy.[24]

---

22. Entrevista a Luis Gay, por Laura Kalmanowiechi, Instituto Torcuato DiTella Oral History Project, 10-11; Torre, *La vieja guardia sindical y Perón*, 95-102.

23. Gambini, *La primera presidencia*, 18-33; Moira MacKinnon, *Los años formativos del Partido Peronista* (Buenos Aires, 2002), 61-99; Page, *Perón*, 160-162.

24. Page, *Perón*, 176-178; Romualdi, *Presidents and Peons*, 56-57; *Periodico Seminal del C.G.T.*, 16 Noviembre 1946, Rollo 5, FSR; *Periodico Seminal del C.G.T.*, 16 Diciembre 1946, Rollo 5, FSR.

Unable to turn Gay, Cipriano Reyes, or other key union bosses, Perón suddenly announced his intention to dissolve the independent *Laborista* party and merge it into a single *peronista* party in mid-1946. Of the *Laborista* deputies, only Reyes formally but fruitlessly resisted. Unwilling to cross their benefactor, and perhaps unaware of the significance of the move, the traditionally apolitical Argentine unions left Reyes out on a limb, where Perón could deal with him at his leisure.[25] While not as openly rebellious as Reyes, Gay nonetheless continued to fight to preserve independence as the head of the CGT until early 1947 when U.S. interference once again played into Perón's hands and provided him with a suitable excuse to effectively eliminate the CGT's tenuous independence.

The "Gay Affair," as it came to be known, centered upon Serafino Romualdi, an Italian expatriate who had attached himself to the AFL, the State Department, and various anti-fascist organizations in Latin America after fleeing Mussolini. After the war, Count Carlo Sforza offered him a post in the Italian Foreign Office, which he turned down to remain with Green and David Dubinski, serving as the AFL's "labor ambassador to all of Latin America." As Green's AFL was looking to regain its prestige and spread its tame, pro-U.S. brand of trade unionism across Latin America, Romualdi's wartime contacts, knowledge of Spanish, and venomous hatred of totalitarianism fit well.[26]

The AFL entrusted Romualdi with the task of establishing an inter-American labor federation that could effectively compete with the *Confederación Trabajadores de America Latina* (CTAL). The CTAL, created in part as a counter to earlier AFL efforts in Latin America, was a left-leaning organization led by Mexican Vincente Lombardo Toledano. With the coming of the Cold War, the AFL sought to challenge the Marxist Toledano and his CTAL as the voice of unionism in the hemisphere, as it was working against the CIO-backed World Federation of Trade Unions

---

25. Messersmith to Braden, 28 October 1946, RG 59, 835.5043; Horowitz, *Argentine Unions*; Page, *Perón*, 176-181.

26. Romualdi, *Presidents and Peons*, 10-39.

(WFTU) in Europe. Since the CIO maintained some affiliation with the suspect CTAL, AFL leaders believed that their efforts on behalf of anti-communist unionism could also curry favor with the Truman Administration, thereby bolstering their union's domestic standing as well as its international one. Described by Toledano as an "agent provocateur," Romualdi was to unite unaffiliated unions and split "moderate" organizations from the CTAL, but the most powerful anti-communist union in the hemisphere was clearly Perón's CGT.[27]

For the unionists of the CGT, the prospect of gaining AFL respect and recognition was an unprecedented opportunity. The CGT, like the AFL, had little use for Toledano's CTAL and leapt at the opportunity to ally itself with the revered Yankee union. Indeed, despite the AFL's "conservative reputation" among Latin American labor circles, the Argentine federation envisioned itself as the logical Latin American spearhead of the AFL's brand of anti-communist unionism. "The English-speaking unionists of the United States," the CGT's newsletter pronounced in July 1946, could not, "as the minority they are, take the initiative to establish any system of hemispheric union cooperation."[28] Well aware that the AFL was working to dismantle the CTAL, the CGT welcomed the opportunity to participate. Although Green and the AFL had considerable prestige in Argentine labor circles, Peronist union leaders nonetheless believed that they could enter as equal partners into a new organization with their North American brethren.[29]

---

27. Romualdi to Woll, 9 September 1946, Romualdi Papers, 5459/1/1, ILGWU; Fishburn to Holland, 23 September 1946, RG 59, 810.5043; O'Donoghue to Secretary of State, 15 October 1946, RG 59, 810.504; Romualdi, *Presidents and Peons*, 42-53; Radosh, *American Labor*, 355-363; Jack Scott, *Yankee Unions Go Home: How the AFL Helped the U.S. Build an Empire in Latin America* (Vancouver, 1978), 201-218; John P. Windmuller, *American Labor and the International Labor Movement* (Ithaca, 1954).

28. Fishburn to Holland, 23 September 1946, RG 59, 810.5043; *Periodico Seminal de la C.G.T*, 1 Julio 1946, Rollo 5, FSR.

29. *Periodico Seminal de la C.G.T.*, 16 Noviembre 1944, Rollo 4, FSR; *Periodico Seminal de la C.G.T.*, 1 Diciembre 1944, Rollo 4, FSR; *Periodico Seminal de la C.G.T.*, 16 Octubre 1945, Rollo 4, FSR; *Periodico Seminal de la C.G.T.*, 1 Julio 1946, Rollo 5, FSR; *Periodico Seminal de la C.G.T.*, 1 Agosto 1946, Rollo 5, FSR.

The AFL had already attempted to extend olive branches to the CGT by offering to base their new hemispheric organization in Buenos Aires, but Perón's increasing hold on the Argentine federation raised questions about its status as a truly independent trade association. To dispel any doubts in this direction, Borlenghi and ambassador Oscar Ivanissevich invited AFL and CIO representatives to visit Argentina in July 1946.[30] The CIO, whose Latin American policies were still dictated by Michanowsky and Potofsky, coldly rebuffed the initiative, but the AFL considered the proposal. Deeming it improper to accept the invitation of a government, Green informed Ivanissevich that the CGT itself should extend the invitation, and in December, Gay did so.[31]

While Messersmith, like Bramulgia, considered the decision to invite the AFL to be a "mistake" and hoped that the "thing would fizzle out," Peronists were convinced that they had an opportunity to showcase the "maturity of the Argentine proletariat, the potential of its unions, and its freedom." Indeed, the CGT press predicted that the AFL delegation would "find it easy to observe the contrast between our democracy and that of the *yanquis*, where at this moment the government and the major political parties compete with each other to put forward anti-worker legislation designed to satisfy the imperialistic capitalists of Wall Street." As Truman was in the midst of his crackdown on John L. Lewis' United Mine Workers and the dreaded Taft-Hartley Act was working its way through Congress, the CGT fully expected to meet AFL representatives incensed with the "*yanqui* plutocracy" and the "American capitalist trusts."[32]

---

30. Bramulgia could only lament that "now I have this mess on my hands." O'Donoghue to Secretary of State, 22 January 1947, RG 59, 835.5043.

31. Romualdi, *Presidents and Peons*, 52-53.

32. Messersmith to Braden, 30 August 1946, RG 59, 835.5043; *Periodical Seminal del C.G.T.*, 16 Enero 1947, Rollo 5, FSR; *Periodico Seminal del C.G.T.*, 16 Enero 1947, Rollo 5, FSR; *El Trabajador de Carne*, Enero 1948, FSR; Interestingly, Peronists in the Chamber of Deputies introduced motions "rendering tribute to John L. Lewis in solidarity" with his fight against the Truman Administration-a gesture that the FBI noted with interest. Hoover to Neal, 11 December 1946, RG 59, 835.5043.

Argentine labor attachés serving in the Washington embassy fed the belief that the United States was ripe for *peronista* overtures, reporting that it was apparently heading for a record year of strikes as Lewis's renegade unionism and a resurgence of "wildcat" strikes belied a hotbed of rank-and-file militancy beneath the timid AFL and CIO leadership. U.S. unionists might, in other words, be willing to join with their Argentine brethren in an international labor alliance that repudiated the extremes of both capitalist plutocracy and communist totalitarianism.[33] Serafino Romualdi, however, had other ideas.

Although Romualdi was not the titular head of the AFL mission who arrived in Buenos Aires in January, he easily overshadowed the rest of the delegation, who lacked his fluency in Spanish and his experience with Latin America.[34] As soon as the delegation landed in Buenos Aires, Romualdi began offering a series of gratuitous insults to Perón. The president had agreed to meet the AFL delegation the morning after its arrival, but Romualdi postponed the meeting, citing jetlag. Even the lodging arrangements were not to Romualdi's taste. Although he had hoped to stay at a hotel close to the Casa Rosada, the Ministry of Labor, and the U.S. embassy, Peronists had provided accommodations at the "more comfortable and spacious" Alvear Palace farther away. Believing that this was an intentional ploy to hamper the movement of the AFL team, Romualdi protested

---

33. Vierya, "Informe sobre el movimiento huelgista ocurrido en los EE.UU. desde 1940 a 1945," AMREC, BA, EEUU 1946, 8, 3; Merlo, "Nuevas actividades de John L. Lewis despues de su derrota en la AFL," 11 Diciembre 1947, AMREC, BA, EEUU 1946, 6, 5.

34. Romualdi's expertise was probably not as complete as either he or the AFL believed. In Buenos Aires, *peronistas* convinced the AFL delegates to remove their coats on a hot day. Romualdi should have known that the "removal of one's coat in public in Argentina was already widely regarded as a symbolic gesture of support for Perón" and the *descamisados*. Photographers captured the spectacle of AFL officials inadvertently giving tribute to Perón. Romualdi, *Presidents and Peons*, 55; see also Romualdi, "The Role of Luis F. Gay and the C.G.T in the Preliminary Work for the Organization of an Inter-American Confederation of Labor," 24 February 1947, Romualdi Papers, 5459/1/4, ILGWU.

vigorously and eventually had his way, "but not without arousing some displeasure on the part of our hosts." Tensions also rose when the AFL delegates were unwilling to accept Perón's agenda for their visit, as it did not provide enough opportunities for the delegation to meet with Argentine unionists.

The most serious confrontation occurred when Romualdi insisted to Perón that the AFL's purpose in Buenos Aires was to "investigate" the status of the Argentine unionism, rather than to "fraternize." Green and the AFL leadership always maintained that the delegation had been sent to assess the CGT, so here Romualdi stood on firm ground.[35] However, since the word "investigate" implied criminal behavior, *peronistas* naturally took umbrage. Conversations between Peronists and AFL delegates deteriorated steadily into accusations and acrimonious, if petty, disputes. Incensed, Perón ultimately threatened to send the AFL delegation home, warning Romualdi, "I know what you are up to" and adding a thinly veiled personal threat in Italian.[36]

Romualdi was "up to" so many different questionable activities in Buenos Aires that it is unclear exactly to which one Perón referred. He may well have suspected that the AFL representative was acting in collusion with Braden and the State Department. Byrnes had promised Romualdi "informal assistance" from U.S. embassies in Latin America. Moreover, the unionist carried letters of introduction from a number of State Department officers and reported directly to the U.S. embassy in Buenos Aires. Although he had not yet forged a full-fledged alliance with Braden by the time of the visit, he was diligently working to do so and had met with Braden weeks before the AFL delegation left for Argentina.[37] Even more suspect, however, were Romualdi's cloak-

---

35. Romualdi, *Presidents and Peons*, 55-56; Gambini, *Historia del peronismo*, 206-208.

36. Page, *Perón*, 179; see also Watrous to Secretary of State, 13 February 1947, RG 59, 835.5043.

37. Byrnes, quoted in Radosh, *American Labor*, 365; see also Memorandum of Conversation, Romualdi and Dreier, 6 June 1946, RG 59, 810.5043; Romualdi, *Presidents and Peons*, 73-74.

and-dagger escapades in Buenos Aires. Using a former Spanish Republican, who happened to be a member of an "embryonic underground as his driver," he dodged police surveillance to meet with "a number of prominent people within the opposition." In the course of his visit, he also re-established old ties with anti-Perón union leaders and dissidents, and probably wrote a letter urging Argentine Socialist Nicolás Repetto to subvert the CGT.[38]

Whatever else he was doing, Romualdi was also trying to stir up dissent within the CGT through Gay and other independent-minded union leaders. Romualdi proudly reported to the U.S. embassy that Gay had reaffirmed that he would continue his fight to preserve CGT independence and integrity. Perón biographer Joseph Page conjectured that the president might have somehow discovered this pledge and acted upon it. Within days, he claimed to have tape recorded conversations that proved that Gay was involved in a treasonous conspiracy with the AFL delegate.[39] Although he never produced these tapes, Perón moved swiftly and decisively against Gay, charging him with "political high treason" and conspiring with Romualdi and Braden to weaken the president and "sell the Argentine workers to American imperialism." The CGT, which as late as January 16 had proclaimed that "the movement needs men like Luis Gay who accumulate jobs, but not pay," echoed the president's denunciations of this latest plot to "separate Perón from the workers."[40] Perón offered to allow Gay quietly to resign, and the CGT accepted his resignation. While Gay went into hiding, the CGT was strongly encouraged to replace him with Peronist Aurelio Hernandez.

It is difficult to envision another scenario whereby the CGT would have allowed anyone to unseat its popular chief without a

---

38. Romualdi, *Presidents and Peons*, 56-57; Watrous to Secretary of State, 13 February 1947, RG 59, 835.5043; see also Romualdi, "Interview with a Group of Members and Leadership of the Following Trade Unions," 28 January 1947, Romualdi Papers, 5459/1/4, ILGWU.

39. Page, *Perón*, 179-181.

40. *Periodico Seminal del C.G.T.*, 16 Marzo 1947, Rollo 5, FSR; *Periodico Seminal del C.G.T.*, 16 Enero 1947, Rollo 5, FSR.

bitter fight. But the president knew well from experience that nationalist appeals to anti-U.S. sentiment virtually guaranteed him victory. Just as he had done with Tamborini after the publication of the *Blue Book*, Perón was able to brand his opponent as a quisling. For union members to stand up for Gay was to stand up for Braden. Whether Romualdi's activities actually precipitated Perón's decision to finally move openly against Gay or merely provided a convenient pretext, the last obstacle to the Peronist control of Argentine labor was effectively removed. In the months following Gay's retirement, the CGT underwent a visible change and its *Periodico Seminal* reflected this new atmosphere. Perón's slogans and sayings became regular features, and paeans to the "Paladin of Social Justice" dominated front pages, as the CGT was thoroughly "captured."[41]

## IV

Still, deposing Gay and cowing other labor leaders created a vacuum that needed to be filled, and in essence, Eva Perón stepped up to replace union leaders as the symbolic and practical link between Perón and the masses to complete the "capture." Perón's lackluster appointees to CGT leadership positions possessed little of Gay's influence or prestige, and he needed a dynamic, charismatic leader who was completely loyal to him to fill the role. By 1947, his wife met both of these criteria. As a woman, she could never become an independent political force or a political threat to him, and her remarkable political savvy soon became apparent. Although she originally had no official title, she opened an office in the Labor Ministry that kept her in regular contact with both government officials and the union chiefs. Perón made his wishes known through his wife and counted upon her to relay them. Within months, however, her role expanded dramatically.[42]

---

41. *Periodico Seminal del C.G.T.*, 24 Febrero 1947, Rollo 5, FSR; see also Hoyt to Mann and Lyon, 7 February 1947, MRIC; Watrous to Secretary of State, 13 February 1947, RG 59, 835.5043.

42. Fraser and Navarro, *Eva Perón*, 83-86; Crassweller, *Perón and the Enigmas of Argentina*, 205-217; J.M. Taylor, *Eva Perón: The Myths of a*

Eva Perón's power over the unions was exercised informally at first. Disgruntled workers approached her as an "extension" of the president, citing abuses or seeking redress of grievances. *Peronista* union bosses in need of re-election petitioned her for assistance and placed themselves further in the Peróns' debt. In addition, she took over some of Perón's duties, giving speeches and attending union rallies. Soon it became clear that her office, rather than that of the Secretary of Labor or the CGT chief, was where workers could turn for aid. Just as before the 1946 election, labor would not be allowed to forget that its gains came directly from Perón.[43]

But her role expanded to preserve Perón's position not only among the union members, but also the *descamisados*. Social welfare in Argentina had been traditionally the realm of a small coterie of aristocratic women. As the president's wife, Mrs. Perón should have been accepted automatically into this *Sociedad de Beneficencia*. However, upper-class *porteña* society spurned the former actress, citing her youth and questionable background. To punish the establishment that had shunned "Evita," *peronistas* nationalized and reconstituted it as the María Eva Duarte de Perón Foundation. Through it, Eva Perón transformed herself into the cult figure who would earn the love and devotion of the masses, and the undying hatred of the oligarchy.

No single, dramatic act transformed her into "Evita," the glamorous and beloved benefactress of the *descamisados*. Instead, it was her constant charitable activities on the behalf of the beleaguered poor. She received virtually anyone in her office and made certain that no petitioner who crossed her threshold left empty-handed. She kept a stack of fifty-peso notes on her desk, handed them out liberally, and when the stack disappeared, called upon her aides to empty their own wallets. Likened by a reporter

---

*Woman* (Chicago, 1981).

43. Marysa Navarro, "Evita and Peronism," *Juan Perón and the Reshaping of Argentina*, eds. Frederick C. Turner and José Enrique Miguens (Pittsburgh, 1983), 15-32; Libertad Demitrópulos, *Eva Perón* (Buenos Aires, 1984), 101-103.

to a "chess master playing twenty-five games at high speed," she dealt with the expectant hordes each day. While the poor had come to expect cold snobbery from the old *Sociedad de Beneficencia*, "Evita" gave compassion and sympathy to even the most diseased or dirty. Denounced by high society as vulgar, these displays nonetheless brought adoration from the heretofore forgotten *descamisados*.

Aside from such haphazard gestures and handouts, the Eva Perón Foundation did have its more systematic programs. The Foundation merged disparate nursing schools into a single institution that provided free education for interns. Her foundation financed the construction of more than a dozen public hospitals to further improve the health care system, imported some of the most modern equipment, and was able to provide free care for the poor. Not only was health care improved dramatically, but it was spread to the interior of the nation, where it was most needed. In addition, the Foundation erected orphanages, nursing homes, *hogares de transito*, low-income housing projects, schools, and similar institutions. Naturally, Perón's and his wife's visages figured prominently among the decor of these projects, lest anyone forget the identity of his or her patrons. Critics denounced these projects as extravagant, and some undoubtedly were, but they did serve valuable functions—assisting the dispossessed and cementing their loyalty to Perón.[44]

The funds for these activities, of course, did not originate with the Peróns. Sra. Perón solicited "voluntary" donations from businesses, unions and individuals to the tune of an estimated $90 million per year. Businesses hesitant to contribute adequate amounts were induced to do so. Chocolates Mu-Mu, for example, was closed by health inspectors for three years until the owners offered a "spontaneous donation." Although such blatantly punitive measures may have been infrequent, most industrialists seemed to understand that there would be consequences for those who

---

44. This analysis draws heavily upon Nicholas Fraser and Marysa Navarro's biography of Eva Perón. Fraser and Navarro, *Eva Perón*, 114-133; Demitrópulos, *Eva Perón*, 96-100; Crassweller, *Perón and the Enigmas of Argentina*, 205-217.

crossed the Foundation or failed to support it generously enough. Sra. Perón claimed to have learned the art of raising money from Miranda, who told her to "give the 'fat cats' a kick and out comes the cash." It naturally followed that "with cash we get social justice." By 1950, the Foundation was a powerful and wealthy force that served, through her, as yet another direct extension of Perón's power.[45]

The third major manifestation of Sra. Perón's talents, as the head of a women's *peronista* party, did not begin to appear until later. Since before his election, Perón had promised to deliver the franchise to Argentine women, and Eva Perón naturally emerged as the standard-bearer for this campaign. When Perón delivered on his promises for women's suffrage, his wife stepped into the role as the head of the women's wing of the Peronist party. This *Partido Peronista Feminino*, a parallel of the new *Partido Peronista*, served Perón well, as he captured 2,441,558 of the 3,816,654 votes cast by women in the 1951 election, the first in which women were eligible to vote. When Peronist women started to enter the Argentine Congress, it only strengthened Perón's standing among the masses—as did nearly everything his wife did.[46]

The emergence of "Evita" added a new dimension to Peronism. As a national leader, Perón at times had to adopt a more conciliatory stance toward his opponents and moderate his activities to build consensus and establish his legitimacy as a head of state. Moreover, he knew well that his every utterance was being monitored by unforgiving critics in Washington. His wife, however, operated under no such constraints and could deliver the same aggressive, militant speeches that Perón had used to radicalize and mobilize the masses. While Perón worked to win over industrialists and gain U.S. favor with moderate rhetoric, his wife maintained and even enhanced the revolutionary flavor that had originally brought them to power. She supplanted the old union chieftains and political functionaries who had previously been

---

45. Lewis, *Crisis of Argentine Capitalism*, 202; see also Fraser and Navarro, *Eva Perón*, 114-133.

46. Demitrópulos, *Eva Perón*, 83-92.

Perón's link to the masses, and simultaneously replaced support for Peronism with adulation. With her sudden and dramatic rise to prominence, Perón's last obstacle to dominance was effectively cleared, as no one could challenge *peronista* control over the unions or the polling booths, and even the Army recognized that Perón's "cult of personality" was, for the time being, insuperable.

If the "Gay Affair" and the emergence of Eva Perón had been almost unequivocal triumphs for Perón, they were also a turning point in the diplomacy of the AFL and CIO. In the aftermath, Romualdi used his underground acquaintances to flee from a scathing *peronista* press campaign and physical threats to Montevideo. He did eventually rejoin the AFL delegation for the last uneventful phases of the tour and returned to the United States to present his findings. Romualdi's report predictably concluded that the CGT was a "puppet" organization that could not be trusted and in fact should be fought vigorously. He catalogued the complaints that he had heard from the independent unionists, detailing the "violence, corruption, bribery, favoritism, and all the illegal methods and pressure" that Perón had used to subvert or eliminate autonomous unionism. Romualdi had to concede that Peronists had indeed delivered "a good number of overdue economic reforms," but added that "social legislation without freedom is inadequate and may even serve as a cover for tyranny." Although the report admitted that there was little formal action "to suppress civil liberties," it argued that Argentina suffered from a "general atmosphere of fear and mutual suspicion" that informally impinged on civil liberties. Matthew Woll personally sent a copy of the report to Hernandez, warning that it "does not cast a favorable light" on the CGT, and Romualdi forwarded it to Braden.[47]

Romualdi and the AFL could no longer view the CGT as a welcome partner but were forced to see the *peronistas* as rivals. Peronism, he argued, posed a very real "danger to the orderly

---

47. Hoyt to Mann, 13 March 1947, RG 59, MRIC; Monsma to Dreier, Lyon, Briggs, and Braden, 22 April 1947, RG 59, MRIC; Romualdi Speech at Rutgers, 9 June 1947, Romualdi Papers, 5459/1/6, ILGWU; Woll to Hernandez, 11 March 1947, Romualdi Papers, 5459/1/1, ILGWU; see also Romualdi, *Presidents and Peons*, 58-63, 72-73.

development of social evolution and social reforms in the rest of our sister republics in the American hemisphere," because "the Perón myth might easily spread all over Latin America, where the economic conditions of the workers are generally speaking deplorable, and where economic reforms are long overdue." Romualdi feared that "if democracy does not find a way to satisfy these just demands," then the masses "will inevitably turn to the first demagogue who will seduce them with catchy slogans and fantastic promises." Like communist propaganda, Perón's "militaristic totalitarian type" "germinates very well in the psychologies of people who are victims of confusion and of political disillusionment and economic suffering."[48] Although the AFL never feared Perón as much as it loathed the communists, Romualdi worked to convince his superiors that leaders who used puppet labor movements as a "club to make a mockery of the democratic process" constituted just as great a threat.

Romualdi derided Argentine laborers for having traded their freedom for bread. Whereas *laissez faire* capitalism offered freedom, but provided no bread, he argued that workers should instead hold out for the bread and freedom that AFL union members claimed to enjoy. Thus, the AFL, like its government patron, attempted to steer a middle course that disdained both totalitarianism and the *laissez faire* alternative that so often spawned it.[49] Unfortunately for the AFL, the patient unionism it condoned and the long-term benefits it promised had little appeal for many Latin Americans who found more hope in the revolutionary alternatives of communist or Peronist radicalism. Just as Green's predisposition against militancy and confrontation had endeared the AFL to the U.S. government, it was as out of touch

---

48. Romualdi, Speech at Rutgers University, 9 June 1947, Romualdi Papers, 5459/1/6; Romualdi, Draft of Memorandum, 12 May 1949, Romualdi Papers, 5459/6/3, ILGWU.

49. Romualdi, Speech at Rutgers University, 9 June 1947, Romualdi Papers, 5459/1/6, ILGWU; see also Romualdi to Leite, 4 March 1948, Carey Collection, LAAC, AULH.

with much of Latin American labor as it was with a good part of the AFL's own rank-and-file.[50]

The CIO, although taking no part in the "Gay Affair," shared much more in common with the AFL than leaders of either union federation would have cared to admit. Although he was cut from a far different cloth than Romualdi, James Carey, long-time Secretary-Treasurer of the CIO, exemplified the "enlightened," internationalist labor leadership of the CIO. Carey's speeches echoed those of Clayton and the most aggressive free traders in the Truman Administration. He regularly served on diverse semi-official committees with progressive businessmen such as Clayton, Paul Hoffman, Owen Young, Gerald Swope, and Nelson Rockefeller, and even advised Truman himself. Carey shared with these men a profound faith in expanded international trade, the ITO, and the Reciprocal Trade Agreements.[51]

He also believed in various social welfare policies that would soften the blows that expanded multilateral trade and regional specialization would inevitably inflict upon workers in "inefficient" industries. This belief put him into an awkward position, as businessmen and unionists in protectionist industries appealed to him, pleading for the CIO to throw its muscle behind tariffs that would protect their interests at the expense of multilateral trade. Carey tended to turn a deaf ear to their pleas, arguing that U.S. labor would eventually benefit far more from "enlightened" multilateralism. Although he did give more attention to the preservation of jobs and wages than did most New Dealers, he was clearly well within the mainstream of the New Deal ethos.[52]

---

50. Craig Phelan, "William Green and the Ideal of Christian Cooperation," *Labor Leaders in America*, eds. Van Tine and Dubofsky, 135-160.

51. James Carey Statement, 8 May 1947, Carey Collection, Box 32, Archives of Labor and Urban History, Wayne State University, AULH; Truman to Carey, 22 June 1946, Carey Collection, AULH; Carey to Clayton, 24 August 1946, Carey Collection, AULH; Batt to Carey, 3 July 1950, Carey Collection, AULH.

52. Carey to State Department, 22 September 1944, Carey Collection, AULH; Kaplan to Carey, 12 June 1947, Carey Collection, AULH; Anthony to Carey, 24 June 1947, Carey Collection, AULH; S. Stroock to Carey, 2 July 1947, AULH; Forstman to Carey, 8 July 1947, Carey Collection, AULH.

Carey and the CIO had started to take a genuine interest in Latin America during the war, when Cordell Hull opened the door for American labor to become a partner of the State Department. The Hull-Carey alliance was a natural one, based upon the mutual needs and beliefs of these kindred spirits. Hull used CIO officials based in U.S. embassies abroad to report developments in Latin American unions and encourage proper union behavior, thereby facilitating the war on fascism. Because, as Carey noted, labor leaders could deal more productively with Latin American workers and moderate Socialists than striped-suit diplomats, they were a more effective conduit for liberal capitalist values. These labor officials were patriotic citizens first and workers second, tending to support U.S. business and government whenever they clashed with Latin American workers. The war effort was an excellent opportunity for U.S. labor leaders to begin to associate the interests of the international working class with those of their government. Although it came to an end with the war's conclusion, the labor attaché program had been a dramatic success for the budding government-union foreign policy consensus.[53]

While the AFL had briefly considered alliance with the CGT, Carey, George Michanowski, Jacob Potofsky, and the CIO unequivocally endorsed Braden's "taking up the cudgels for the cause of democracy" against Perón. Potofsky, head of the CIO's Latin American Affairs Committee (LAAC) publicly proclaimed Perón to be a fascist "cancer" and his Argentina to be an "outlaw in the family of nations" in 1945.[54] In this, the CIO echoed both the CTAL and the U.S. government. Like their AFL counterparts, CIO officials downplayed the significance of the bread-and-butter gains that Perón had delivered to the Argentine working class and focused instead upon his subversion of independent unionism. Without independence, CIO leaders argued, any other benefits were

---

53. Gallarza Memorandum, 20 January 1943, Carey Collection, AULH; Hull to Carey, 4 September 1943, Carey Collection, AULH; Franklin to Carey, 9 April 1948, Carey Collection, AULH; Scott, *Yankee Unions*, 201-208.

54. Michanowski to Byrnes, 2 July 1945, Byrnes Papers, Box 488 Folder 3, Clemson; Potofsky Press Release, 19 January 1945, Carey Collection, AULH.

peripheral, and in all likelihood temporary. Although this assessment was later proven to be valid, by almost any measure, the CGT had accomplished more for its rank-and-file than the AFL or CIO had within the New Deal order. When Carey and other CIO leaders denounced the state of Argentine unionism, they were forced to ignore labor's very real representation in the *Camara de Diputados* and Perón's cabinet, even as they bemoaned the fact that there were no unionists sitting in the U.S. Congress or Truman's cabinet.[55]

A second irony can be found in the LAAC's "Plan for the Economic and Social Development" of Latin America, which catalogued CIO recommendations for effective national union development. Perón and the CGT had already taken almost all of the steps the CIO advocated.[56] Interestingly, at least one member of the CIO recognized this discrepancy and tentatively called for a re-evaluation. Perón had done much for workers "and not just on paper," his report argued, and "though basically dictatorial" his government has "given up some of its abuses." Even if Perón himself was unpalatable and had suborned independent unionism, "there have been strikes all the time" and "whether we like it or not, we are not in a position to tell the Argentine workers what to think and to do, and certainly not by way of ordering them around." The author proposed that the CGT might make a useful ally against the AFL and that it needed to be shown that "there are not only 'Yankee Imperialists' in the US, but also honest and hard working people like themselves." Still, the vast majority of the CIO remained firmly wedded to Braden and Truman, who lauded Potofsky's rejection of totalitarianism and "contribution to the strengthening of American traditions."[57]

---

55. Latin American Affairs Committee Memorandum, 16 August 1946, Carey Collection, AULH; Potofsky Press Release, 5 May 1950, Carey Collection, AULH; Carey to State Department and Bureau of the Budget, 22 July 1947, Carey Collection, AULH.

56. LAAC, "Plan for the Economic and Social Development of the Countries and Territories of Latin America," 18 May 1949, Carey Collection, Box 84, AULH.

57. Unsigned Memorandum, 16 August 1948, Carey Collection, AULH;

When Ivanissevich invited U.S. unionists in late 1946, the CIO had summarily rejected the offer. "Perón of Argentina," the *CIO News* announced in late-1946, "will not be able to use a CIO delegation to whitewash his fascist regime."[58] This posture was not remarkable. Murray and Carey had maintained close relations with the pre-Perón leadership of the CGT, and helplessly watched its power erode in the face of the Peronist surge. It is hardly surprising that Murray's CIO, with its relatively tolerant view of communism and close relationship with the CTAL, opted to see "fascists" such as Perón as the true enemy. The members of the LAAC considered Peronism to be, like the AFL, a threat to CIO dominance in Latin American labor circles, as Perón was "sparing no effort or expense to achieve the objective of creating an inter-American labor movement as a corollary" to his "Third Position." If possible, the CIO's Latin Americanists feared Perón's capacity for international mischief even more than the AFL. As one of them explained:

> . . . labor attachés, sometimes two or more, are attached to every Argentine Embassy as a special task force to gain labor's sympathy and to draw the union movement into the new Peronist labor organization. They are indefatigable . . . It must be said that the efforts to draw the Latin American labor movement into the Perón orbit have failed so far. However, the Argentine propaganda line of denunciation of Yanqui Imperialism, racial discrimination and exploitation of Latin American workers by American corporations will have considerable impact.[59]

---

Truman to Potofsky, 4 May 1950, Papers of Jacob Potofsky, 5619/133/17, ILGWU.

58. Swayze to Mulliken, 13 November 1946, RG 59, 835.5043.

59. Kyne and Schwarz Report, 27 October 1949, Carey Collection, AULH; Joel Horowitz surmises that Perón was sending independent-minded CGT officials abroad to simply remove them from the picture. If so, Perón was adroitly killing two birds with one stone. Horowitz, *Argentine Unions*, 225-226.

As early as September 1946, Perón had started to deploy labor attachés—loyal representatives of the CGT across the hemisphere with the express purpose of "spreading the revolution of June 4." At the inauguration of this offensive, Perón announced that his attachés were to be "apostolic missionaries of peace," not "soldiers of conquest," intermediaries between "Argentine workers and the working masses of all nations, especially those of the Americas," and educators who would bring "knowledge of the revolutionary work" being done in Argentina. Peruvian Ambassador C. E. B. Ledgard, alarmed at this development, warned his own government that there was "nothing subtle in the words of the Chief of State," as he recognized the mischief that this cadre of provocateurs could cause outside Argentina.[60]

The Peruvians were not alone in their fears, as CIO commentators went so far as to consider Latin American labor to be divided into three distinct "camps:" the CIO/CTAL, Peronist, and AFL.[61] While the CIO would never be able to convince the State Department that it was as anti-communist as the AFL, or that the Peronists were as great a threat as the communists, its stance can probably be at least partially explained as an attempt to curry favor with Bradenist hard-liners in the Truman Administration. It is very significant that before rejecting the Argentine invitation, Michanowsky, in the spirit of independent unionism, phoned Braden's home four times in one day, asking "what should be done in this connection."[62]

The CIO's efforts to endear itself to the State Department were, to some degree, doomed to failure from the onset. Partially because of the Cold War and partially due to the last remnants of CIO militancy, the U.S. government naturally opted for the AFL to be its labor spearhead in Latin America. It quickly became very clear that U.S. policymakers did not want the CIO to be especially

---

60. Ledgard a Ministro, 3 September 1947, AMRE, Lima, 5-1-Y/107.

61. Schwarz to Potofsky, 7 February 1949, Carey Collection, Box 84, AULH; Schwarz to Carey, 21 February 1949, Carey Collection, Box 84, AULH.

62. Romualdi had also. Braden to Briggs, Mann, and Spaeth, 27 August 1946, RG 59, 835.5043.

active in Latin America. When CIO leaders offered to restart the wartime labor attaché partnership with the State Department, Braden's replies to Michanowski and Potofsky were lukewarm negatives. Although he professed agreement with the sentiment, he asserted that "it would be very difficult to carry out such a project at this time without giving the impression that this government was attempting to practice an indirect form of intervention in the internal political affairs of other American Republics." "I feel that the government should be especially careful not to invite such accusations gratuitously," he commented, "in view of the present Argentine situation."[63] Braden's note was dated only weeks after the release of the *Blue Book* and just months before he started putting the Department's resources at Romualdi's disposal. On the other hand, Byrnes warned his embassies to "avoid any formal sponsorship of Romualdi's activities," if only because doing so "might give rise to charges that the State Department is favoring the AFL over the Congress of Industrial Organizations." Although the State Department did not want to openly snub the CIO, Romualdi's AFL had assumed overt government patronage.[64]

The fate of the CIO in many ways paralleled what was happening to the CGT. Both had hitched their carts to political movements and charismatic leaders that had allowed them to win unprecedented victories. However, once Perón and the New Dealers had established themselves, neither had much use for militant union federations that might rock the ship of state. Thus, Perón purged independent unionists and replaced them with pliable cronies, as the U.S. government gave its nod to the AFL and ostracized loose cannons such as Lewis. Ironically, just months after the "Gay Affair," the CIO explored the possibility of bringing Latin American workers to the United States, but the State Department rebuffed Carey, arguing that "under the present

---

63. Braden to Kellogg, 6 March 1946, Carey Collection, AULH.

64. Byrnes to Certain American Diplomatic Officers in Other American Republics, 11 June 1946, RG 59, 810.504; see also Radosh, *American Labor and U.S. Foreign Policy*, 368-369; Braden to Briggs, Mann, and Spaeth, 27 August 1946, RG 59, 835.5043.

conditions of unusual industrial unrest, it would be difficult for these representatives to get anything but a confused impression of employer-employee relationships in the United States."[65] The CIO tamely acquiesced, apparently unaware of the irony. While the CIO derided the CGT for allowing itself to be dominated by Perón, the Argentine unionists had at least been permitted to invite foreign unionists into their nation. Increasingly blinded by and subordinated to their patrons' interests, the U.S. unions had, like the CGT, sold their vaunted freedom for bread.

## V

Taken together, the promulgation of the Five-Year Plan and Perón's "capture" of the CGT illustrated just how far the Argentine revolution of 1943 had deviated from the privatist corporatism of the United States and its New Deal order. The Five-Year Plan reinforced U.S. fears that Perón was not to be easily deterred from his statist path to development, and even six months of Messersmith's cajoling and lecturing was not going to divert him. Indeed, Perón appeared to be stronger than ever, as his wife became a key part of Peronism's "two-cylindered machine."[66] Still, representatives of the New Deal order had not rested all of their hopes on Messersmith.

In this context, Romualdi's visit, and the "Gay Affair" constituted a far more fundamental attempt to derail Perón than anything since the *Blue Book*. U.S. policymakers and their labor allies had hoped that CGT support might be cut out from under Perón, eroding one of the "two pillars" of Peronism, but like the *Blue Book*, Romualdi's efforts backfired miserably. Still, Romualdi's blundering in Buenos Aires should be understood within the larger context of labor history in both North and South America. The AFL and CIO had fallen almost completely into line with the New Deal vision of capital-dominated corporatism and had been "captured" in their own fashion but refused to recognize their

---

65. Herling to Carey, 11 March 1946, Carey Collection, AULH.

66. Griffis to Truman, 1 March 1950, PSF, Foreign Affairs, Argentina, HST.

plight. The CIO's condemnations of Peronism, in particular, must have confused or amused *peronistas*, who were still reaping the benefits of government sponsorship, even as the Truman and the U.S. Congress debated some of the most stringent anti-union legislation of the twentieth century.[67] Still, while U.S. leaders were engaging in this fruitless challenge to Perón's control over his nation, Peronists were preparing their own challenge to U.S. hegemony in the Western Hemisphere.

---

67. Hoyt to Braden, Wright, Mann, Briggs, and Woodward, 25 March 1947, RG 59, MRIC.

# CHAPTER 6

## "INTO THE JAWS OF THE WOLF:" PERONIST DIPLOMACY AND THE INTER-AMERICAN SYSTEM

> We cannot talk of an important building up of commercial intercourse . . . on an exclusively private initiative basis, because the problems which we are facing are of such magnitude that they escape the scope of private solutions. If the state does not intervene directly or indirectly to give definite aid to these problems through a complete and new presentation of the situation, Chilean-Argentine difficulties will continue which hinder normal and even greater development. We must attack the evil at its root if we wish to exterminate it.
>
> Julio López Muñiz, 4 April 1948[1]

## I

While Perón's domestic activities caused consternation in Washington, in December 1946, the State Department's worst fears were realized as he inaugurated a new diplomatic gambit calculated to strike directly at the weakest points of the "Inter-American system." Rhetorically, Perón's "Third Position" between capitalism and communism was just one of many neutralist, nationalist foreign policies during the Cold War. However, it must also be seen as at once both a campaign to subvert U.S. hegemony over the hemisphere and one to advance his domestic agenda. The threat of the "Third Position" manifested itself on several levels. On the one hand, Perón was elevating himself to the status of a full-fledged rival to the United States for the hearts and minds of South America. On the other, he was taking powerful steps to draw neighboring nations into his web of bilateral barter and statist

---

1. Bowers to Secretary of State, 23 April 1946, RG 59, 625.3531.

economic control-away from the U.S.-sponsored "Inter-American system." Although Perón's efforts ultimately failed, and failed almost completely, this does not diminish the significance of either his ideological offensive or the U.S. response.

Riding high with full coffers and unbridled optimism, Perón and Miranda negotiated commercial agreements with neighboring states that promised to grant Argentina access to vital mineral wealth, forge customs unions, and strengthen political and economic links among South American nations. In the process, they threatened to make U.S. leaders pay dearly for their preoccupation with Europe and the Cold War. Will Clayton had offered Latin America *laissez faire* at Chapultepec; Perón was offering cash on the barrelhead, alliance, and a new economic model. A GOU manifesto written in 1943 had asserted that "Paraguay is already with us. Chile and Bolivia will follow." In late 1946, Perón tried to make good on that promise, even as *peronistas* denied any "intent to form an anti-U.S. coalition."[2]

Although the prospect of Peronist economic and political expansion was the "threat which gives us the worst case of cold shivers," it was one they could not directly oppose.[3] Well aware that any serious attempt to block Perón's treaties might well boomerang, the State Department trod lightly, working quietly behind the scenes to dissuade Argentina's potential partners. No longer was the provocative bluster of Hull and Braden the vehicle of policy, but backroom manipulation and the intangible economic and political influence of a superpower. Indeed, while Perón's ill-advised alliance building floundered, it is perhaps more remarkable that U.S. statesmen were able to rebuff his challenge as effortlessly as they did.

---

2. Justo, *Argentina y Brasil*, 43; Antonio Cafiero, *La política exterior Peronista, 1946-1955: sobre la falacia del "mito aislacionista"* (Buenos Aires, 1997), 40; see also Goñi, *Perón y los alemanes*, 121-122.

3. Ray to Secretary of State, 5 January 1948, RG 59, 711.35.

## II

While Argentina had parlayed its wartime neutrality into massive financial reserves and "more money than [Perón] knows what to do with," Chilean association with the Allies had cost that nation from $100 to $500 million.[4] To efficiently fight the "warehouse war," U.S. procurement agencies had stockpiled vital Chilean mineral exports such as copper and nitrates by setting low price ceilings for these goods. What financial reserves Chile did acquire from the war were rapidly dissipated in the inflationary postwar period, placing Chile "high on the critical list of countries suffering from a dollar shortage."[5] Although this might have otherwise called for an austerity program, Radical party leader Gabriel González Videla, elected to the presidency in September 1946, had other ideas.

Thanks to the vagaries of Chilean politics, González Videla's position was at best tenuous. He had unified the Chilean leftist parties into a "Popular Front" and achieved a narrow plurality by calling for his own costly industrialization scheme dedicated to "economic independence." Furthermore, he pledged to strengthen rural unionism through a controversial "peasant unionization" (*sindicalización campesina*) scheme. The new president also entered office owing favors to the powerful Chilean Communist Party, which had effectively swung the election in his favor, and granted the communists three Cabinet seats. Proclaiming that "powerful foreign enterprises exploit cheap labor in Chile with the same imperialistic attitude with which they exploit Chinese, Hindu and African labor," his rhetoric echoed that of his Communist allies and the Peronists across the Andes.[6]

---

4. Memorandum of Conversation, Braden and Berreta, 12 February 1947, PSF, Foreign Affairs, Marshall File, HST; see also Brian Loveman, *Chile: The Legacy of Hispanic Capitalism* (New York, 1979), 282-287.

5. *Current Economic Developments* #114, 2 September 1947, HST.

6. Braden to Bowers, 10 May 1946, RG 59, 825.00; see also Jauregui a Secretario de Aeronautica, 22 Febrero 1947, AMREC, BA, Chile 1946, 7, Convenio, Legajo 2, 3; Guiraldes a Bramulgia, 6 September 1946, AMREC,

As if these problems were not enough for the new government, Perón and Miranda had not exempted Chile from their campaign to utilize the international food shortage to their benefit. The U.S. ambassador in Santiago, Claude Bowers, reported to Braden in autumn 1946 that "the Perón regime is getting tough with Chile" by cutting off badly needed edible oil shipments.[7] Bowers pressed Braden to send 50,000 tons of soybean oil to Chile to relieve the pressure and stymie Miranda, whom he sarcastically branded "the great mind in charge of Perón's economic program." Doing so, he claimed, would "make friends for us at the expense of the Peronists" and prevent González Videla from making concessions to the Argentines under duress. "Most unfortunately, we can do nothing here," Braden replied, citing domestic shortages in the United States. Apparently abandoned by the United States and with "Wall Street creditors" hounding them for debt payments, Chilean negotiators turned to comprehensive negotiations with Argentina.[8] Two weeks later, Argentine Vice President Hortensio Quijano and González Videla announced an agreement over food shipments, and to Bowers' astonishment, González Videla added that he was dispatching Senator Jaime Larraín Moreno to Buenos Aires to put the finishing touches on extensive "economic arrangements concluded here in principle some days ago."[9]

The "economic arrangements" were much more far-reaching than even Bowers could have imagined. The Argentine-Chilean Trade Agreement was signed on December 13, and Larraín deemed it "the most important signed by Chile in its life as an independent nation." The main provision of the treaty was the

---

BA, Chile 1946, 7, 1; J. Guzman Hernández, *Gabriel González Videla: Biografía y Análisis Crítica de su Programa* (Santiago, 1946).

7. Bowers to Braden, 2 October 1946, Bowers MSS II, Folder 6.

8. Bowers to Braden, 2 October 1946, Bowers MSS II, Folder 6; Braden to Bowers, 31 October 1946, Bowers MSS II, Folder 6; Bowers to Truman, 14 July 1947, PSF, Foreign Affairs, Chile, HST.

9. Bowers to Secretary of State, 16 November 1946, RG 59, 835.503125; see also *La Nación*, 15 November 1946, 1.

creation of a customs union that provided for duty free importation of most goods across the *cordillera*. These tariff concessions were not to be applied to other nations, with the possible exception of limitrophe countries that might later enter the union—paving the way for other nations to enter a regional bloc. The Argentine city of Mendoza and the Chilean port of Valparaiso were to become "free trade zones" between the nations to further encourage trans-Andean commerce.

Perón sweetened the pot by offering $175 million in loans and developmental credits to Chile at low interest rates—"the biggest in Latin American history, five times the total war and postwar financial aid which Chile" received from the United States.[10] Twenty-five million dollars was to be used to redress adverse trade balances, and the rest was earmarked for public works and industrial development projects in Chile. A joint Argentine-Chilean committee was to be created to administer and oversee the loans, while IAPI would receive 50 percent of any profits. Furthermore, the treaty stipulated that the "production of Chilean industries benefiting from the Argentine financing may be purchased in whole or in part by Argentina" once "Chile's domestic needs had been met."[11]

The public works loans merit special notice. The treaty specified that these funds were to be utilized exclusively "to promote and coordinate Argentine-Chilean commercial exchange." Naturally, a major focus was to be new roads and rail lines across the Andes, linking Chilean and Argentine transportation networks. For example, northern provinces in Argentina would be tied into Chilean ports, giving these regions better access not only to the Chilean market, but also to new markets in the Pacific. Argentines also contemplated the construction of a *frigorifico* in Valparaiso-granting their beef better access to Pacific nations. Given the

---

10. Carleton Beals, "Chile, Copper and Communism," *Latin America in the Cold War* ed. Walter M. Daniels (New York, 1952), 150-151.

11. Gilmore to Braden, Smith, Lyon, Mann and Wells, 27 December 1946, RG 59, MRIC; Bowers to Secretary of State, 19 December 1946, RG 59, 625.3531; see also W.E.D. to Secretary of State, 7 November 1946, RG 84, BA.

extraordinary powers being granted to the Argentines, it appeared likely that Perón and Miranda might be able to guide Chilean development along the same path they were taking Argentina. Even if they were not able to exercise undue influence, the Chileans would be forced into a far more statist approach to meet the structural demands of the treaty. At the very least, Argentina and Chile would be engaging in joint projects designed to tighten bonds between their individual nations, outside the framework of the "Inter-American system," and independent of the United States.[12]

Almost every aspect of the treaty mystified Bowers. He had informed González Videla in November that U.S. aid would be forthcoming soon, and the president had responded that he had no intention of accepting any money the Argentines offered. Furthermore, González Videla had been a fierce opponent of Perón and had been the author of "powerful" speeches in the Chilean Senate in "denunciation of the Perón regime." The principal Chilean negotiator, Jaime Larraín, a member of the traditionally conservative, aristocratic elite, also possessed strong anti-Peronist credentials. González Videla and Larraín, however, reversed their stances almost overnight and pushed for ratification. Larraín contrasted this accord with U.S.-sponsored Export-Import bank loans, arguing that in all respects the former was superior, while González Videla pronounced the pact to be "intelligently realistic" and the "first step toward the effective unity of the American nations."[13]

---

12. Desmara to Belmonte, 4 Febrero 1947, AMREC, BA, DE, Chile 1947, 15, 1; Dardalla a Cavagna Martínez, 18 Marzo 1947, AMREC, BA, Chile 1946, 10, Convenio, 2, 3; see also Bassi to Sosa Molina, Mayo 1947, AMREC, BA, Chile 1947, 10, Convenio, Legajo 2, 3; Pero a Bramulgia, 16 Junio 1947, AMREC, BA, DE, Chile 1947, 15, 1; Halle Barceló a Perón, n.d., AMREC, BA, DE, Chile 1947, 15, 1; Camara de Senadores de la Nación, *Diario*, 24 Agosto 1946, 1083-1086.

13. Bowers to Braden, 18 December 1946, Bowers MSS II, Box 6; El Mercurio, 12 Diciembre 1946, 1; see also Argentine Embassy Santiago to Bramulgia, 23 Diciembre 1946, AMREC, BA, Chile 1946, 10, Convenio, Legajo 1, 1; Bowers to Braden, 6 March 1947, Bowers MSS II, Box 6; Leonor A. Machinandiarena de Devoto provides an excellent analysis of Argentine-Chilean relations during this period, especially the treaty and its aftermath. Leonor A. Machinandiarena de Devoto "La influencia del justicialismo en

Naturally, the surprise announcement of the treaty's signing provoked a flurry of speculation and gave renewed life to Braden's warnings about the "southern bloc." Virginia Prewett of the *Chicago Sun*, an old enemy of Perón, wrote that the treaty contained secret provisions that among other things, gave Argentina control over Chilean petroleum in Patagonia. The Chilean government quickly dispelled this myth. More importantly, the *New York Times* correspondent in Buenos Aires blasted the pact, likening it to "the occupation of Czechoslovakia by Hitler and the Austrian *Anschluss*." Argentines and Chileans quickly rallied to defend their actions. The Chilean chargé in Buenos Aires dismissed the charge as the "arbitrary and biased" judgment of a "bad correspondent of a North American newspaper," and the Argentine response was even more venomous, contending that the accusations were the "malicious and capricious" "nightmares of a sick mind." Little could have been calculated to better unite the two nations behind the pact than attacks from the north that simultaneously accused Argentina of fascist expansionism and Chile of subservient acquiescence to foreign pressure.[14]

The State Department's reaction was by and large similar to, if not as extreme as, the *New York Times* report. Braden cited the treaty as another Peronist attempt to forge "hegemony over lower South America," which "the Chileans deplored, but were helpless to resist." Bowers had similar fears. Although he did not doubt that the Chilean oligarchy—"industrialists, merchants, agriculturalists and rightist members of Congress"—recognized that the treaty was "against Chile's best interest," he feared that Chile's weak financial situation had thrust the nation into the Peronist orbit. The idea that Chile had been coerced into the arrangement was given further credence by an ORI study in early 1947 that showed that Argentina was Chile's only supplier of almost twenty

---

Chile, 1946-1952." (Tesis de Doctorado, Universidad de Buenos Aires, 1995), Capítulo 2; Machinandiarena de Devoto y Carlos Escudé, "Las relaciones Argentino-Chilenas, 1946-1953, y las ilusiones expansionistas del peronismo," *Argentina-Chile: Desarrollos paralelos.* ed. Torcuato DiTella (Buenos Aires, 2000), 181-200.

14. Simmons to Secretary of State, 13 December 1946, RG 59, 625.3531.

agricultural products. The "quasi-monopolistic character" of Argentine essential agricultural exports to Chile, the ORI reported, granted Perón disproportionate leverage, strengthening the thesis that he was engaged in a campaign of aggressive economic expansion.[15]

The pact was also a blow to the principles of multilateralism, despite its superficial appearance to the contrary. "While the reduction of trade barriers is in line with the efforts of the United States to remove trade barriers," Bowers noted, the Argentine-Chilean Treaty was highly discriminatory and perhaps even autarchic. Tariffs were lowered or eliminated between the two nations, but these benefits were not being extended to third parties—clearly violating both the U.S.-Chilean Reciprocal Trade Agreement and the principle of the most favored nation. Indeed, the preferential treatment that was to be given to Argentina was the antithesis of U.S. policies, and a dangerous development, reminiscent of the exclusionary treaties of the 1930s. A true customs union, the proposed ITO charter stated, "required the adoption of a common tariff as regards third countries." Since Argentina and Chile would not be aligning their tariffs, the treaty fell short on this score.[16]

Nonetheless, the potential implications of the pact appeared to be monumental. González Videla, whose alliance with the communists had already raised eyebrows in Washington, had apparently been coerced into a deal with Perón that was in direct contradiction to the principles of liberal capitalism. Because Argentina lacked the mineral resources to fulfill its industrialization scheme, it was using its wealth to buy access to Chilean copper, coal, and other subsoil products. Moreover, Chile would be drawn into extensive state-trading and the role of the most offensive

---

15. Braden to Acheson and Marshall, 13 February 1947, PSF, Foreign Affairs, Marshall, HST; Bowers to Secretary of State, 19 December 1946, RG 59, 625.3531; Atwood to Hussey, Schnee, and Gilmore, 6 March 1947, RG 59, MRIC.

16. Bowers to Secretary of State, 19 December 1946, RG 59, 625.3531; Gilmore to Braden and Mann, 18 December 1946, RG 59, 625.3531.

*peronista* creation, IAPI, would be even further strengthened and expanded.[17]

The most intriguing aspect of the proposed accord, however, was its role in Perón and Miranda's industrialization scheme. The Argentine War Department had long called for the construction of a copper smelter in Argentina for the manufacture of shell casings and cartridges. To placate the Army and generally push along the industrial program, Perón had authorized *Fabricaciones Militares* to commence negotiations with representatives of Allis-Chalmers for the building of a high-capacity primary smelter in August 1946. Allis-Chalmers had reluctantly taken part in the discussions, believing them to be nothing more than the unrealistic whim of foolish militarists and exaggerated nationalism of amateur planners. Although extremely dubious of the project's feasibility, Allis-Chalmers agreed to provide technical assistance lest the Argentines take their business to another firm.

Messersmith also considered the project to be "unsound" and yet another manifestation of misguided *peronista* nationalism. He urged Perón to abandon his plans for a large smelter and to focus on a secondary facility with a much smaller capacity, suggesting to his superiors that Perón would scrap the project when his financial reserves dwindled. Until then, it would not be wise to senselessly antagonize the regime by protesting. Unbeknownst to the ambassador, however, Perón had a plan to secure cheap imports of large quantities of copper through his negotiations with the Chileans and was bidding to take a significant step toward economic diversification in the process. An Argentine copper industry based upon Argentine resources was undeniably "unsound," but with large quantities of cheap Chilean copper, it might have been far more feasible.[18]

---

17. Bowers to Braden, 23 December 1946, Bowers MSS II, Box 6; Perón, Bramulgia and Lagomarsino to Congreso de la Nación, 11 Marzo 1947, AMREC, BA, Chile 1946, 7, Convenio, Legajo 2, 3.

18. Messersmith to Secretary of State, 21 August 1946, RG 59, 821.60; Winsnes to Messersmith, 21 August 1946, RG 59, 835.60; Messersmith to Winsnes, 21 August 1946, RG 59, 835.60; Messersmith to Secretary of State, 13 November 1946, RG 59, 835.60.

Although Messersmith was close enough to have perceived this coordination of *peronista* internal and foreign policies, he did not appear to have done so. Mere days before the announcement of the pact, he informed Clayton that "the Argentine Government is not interested in strengthening, through the kind of commercial accord the Chileans want, the present Chilean Government." The ambassador was as shocked as Bowers when the pact was signed, but immediately set to work trying to exonerate Perón and defuse Braden's accusations. He claimed that the treaty had been a Chilean initiative and that the Chileans had gone "very far toward permitting Argentine exploitation of certain minerals and fuel" as a lure for desperately needed loans. It was impossible, he argued, to see anything "sinister" in Argentine acceptance of generous Chilean offers.[19]

For his part, Miranda argued that the treaty represented the natural unification of two complimentary nations for the benefit of both. "Chile needs to increase its standard of living," he asserted, "and we can offer the means to do so, while we need certain products. If we have these products so close at hand, why should we look for them across the ocean?"[20] With the Argentine and Chilean populations linked into a single market, both nations could industrialize more quickly and effectively. Argentine and foreign economists had long recognized that one of the foremost impediments to Argentina's industrialization was the size of its domestic market. Argentina's population of thirteen million was insufficient to absorb large quantities of manufactured goods. Therefore, Argentine industrialists would never be able to employ the mass production or economics-of-scale that had so facilitated U.S. industrialization as long they were forced to rely upon such a small domestic market. Furthermore, Argentine industrial goods would never be able to become competitive without at least temporary protection from international competition. Even anti-

---

19. Messersmith to Clayton, 3 December 1946, RG 59, 625.3531; Messersmith to Secretary of State, 5 March 1947, RG 84; BA; see also Messersmith to Secretary of State, 11 March 1947, RG 59, 835.50.

20. Tewksbury to Secretary of State, 10 January 1947, RG 59, 625.3531.

Peronist businessmen could see the potential benefits of Miranda's efforts, as did the State Department, which understood well that "Argentina is too small a market to support all of the industries which would be needed to give her any degree of industrial independence," but that a "larger economic bloc" might help overcome these obstacles.[21]

The pact also promised to overcome the other major impediment to Argentine industrialization: its lack of mineral wealth for heavy industry. Although Patagonian oil reserves showed promise, Argentina possessed minimal quantities of coal, iron, copper, tin, and other vital raw materials. Chile, Bolivia, Peru, and the other nations of South America had these minerals in abundance. As North Americans had pointed out for years, all that was necessary was the capital to extract them. Perón and Miranda dedicated themselves to supplying it, and for the time being, seemed to be in a position to do so.

Optimally, economic independence from the United States and Great Britain was possible for Chile as well as Argentina, because their "dependence on foreigners will have disappeared and [they would] be able to meet [their] own requirements." Argentina, Miranda argued, would assist in the true economic development of Chile, whereas the "eternal vested interests" had over the centuries warped and hindered Chilean and Argentine national development. Although Europeans and North Americans wanted to perpetuate Latin American underdevelopment to their own benefit, "we need a prosperous and proud Chile." In short, Miranda asserted confidently, "my greatest aspiration and, of course, that of General Perón, is our emancipation from foreign tutelage."[22]

As eager as Miranda was to eliminate "foreign tutelage," he was at least as interested in the elevation of Argentina. "It is my desire," he told a Chilean journalist with his usual candor, "to

---

21. *Zig-Zag*, 23 Enero 1947, AMREC, BA, Chile 1946, 10, Convenio, Legajo 2, 4; "Argentine Post-War Economic Policies," 2; see also Interview with Torcuato DiTella, *Zig-Zag*, 6 Febrero 1947, AMREC. BA, Chile 1946, 10, Convenio, Legajo 2, 4.

22. Tewksbury to Secretary of State, 10 January 1947, RG 59, 625.3531; *Zig-Zag*, 23 Enero 1947, AMREC, BA, Chile 1946, 10, Convenio, Legajo 2, 4.

economically recreate the Viceroyalty of the Plata," when Buenos Aires was the glorious economic center of the Southern Cone within the Spanish Empire.[23] Although he denied that he had any wish to dominate neighboring states politically, he clearly hoped to restore Buenos Aires as the economic hub of the region. The shared prosperity of this new "Viceroyalty" would effect dramatic changes in all participating nations, bringing higher standards of living, and the same "social peace" that the Peronists had brought to Argentina. The challenge to U.S. economic and political hegemony in the region and the "Inter-American system" could hardly have been clearer.

Regardless of the treaty's origins or the motivations in creating it, the State Department sought an effective means to block its implementation. Bowers argued that the U.S. should not interfere but instead "should make clear that this is a Chilean problem which Chile must decide."[24] In short, he wanted to let the Chileans themselves "make the fight" against the pact. Because the trade agreement was already "puzzling Chileans and causing uneasiness," there was a good chance that if the State Department did nothing at all, opposition to the treaty would develop on its own. The key, then, was to keep a low profile and do nothing that might be interpreted as *yanqui* coercion. The U.S. government should express interest in the agreement but decline to comment publicly or show serious disfavor in private. Instead, González Videla, already embattled, should be quietly reminded that Chile was on the verge of violating its agreements with the United States and left to ponder the consequences. By working behind the scenes, the State Department could achieve far more than it could with counterproductive bluster that would only exacerbate Chilean nationalism.[25]

---

23. *Zig-Zag*, 23 Enero 1947, AMREC, BA, Chile 1946, 10, Convenio, Legajo 2, 4.

24. Bowers to Secretary of State, 4 January 1947, RG 59, 625.3531.

25. Bowers to Braden, 18 December 1946, Bowers MSS II; Bowers to Braden, 23 December 1946, Bowers MSS II.

Bowers' advice was heeded, and the State Department issued nothing more than ominous silence. The policy paid quick dividends. Just weeks after the announcement of the treaty, Bowers was able to report that "I see ample evidence that González Videla is becoming apprehensive over our reaction, and the fact that we remain silent but clearly interested is causing him some concern." Just as important than his concern, however, was "that of Chileans in business and political circles."[26] Roberto Vergara of the Chilean Fomento Corporation broached the topic with two State Department officers, asking "whether the Department has taken a stand with respect to the Agreement." When he was told that the Truman Administration was "not alarmed," Vergara "said he had reason to believe otherwise" and that other conversations had convinced him that "we had taken a very strong position on this matter."[27]

Larraín, who had not spoken to Bowers in his eight years as ambassador, suddenly approached him in early January. According to Bowers, "he made it quite clear that Chile is concerned" about the U.S. reaction, asserted that no harm had been intended toward the United States, and stated that he would very much like to go to Washington as soon as possible to explain the situation to Byrnes, Clayton, and Braden. Bowers chortled that Larraín's uneasiness was "convincing proof" that "our silence on the Argentine treaty is effective." The Peruvian ambassador in Santiago concurred, commenting on the wisdom of allowing the "Chilean opposition to develop without subjecting the opponent of the treaty to the demagogic charge of Yankee pressure."[28]

Bowers did break his silence once, and in a decidedly threatening fashion. Byrnes instructed Bowers to approach the Chilean Government and "discuss informally" with González Videla the two points that most concerned the Truman Administration.

---

26. Bowers to Braden, 23 December 1946, Bowers MSS II.

27. Memorandum of Conversation, Vergara, Schnee, and Brundage, 9 January 1947, RG 59, 625.3531.

28. Bowers to Braden and Byrnes, 3 January 1947, RG 59, 625.3531; Bowers to Byrnes and Braden, 31 December 1946, RG 59, 625.3531.

First, the 1938 trade agreement between the United States and Chile supposedly provided "reciprocal, unconditional and unlimited most-favored-nation treatment." Byrnes was curious to know how the Chileans were going to reconcile this provision with the blatantly discriminatory features of the Argentine-Chilean pact. Second, Bowers was to remind the Chileans that they had "large and special responsibilities to conform [to the] ITO Charter," as they had participated in the drafting of that document. Because the pact was little more than the "extension of discriminatory preferences under the mere guise of a customs union," Chile was in the process of jeopardizing its position in the ITO. Bowers did not make threats, rattle sabres, or otherwise brandish a "big stick," but the implicit threats were crystal clear.[29]

The response was almost immediate. Within a week of Byrnes' message, the Chileans unilaterally eradicated the offending article from the treaty. Larraín announced that the Chilean chancellery had eliminated the feature to ensure compliance with the ITO Charter and would extend tariff concessions to other states. He carefully avoided mentioning the U.S. protests and privately requested that Bowers and the State Department do nothing "to give impression that [the] treaty was being modified in any way as a result" of them. While Bowers agreed wholeheartedly, anonymous State Department sources leaked to journalists that "as a result of U.S. representations to Chile and Argentina, an amendment had been drawn up eliminating objectionable features of treaty." Bowers was incensed at the "deplorable" leak and how it had compromised the Chilean government, but González Videla rode out the controversy.[30]

On a more positive note, Bowers' faith that Chilean opposition would inflict a "severe pummeling in the debate which is to come" was soon rewarded. Fernando Aldunate of the

---

29. Byrnes to Embassy Santiago, 17 December 1946, RG 59, 625.3531; Byrnes to Embassy Santiago, 4 January 1947, RG 59, 625.3531.

30. Bowers to Secretary of State, 13 January 1947, RG 59, 625.3531; see also NWC to ARA, 23 January 1947, RG 59, 625.3531; Gilmore to Smith and Lyon, 6 February 1947, RG 59, 625.3531.

Conservative Party informed him in May that he was planning a "major attack" against the treaty in the Senate. Not only was Peronist Argentina an unsavory partner, but the treaty was going to force Chile into "dangerous" statist controls like Perón's. Fellow Conservative, Eduardo Cruz Coke, echoed this assessment and claimed that the pact would never be ratified, but Bowers feared that "this may be wishful thinking." More significantly, the senior statesman of the right-center Liberal Party, Arturo Alessandri, announced his own misgivings. While Alessandri was somewhat "amused" by suggestions that Chile was falling into a "southern bloc," he was also "fully cognizant of the plans of Perón" and would not be duped. Bowers noted, however, that Alessandri and most other senators were subordinating the treaty to domestic concerns, most significantly, peasant syndicalization. If González Videla did not back down on this project, centrists would defeat his treaty. On the other hand, the Communists were backing the treaty "to harm Chile-United States relations." While Bowers claimed that he had "not talked to a single Chilean who does not express fear and opposition to the treaty as a bad thing for Chile," he hedged his bets by conceding that it would "pass or be defeated by a narrow margin."[31]

Peronist assessments mirrored Bowers in some ways. The Argentine embassy in Santiago reported that González Videla's Radicals, the Communist party, and many Liberals supported the pact, whereas Conservatives and Salvador Allende's Socialists opposed its ratification. It reported its own wishful thinking that "the great majority of articles" appearing in the Chilean press were "frankly favorable" to ratification. While the Communist *El Siglo* hailed the pact as a step "toward the formation of an anti-imperialist bloc," other papers were more critical. *El Mercurio* ran a series of editorials by René Silva Espejo, blasting the treaty. Espejo attacked

---

31. Bowers to Braden, 21 April 1947, Bowers MSS II; RPA to ARA, 17 January 1947, RG 59, 625.3531; Bowers to Braden, 31 March 1947, Bowers MSS II; Bowers to Armour, 9 September 1947, Bowers MSS II; Guiraldes to Bramulgia, 6 Marzo 1947, AMREC, BA, 10, Convenio, Legajo 2, 4; Embajada Santiago a Bramulgia, 13 Marzo 1947, AMREC, BA, 10, Convenio, Legajo 2, 4.

Miranda's statement that "we are interested in capitalizing Chilean industries that produce what Argentina needs" and called upon patriotic Chileans to rise up and defeat the self-serving Argentines. *Zig-Zag* weighed with its prediction that Chile was throwing itself into "the jaws of the wolf." Nonetheless, Argentines remained confident that once González Videla rallied the Liberals, he would be able to secure ratification.[32]

In spite of their optimism, Argentine officials recognized well that prospects for the treaty were dimming and that dark clouds had started to appear on the horizon. Foremost among these were subtle indications that González Videla was having second thoughts. The embassy reported that in his speeches, he was no longer referring to Argentina as a "sister nation" or a "friendly country," but simply as "the Argentine Republic." Even more telling, he had not submitted the treaty for a final vote in Congress. The Argentines were well aware that any "delay in approval of the treaty" "undoubtedly favors the U.S., which does not want to lose its economic dominance here." Finally, Argentines sensed that the State Department was "counterattacking," as the Export-Import Bank finally approved a small but suggestive $5.3 million loan to Chile.[33]

Still, Perón was unwilling to allow the treaty to fade away. In July, he promised Chileans that "as an incentive to ratification," Argentina would not build synthetic nitrate plants and would instead rely upon Chilean nitrate exports "at world market price."

---

32. Luti to Bramulgia, 21 Noviembre 1946, AMREC, BA, Chile 1946, 10, Convenio, Legajo 1, 1; Luti to Bramulgia, 30 December 1946, AMREC, BA, Chile 1946, 10, Convenio, Legajo 1, 1; Memorandum a Miranda and Bramulgia, Febrero 1947, AMREC, BA, Chile 1946, 10, Convenio, Legajo 2, 3; Luti a Bramulgia, 21 Marzo 1947, AMREC, BA, Chile 1946, 10, Convenio, Legajo 2, 3; Lopez Muñiz a Bramulgia, Septiembre 1948, AMREC, BA, Chile 1946, 10, Convenio, Legajo 2, 3; *El Mercurio*, 20 Diciembre 1946; *Zig-Zag*, 27 Diciembre 1946; *El Siglo*, 1 Enero 1947; *La Hora*, 7 Enero 1947; *La Nación*, 7 Febrero 1947.

33. Memorandum a Bramulgia and Miranda, Febrero 1947, AMREC, BA, Chile 1946, 10, Convenio, Legajo 2, 3; see also Guezales a Hoyos, 29 May 1947, AMREC, BA, Chile 1947, 4, 1.

After World War I, Chilean nitrate sales had catastrophically plummeted as surplus gunpowder replaced their produce on the international market. Chileans had vowed to "remember for years, remember with tears" this disastrous episode and had every reason to fear that peace and the emergence of cheap synthetic fertilizer would again threaten this major export. Because Argentine planters required fertilizer, and an Argentine arms industry would require nitrates for gunpowder production, this offer had appeal on both sides of the Andes. Nevertheless, the State Department continued its silent treatment, and Bowers informed his British counterpart that he doubted that Washington "will instruct us to protest unless prospects of the treaty brighten considerably."[34]

Although Perón was pressing for a conclusion, González Videla soon faced another crisis that ultimately decided the fate of the pact. Even though the Communist Party had supported his candidacy and been vital in securing his victory, he was leaning toward moderation. Chile's deteriorating economy and skyrocketing inflation were forcing him to renege on his more costly campaign pledges, and his popularity was in decline. In municipal and local elections held in April 1947, his Radicals were mauled, losing 125 *corregidores*. While one third of these seats went to Conservatives intransigently opposed to González Videla, the remainder went to the Communists—an illustration of the increasing polarization of the nation.[35] Reeling from this popular repudiation of his party and fearing the newfound strength of his erstwhile Communist allies, González Videla turned to moderate Radicals and Liberals for backing when Communists and radicalized *campesinos* initiated a paralytic general strike and a major coal strike on October 4. The timing of the strike was perfect, as it

---

34. Bowers to Secretary of State, 14 July 1947, RG 59, 625.3531; *Review of the River Plate*, 18 July 1947, 7-8; Bowers to Leche, 2 October 1947, Bowers MSS II; see also Bassi a Sosa Molina, Mayo 1947, AMREC, BA, Chile 1946, 10, Convenio, Legajo 2, 3.

35. Embajada Santiago a Bramulgia, 10 Abril 1947, AMREC, BA, Chile 1947, 4, 1; see also Embajada Santiago a Bramulgia, 4 Agosto 1947, AMREC, BA, Chile 1947, 4, 1; Hoyos a Anadon, 21 Agosto 1947, AMREC, BA, Chile 1947, 4, 1.

placed the country in "grave peril," with perhaps ten days of coal left in the national stockpile.

Bowers frantically tried to convince his superiors that the floundering president was neither a fascist (although he was contemplating alliance with Perón) nor a communist (despite his dalliance with them). He reported that Moscow, through several Yugoslav agents, was directing the strike to "overthrow the government and obtain control of the production [in order to deprive the United States] of strategic raw materials." González Videla seemed helpless to stop the strike without more coal with which to weather the storm and pleaded with Truman for emergency shipments of coal that would permit him to break the strike. Bowers endorsed and relayed his appeal.[36]

Washington again responded, as no one understood the infuriating and crippling impact of a major coal strike better than Truman. With a promise of forthcoming coal shipments from the United States, González Videla opted finally to "put an end to political control that the Communist Party has over the vital industries of the country" by sending troops into the mines and decisively breaking the strike. He "expressed his deep appreciation" to Bowers and "almost with tears in his eyes, said that his government wanted to work in closest cooperation with the United States." He not only removed the remaining Communists from government positions but outlawed the Communist Party with the Law for the Permanent Defense of Democracy and broke off relations with the Soviet bloc.

Washington was quick to reward their new ally's turnabout, as larger Export-Import Bank loans started to pour into Chile. Naturally, these loans stipulated the "exclusive use of United States purchased capital goods for the Chilean industries receiving Bank credits and even that U.S. carriers ship goods to Chile." Anaconda Copper suddenly announced that it would be investing $130 million more into the Chilean copper industry. U.S. policymakers and businessmen were finding González Videla far more pliable and

---

36. Bowers to Truman, 14 July 1947, PSF, Foreign Affairs, Chile, HST; Claude Bowers, *Chile Through Embassy Windows* (New York, 1958), 166-175; Loveman, *Chile*, 288-291.

were rewarding him accordingly. The October coal strike and the timely U.S. response was also a decisive turning point in the Argentine-Chilean Trade Agreement.[37]

González' sentiments toward the treaty cooled as his closer ties with the *yanquis* necessitated a new approach toward Perón. Taking the advice of the Conservative Party, he stopped maneuvering for a ratification vote and instead worked to amend the treaty to "remove any vestige of Argentine influence in Chile." His representatives in Buenos Aires submitted a number of amendments to the treaty that weakened Argentine control over the dispensation of the loans. Although González Videla still saw some value in acquiring loans, tariff concessions, and markets, he was basically looking for "a way out of the entire treaty." The Conservative opposition became a "blessing" as it gave him a pretext for "letting [the] treaty languish." His only remaining interest in the treaty now was to ensure Chile did nothing to "prejudice her relations with [the United States] or the world bank by proceeding with the treaty when she would quite possibly be left holding the bag."

By 1948, it was entirely possible that all Perón could give Chile was trouble. Perón's Five-Year Plan, nationalization campaign, and arms purchases were draining his coffers faster than IAPI could refill them, as Bowers was more than happy to relate to González Videla. Although Chile "lacked the technical services" to ascertain whether Perón had enough money left to fulfill the loan pledges, the State Department did and was predicting Argentine bankruptcy by 1949. Thus, confident of U.S. backing, the reinvigorated González Videla decisively cast his lot with Washington.[38]

---

37. Memorandum of Conversation, Bowers and González Videla, 24 December 1947, Bowers MSS II; Unsigned Memorandum on Chile, undated, AMREC, BA, Chile 1947, 4, 1; see also Loveman, *Chile*, 286-292; Francis Parkinson, *Latin America, the Cold War, and the World Powers, 1945-1973: A Study in Diplomatic History*. (Beverly Hills, 1978), 13-14.

38. Bowers to Armour and Daniels, 18 November 1947, RG 59, 625.3531; Memorandum of Conversation, Bowers and González Videla, 2 December 1947, Bowers MSS II; see also Tascheret a Hoyos, 2 Septiembre 1947, AMREC, BA, Chile 1947, 4, 1; Bowers to Secretary of State, 20 November

*Peronistas* recognized the shift in the Chilean attitude immediately. González Videla was now uniting with Conservatives and Liberals "in an anti-communist alliance, supporting North American interests, and at the same time, opposing good relations with Argentina," Argentine diplomats reported, as he renounced reform to forge an alliance with the "large landowners and directors of American businesses." Rather than pursue a reformist course, they argued, he had hitched his wagon to the traditional oligarchy, and in the international sphere, forged a similar entente with U.S. "imperialists."[39] Ambassador López Muñiz reported that González Videla's turnabout could be attributed simply to "the United States of North America, which makes millions of dollars of loans conditionally, with diverse demands upon internal order" to carry nations "down paths chosen by Washington."[40]

Perón was quick to accuse the State Department of subverting the pact. In a speech before Congress, Perón announced in May 1948 that "foreign interests" had "secretly interfered" in Argentina's dealings with Chile and Bolivia. On hearing this, U.S. Ambassador James Bruce, drawing his own conclusions, reported to his superiors that "the communists have in some way unknown to us persuaded the Argentine government that the State Department was instrumental in causing the non-affirmation of the Argentine trade agreement with Chile." Acting Secretary of State Robert Lovett informed Bruce that he could "categorically deny any statements indicating" that the U.S. government "has exerted pressure to prevent ratification." Lovett added confidentially, however, that the State Department "did object in informal discussion." While there can be no doubt that U.S. actions had hindered the treaty, there was no tangible proof that they had

---

1947, RG 59. 625.3531.

39. Varas and Pallas a Lopez Muñiz, 9 Septiembre 1948, AMREC, BA, Chile 1948, 7, 5; Portela a Lopez Muñiz, 17 Marzo 1947, AMREC, BA, Chile 1948, 7, 5.

40. López Muñiz a Anadón, 15 Abril 1948, AMREC, BA, Chile 1948, 6, Copias de las notas de la embajada argentina en Chile.

actively sabotaged it. Perón would not charitably be given another *Blue Book* to turn to his own advantage.[41]

Still, he was not yet prepared to abandon the treaty either, even after González Videla contradicted his accusations against the United States.[42] In a last-ditch effort, Perón appealed to the Chileans to abandon their attempts to modify the treaty, which were "becoming a joke." Perón reaffirmed that no imperialism or domination had been intended, but he had only sought to forward Chilean industrialization so Chileans could purchase more from Argentina. Furthermore, he asserted that he was willing to put aside old, petty border disputes in Antarctica and the Beagle Channel Islands that had plagued the nations for decades. With regard to the Beagle islands, Perón lightheartedly suggested that the "pair of big rocks of no value or importance" should be dynamited or turned over to the Chileans if they actually cared enough to bother claiming them. Perón concluded by stating that he was only trying to correct the "incomprehensible error" by which Chile, "the land of the great O'Higgins," and Argentina, that of "the great San Martín," were not a "single country." Perón's reference to heroes of the independence movement might have been intended to inspire feelings of international brotherhood, but it hardly reassured Chileans to learn that Perón considered Chilean independence to be nothing more than an "error." As a final attempt to resurrect the treaty, Perón's interviews were an abject failure.[43]

Within months, the traditional suspicion and mistrust between Argentina and Chile returned. Chilean officials reported to Bowers that they had evidence that *peronistas* had aided in a coup

---

41. Bruce to Secretary of State, 22 April 1948, RG 59, 711.35; Lovett to Embassy Buenos Aires, 9 April 1948, RG 59, 625.3531; see also López Muñiz to Anadón, 4 Mayo 1948, AMREC, BA, Chile 1948, 6, Copias de las notas de la Embajada argentina en Chile; Memorandum of Conversation, Bowers and González Videla, 2 December 1947, Bowers MSS II.

42. López Muñiz to Anadón, 4 Mayo 1948, AMREC, BA, Chile 1948, 6, Copias.

43. Bowers to Secretary of State, 22 June 1948, RG 59, 625.3531; Davis to Mills, 30 July 1948, RG 59, 625.3531.

attempt made by Perón's friend, General Carlos Ibañez del Campo, in November. They also accused him of fomenting war between Chile and Bolivia. Other accusations were more bizarre, suggesting that Perón was training alpine troops and recruiting ex-Luftwaffe pilots in Switzerland for a trans-Andean invasion. With the Communists and the treaty decisively beaten down, González Videla needed to convince Washington that there was still a threat to Chilean democracy, and Perón fit the bill, as Argentine-Chilean relations had gone full circle in just three years.[44]

With the Argentine-Chilean Trade Agreement dead, Chilean communism thwarted, and Perón's challenge rebuffed, U.S. interests had been served. Perón had tried fruitlessly to induce a neighboring nation to undertake a state-guided industrial scheme similar to his and join him in his efforts to stand against the United States. With a minimum of effort, the State Department had helped to prevent the defection of Chile from the "Inter-American system." Although the communist menace was the threat that prompted the United States to dramatic action, Perón was checked at the same time. Furthermore, U.S. policymakers had learned that "Argentina's emergence as a creditor nation" represented a novel but genuine threat to U.S. interests in South America.[45]

## III

Still, Chile had only been the first of Miranda's targets. Chronically unstable and traditionally impoverished Bolivia was, on the surface, an even more vulnerable target, and in the wake of Gualberto Villarroel's downfall, this was especially true. Although the State Department viewed the overthrow of Villarroel as a blow to Perón, fascism, and the "southern bloc," Peronists were

---

44. Bowers to Secretary of State, 30 November 1948, RG 59, 725.35; Memorandum of Conversation, Rodriguez, Mills, Green and Davis, 29 December 1946, RG 59, 725.35; Daniels to Bowers, 30 December 1948, Bowers MSS II; Bowers to Secretary of State, 31 December 1948, RG 59, 724.35.

45. Memorandum I for the Secretary, January 1947, RG 59, Records of the Deputy Assistant Secretaries of State for Inter-American Affairs (RDAS), Subject File, Policy-Position Papers.

undeterred. Hedging his bets, Perón simultaneously sheltered Víctor Paz Estenssoro and other MNR exiles in Buenos Aires at the same time he opened negotiations with the new *junta* and President-elect Enrique Hertzog. The *peronistas* had no illusions in this regard. They recognized that with the fall of Villarroel and the restoration of the oligarchy, the "United States will have great influence in the new government," but understood full well that Bolivia remained economically dependent on Argentina and therefore vulnerable. As one Peronist official put it, "no one can replace us."[46]

The Argentine embassy in La Paz had high hopes and preached optimism. Ambassador Mariano Buitrago Carrillo was easily the most zealous. The chaotic post-coup period was an "exceptionally favorable time" "to enter Bolivia and penetrate economically to make a change in its social attitude," he posited. He urged his superiors to present the Bolivians with a comprehensive trade treaty as soon as possible. The new leaders, he argued, were "men of mediocrity" who lacked political skill or strong ideological motivation and would leap at the prospect of guaranteeing their nation's food supply, securing markets, and receiving loans.[47]

Although U.S. ambassador Joseph Flack breathed easier with the Villarroel regime gone and the *rosca* back in control, he remained wary. Counterrevolution was always a possibility in Bolivia, and U.S. officials were well aware that "Bolivia's attitude toward Argentina must take into consideration its present economic dependency on that country." In December, Bolivian officials reported to Flack that Argentine troops were massing on the border, preparing for invasion. Flack dismissed the accusations, but relayed them to Acheson, who attributed them merely to the "nervous state of mind" of the Bolivian government. Even if

---

46. "Movimiento Revolucionario de Bolivia," 21 Julio 1946, AMREC, BA, Bolivia 1946, 1, 1, Anexo 2, Parte 1.

47. Buitrago Carrillo, Memorandum, 28 Noviembre 1947, AMREC, BA, Bolivia 1947, 1, 2; Rios Mármol, "Informe Politico y Económico del Consulado en Santa Cruz," 1 Agosto 1947, AMREC, BA, Bolivia 1947, 1, 1.

officials in the United States firmly believed that Perón was trying to assemble an autarchic "southern bloc," they knew full well that he would not dare to try to do it with military force or open aggression.[48]

They were, however, far more fearful that Perón was applying economic pressure on Bolivia. Argentina had agreed to supply Bolivia with sixty thousand tons of wheat throughout the course of 1946, but by December, only seven thousand tons had arrived. Even worse, in the months following the coup, Argentine beef shipments dropped dramatically. Although Bolivia had been receiving twenty-five railroad cars of cattle per week, by December only five were crossing the border weekly. While Bramulgia claimed that the poor condition of the Argentine rail system was at fault, the Bolivian ambassador to Argentina found "it hard to believe that such a high percentage of Argentina's cattle cars could have been worn out in such a brief period of time." It did not come as a surprise when the *junta* petitioned Washington in early 1947 for emergency shipments of edible oils and 50,000 tons of wheat. The State Department responded to the Bolivian appeal with "assurances of assistance" to "in effect nullify Argentina's economic pressure." When the Argentines learned of Washington's willingness to supplant them in the Bolivian market, they suddenly promised to increase their own shipments, and even Messersmith did not try to vindicate the *peronistas* on this occasion.[49]

Having secured assistance once, Hertzog's government launched a barrage of accusations against Perón probably calculated to draw more concessions from Washington. In mid-December, a Bolivian cabinet minister warned Flack that "no exportation to Bolivia will be permitted [by Perón] after January first" unless

---

48. Espy to Flack and Wells, 6 October 1946, RG 59, 624.3531; Acheson to Embassy Buenos Aires, 3 December 1946, RG 59, 724.35; see also Flack to Secretary of State, 3 December 1946, RG 59, 724.35.

49. Messersmith to Secretary of State, 12 December 1946, RG 59, 724.35; Orloski to Secretary of State, 16 January 1947, RG 59, 624.3531; see also Orloski to Secretary of State, 20 December 1946, RG 59, 624.3531; Flack to Secretary of State, 10 January 1947, RG 59, 624.3531; Flack to Secretary of State, 13 December 1946, RG 59, 724.3531.

Bolivia was prepared to negotiate an "overall trade treaty and a customs union" with Argentina. Although this news initially alarmed U.S. officials, it eventually became known that this was merely his "personal opinion" and that no such ultimatum had been delivered. False alarms of this sort did little to convince U.S. officials that the *junta* earnestly feared Perón's machinations, and the State Department began to view subsequent Bolivian pleas as little more than poorly disguised attempts to curry U.S. favor. The State Department never took the Argentine-Bolivian negotiations as seriously as they did the Argentine-Chilean Trade Agreement, and, except for Braden and some of his colleagues in the Division of North and West Coast Affairs, were well aware of Bolivian ulterior motives. So although officials such as Carlos Hall and James Espy worked furiously to incite the Department to "help Bolivia to extricate itself from the position that it must either accede to" Perón's "demands or suffer starvation," their appeals fell on deaf ears.[50]

Still, Miranda's emissaries approached the *junta* in December 1946, just days after inking a deal with Larraín. The Argentines predictably proposed a customs union and showed interest in "obtaining the total production" of Bolivian tin, iron, and lead in exchange for food shipments and loans. Furthermore, the *peronistas* requested permission to establish a branch of IAPI in La Paz. The *junta* duly reported these propositions to Flack, undoubtedly hoping that Argentine competition might convince the United States to pay higher prices for mineral imports. They further raised the ante by warning that if IAPI established a foothold, "the economy of Bolivia would come under the complete domination of Argentina within from two to five years."[51]

In March 1947, however, negotiations began in earnest as Miranda dispatched his "principal subordinate" Carlos Devries to

---

50. O'Donoghue to Secretary of State, 3 January 1947, RG 59, 724.35; Espy to Hall, 5 May 1947, RG 59, 724.350.

51. Orloski to Secretary of State, 16 January 1946, RG 59, 624.3531; see also O'Donoghue to Secretary of State, 3 January 1947, RG 59, 624.3531; Flack to Secretary of State, 13 December 1946, RG 59, 724.3531.

La Paz. Whereas Hertzog's government tried to assert that Devries' arrival had been a "complete surprise," Messersmith commented that it was highly unlikely that Miranda would have sent IAPI's vice president "unless the ground had been well prepared for such a mission." Furthermore, it took the two sides less than a week to agree upon a draft treaty. Although the *junta* had informed the State Department that it wished to limit its contact with Argentina to simple barter, the draft treaty was remarkably comprehensive.[52]

The major points of the treaty were familiar. Duty-free importation of many products was guaranteed to both nations, and Bolivia agreed to provide the Argentines with large quantities of tin, lead, wolfram, coca, and other products. IAPI would provide substantial loans to "stimulate industry and commerce" that would be administered by mixed commissions of Argentines and Bolivians. Although some loans were earmarked for public works programs, most were geared toward enhancing Bolivian mining and exporting capacity. IAPI and Miranda, of course, would be handling the financial and commercial aspects of the pact's implementation. Hertzog professed his loyalty to free enterprise and his unwillingness to turn over such great economic powers to governmental entities, but nonetheless signed the treaty.[53]

Perón's and Miranda's motivations were far clearer. Just as they were negotiating for the construction of a copper mill that would have utilized Chilean copper, so too were they receiving bids from U.S. and European firms for the construction of a high-capacity tin plate and steel mill. Although Messersmith and representatives of Allis-Chalmers tried again to dissuade *peronistas* from this "uneconomic" venture, and to convince the Argentines to lower their sights, Perón and his generals refused to be deterred. But in addition to this dovetailing of foreign policy and domestic

---

52. Messersmith to Secretary of State, 4 March 1947, RG 59, 624.3531; see also Embassy La Paz to Secretary of State, 27 February 1946, RG 59, 624.3531.

53. Flack to Secretary of State, 9 March 1947, RG 59, 624.3531; see also Hertzog, "Mensaje al Congreso Ordinario de 1947," AMREC, BA, Bolivia 1947, 1, 1; Flack to Secretary of State, 4 March 1947, RG 59, 624.3531.

industrialization efforts, there were even greater ramifications to the pact.[54]

Argentines had long worked to gain access to the "gigantic" quantities of iron ore in the Bolivian region of Mutún and planned to use industrial credits to develop these resources. Various Brazilian governments in the past had blocked every similar Argentine effort in order to "impede Argentine utilization" of Bolivian iron. Nonetheless, Peronists pressed with renewed vigor. U.S. and British firms had contemplated investment in Mutún, but studies had shown it to be uneconomic, due to the cost of shipping the low-quality ore to Liverpool or the United States. Because Argentina already had a fleet of ships on the Paraguay River and would not have to make any trans-oceanic voyages to process the ore, there was no reason why this Bolivian iron could not augment the *peronista* industrialization and rearmament scheme. Although the Brazilians could be counted upon to resist this development once again, Peronists were confident that they had the most to offer. Bolivian commerce with Brazil was "artificial," they argued—a conscious effort on the part of Brazil to prevent Argentine-Bolivian ties—but the Argentine and Bolivian economies were "naturally" complementary. If Bolivia could be weaned from the United States and Brazil, Peronists hoped to alter the balance of power in South America.[55]

Despite, or perhaps because of the benefits that Argentina would gain from the pact, Hertzog probably never intended to allow the treaty to go into effect. Bolivian officials constantly fed Flack and Braden tales of Argentine perfidity. According to one report that came from a "high-ranking official Bolivian source," Buitrago had been making inflammatory speeches against the United States. Apparently, Buitrago claimed that:

---

54. Messersmith to Secretary of State, 21 August 1946, RG 353, RIIC-ARG; Messersmith to Clayton, 9 October 1946, RG 59, 835.24; Messersmith to Clayton, 12 September 1946, RG 353, RIIC-ARG.

55. Carles, "Sobre infiltración Brasileña en Santa Cruz de la Sierra," 9 Septiembre 1946, AMREC, BA, Bolivia 1946, 1, 11, Anexo 1; see also Mármol to Bramulgia, 7 Septiembre 1948, AMREC, BA, Brasil 1948, 3, 2; Galbraith to Secretary of State, 24 November 1947, RG 59, 835.503124.

> Argentina has a particular interest in establishing close ties with Bolivia because this is the easiest place for the infiltration of Yankee imperialism which had to be combated in South America; since Bolivia was a bridge-head of this imperialism which had to be neutralized.[56]

Also telling is the Bolivian foreign minister's opinion, expressed to Flack, that "Miranda is arch-fiend." The Hertzog administration, which was supposedly considering a customs union with Perón's Argentina, seemed quite intent upon discrediting its prospective partners, although it was certainly possible that the conflicting accounts were indicative of a split in the hastily assembled cabinet. The Bolivian motivation became even clearer in May when the head of the Bolivian Central Bank disclosed to Flack that had the U.S. not committed the "regrettable error" of being "dilatory" during the last tin contract negotiations, the Argentine-Bolivian pact would never even have been considered.[57]

Negotiating with Perón, however, in addition to increasing pressure on U.S. negotiations for tin, also allowed Hertzog to reap further benefits. So long as there was hope of reaching an agreement with Hertzog, the *peronistas* had no reason to support Paz Estenssoro and the MNR exiles in Argentina. Peronists must have been tempted to help the exiles return to Bolivia, as they were the only Bolivian faction "which could respond to our overtures for the formation of a bloc" against the "Yankee and Brazilian imperialisms aligned against us."[58] According to Paz Estenssoro, "in the beginning, Perón had received them with open arms." The U.S. embassy in Buenos Aires even received information, albeit unverified, that Paz Estenssoro and the MNR refugees were

---

56. Flack to Secretary of State, 27 December 1947, RG 59, 724.35.

57. Flack to Secretary of State, 9 June 1948, RG 59, 724.35; Espy to Hall, 2 May 1947, RG 59, 724.35; see also Flack to Secretary of State, 20 March 1947, RG 59, 624.3531.

58. Rios Marmol a Bramulgia, 31 Agosto 1948, AMREC, BA, Bolivia 1948, 1, 2.

promising to support the *peronistas* if they ever managed to return to power in Bolivia. After the negotiations with Hertzog seemed to be bearing fruit, however, "it was," according to Paz Estenssoro, "almost impossible for any of the MNR exiles to get in touch with any important Argentine official."[59]

Another sign of Peronist goodwill was its handling of Elías Belmonte Pabón's long-awaited return to Bolivia from his exile in Europe. Belmonte, whom U.S. intelligence services believed to have been a Nazi supporter during the war, might have been welcome in Villarroel's Bolivia, but not in Hertzog's. When it became known that he was on board a ship sailing for Buenos Aires in early 1947, Bolivians feared the worst. Belmonte still held the loyalty of some in the Bolivian army and, on South American soil, represented a potential threat to Hertzog's government. Bolivians appealed to Perón and urged him not to allow the "notorious" war criminal to disembark. The Argentines appeared willing to cooperate until they learned that Belmonte required immediate appendix surgery. He was taken off his ship and given treatment for his ailment, but although some may have feared that this was a weak *peronista* ploy to allow Belmonte to join his allies in Argentina, he was returned to his ship and sent on his way as soon as his health permitted. If Perón was planning intrigues in Bolivia, Belmonte might well have proven useful, but instead he opted for cooperation with the Hertzog government.[60]

---

59. Robert J. Alexander, *The Bolivaran Presidents*, 16-17; see also Messersmith to Burrows and O'Donoghue, 5 December 1946, RG 84, BA; Mármol to Bramulgia, 31 Agosto 1948, AMREC, BA, Bolivia 1948, 1, 2; Foianini. "Refutación," 27 Febrero 1946, AMREC, BA, Bolivia 1946, 1, 1; Buitrago Carrillo to Bramulgia, 5 Mayo 1947, AMREC, BA, Bolivia 1947, 1, 1; Sosa Molina to Perón, 16 Octubre 1948, AMREC, BA, Bolivia 1948, 1, 1, Parte 3.

60. Embassy La Paz to Bramulgia, 6 Febrero 1947, AMREC, BA, Bolivia 1947, 1, 8; La Rosa, "Noticia," 11 Febrero 1947, AMREC, BA, Bolivia 1947, 1, 8; Anaya to Sosa Molina, 22 Febrero 1947, AMREC, BA, Bolivia 1947, 1, 8; Desmaras a Embajada Buenos Aires, 28 Febrero 1947, AMREC, BA, Bolivia 1947, 1, 8; Belmonte's mother had even written Perón, begging him to provide shelter for her son, whom she claimed, was the victim of a "cruel international conspiracy." Flora de Lardon to Perón, 15 Febrero 1947, AMREC, BA, Bolivia 1947, 1, 8.

Like the Chileans, Bolivia was quick to sign the treaty, but slow to ratify, as opposition quickly mounted. Chilean envoys protested that the diversion of Bolivian trade through Argentina would "dry up" the Chilean port of Arica which had long served land-locked Bolivia. The Brazilians, predictably, were even more adamant in their fears of the "establishment [of an] Argentine zone of influence" in "territories near its border."[61] Domestic opponents soon surfaced as well, as industrialists and agricultural elites complained of the treaty's "far-reaching implications." In addition to the predictable opposition of the *rosca*, the leftist PIR (*Partido de la Izquierda Revolucionaria*) weighed in against the pact and in favor of U.S. investment. The State Department did nothing to sandbag the treaty, simply because there was no need. Hertzog himself was busily trying to amend it so drastically that in Flack's opinion, it "may not be acceptable [to] Argentines."[62]

Buitrago and the Argentine embassy in La Paz must shoulder some blame for the defeat of the treaty, as well. In October, reports surfaced that they had bribed journalists to print favorable assessments. As part of his efforts to assist in the ratification process, Buitrago allegedly made payments not only to newspapermen, but possibly to politicians. The Peronists immediately worked to control the damage by recalling the ambassador and dispatching Miranda to Bolivia in an effort to undo the damage. The "economic czar" publicly renounced the ambassador's actions, and vehemently denied that he had been acting under orders from the Casa Rosada. Since many Bolivians had already concluded that Miranda had financed the entire

---

61. The Brazilians apparently also made a counterproposal to Hertzog, promising economic aid to keep Bolivia out of the Argentine orbit. It included financing a $60 million rail line in Bolivia. Braden's friend, William Dawson, argued that because U.S. leaders were doing nothing to block this pact, "Brazil might conceivably be considered as pulling our own chestnuts out of the fire." Dawson did, however, note that if Brazil had the funds to make these extravagant promises for "primarily political purposes," it should not be applying for (and receiving) Ex-Im Bank loans. Dawson to Wells, Braden and Briggs, 19 March 1947, RG 59, 724.35.

62. Flack to Secretary of State, 20 March 1947, RG 59, 624.3531.

operation, his denials had little credibility. Miranda lost even that when the Hertzog government accused him of covertly shipping arms to MNR rebels soon thereafter. Regardless of the genesis of these fiascos or the veracity of the accusations, the mere appearance of such impropriety hardly helped the chances of ratification.[63]

By the end of 1947, the treaty had more or less died. Subject to bitter debate in the Bolivian Congress, it had not fared well. If Bolivia were to open its borders to Argentine products, it would have to do so for other nations or risk violating a number of existing treaties. More significantly, Hertzog and his colleagues had reinterpreted the provisions dealing with their obligatory mineral export quotas to Argentina. Although it had been understood that the Bolivian government would sell fixed quantities of tin, wolfram, and other ores to Argentina, the head of the Bolivian Central Bank traveled to Buenos Aires to inform Miranda that his government could not consider itself bound to do so. In addition to restoring its freedom to negotiate unimpeded with the United States, this served to make the pact more unpalatable to the Argentines. When the Bolivian Congress recommended sixteen changes to water down the treaty in October, the Argentines refused to accept any of the revisions.[64]

Perón and Miranda did not give up entirely. Although the Five-Year Plan was rapidly draining the Argentine treasury, Miranda increased the amount of the loans to eight hundred million pesos. At the same time, Bolivians again cried that he was deliberately slowing food deliveries to encourage ratification. These efforts were futile. The U.S. embassy in La Paz informed the Department in late October that "the treaty will fall far short of its

---

63. Santiago Arce to Bramulgia, 25 Octubre 1947, AMREC, BA, Bolivia 1947, 1, 1; *El Diario*, 24 Octubre 1947, 1; *El Diario*, 25 Octubre 1947, 1; Ray to Secretary of State, 22 July 1948, RG 59, 724.35; see also Buitrago Carrillo Memorandum, 28 Noviembre 1946, AMREC, BA, Bolivia 1946, 1, 10.

64. Flack to Secretary of State, 6 March 1947, RG 59, 624.3531; Flack to Secretary of State, 20 March 1947, RG 59, 624.3531; Flack to Secretary of State, 4 November 1947, RG 59, 724.35; Espy to Hall, 22 April 1946, RG 59, 624.3531.

original scope" at the same time it warned that as a result, "Argentine efforts to resolve Bolivia's food difficulties will be a mere gesture." Notably, when Perón and Hertzog met soon thereafter, they apparently did not even discuss the treaty.[65]

By 1948, the treaty had languished, and the State Department had done almost nothing to derail it. When Perón made his grand claim that "foreign interests" had sabotaged his Bolivian and Chilean pacts, Lovett informed his ambassador in Buenos Aires that there had been nothing done in Bolivia that could be construed as interventionism. Buitrago, embittered by recent events, confirmed this opinion. Ironically, by the time Perón announced that his efforts were being blocked by foreigners, his own government was souring on the treaty. His ambitious Five-Year Plan was draining Miranda's coffers, and the prospects for a tin-plate mill were dimming. Hertzog started to show interest in exporting greater quantities of tin to Argentina throughout 1948, but by this time the Argentines were becoming aware that they were unable to fulfill the loan provisions.[66]

## IV

Peru, a third potential member of a "southern bloc," was yet another battleground between the Argentine and North American visions. *Peronista* Ambassador Hugo Oderigo reported that Peru had been torn by the emergence of Perón. Although the Andean nation traditionally followed the U.S. lead, according to Argentines, the United States was "absorbing the economy of the country without bringing progress or assuring the economic liberty of the people." Although he acknowledged that for the time being, the U.S. held the upper hand in Peru, there was a burgeoning

---

65. Embassy La Paz to Secretary of State, 21 October 1947, RG 59, 624.3531; see also Flack to Secretary of State, 4 November 1947, RG 59, 724.35.

66. Lovett to Embassy Buenos Aires, 9 April 1947, RG 59, 625.3531; see also Formichelli to Bramulgia, 20 Enero 1948, AMREC, BA, DE, Bolivia-Brasil 1947, Legajo 1; Formichelli to Bramulgia, 8 Junio 1948, AMREC, BA, Bolivia 1948, 1, 2; Formichelli to Bramulgia, 24 Diciembre 1947, AMREC, BA, DE, Bolivia-Brasil 1947, Legajo 1; Memorandum, "Rafael Ordica en Bolivia," 10 Diciembre 1948, AMREC, BA. Bolivia 1948, 1, 1.

undercurrent of resentment. "It is very common," he related, "to hear people repudiating the North Americans," even if they "do it very quietly." Even more satisfying was the apparent growth in Peru of the sentiment, "what we need here is a Perón."[67]

Peronists worked hard to encourage this spirit and stop the Peruvian "gravitation toward the United States." The embassy published and distributed pamphlets, booklets, and magazines detailing Perón's "social work, solution of economic problems, recuperation of the country, and orientation in international politics." It also broadcast a weekly radio program, the "Voice of Argentina," to retell the "principal accomplishments of our country, accompanied by music." *Peronistas* believed that if the Peruvian people simply understood Perón's accomplishments, they would no longer content themselves with the traditional order.

> Argentina has the attention of the world at this time, and especially that of the Americas, owing to the enormous transformation it has effected . . . Naturally, Peru is interested, which raises the need for them to better understand the factors that have made possible the great changes in our country in such a short period of time.[68]

Although this propaganda campaign was directed toward universities, unions, and the masses, *peronistas* also cultivated Peruvian Army officers. According to Oderigo, a number of generals, some of whom served in President José Luis Bustamante i Rivero's cabinet, "admire the personality of General Perón and his important achievements in the social field that have permitted Argentina to become a strong, sovereign, and proud nation." This social and cultural offensive was, of course, accompanied by economic overtures as *peronistas* began to press Bustamante for a comprehensive trade agreement.[69]

---

67. Oderigo to Bramulgia, 21 Marzo 1947, AMREC, BA, Peru 1947, 12, 1; Oderigo to Bramulgia, 16 Septiembre 1947, AMREC, BA, Peru 1947, 12, 1; Memoria Anual, 1947, AMREC, BA, Peru 1947, 12, 5.

68. Memoria anual, 1947, AMREC, BA, Peru 1947, 12, 5.

69. Oderigo to Bramulgia, 21 Marzo 1947, AMREC, BA, Peru 1947, 12, 1;

Still, Bustamante himself had no illusions about the nature of Peronism, and his administration had long since dedicated itself to a close alliance with the United States. Peruvian diplomats had looked upon "Argentine penetration" of Bolivia with alarm since the days of Villarroel, when ambassador Garland had reported to his superiors that "as you undoubtedly well know," Argentines were pursuing "political and economic hegemony over Bolivia and Paraguay." If successful, Garland argued, Peronists would utilize these states as a "base of operations" for the future penetration of Chile and Peru with the obvious object "of seeking to confront the great North American power" and "counter and diminish the enormous influence which it exercises."[70] When Miranda negotiated the pact with Chile, cash-starved and deeply indebted Peru—which had not received aid of any sort from Washington in years despite its loyal support of the Allies during the war—could not but take notice.

Ambassador Ledgard was stunned that Argentina had almost instantaneously gone from "a debtor nation to a creditor nation" that even the British and Spanish owed. "This county," he announced, is certain "not to be disposed to merely sell us wheat and meat on credit," but will want "something like participation in the development of extractive industries" such as coal or oil. Although he was clearly warning his government to expect a determined trade mission from Argentina, whose "political and economic importance grows every day," he reflected Peruvian desperation when he suggested that "if all of the financial aid [Peru] requires cannot be obtained from the United States," it should look seriously at the possibility of acquiring Argentine credits.[71]

Ledgard, serving in Buenos Aires, had been impressed by the sudden transformation Perón had affected, but other Peruvian diplomats better reflected the sentiments of their government.

---

Memoria Anual, 1947, AMREC, BA, Peru 1947, 12, 5; Oderigo to Anadón, 5 Septiembre 1947, AMREC, BA, Peru 1947, 12, 1.

70. Garland a Ministro, 7 June 1946, AMRE, Lima, 5-7-Y/35.

71. Ledgard a Ministro, 10 Diciembre 1946, AMRE, Lima, 5-1-A/523; Ledgard a Ministro, 9 Diciembre 1946, AMRE, Lima, 5-1-A/519.

Garland, lamenting that "Chile fell easily into the Argentine orbit," reminded his superiors of earlier Argentine intrigues in Bolivia and Uruguay and warned that Perón was on the verge of bringing Bolivia into his "southern bloc." Ambassador Javier Correa went even further, warning that "it cannot be doubted that the Inter-American system will suffer a serious blow" if this "Argentine offensive against U.S. positions in South America" met with any success. Although Chilean officials had already made a preliminary invitation for Peru to join the customs union, this was "a moment of highest importance," as any dalliance with Perón could prejudice Washington against Peru. Whereas Hertzog hoped to draw concessions from the State Department by negotiating with Perón, Bustamante's government hoped to impress U.S. officials with its honesty and loyalty by openly spurning Argentine overtures.[72]

In early 1947, Miranda predictably made his overture, offering tariff reductions, barter, and a two hundred-million-peso credit that was to be administered in the usual fashion. He hinted that the loan could be doubled if the Peruvians were willing to promise additional iron, coal, lead, zinc, and oil exports to Argentina. These loans were to be primarily directed toward increasing production of iron and other minerals and were, of course, to be state-to-state. Miranda's motivations were again quite clear. Argentina had long needed increased amounts of oil, but the true lure was coal and iron that could fuel an Argentine steel industry. Nonetheless, Bustamante tried to stall the Argentines and avoid any commitment, hoping beyond hope for U.S. assistance and aid.[73]

For some in the State Department, these negotiations had an added significance. Ambassador Prentice Cooper reported that the Argentines were indeed attempting to use the loans to gain a voice in the Peruvian oil industry. Because a Standard Oil subsidiary,

---

72. Garland a Ministro, 30 Diciembre 1946, AMRE, Lima, 5-7-Y/65; Correa a Ministro, 23 Diciembre 1946, AMRE, Lima, 5-4-Y/50; Correa a Ministro, 29 Diciembre 1946, AMRE, Lima, 5-4-Y/52.

73. O'Malley to Secretary of State, 3 March 1947, RG 59, 623.3531; Cooper to Secretary of State, 12 March 1947, RG 59, 623.3531; Cooper to Secretary of State, 14 March 1947, RG 59, 623.3531.

International Petroleum Corporation, owned a good percentage of the oil producing and refining facilities in Peru, this could easily "work against American interest[s]." Even more disastrous, the Argentines were apparently looking to secure a Peruvian petroleum export quota of eight hundred thousand tons per year that might feasibly do irreparable damage to U.S. firms. To prevent this eventuality, Cooper informally requested that the Peruvian government allow him to view and comment on any treaty prior to its signing. Bustamante agreed and kept him well informed of every Argentine move that hinted of economic pressure. When Cooper was told that Miranda had almost doubled the price of wheat to apply pressure and "further weaken Peru's exchange position," he urged his superiors to heed Bustamante's calls for aid. He pleaded with his superiors to send emergency food shipments to negate this "hard bargaining on the part of Argentina," and even requested that U.S. banks be encouraged to offer loans to Peru.[74]

When the Peruvian government appealed for credits and wheat, Acheson regretfully turned down any long-term guarantee, citing the "world supply situation and relief needs." Still, throughout 1947, Cooper was more successful in arranging a number of food shipments that did allow Bustamante to hold the Argentines at bay. In October 1948, however, Bustamante's government fell to Perón's personal friend, General Manuel Odría, and the Argentines renewed their interest in a treaty. Concerned that a commercial pact might materialize and cement political ties between these two natural allies, the State Department waded in. Fearful that offering U.S. wheat at this late date would be interpreted as a blatant intervention "that would be pretty difficult to justify," embassy officials moved quietly to arrange a sale of Canadian wheat to Peru. Ambassador Harold Tittmann presented a memorandum to the Peruvian Foreign Office that was intended to discourage Odría from allying himself with Perón.

> The Embassy left [the memorandum] with [the Foreign Minister] with some confidence that 'the informal approach'

---

74. Cooper to Secretary of State, 22 March 1947, RG 59, 623.3531; U.S. Embassy Lima to Secretary of State, 7 April 1947, RG 59, 623.3531.

would dissuade the Peruvian Government from completing an arrangement with the Argentine Government. Ambassador Tittmann understands that the memorandum was before the Ministers 'with good effect' when they decided to abandon the Argentine project.[75]

Although the State Department was exuberant that this quiet intervention succeeded in dissuading Odría, it nonetheless feared that the memorandum might eventually fall into Argentine hands and had to decide "whether we should or can cover ourselves" from this eventuality. T. R. Martin succinctly recommended that, "since the worst we appear to have done on the record, is to protect American interests," "we should merely hope for the best." He added a warning that "we should certainly stop trying to sell Canadian wheat or arrange for a Canadian loan." Despite their fears of "political repercussions" "which might have been serious," if Perón learned of the intervention, the matter never appears to have become public information. Off the record, Tittmann had undoubtedly reassured Odría and his ministers that they had far more to gain from a close alliance with the United States, in what was one of the first, tentative steps toward the formation of a very close working relationship throughout the 1950s.[76]

Again, the State Department had utilized quiet persuasion to impede Argentine economic expansion as the prospects for Perón's third initiative faded. While Perón had accused Washington of subverting his overtures to Chile and Bolivia, he never recognized the blatant interference that had undercut what might have been his most promising potential alliance.

## V

---

75. Martin to Tewksbury, 21 March 1947, RG 59, 623.3531.

76. TRM to RSA and HHT, 14 February 1949, RG 59, 623.3531 (misfiled in 625.3531); Martin to Tewksbury, 31 March 1949, RG 59, 623.3531 (misfiled in 625.3531).

What appears out of these inter-American relations in the 1946-1948 period are several consistent patterns and themes. South American nations repeatedly attempted to gain the attention of the Yankee colossus by reporting incidents of Argentine economic pressure or political expansion. This can especially be seen in late 1946 and early 1947 when the upper echelons of the State Department were bombarded regularly with appeals for emergency aid to counter real or imagined *peronista* threats. The State Department examined each situation as it arose, but there were several attempts to solve the problem with a stroke of the pen.[77]

The first proposal, authored by Clayton at the end of 1946, was little more than a calculated bluff. Recognizing that "insecurity in Uruguay, Bolivia, Brazil and Peru" regarding "wheat and flour imports places these countries in weak bargaining position with Argentina," he suggested that the State Department unilaterally state its intent to "supply [the] minimum requirements" of every nation in South America. This would "so strengthen their position vis-à-vis Argentina that latter would see little or no gain in [the] continuance [of its] present tactics." Such an approach, he argued, might well lead *peronistas* to adopt a more "reasonable attitude."[78] Clayton noted that due to the global food shortage the State Department would be unable to underwrite this pledge if the bluff was called, but hoped that the announcement itself would be enough. Messersmith argued against such a course, suggesting that South American nations, assured of an alternative source of food, would immediately stonewall Perón. Since the State Department would not be able to fulfill the promise, the United States would lose prestige and credibility and hand Perón more victories.[79]

The second proposal from the Office of American Republics Affairs was far more radical and far-reaching. According to this

---

77. Smith to Braden, 20 September 1946, RG 59, 810.61311.

78. Clayton to Embassy Buenos Aires, 23 September 1946, RG 59, 835.61311.

79. Messersmith to Secretary of State, 24 September 1946, RG 59, 835.61311.

proposition, "all non-political considerations—of classical economics and the like—must be subordinated to the over-riding exigencies" of containing Perón. Because the Argentines were "driving country after country to political subservience" through their "economic stranglehold" on South America's food supply, the solution was to make Perón's neighbors and Great Britain agriculturally self-sufficient. The United States could accomplish this by offering loans, technical assistance, improvement of food-conservation methods, and shipments of seed. Sounder minds shot down the proposal as well, arguing that even if the program was "economically feasible," it was the antithesis of U.S. global goals of regional specialization, maximization of world trade, and efficient multilateralism. Not only would the British need to maintain the Imperial Preference system but driving other nations to autarchic self-sufficiency was at best foolhardy. Like Clayton's proposition, this one died stillborn, and the State Department was forced to deal with the problem of Argentine economic expansionism piecemeal.[80] What was notable about this outlandish proposal was that some elements of the State Department were so fearful of *peronismo* that they were apparently willing to overhaul the State Department's entire global economic program to contain it.

Unable to arrive at a comprehensive policy to deal with Argentina's powerful position as a food exporter in the immediate post-war period, the State Department nevertheless ably combated the threat until the food crisis ebbed. Even though the State Department rarely responded tangibly to these appeals, merely intimating that Yankee economic power might be brought to bear often proved to be sufficient to "spike the deal."[81] Even though Washington chafed under the Good Neighbor pledges of non-intervention, it found ways to enforce its will. It is something of a testament to the strength of U.S. hegemony in the Western Hemisphere that Perón's relatively adroit attempts to strike at its weakest point were so effortlessly rebuffed. The State Department was able to maintain its minimalist approach to South America

---

80. Gilmore to Mann, 15 October 1946, RG 59, 835.50.

81. Maleady to Secretary of State, 10 September 1947, RG 84, BA.

without making serious concessions or adopting a truly constructive policy. As Stephen Rabe noted, U.S. policymakers were unwilling to seriously consider broad measures to improve Latin American economic conditions that could preclude the development of communist or nationalist menaces but were content to do damage control for oligarchies like the Bolivian *rosca* whenever such a danger arose. While an economically united, strong "United States of Europe" was deemed vital to the American way of life and the New Deal order, the New Dealers needed a weak, divided and subordinate Latin America that accepted privatism. Thus, at the same time they were pushing European collaboration and economic integration, the State Department resisted every Peronist initiative outright. Although these minor, quiet U.S. "interventions" were camouflaged during the 1940s, the day was soon coming when subtle, peaceful policies were no longer sufficient to preserve the unified hemisphere and combat economic nationalism like Perón's.[82]

The full implications of Perón's industrialization program also become apparent through his international intrigues. Although observers could paint dreams of heavy industry in Argentina as unpractical, if not fantastic, there was clearly method to the madness. Even though Argentina lacked the mineral resources to become a classic industrial power, South America as a whole possessed them in abundance. As U.S. businessmen were fond of proclaiming, all that was needed was the capital to exploit these resources. Perón's government had it for a time. U.S. businessmen and diplomats may have sneered at Argentine attempts to contract for tin plate mills, copper smelters, and steel plants, but the Peronists obviously had ideas that they believed might have made these grand projects feasible.[83]

---

82. Rabe, "The Elusive Conference," 279-294; Hogan, *The Marshall Plan*.

83. For example, the Republic Steel's representative told a Department officer that his firm was bidding to build an Argentine steel mill at the behest of the government. When informed that such a project was "economically unsound," the businessman said, "Of course, but the trend nowadays in most countries was to have their own steel industries." Memorandum of Conversation, Lyon and Stephan, 2 December 1947, RG 59, 835.5034.

In this respect, Braden and his backers may have been correct in warning of the implications of Perón. He clearly had a somewhat coherent plan for national development and the centralized organization to carry it out. There can also be no doubt that this program was one that directly defied the United States. Even if Braden overreacted to the "southern bloc," it was, for a time, the major threat to U.S. interests in South America. From the standpoint of preserving U.S. hegemony, the State Department did well to take Perón's gambits as seriously as they did.

# CHAPTER 7

## THE CHANGING OF THE GUARD, JANUARY-JULY 1947

> Permit me to note that the opposition that Mr. Braden is encountering . . . owes principally not to a difference between the objective which he proposes and that of his opponents, but to a question of method or procedure to attain the same end.
>
> Luis Luti, 30 January 1946[1]

### I

In the wake of Perón's abortive alliance building at the end of 1946, Messersmith's heretofore unsuccessful campaign to sell his government on his new appraisal of Perón ground to a complete halt. He had attempted to portray Perón as a well-intentioned opportunist, but these initiatives demonstrated that the Argentine was unrepentant and, in some ways, more dangerous than Braden had originally guessed. For Braden, however, they seemed to prove that he had been correct all along in warning of Perón's "Nazi tendencies" and expansionist ambitions. The stage was set for the outbreak of full-fledged bureaucratic warfare between Messersmith and Braden as these two strong-willed antagonists drew battle lines and mustered allies for the brawl that ultimately ended the illustrious careers of both. As Messersmith continued to enthusiastically present the carrot to Perón, attempting to lure him to abandon state corporatism, Braden branded his ambassador an appeaser. In Braden's eyes, Messersmith had been hoodwinked by the charismatic Perón and had abandoned the guiding principles of U.S. foreign policy in the process.

---

1. Luti to Cooke, 30 Enero 1947, AMREC, BA, EEUU, 1946, 8, 2.

When Truman opted to end their conflict by removing both warring diplomats in mid-1947, it brought an opportunity to better enact the approach formulated in April 1946. New Ambassador James Bruce was dispatched to Buenos Aires to complete the task started by Messersmith and was to give an outward appearance of friendliness at the same time he fomented dissent within Perón's own coalition and cabinet. The State Department had accepted that Perón would be in power for the foreseeable future, and to some extent Messersmith's assertions that he could serve as a bulwark against even more radical nationalists and communists, but it was far from content with his continued experiments in statist corporatism. On the other hand, Bruce's efforts to tear the wheels out from under Peronism ultimately proved to be far more effective than Braden's as he came to represent a synthesis of the two approaches.

## II

The first salvos of the Messersmith-Braden feud were fired in mid-1946, and in retrospect, were probably inevitable. Although the two men had enjoyed a certain mutual respect during the war, Perón was simply too divisive. Braden would not rest until Argentine "fascism," personified in his mind by Perón, had been eliminated, whereas Messersmith had linked his career and prestige to rapprochement. Both protagonists had a high personal stake in the affair and were confident that their superiors endorsed their stance. Needless to say, neither was willing to tolerate compromise.[2]

Difficulties between the two diplomats dated back to the closing days of Messersmith's tenure in Mexico when, to avoid a diplomatic incident, he had facilitated the landing of a shipment of Brazilian cattle that later proved to have been infected with *aftosa*. To prevent the spread of the disease across the Rio Grande and preserve U.S.-Mexican harmony, the Truman Administration spent more than one hundred million dollars to assist Mexican efforts to purge their herds of the disease. Even biographer Jesse Stiller,

---

2. Stiller, *George S. Messersmith*, 240-242.

usually sympathetic to Messersmith, concluded that the ambassador probably had "presented [Washington's] objections with insufficient emphasis" to Mexico City. Acheson and Braden were far less charitable. In Acheson's confused account of the episode, the bulls were landed with "Messersmith's collusion, if not consent," whereas Braden later blamed the entire fiasco on Messersmith's "insubordination."[3]

Despite this debacle, Messersmith was given the critical posting in Buenos Aires and had reason to believe that he still enjoyed the support of his superiors. Before leaving for Argentina, he had spoken at length with both Truman and Byrnes and was convinced that they shared his views and trusted his judgment. After all, they had asked that he take the crucial and difficult job in spite of his deteriorating health. Secure in the knowledge that he had been given a mandate for rapprochement, Messersmith forged ahead, "rightly and properly brooking no authority other than [his] own."[4] With Clayton and other senior officials behind him, he had little concern for Braden. After all, Truman, Byrnes, and Acheson had excluded Braden from the White House conference in which Messersmith was given his instructions, tacitly suggesting that the assistant secretary could be overlooked. Ironically, the ambassador had been so convinced that Braden was about to be put out to pasture that he had sent unsolicited advice to his superiors, urging that Braden be retained for the good of the Argentine policy. He would soon have cause to regret that action.[5]

Just as he thought he could be confident in the support of his superiors, Messersmith had the backing of the other foreign

---

3. Stiller, *Messersmith*, 242-243; Dean Acheson, *Present at the Creation* (New York, 1954), 189-190; Braden, *Diplomats and Demagogues*, 359; see also M. Ugarte to Bramulgia, AMREC, BA, Mexico 1947, 12, 5.

4. Bohan, "The Department of State-A Study of Futility," Bohan Papers, Reference File, HST.

5. Messersmith to Byrnes, 15 June 1946, in *FRUS* IX, 258-259; see also Messersmith Memorandum, 25 January 1947, RG 59, 711.35; Messersmith to Byrnes, 30 October 1946, Messersmith Papers, 1813; Stiller, *George S. Messersmith*, 220-230.

service officers in Buenos Aires.[6] In December, he polled his underlings to get their opinions on whether there ever had been or still was a valid "Case against Argentina." Almost the entire embassy staff, many of them veterans of both Hull's and Braden's crusades, supported Messersmith's stance. Although it must not be forgotten that these individuals were serving directly under him and were naturally inclined to see things his way for that very reason, their comments and assessments are telling, as the embassy staff went on the record against their assistant secretary of state.

Howard Tewksbury, Messersmith's astute economic counselor, blamed both U.S. and Argentine decisions for the poor relations and singled out Braden's speeches as the most destructive factor. While he admitted that Argentines had somehow repudiated "democratic principles" by electing Perón, he made it clear that attacks from the north only strengthened Argentine nationalism and its foremost spokesman. Not surprisingly, he praised the "complete change in the official attitude of the Argentine government" since Messersmith's arrival in Buenos Aires.[7]

Another aide, Joseph Apodaca, echoed this assessment and went so far as to argue that "viewed dispassionately," Perón's program was "entirely compatible with the maintenance of free enterprise, private initiative, and the principles of capitalism." However, individuals such as Miranda and Figuerola, the "brains behind the throne," were subverting the regime. These economic nationalists were "confusing and befuddling" Perón in an attempt to contaminate him with the "same sort of psychosis" that had long ago infected them. The solution, Apodaca suggested, was exactly what Messersmith was doing—encouraging Perón to rid himself of these sinister influences and their destructive ideas. Echoing

---

6. Messersmith's position with his superiors was not nearly as strong as he believed it to be. Messersmith shared the common opinion that Acheson had very little knowledge of Latin America and emphatically told the undersecretary so on at least one occasion. The ambassador's haughty demeanor had also made an impression on Truman. According to Truman, Messersmith had on one notable occasion called "to tell me how to run the gov[ernmen]t." Stiller, *Messersmith*, 220, 236.

7. Tewksbury to Messersmith, 6 December 1946, Messersmith Papers, 1826.

Messersmith's call to be a "good friend" to the president, Apodaca pleaded that the State Department must assist Perón and moderate Argentines lest the dangerous ideologues triumph.[8]

Gerald Smith also attacked Braden's thesis directly and questioned whether there even was a "Case against Argentina." Argentina, he asserted, had been singled out for its neutrality and late declaration of war, he claimed, but a number of Latin American nations had made their own declarations less than three months earlier, if at all. He ridiculed Braden's belief that ninety thousand Germans and twelve million dollars of German investments in Argentina were "a serious threat to peace and security of the world." "Any fair-minded person" could only conclude that the "Case against Argentina" was overblown, the Argentines were "intensifying their efforts" to comply with U.S. dictates, and Braden's "be tough" policy had failed.[9]

Kenneth Oakley took these arguments a step further. "Many persons superficially familiar with the 'Case against Argentina'" he argued, "believe that Buenos Aires during the war was a hotbed of the most effective espionage and sabotage. It was a hotbed, but it was not effective," as German agents in Argentina had not caused any real damage to the war effort. Arguing that the charge that Perón and the Germans had been responsible for the 1943 coup in Bolivia was equally groundless, he concluded that Argentina had not given appreciable "aid and comfort to the enemy." Oakley then turned to the question of whether the Perón regime was "Nazi-Fascist inspired." He knew of no political prisoners in Argentina and reminded Messersmith that the president had released a number of potential revolutionaries whose "freedom represented a positive and considerable threat" to the government. If there was a fascist economic program, he, like Apodaca, blamed it upon Perón's "bad and incompetent" advisors, rather than the president, who was a "moderately intelligent man with an extraordinarily likeable personality, an almost limitless ambition, no

---

8. Apodaca to Messersmith, 5 December 1946, Messersmith Papers, 1825.

9. Smith to Messersmith, 4 December 1946, Messersmith Papers, 1823.

political education worthy of its name, and with basic convictions readily subject to change."

Oakley naturally had little use for Braden, his exaggerated *Blue Book* accusations, and his fears of a "southern bloc." Considering the *Blue Book* to have been little more than "yellow journalism" that had "failed to convince Latin Americans that Perón was to be feared," he ridiculed fears that Argentina was a military threat to the peace of South America by citing Braden's own assessments of Argentine armament levels. Because Argentina could not assemble a "southern bloc" by force, the U.S. had only to fear binding treaties and customs unions. But even this was no real threat due to the nationalism, protectionism, and mistrust of Argentina that dominated the region. He wryly cautioned his countrymen that reducing trade barriers was generally a good thing and very difficult under any circumstances, as anyone familiar with Hull's efforts in the 1930s should have known. In short, the "Case against Argentina" "sadly fails to add up to a reason to refuse our cooperation with Argentina."[10]

Even if Messersmith was buoyed by this show of solidarity at the embassy, the leading proponent of the "Case against Argentina" had equally valid reasons to believe that he spoke for the State Department. Braden interpreted his retention in office as a sign of support. After all, anyone who knew Braden knew that unseating Perón had become almost an obsession and that he would never be party to any arrangement that smacked of "appeasement." Truman and Byrnes were allowing Braden single-handedly to forestall the negotiation of a vital hemispheric defense pact—a position that brought the administration into conflict with both the Army and Senate. Braden thought he possessed even more concrete proof that his superiors approved of both his program and his tactics. Byrnes, in his weekly press reports, periodically directed a blast in Perón's direction and referred regularly to Argentine "fascism." Most importantly, when Braden presented Truman with three policy alternatives to deal with Perón on July 12, the president emphatically endorsed his hard line.[11] Braden later

---

10. Oakley to Messersmith, 12 December 1946, Messersmith Papers, 1832.

11. Braden, "Memorandum of the Argentine Situation to President Truman,"

claimed that on one occasion, Truman had "observed that George [Messersmith] was an s.o.b. and would be fired." Thus, he proceeded, confident that the president shared his opinions. Before the end of 1946, Braden would be attacking his insubordinate and apparently wrong-headed ambassador as vigorously as he had attacked Perón a year earlier, and with the same certainty that he would be vindicated.[12]

Braden seems to have fired the first shots as early as July 1946 in an attempt to bring his ambassador into line. He sent his "Memorandum on the Argentine Situation" to the embassy, noting that Truman had endorsed a "get tough" policy toward Perón. Messersmith sent a flurry of dispatches in response, claiming that he had not in his many years of service received a communication "which has caused me in certain respects more concern." Denying that he was in any way "selling out" or "'toadying' to Perón," Messersmith reiterated that he was only facilitating rapprochement at the Department's behest and went on to claim that if anyone had erred, it was Braden, whose interventionism had caused no small part of the damage that needed repairing.[13]

The struggle between the strong-willed adversaries intensified and escalated as both appealed to their superiors. Acheson vainly tried to patch the cracks by offering false reassurances to Messersmith that no one was trying to undermine his position or have him removed. Acheson also tried to smooth over the difficulties by insisting that there was no fundamental difference between the two positions. The only area where the two disagreed was what comprised "adequate compliance" with the Chapultepec resolutions. He reminded both that Truman himself would decide if and when Perón had complied, so it was pointless for either of them to expend energy trying to make that decision. Unfortunately, this did not satisfy either diplomat: Braden was set

---

12 July 1946, PSF, Foreign Affairs, Argentina, HST.

12. Jesse Stiller, *Messersmith*, 232-250, 255.

13. Messersmith to Secretary of State, 26 July 1946, in *FRUS* IX, 285-286; Messersmith to Secretary of State, 15 August 1946, in *FRUS* IX, 297-298; Messersmith to Secretary of State, 16 August 1946, in *FRUS* IX, 302-303.

upon crushing Perón and his defiant ambassador, and Messersmith was equally determined to succeed in his mission and stop the calumny that was sullying his name.[14]

Messersmith, at least, seems to have interpreted Acheson's mandate to mean that he had to convince Truman, Byrnes, and Clayton that Perón was a worthy partner and a potential ally. Although he claimed that he did not want to become an "apologist for or a defender of the Argentine Government," he very quickly became one, as his dispatches degenerated from reasonably objective, highly detailed assessments (which had earned him the nickname "Forty-Page George") to favorable publicity reports for Perón. Despite this, it is probably somewhat unfair to conclude that "Messersmith fell under Perón's spell as soon as he had landed in Buenos Aires."[15] Messersmith was a career diplomat with a well-earned reputation for toughness. While Perón's charisma was legendary, and he undoubtedly had succeeded in manipulating or duping the ambassador from time to time, Messersmith was no one's lackey. Yet, as Stiller noted, a discernable change in both the tone and content of Messersmith's reports can be seen in late 1946 and early 1947 as Braden's attacks intensified.[16]

Messersmith's assessment of the threat of communism in Argentina was the most notable change. Even though he had earlier agreed with Braden in dismissing Soviet intrigues as almost unworthy of attention, by October, he had become "very deeply preoccupied" with the "tremendous play" being made by the Soviets in Argentina. He warned that the Soviet penetration would come to naught, only "if we handle this thing right," and suggested that further hostility toward Argentina could only drive Perón into

---

14. Acheson to Messersmith, 29 August 1946, RG 59. 835.00; Memorandum of Conversation, Burrows and Spaeth, "on or about June 24," Messersmith Papers, 1794; see also Messersmith to Byrnes, 30 October 1946, Messersmith Papers, 1813; Messersmith to Truman, 5 October 1946, PSF, Foreign Affairs, Argentina, HST; Escudé, *Gran Bretaña, Estados Unidos*, 198-214.

15. Messersmith to Simmons, 3 March 1947, RG 84, BA; Joseph Tulchin, *Argentina and the United States*, 94.

16. Stiller, *George S. Messersmith*, 255-256.

the waiting arms of the Soviets. He added an interesting touch by suggesting that the Soviets were showing "an unusual interest in getting in touch with" corporations being targeted for "denazification," as these firms "have special resentments with respect to us." Interestingly, at the same time the Central Intelligence Group was notifying Truman that South America in general, and Argentina in particular, were in no real danger from communism, Messersmith was issuing alarmist warnings.[17] Perón may not have played his "Russian card," but Messersmith was playing it on his behalf.

The ambassador also stepped up his warnings that the British were moving to snatch the entire lucrative Argentine market and would succeed if Braden's antagonism did not abate. While Messersmith had always been a proponent of an Anglo-American united front against Argentine nationalism, he abruptly changed his tune in October. He informed Clayton that the British were giving "lip service" to cooperation, at the same time they used Argentina as the "spearhead against what they consider too great economic penetration by us in this hemisphere." Messersmith further warned that with the signing of the Miranda-Eady Treaty (which, of course, he had facilitated), Britain was now in perfect position to strengthen its commercial ties with Perón as the U.S. dallied. He presented no evidence to support this new interpretation of British designs but did counsel Clayton to be careful lest U.S. policy "create a very unfavorable position for ourselves" in Argentina.[18]

Even though Messersmith had always declared that Perón was not trying to assemble an autarchic bloc, he now warned that U.S. antagonism might drive the Argentines to it. Just as Braden's policies were pushing Perón into the hands of the Soviets and the

---

17. Messersmith to Clayton, 31 October 1946, Messersmith Papers, 1815; Messersmith to Clayton, 2 October 1946, RG 59, 611.3531; see also Messersmith Memorandum, 25 January 1947, RG 59, 711.35; Central Intelligence Group, "Soviet Objectives in Latin America," 10 April 1947, PSF, Intelligence File, CIA Reports, 1947, HST.

18. Messersmith to Clayton, 31 October 1946, Messersmith Papers, 1815; see also Messersmith Memorandum, 25 January 1947, RG 59, 711.35; MacDonald, "The U.S., Britain, and Argentina," 183-199.

British, they were encouraging him to engage in an adventuristic foreign policy. A "southern bloc" was not the ambassador's only fear. Out of desperation, Perón might try to form a Hispanic bloc, incorporating most of Latin America and Falangist Spain, or simply ally himself with Franco.[19]

Still, Messersmith's most unlikely turnabout came in his assessment of Miranda. He had throughout his tenure reported that Perón's "economic czar" was "quite unfriendly or at least deeply critical of the United States." In March 1947, however, he tried to sell a "completely changed" Miranda as "one of the principal exponents" of "close collaboration with the United States" and claimed him to be one of the "two most capable men in the Argentine cabinet." When Miranda informed him that he would be cutting military spending by half within a year, Messersmith advertised this development to repudiate Braden's claims that Peronist Argentina was militaristic and expansionist. To defeat Braden, Messersmith was suddenly exonerating the one Argentine that the State Department and the embassy staff had long since singled out as the most dangerous *peronista*.[20]

Some of Messersmith's other proclamations are similarly suspect. His defense of the Five-Year plan is a case in point. While the plan was certainly not as malevolent as Braden's allies asserted, Messersmith downplayed or ignored measures that he privately thought unwise, dangerous, or unsound. He was, on the whole, remarkably tolerant of statism for a U.S. official, but the Five-Year Plan clearly surpassed anything he had ever endorsed. He notified Byrnes that the Argentine industrialists' society, the UIA (which Perón had dissolved in 1946), had reconstituted itself and its formerly hostile members were backing the plan. This was at best a distortion. A number of "collaborationists" like Miranda had always served in the UIA's leadership, but most important industrialists still despised Perón. The UIA that had been recreated from the ashes of the old was but a shadow of the earlier

---

19. Hoyt to Briggs, Wright and Mann, 19 March 1947, RG 59, MRIC-ARG.

20. Messersmith to Secretary of State, 12 March 1947, Messersmith Papers, 1857.

organization. Even Perón conceded that Argentine businessmen were not cooperating with the Five-Year Plan. Messersmith accused pro-Braden journalists of "sending up the most screwy kind of stuff," but was sending some very suspect interpretations of his own to Washington.[21]

These efforts achieved little but provided more and more ammunition for Braden and grist for journalists' mills as Messersmith became openly insubordinate. He started sending his dispatches over Braden's head and was increasingly critical of his iconoclastic superior. Unfortunately, more than fifty of his inflammatory letters apparently made it into Braden's hands, with predictable results. By 1947, the antics of Messersmith and Braden were overshadowing the Argentine policy itself and causing an unnecessary headache for an administration that was trying to cement consensus for the Marshall Plan and the Truman Doctrine. Although Byrnes had tolerated or ignored the feud, either hoping it would simply fade away or fearing the attention that would be drawn by any strong action, his retirement in early 1947 paved the way for Truman to cut the Gordian knot.[22]

### III

In June 1947, new Secretary of State George Marshall ended the feud by simply eradicating it. On the fourth, Messersmith was informed that his resignation had been accepted. He had not tendered one and was "completely in the dark as to what has been happening." Soon thereafter, Braden was likewise surprised to discover that Truman had accepted his resignation as well. In his memoirs, Braden claimed that he had voluntarily submitted his resignation earlier but had delayed in making it public to be certain Messersmith was fired first. Supposedly, he was only surprised that

---

21. Messersmith to Cabot, 28 September 1946, Cabot Papers, Argentina, HST; see also Messersmith to Clayton, 21 October 1946, RG 59, 835.50; Messersmith to Byrnes, 30 October 1946, Messersmith Papers, 1814; *Review of the River Plate*, 28 March 1947, 12; Lewis, *Crisis of Argentine Capitalism*, 155-157.

22. Stiller, *Messersmith*, 256-259.

Marshall's office had leaked the news prematurely. Whether Braden submitted to his fate voluntarily or not, both men and their bickering had become a colossal and unnecessary embarrassment to an administration that hardly needed another one.[23]

Although it was virtually inevitable that both men had to go sooner or later, the timing of the firings is interesting. Truman and Marshall, who had been in office for several months, appear to have been willing to allow the feud to continue unmolested until they were spurred into action, at least in part, by a bold British initiative. On May 16, Marshall was informed that Great Britain was in the process of selling Perón one hundred Meteor jet fighters and thirty Lincoln bombers. Messersmith had informed Acheson in mid-1946 that "Argentina has nothing that approaches a modern first-line military plane," but Perón was taking a major step to rectify that deficiency.[24] While Whitehall had announced that it was opting out of the "Gentlemen's Agreement" arms embargo a month earlier, it had also pledged to limit sales to Argentina to "certain spare parts and replacements." Sir John Magowan tried to joke about the deal, jibing that "You want to see British exports increased, don't you?" Marshall, however, was furious at this "dramatic British intervention," and vaguely threatened Whitehall with retaliation.[25]

Even George Kennan, who only rarely concerned himself with Latin America, took notice of this deal, its implications for the balance of power in South America, and the future of the arms standardization program. With the doors opened to arms infusions from England, Sweden, and even the Czech Skoda Works, the State Department had to lift its unilateral embargo and hold the Inter-American Defense Conference quickly. The U.S. Navy joined the Army and Messersmith in calling for an end to the embargo, for it was on the verge of selling a cruiser, four destroyers, three submarines, and their own planes to Argentina. Braden, who was

---

23. Messersmith to Truman and Marshall, 6 June 1947, Messersmith Papers, 1893; Braden, *Diplomats and Demagogues*, 369-370.

24. Messersmith to Acheson, 6 June 1946, Cabot Papers, Argentina, HST.

25. Memorandum of Conversation, Lyon and Magowan, 5 May 1947, RG 57, 635.4131; Marshall to Bevin, 17 May 1947, RG 59, 735.4113.

blocking any effort to hold the conference or sell arms, had to go, and Messersmith had to follow lest the charge of "appeasement" taint the Truman Administration as it was staining the ambassador.[26]

But if Messersmith's "appeasement" was one major problem, Braden had his own crosses to bear, as red-baiting opponents found him to be an easy target. Despite his conservatism, Braden had always enjoyed the backing of leftists who believed that Perón's and Franco's brand of "fascism" represented the greatest threat to peace in the post-war period. This had naturally opened him up to charges of being soft on communism. Vandenberg, Connally, and other Cold Warriors had long argued that his campaign against Perón was ripping apart the hemisphere at a time when it needed to be united against the communist menace. "Our Braden-dictated policy," one newspaper concluded grimly, "has suited the Commies to a 'T.'"[27]

But Braden had ably rebuffed these challenges until March 1947, when Congressman Alvin O'Konski of Wisconsin unleashed a savage barrage on the floor of Congress. Presaging the revelations of Joseph McCarthy, O'Konski informed the House of Representatives that "what I will say to you is so fantastic that it will be difficult to believe." He began by detailing the career of Braden's trusted friend and "selected protégé," Spanish Republican refugee Gustavo Duran. This "notorious communist," O'Konski argued, had personally assisted Braden in "creating a feeling of suspicion between the countries of South America and the United States, enabling the Soviet government to enter into favorable trade negotiations with the Republic of Argentina." All of Duran and Braden's activities in Argentina were, in short, "in complete accord with the Communist fellow travelers and pink journalists in America and the State Department."

---

26. Kennan to Johnson, 30 July 1947, RG 59, Records of the Policy Planning Staff, 1947-1953, Country and Area Files; Messersmith to Marshall, 21 February 1947, Messersmith Papers, 1851; Briggs to Acheson, 13 June 1946, RG 59, 835.24.

27. *Times Herald*, 18 June 1946; see also Drago to Embajador, 6 Diciembre 1946, AMREC, BA, EEUU 1946, 8, 1; Stiller, *Messersmith*, 237-260.

O'Konski then laid out his unlikely version of Braden's campaign against Perón. According to the congressman, Braden had been duped by Duran and the communists. Duran was an old acquaintance of Jacob Potofsky, the Russian immigrant who had for a time worked with Sidney Hillman to improve U.S.-Soviet relations. As head of the CIO's Latin American Committee, Potofsky had maintained close contact with Mexican communist chieftain Lombardo Toledano. Toledano, following orders from Moscow, had urged the State Department to do "something more than words" to prevent Perón's ascension. According to O'Konski, Braden, manipulated by Duran and Potofsky, had responded by issuing the "infamous" *Blue Book*. With the "seeds of dissention" between the U.S. and Latin America well sown, the communists had to cover their tracks. At this point, Moscow, "in true Marxian style," started to attack Braden for his "imperialistic" intervention "to hide the real object and purpose." "So today," O'Konski maintained, "the communists are using their *Blue Book*, issued by our own State Department, as a basis to poison the South American people against the United States." As a result of this perfidious communist plot, "anybody can get elected to any office in South America merely by denouncing Braden."

In closing the speech, O'Konski made his true objective known.

> We are now being told by our State Department that we must stop Communism in Greece. To that I answer . . . let's first oust the communist stooges and their dupes in the State Department. . . Let's begin with Braden.[28]

O'Konski and those who echoed his ludicrous accusations and innuendos did succeed in making Braden's retention increasingly costly. Although he may have been a valuable tool to keep Perón in line, he was opening the Truman Administration to serious criticism. In light of efforts to secure a Cold War

---

28. O'Konski Speech, 13 March 1947, AMREC, BA, EEUU 1946, 6, 1; see also unsigned Top-Secret Memorandum, 5 March 1947, James Bruce Papers, University of Maryland Library, College Park, MD.

consensus, Braden's service was becoming far more trouble than it was worth. He was becoming a lightning rod for criticism that inevitably reflected poorly on the administration, whereas Messersmith was failing in his mission to convert Perón and helping to make a mockery of the State Department in the process. Although Merwin Bohan claimed that "you can't tell me that [Braden] didn't deserve more from the U.S. government *and* from Dean Acheson," Marshall and Truman washed their hands of both diplomats, more or less simultaneously, hoping for an end to the sensationalism that had characterized U.S.-Argentine relations for the past several years.[29]

Concurrently, Truman announced that Argentina had been adequately "denazified." This too appears to have been an almost entirely arbitrary decision. Just months earlier, Truman, Acheson, Vandenberg, and Connally had met with Argentine ambassador Oscar Ivanissevich at the White House to discuss "denazification." At this show of bipartisan unity, Truman had informed the Argentine that for relations to be normalized, Perón still had to deport twenty or thirty important Nazis. In spite of the fact that Perón did next to nothing in the next two months to expedite the deportation of these "agents," Truman had no qualms about announcing that Argentina had at last "complied." Ironically, it was only with Messersmith's fall that his mission to formally normalize relations succeeded.[30]

## IV

Without the Messersmith-Braden feud to cloud the issue, U.S. policymakers were able to more clearly define their goals, as officials in Buenos Aires and Washington coordinated their actions to effectively implement the strategy, they had developed in 1946.

---

29. Bohan Oral History, 46; see also MacDonald, "The US, the Cold War, and Perón," 407; May, "The Bureaucratic Politics Approach," 154-155.

30. Memorandum of Conversation, Vandenberg, Connally, Ivanissevich, Acheson, and Truman, 31 March 1947, RG 59, 711.35.

In this task, new ambassador James Bruce quickly discovered that he had unexpected allies in the Argentine Army who had little use for Eva Perón or her ally, Miranda. Washington recognized the potential implications of this rift and, having finally discovered a "good stick," shifted its policies to exploit and widen it.

Bruce, a dairy executive, was one of the New Deal's many businessmen-cum-diplomats who had little experience with formal diplomacy. He agreed to take what Truman described as "the most difficult diplomatic post I've ever asked anyone to take" despite possessing almost no knowledge of Argentina, but with the promise that if he was successful, he would be named ambassador to England. His chief virtue seemed to be his campaign contributions to and indefatigable work on behalf of the Democratic Party, which made him an unlikely candidate to succeed where professionals like Braden and Messersmith had failed. Therefore, he relied heavily upon his skilled and far more knowledgeable subordinate, Guy Ray.[31]

In an unusually long and candid dispatch, Ray laid out their assessment of the Argentine situation. Acknowledging that Perón "has many Nazi-Fascist ideas," Ray nonetheless asserted that he was better categorized as an opportunistic "man on horseback" who simply "loves power." Perón was not "the absolute dictator he is so often depicted as being," but a traditional *caudillo* who was "saddled" with "unscrupulous" counselors like Miranda and a wife who "could be briefly and accurately described as a national Argentine headache." Because of the weakness of the democratic opposition, a sad product of its own ineptitude and selective *peronista* repression, Ray reiterated that Perón was in power to stay.[32]

According to Ray, the U.S. now faced two choices. The State Department could either give him a "cold shoulder" that would "succeed in making him aware of our moral disapproval of him and his Government," but would also fail "to accomplish anything useful," or it could be "completely friendly" in order to

---

31. James Bruce, *Memoirs* (Baltimore, 1997), 245-246.

32. Ray to Secretary of State, 5 January 1948, RG 59, 711.35.

"obtain what advantages and concessions we can from him." Ray prophesied that "if we play our cards right, we can strengthen Perón in defending himself against the extreme nationalists," and in the process, turn Argentina in the proper direction.[33] Since he was advocating an end to Braden's crusade, Ray felt the need to defend himself from potential charges of appeasement. He stated that no one should deduce "that we have gone overboard and think the set-up here is perfect." Indeed, "we all know it is lousy," that "Perón's basic philosophy is totalitarian," and that "IAPI is rotten almost beyond the point of description." In short, "we think we understand pretty well what kind of people we have to deal with."[34]

While some might have believed that cultural missions and exchanges might warm Argentines to the concept of U.S. hemispheric leadership, Ray reasserted that economic issues were the key. Even if Perón's authoritarian methods were unpalatable and Argentine culture had little in common with that of the United States, "history does not record a single instance where cultural relations were a determining factor in provoking or preventing a war or deciding on which side a nation would line up in the case of war." Certainly "no one," he claimed, would "argue that Germany, Japan and Italy lined up together during World War II because of cultural sympathies or admiration for each other's blue eyes."[35] In short, "so long as IAPI, unfair treatment and obstruction of business and arbitrary controls and restrictions continue, our relations with Argentina will inevitably remain difficult." Ray was confident that if IAPI was proven to be ineffective, Perón would abandon statist corporatism and Miranda with it. Thus, the United States should do nothing that might strengthen Argentina's financial position so long as Eva Perón, Miranda, and their *mirandistas—*

---

33. Dearborn to Tewksbury, Ohmans, Martin, Woodward, and Wright, 22 September 1947, RG 59, ARA, Argentina; Ray to Secretary of State, 5 January 1948, RG 59, 711.35; see also Truman to Bruce, 9 December 1948, HST, PSF, Foreign Affairs, Argentina File, HST.

34. Ray to Dearborn, 12 April 1948, RG 59, 735.41.

35. Ray to Secretary of State, 5 January 1948, RG 59, 711.35.

Peronism's "worst elements"—were a significant part of the government.[36]

Bruce ignored almost all of Messersmith's analyses, believing firmly that by the end of his tenure, he was "in effect, 100% on the *peronista* side." But he explicitly rejected his predecessor's *volte face* regarding the "economic czar," arguing that Miranda "is a nimble-witted, shrewd man," whose "word is not to be relied upon." Even worse, Bruce claimed that "one would have to search history to find a man who has been of such disservice to his country as this man has been to this nation." Unfortunately, Perón soon reaffirmed his faith in Miranda by naming him President of the newly created National Economic Council (NEC). Imbued with broad but vague powers, the NEC was another of Perón's attempts to centralize the Argentine economy under the auspices of a technocratic body. Although U.S. policymakers hoped that this was a "kick upstairs" as a "step preparatory to getting rid" of him altogether and were relieved that his duties at the Central Bank and IAPI were to be handed over to underlings, they also dreaded the state corporatist mischief he might be capable of in this new office.[37]

On the other hand, Bruce soon discovered that there were those within the Peronist camp who had little use for Miranda, IAPI, or the "extremists." The first of these was Foreign Minister Bramulgia. Miranda had assumed most of the authority to negotiate treaties and commercial accords, leaving Bramulgia with a largely symbolic post. Scorned by Eva Perón, who harbored an old resentment against him, Bramulgia nonetheless had her husband's respect and the full support of the U.S. and British governments. Indeed, Whitehall and Washington regarded him as Peronism's most "reasonable and understanding and constructive element." Ray praised Bramulgia's handling of the British

---

36. Ray to Secretary of State, 5 January 1948, RG 59, 711.35; see also Bruce to Secretary of State, 26 December 1947, RG 59, 835.4131; MacDonald, "The US, the Cold War, and Perón," 408-409.

37. Bruce, *Memoirs*, 235; Bruce to Secretary of State, 26 September 1947, RG 59, 611.3531; Bruce to Secretary of State, 6 October 1947, RG 59, 835.50; OIR, "Argentine Foreign Policy," 29 July 1947, RG 59, Report #4714.

negotiations, if only because "the Argentines gave in on most points and the British gave in on none of importance." As Acting Secretary of State Robert Lovett lamented, however, "Bramulgia with complete sincerity has indicated that drastic action would not be taken" on a number of occasions but had "been unable to prevent final action sponsored by Miranda."[38] So although Bramulgia had international respect, he had no real constituency in Argentina, and therefore was a partner of limited utility.

On the other hand, Miranda had also alienated the CGT, one of the "pillars" of *peronismo*, by arguing that the unions were hindering economic growth. The CGT, he claimed, had grown fat on Perón's generous treatment, as the higher wages and increased benefits being given to workers were an excessive drain on capital accumulation. He compared Argentine workers' absentee rates and productivity with those of their U.S. counterparts and found his countrymen lacking. Not only was this directly impeding industrialization, but improved wages were increasing domestic food consumption, with a resultant loss in exportable surplus— thereby thwarting IAPI. In one case, a sugar workers' strike in Tucumán so paralyzed that industry that Miranda grudgingly was forced to spend $10 million of foreign exchange to import what should have been produced domestically. After several such episodes, he tried to convince Perón to roll back his labor reforms. While he was unsuccessful, he nonetheless had made enemies in the labor movement. Even though the CGT's hostility to Miranda was promising, there was simply no way for Washington to exploit it. The "Gay Affair" had embittered the CGT so thoroughly against the United States government, that there was no hope of cooperation in the immediate future. So while Washington was reluctantly forced to concede control over Argentine labor to Perón, the Argentine Army offered far greater promise.[39]

---

38. Ray to Dearborn, 12 April 1948, RG 59, 735.41; Lovett to Embassy Buenos Aires, 5 December 1947, RG 59, 835.6363; see also Callum MacDonald's very effective use of the concept of "extremists" and "moderates" to analyze the Anglo-American response to Peronism. MacDonald, "The U.S., Britain, and Argentina," 183-199; and "The U.S., the Cold War, and Perón," 405-414.

39. Ordway to Secretary of State, 29 November 1948, RG 59, 835.50; Greenup

## V

At first glance, the State Department and the *Ejército Argentino* seemed to be strange bedfellows. The Army, thought to be a bastion of "Prussianism" throughout World War II, had traditionally been the foremost enemy of democracy in Argentina. It had risen from the barracks to overthrow civilian leadership on a number of occasions and was most recently responsible for the 1943 coup that brought Perón to power. Furthermore, Perón had largely rid the Army of officers who were ideologically distant from his position in the intervening years. However, on closer inspection, there were important areas where Washington and the *Campo de Mayo* could find common ground.

The first of these was their mutual distaste for Sra. Perón and Miranda. Socially conservative, the Army had never thought highly of Perón's dalliance with the ex-actress. Although Perón's marriage to Eva Duarte had legitimated their relationship, her role in politics never sat well in the barracks. The Army, like high society, did not accept the principle of women's participation in politics, and specifically, that woman's participation in the inner councils of state. Army cadets scornfully jeered and disrupted newsreels that featured the First Lady, and the officer corps seemed to agree with the sentiment.[40] In 1947, military leaders went so far as to approach Perón, trying to persuade him to keep his wife from "meddling" in domestic and foreign affairs. Ray and Bruce also had little use for her inflammatory rhetoric and demagoguery, but she aroused Yankee ire primarily because she seemed to be Miranda's patron.[41]

Ray understood quite well that Minister of War Humberto Sosa Molina "and the military elements in general thoroughly detest

---

to Secretary of State, 28 December 1948, RG 59, 835.50.

40. Fraser and Navarro, *Eva Perón*, 105.

41. OIR, "Probable Argentine Policy," 15 February 1949, HST, Intelligence File, CIA Reports, Box 255, HST; Potash, *Army and Politics: Perón to Frondizi*, 94-96.

Miranda."[42] His close ties with Eva Perón aside, Miranda had shot down an arms purchase with the Czech Skoda Works in 1946, claiming that the government lacked the funds—a highly suspect assertion during the heady early days. Soon thereafter, he attempted to persuade Perón to pare the size of the Argentine Army from 100,000 men to 70,000 and reduce military expenditures by fifty percent. Miranda's arguments had some merit: the British aviation purchase had cost approximately £2.6 million that could have been better used elsewhere. Since U.S. hegemony shielded the hemisphere from attack from the outside and the "Inter-American system" prevented war within, Miranda argued that massive arms expenditures were both unnecessary and counterproductive.[43]

Needless to say, this attitude brought him into conflict with General Sosa Molina and the generals. While Braden recalled that Sosa Molina had a "long record of pro-Nazi sympathies," he was a proponent of civilian rule, unlike some in the military. He had presided over the 1946 election and possessed a reputation for fairness and honesty. Bruce described him as a "friend of mine" and believed that he "generally saw eye to eye" with the *peronista* officer. Entrusted to return the Army to the barracks, revive its nominally apolitical professionalism, and restore military parity with Brazil, Sosa Molina was as much Perón's link with the officer corps as his wife was with the unions.[44]

Sosa Molina, the head of *Fabricaciones Militares*, General Manuel Savio, and most Army leaders agreed upon a two-pronged approach to the modernization of the Armed Forces. First, they acknowledged U.S. hegemony and hoped to participate in the

---

42. Ray to Secretary of State, 22 July 1948, RG 59, 724.35.

43. Messersmith to Secretary of State, 12 March 1947, Messersmith Papers, 1857; Tewksbury Report, 8 April 1947, RG 353, RIIC-ARG, Box 10; Paz and Ferrari, *Política Exterior Argentina*, 154; Potash, *Army and Politics: Perón to Frondizi*, 77.

44. Braden to Messersmith, 6 August 1946, RG 59, 835.002; Bruce, *Memoirs*, 280; Potash, *Army and Politics: Perón to Frondizi*, 55-59; Alain Rouquié, *Poder militar y sociedad política en la Argentina* (Buenos Aires, 1983), 72-77.

hemispheric arms standardization program, recognizing that U.S. surplus equipment was a bonanza waiting to be tapped. Sosa Molina had visited Washington to consult with Secretary of Defense James Forrestal, and the two had reached several agreements in principle on this and other subjects. But, like Perón himself, these men were unwilling to put their fate entirely in Washington's hands. Thus, they hoped to create an independent arms industry and tried to sell Washington on the idea of Argentina as a "southern bastion of the 'arsenal of democracy.'"[45]

Their ultimate goal was to standardize their equipment with that of the United States, buy what Washington was willing to sell, and then produce their own weapons to U.S. specifications. To do so, however, they required good relations with the Yankee colossus and the industrial capacity to support an arms industry. Therefore, the Army had backed Miranda's Argentine-Chilean Trade Agreement as a precursor to the establishment of a copper mill to produce shell casings. Large quantities of cheap Bolivian tin and Peruvian oil, iron, and coal would also have been major assets. Although there was this confluence of interests between the Army and Miranda, difficulties arose over the steel mill project.[46]

In late 1947, Savio and *Fabricaciones Militares* took bids for the construction of a steel mill and an adjoining tin plate mill. Two British companies submitted bids for the construction, but the best offer was from a U.S. firm, ARMCO. Inexplicably, Miranda turned ARMCO away and gave the contract to an obscure company, Amer-Ind, whose bid was substantially worse than ARMCO's. Incensed, the High Command went to Perón, who ordered the cancellation of the contract in, as the ORI put it, "an atmosphere of a *coup d'etat*."[47] Subsequently, Savio learned that

---

45. Oakley to Secretary of State, 25 July 1947, RG 43, Records of U.S. Participation in International Conferences, Commissions, Expositions, and Committees, Inter-American Conference for the Maintenance of Continental Peace and Security, Rio de Janeiro, 1947, Box 3; see also Bruce, *Memoirs*, 258.

46. Martin to Atwood and Tewksbury, 21 July 1947, RG 59, MRIC; Potash, *Army and Politics: Perón to Frondizi*, 77-80; Lewis, *Crisis of Argentine Capitalism*, 149; Paz and Ferrari, *Política Exterior*, 144-147.

47. ORI, "Probable Argentine Policy" 15 February 1949, Intelligence File, CIA

almost $2 million earmarked for the construction of the mill had inexplicably disappeared. He accused Miranda, who had used his own business partners as go-betweens on the Amer-Ind deal, of corruption. Perón promptly turned the project over entirely to Savio's *Fabricaciones Militares*, who agreed to forget the missing money "to prevent the matter from becoming a national scandal."

Bruce reported that the discontent ran even deeper. Perón had canceled the Amer-Ind contract, the ambassador asserted, because "he was told by the Army that if he did not do so the Army would put in a new President."[48] Indeed, Perón was away in Córdoba when news of the scandal broke, and several generals approached Bruce to inform him that "on Monday we are going to put President Perón out of the presidency, and we want to ask your advice on who we should put in his place." Bruce, "completely at a loss," claimed that "nothing you have told me convinces me that Perón is a part of the attempted theft." Instead, he suggested that it was in all likelihood Miranda's doing. He recommended that the generals contact Perón by telephone. They apparently took the recommendation and were mollified when the president pleaded ignorance and promised to turn the project over to the Army.[49]

The State Department could not have been happier. First, at the height of the crisis, Army officers had come to Bruce, asking for his support against Miranda. It was a good sign that the Army was making friendly overtures and looking for assistance and advice at the U.S. embassy in the first place. Just as important, however, U.S. embassy personnel believed that "it might be a very healthy development to have some of Miranda's operations aired

---

Reports, 1948, HST.

48. Ray to Lyon, 17 November 1947, RG 59, 835.50; Bruce to Secretary of State, 2 December 1947, RG 59, 835.656; Watrous to Secretary of State, 31 December 1946, RG 59, 835.602; Dearborn to Atwood, Woodward, Daniels, and Armour, 15 December 1947, RG 59, ARA, Memoranda on Argentina; Embassy Buenos Aires to Secretary of State, 12 February 1948, RG 59, 835.602.

49. Bruce, *Memoirs*, 275-277.

publicly."[50] Even if the specific aspects of the steel mill debacle were not publicized, the embassy could content itself in the knowledge that at least Perón and the Army had seen this side of IAPI and Miranda.

Miranda had always claimed that the high prices IAPI charged for Argentine food sales abroad were to compensate for the "black market" prices it had to pay for American industrial imports. In reality, the embassy claimed, "Miranda and his associates who have been dealing with all sorts of jackleg concerns and small people, taking commissions and splitting profits on sales to his own government," and this practice was to blame for the high prices Argentina was paying. If IAPI was shown to be as rife with graft and "shady dealings" as Bruce believed it to be, Perón might be convinced to jettison both. Regardless, the embassy was pleased that "Miranda is in a precarious position and the Army is determined to effect his downfall."[51]

Miranda tried to defend himself from these charges, claiming that he was already so wealthy that he had no reason to steal from government coffers unless he wanted to "pass my life eating thousand-peso bills until I die," but IAPI's operations were indeed profoundly riddled with corruption and graft.[52] In all likelihood, it was not the only *peronista* institution guilty of this particular charge. The Eva Perón Foundation, in addition to its other functions, also apparently served as a pipeline to Swiss banks. By the time of Perón's fall in 1955, he and his wife had funneled approximately $700 million out of the country. Paul Lewis speculated that as much as $2-3 billion of government funds was "drained off" in this fashion by the *peronistas*. Bruce believed that Miranda, the "dirtiest crook in the Western Hemisphere," had managed to abscond with more than $30 million. With so much of the nation's economic transactions being carried out by secretive

---

50. Watrous to Secretary of State, 31 December 1947, RG 59, 835.602.

51. Ray to Lyon, 17 November 1947, RG 59, 835.50; Dearborn to Atwood, Woodward, Daniels, and Armour, 15 December 1947, RG 59, MRIC, Argentina.

52. Burrows to Secretary of State, Enclosure 1, 11 April 1947, RG 59, 835.61.

operations like IAPI and the Eva Perón Foundation, the Army's complaints seem to have been well founded.[53]

But just as Miranda and IAPI were hindering the creation of an Argentine munitions industry, they were also impeding the Army's efforts to gain access to U.S. arms. Even though Braden's departure had opened the door for arms sales to Argentina, the State Department was hesitant to give Perón aid until he made changes in the government's economic program. If Argentina wanted to become the "southern bastion of the 'arsenal of democracy,'" it had to show itself to be in accord with U.S. principles of liberal capitalism. Whereas Braden had hoped to use the arms embargo as a stick to punish Perón, Bruce and Ray saw the lifting of the embargo as a carrot that could lure the Argentine military to actively support the "Inter-American system." The principle remained the same. To acquire weapons, the Army would use its ample persuasive power to move Perón in the "proper" direction.

At the same time, he vigorously opposed giving Perón any economic aid, Ray openly advocated arms sales, arguing that "the armed forces are anxious to have our cooperation" and that "we have little or nothing to lose by offering Perón some cooperation" in this regard. "On the contrary," he asserted, "it offers the best hope of getting the armed forces and military leaders on our side." If successful, "we will have an excellent opportunity of using our influence on the military and naval forces of Argentina."[54] Sosa Molina was to be given enough U.S. aid to whet the Army's appetite, and he was expected to pressure Perón toward moderation. Since this involved attacks upon the "extremists" that he and his colleagues were already undertaking for their own reasons, in this instance the U.S. State Department and Argentine Army found common ground.

Sosa Molina's conciliatory approach paid quick dividends. In September, an embassy official in Belgium noticed that hundreds of U.S. tanks were being loaded onto ships destined for Argentina.

---

53. Lewis, *Crisis of Argentine Capitalism*, 201-205; Bruce, *Memoirs*, 276.

54. Ray to Secretary of State, 5 January 1948, RG 59, 711.35.

The Belgians had obtained the tanks as scrap metal from the British, who had originally received them through Lend-Lease. Suspecting that this was another Belgian attempt to circumvent the arms embargo, the embassy in Brussels reported it to Washington. Although Marshall did chide the Belgians for selling military equipment that had been paid for by U.S. taxpayers, he had no complaints about Belgian military sales to Argentina in general and raised no serious objections. Because Argentina was due to receive weapons soon anyway and these tanks were made to U.S. Army specifications, there was no problem. If the Belgians could use "scrap metal" to procure foodstuffs from Argentina, so much the better. In October, Bruce himself intervened on behalf of the Argentines, persuading his government to sell 88mm anti-aircraft guns to Argentina to undercut a potential deal with Skoda. These gestures of amity cost the U.S. little or nothing, illustrated to Sosa Molina that cooperation with the United States could provide benefits, and were the clearest sign that "Bradenism" was for all intents and purposes dead.[55]

This new approach and Sosa Molina's leverage in the Perón government also paid off when Argentina's oil policies were reconsidered in 1947. Perón had spent 1946 trying to make good on his pledges to ease restrictions on the U.S. and English oil companies operating in Argentina, but these firms had been experiencing constant pressure from labor decrees and state competition. The Argentine state oil corporation, *Yacimientos Petrolíferos Fiscales* (YPF) was a powerful nationalist symbol representing independence from foreign exploitation. Although YPF had operated efficiently for its first decade, by the late-1940s its productivity had slipped just as Argentina's fuel needs had expanded dramatically. To reinvigorate Argentine oil production and tap potentially huge oil fields in Patagonia, Perón was negotiating with Standard Oil. However, he could not comply with Standard's requests simply to grant drilling and refining

---

55. Godley to Secretary of State, 10 September 1948, RG 59, 835.24; Marshall to Embassy Brussels, 24 October 1947, RG 59, 835.24; Secretary of State to Embassy Brussels, 29 May 1948, RG 59, 835.24; Potash, *Army and Politics: Perón to Frondizi*, 81.

concessions, for to do so would curtail YPF's operations and be a symbolic surrender to foreign exploitation. Standard predictably had no intention of entering into the "mixed company" arrangement that Perón sought either. When news of Perón's negotiations with Standard came to light, *peronista* nationalists rose to defend Argentine sovereignty, and pressed for expropriation of the private companies.[56]

Bolstered by this congressional pressure, nationalists in Perón's cabinet took up the call and presented a plan to expropriate all foreign oil companies by December 13, the Petroleum Day holiday. The administrators of YPF informed the foreign firms that their contracts to drill would be allowed to expire, and Perón's Minister of Commerce José Barro, one of Eva Perón's allies and a *mirandista*, led a fight for cabinet approval of the decision. Only Perón, Bramulgia, and Miranda resisted the call for expropriation. Miranda's stance against his fellow nationalists was somewhat uncharacteristic, and Bruce was astonished to "find him on the right side of the fence" for once. Like Perón, however, the "economic czar" recognized the need for the foreign oil companies. Although Perón and Bramulgia had both pledged to Bruce that no action would be taken against the oil firms, an impasse had been reached. Perón did not dare to alienate nationalist sentiment by negotiating settlements with the oil companies, and the nationalists could not proceed with their plans without the president's backing.[57]

The stalemate was finally broken when Sosa Molina weighed in. The war minister had been a lukewarm supporter of expropriation at the onset, but he radically altered his position after conversations with Bruce, Ray, and General Willis Crittenberger, who was visiting Buenos Aires to discuss arms standardization and sales. While it is impossible to know exactly what was said at their meetings, Bruce later recalled his own conversation with Sosa

---

56. OIR, "Relations of the Argentine Government Petroleum Corporation with the Foreign Oil Companies," 15 August 1947, RG 59, Report #4193; Potash, *Army and Politics: Perón to Frondizi*, 68-70.

57. Bruce, *Memoirs*, 279; see also Bruce to Secretary of State, 26 September 1947, RG 59, 611.3531; Potash, *Army and Politics: Perón to Frondizi*, 71-73.

Molina. Bruce told the war minister that although "you and I have been working right along together for closer Western Hemisphere understanding," this resolution "is very likely to shatter the friendly relationship we have established between our two nations." Stunned, Sosa Molina responded that he had only supported the measure because "my habit has always been to be against anything Miranda is for, and for everything he is against." When he learned how serious the matter was, he reassured Bruce that "all we have to do is call up the President and have another Cabinet meeting and we will rescind it."

As Richard Potash posited, 'Sosa Molina's subsequent warning to the cabinet that [expropriation] could damage the interests of Argentina was an understandable position for one whose consuming interest ever since he took office had been to replace the Army's outmoded equipment."[58] Nonetheless, one day after it had passed the expropriation measure and less than fifteen hours after Bruce had spoken to Sosa Molina, Perón reported that the cabinet had unanimously rescinded the measure. The significance was not lost upon U.S. policymakers who now understood that "Sosa Molina appears to hold the balance of power and will probably exert an influence favorable to U.S.-Argentine cooperation." In what must be considered a radical turnabout, the State Department had come to consider the generals to be benevolent, extremely powerful allies who were simply "trying to do an honest and patriotic job."[59]

Since U.S. leaders now had ample evidence that the Army held a whip hand over Perón, they had at last found a worthy Argentine opposition behind which they could throw their weight. Sosa Molina and the Army had twice assailed the "extremists" and emerged victorious. For want of a democratic alternative to Perón, U.S. policymakers turned their attention to the Army. Bruce now

---

58. Bruce, *Memoirs*, 279-280; Potash, *Army and Politics: Perón to Frondizi*, 75.

59. ORI, "Probable Argentine Policy," 15 February 1949, HST, Intelligence File, CIA Reports, Box 255, HST; Embassy Buenos Aires to Secretary of State, 12 February 1948, RG 59, 835.602.

understood that "at some point Perón will have to clean out Miranda and the other crooks associated with him or else the Army will probably clean out Perón." While "at the moment we do not know which way the cat is going to jump," he argued that "when it does the chances are that we will land with it on a better spot than the one we left."[60]

Whether the diplomats understood it or not, a new doctrine was evolving, as the State Department came to understand that the most effective counter to revolutionary nationalists like Perón was local military establishments. As Edward Miller, soon to become assistant secretary of state, noted, "in Latin America, it is better to have the military with you than against you, because they usually decide the issue."[61] The case of Argentina in the 1940s is more of a harbinger than a perfect example. Still, it is significant that the State Department could not find common ground with groups that were dedicated to economic redistribution and industrial diversification—like the *peronista* unions. Because Argentina would never be a military threat to the United States, arms sales to Perón's Army did not jeopardize any important U.S. interests. Ray and Bruce understood this, as did their superiors. So rather than addressing the need for economic reform in Latin America, jeopardizing U.S. neo-colonial control, and reassessing its economic policy, the State Department did what it had to do to preserve the economic order that was at the core of U.S. hegemony.

## VI

Taken together, the Messersmith-Braden feud and Bruce's emergence demonstrate the full evolution of U.S. policy. Messersmith's and Braden's inflexible positions and interpretations did not lend themselves well to the subtle maneuvering and dispassionate analysis that were necessary for U.S. statesmen to

---

60. Bruce to Secretary of State, 2 July 1948, RG 59, 835.50.

61. Miller to George S. Franklin, 31 January 1949, Edward G. Miller Papers, Correspondence File, Nomination File, HST.

destabilize Perón's Argentina. Remarkably, and despite all appearances to the contrary, however, U.S. policy toward Perón did not suffer terribly as a result of the Messersmith-Braden feud. As U.S. efforts to head off Perón's foreign policy offensives illustrate, the State Department managed to act, and act effectively, even at the height of the bureaucratic struggle. Although it may have been embarrassing, the Messersmith-Braden feud created little more than a ripple in the course of U.S.-Argentine relations.

Another aspect that must not be forgotten is that these two powerful diplomats differed on their assessments of Perón and came to despise each other, but neither questioned the merits of the "Inter-American system" as a hemispheric order, or the need for global liberal capitalism. As Messersmith came to believe that Perón could "be bought" and used as a vehicle to bring U.S.-style capitalism to Argentina, Braden persisted in his belief that the president had to be unseated before the hemisphere could be made safe for democracy.[62] Braden, the traditional Republican conservative, and his left-wing allies like Henry Wallace and Potofsky were themselves on the fringes or outside of the centrist New Deal order, and could see no redeeming features in the Peronist program. For traditional New Dealers such as Messersmith, however, Perón's state corporatism might in time be adapted into a more acceptable, privatist variant. In the end, the feud amounted to little more than a tragicomic sideshow with little lasting impact on the course of U.S.-Argentine relations or the evolution of U.S. policy toward Latin America. When Truman simply fired both of them in June 1947, the path was cleared for the implementation of the Department's new, more subtle approach to Perón.

With relations now fully normalized and a dispassionate ambassador directing U.S. policy, the State Department would be able to far more effectively exploit Perón's weaknesses. Despite formally normalizing relations, the State Department was not prepared to become Perón's "reluctant partner," and Bruce loathed

---

62. Weil, "Can Perón Be Bought?" *Inter-American Economic Affairs* VI (Summer 1950), 27-36.

Perón almost as much as Braden ever had.[63] However, he cloaked his repugnance to better deal with the Argentines. For Bruce and his superiors, it did not really matter whether Perón was replaced or if he could be convinced to become a conventional leader, so long as the experiments in state corporatism ceased. U.S. policymakers had not moved into partnership with Perón; they simply recognized that they had to work quietly and preserve the illusion of amity lest Argentine nationalism resurface to the detriment of the United States. The Truman Administration needed cool, level-headed functionaries to carry out such an approach, not stubborn idealists like Braden and Messersmith.

---

63. Rita Giacalone, "From Bad Neighbors to Reluctant Partners: Argentina and the United States, 1946-1950," (Unpublished Ph.D. dissertation, Indiana University, 1977).

# CHAPTER 8

## THE BEGINNING OF THE END OF THE PERONIST CHALLENGE: AUGUST 1947-DECEMBER 1948

> While the situation here is critical, it may work to our advantage in the long run. We would like to emphasize, however, that it will antagonize even the Argentines who are our friends if we appear to gloat over Argentina's present discomfiture. It would be a mistake for us to permit the impression that we are deliberately bringing pressure on Argentina to bring the Administration to its knees and possibly force Perón out. Such action would alienate all sectors of local opinion.
>
> James Bruce, 2 July 1948[1]

### I

The period from late 1947 through the end of 1948 should be seen as the culmination of U.S. strategy under Bruce's guidance, and the beginning of the end of the *peronismo* that had challenged U.S. hemispheric dominance. The economic crisis that beset Argentina in 1948 was one primarily of Perón's making, but external factors also played a role in the decline of the New Argentina. In September 1947, the British government announced that it was ending its policy of sterling convertibility, and for Perón, this was nothing short of devastating. Without convertibility and the ability to garner foreign exchange or buy goods from the United States, Perón either had to roll back his industrialization program or risk bankruptcy by continuing his lavish spending. When Perón and Miranda, expecting to be saved by the Marshall Plan, opted for the

---

1. Bruce to Secretary of State, 2 July 1948, RG 59, 835.50.

latter course, they were gambling heavily with not just their own but Argentina's future.

Unfortunately for the *peronistas*, Marshall Plan dollars never came. The European Recovery Program (ERP) called for massive foreign aid to rebuild Europe, but many of the dollars sent to Europe were to be used, through offshore procurements in the dollar area, as a means for Europe to acquire raw materials. However, the Economic Cooperation Administration (ECA), the organization that administered ERP funds, was dedicated to promoting multilateral trade, liberal capitalism, and privatist corporatism. Therefore, it adopted a policy calculated to "beat the Argentine to its knees" by denying Perón offshore procurement.

Interestingly, Bruce and his superiors urged Truman to end the ECA's open campaign against Peronism. Although the State Department had long dreamed of the day when he would be forced to curtail his economic experiments due to financial constraints, the ECA's efforts to hammer nails into Perón's coffin threatened not only to weaken him economically but to strengthen him politically. To eliminate the possibility that he might be able to transform economic defeat into political victory, Bruce urged the ECA to end its formal discrimination against Argentina, as Byrnes had ended Braden's embargoes two years earlier. Although both the State Department and the ECA sought to end Perón's experiments in state corporatism, for Bruce it was not enough for the Peronist economy to fail, it had to fail because of its own flaws, not as a result of U.S. pressure.

## II

Although the failure of the Peronist economy remains the subject of great debate, in all likelihood, it collapsed largely as a result of the effort to transform the nation. In this regard, Perón's labor constituency proved to be a double-edged sword, as the militancy that had served Perón the candidate so well was an impediment to President Perón. He had rebuffed Gay's and Reyes' challenges in order to "capture" the CGT, but he still had to provide an outlet for labor's economic demands. By 1948, however, the Peronists' extravagant labor reforms had started to exact a price on economic development.

In 1945, the heyday of pro-Perón upheaval, there had been more than forty thousand strikes in Argentina, resulting in the loss of over a half million days of work. Thanks to Perón's tolerance, however, 334,000 strikes, costing 1,813,000 workdays, occurred during 1946. These numbers swelled annually, as Argentine workers took advantage of their powerful unions to defy industrialists openly, hinder production, and further augment their wages. As absenteeism and workplace disruptions increased, productivity fell. Miranda repeatedly chastised workers, asking them how he could redistribute wealth if Argentines produced nothing to distribute. The "economic czar" had initiated profit sharing in the old ITT properties as a flagship of *peronismo* but was appalled to find that even when workers had a stake in their corporation, they showed little zeal. Even Perón joined Miranda in the chorus of businessmen, fruitlessly appealing to workers' patriotism to improve their shop floor performance.[2]

Still, Argentine workers had valid complaints. Despite the spate of Peronist activities to better their lot, rampant inflation negated many of these gains. According to official government statistics, the costs of rent, electricity, clothing, and food had more than doubled in less than a year and a half. While nearly every nation suffered from an inflationary spiral in the post-war period, Argentina's was unusually pronounced and was in part a direct result of Perón's free spending and the Central Bank's easy money policies. For Perón to contain the inflation that was crushing the lower classes, he would have been forced to roll back the same policies that were fueling industrialization and raising wages. Stuck with this dilemma, Perón simply pressed forward, unwilling to take the steps that might salvage his economy but undermine the goals of his revolution.[3]

---

2. *Review of the River Plate*, 17 January 1947, 9; *Review of the River Plate*, 25 July 1947, 13; Watrous to Secretary of State, 7 August 1947, RG 59, 835.504.

3. Apodaca, "Current Economic Review of Argentina," 20 April 1949, RG 59, 835.50.

As serious as the decline of industrial production was, the effect of Peronism on the *pampas* proved to be even more devastating. Although Argentine agro-pastoral production had been in decline for some time, it plummeted catastrophically under Perón. In the first three years of his administration, Argentine wheat exports dropped from twenty-two percent of the world supply to eleven percent. To some extent, this was a result of Miranda's stiff bargaining techniques and bumper crops in other nations, but Perón's labor decrees had played a role in this decline as well. As the rural poor flocked to Buenos Aires to partake of the industrialization drive, fields were left unsowed. In 1945, 34.7 percent of the Argentine populace had been engaged in agriculture, but after four years of Peronism, this figure had dropped to only 25.6 percent as over half of Argentina's 150,000 sharecroppers simply left the land and moved to urban centers. Although this migration to the cities was a boon for industrialization and union membership, it cost Argentine agriculture dearly. In the early years of the war, Argentines planted wheat and corn on over thirteen million hectares but by 1948 they were planting on less than nine million. Other crops suffered similar declines. Since Perón's buying power was directly dependent upon his food exports, this boded ill for the industrialization program.[4]

Part of the decline of Argentine agriculture also must be attributed directly to IAPI. Large landowners had always complained that IAPI's practices were starving them out, and since Miranda sold sunflower oil overseas for more than ten times the amount he paid farmers, their complaints had some merit. In protest, *hacendados* either left fields fallow or violated the law and simply refused to sell their produce to IAPI, decreasing exportable surpluses. Furthermore, Peronists instituted a complex series of

---

4. Carlos F. Diaz Alejandro, *Essays on the Economic History of the Argentine Republic* (New Haven, 1970), 440-441; DiTella and Zymelman, *Las etapas del desarrollo*, 500-510; Edward J. Chambers, "Some Factors in the Deterioration of Argentina's External Position," *Inter-American Economic Affairs* VIII (Winter 1954), 28-35; Fodor, "Perón's Policies," 153; Lewis, *Crisis of Argentine Capitalism*, 190; Daniel Lewis, "Internal and External Convergence: The Collapse of Argentine Grain Farming," *Latin America in the 1940s: War and Postwar Transitions*, ed. David Rock (Berkeley, 1994), 209-223.

regulations for rural workers and unionists that further hindered agriculture. Farmers, for example, had to hire and pay high wages to rural union members to perform tasks that family members or friends had always done. The *Review of the River Plate* published a letter from one grower that illustrated how all factors conspired against the farmer. Because IAPI's prices were so low and the price of union labor so high, this farmer asserted that he could only turn a profit on high-yield crops from his most fertile fields. As a result, he had been compelled to leave most of his crop unharvested, resulting in "twenty tons of rye lost to the country, to me, and to Europe."[5]

At the same time food production was in decline, urban Argentines were consuming more, leaving Miranda with ever smaller surpluses to peddle abroad. Argentine meat consumption increased at a rate of almost one hundred thousand tons per year during the first Perón presidency, and by 1950, the Peronists were exporting less than twenty percent of their meat and eating the rest. Even though meat production had risen, Argentine internal consumption had far outpaced the increase, as it did with grain. Almost half of Argentine grain was exported before the war, but by 1950 Argentina was selling less than a quarter of its produce abroad. With production slipping and domestic consumption rising dramatically, Argentine exports and profits from the international trade plummeted.[6]

Serious as these problems were, perhaps the most damaging aspect of the Peronist economic program was the depletion of $1.5 billion of accumulated financial reserves, as Miranda and IAPI went through Argentine gold, dollar, and sterling reserves like there was no tomorrow. In part, this was because they did not believe there would be. Peronists had predicated the Five-Year Plan on the

---

5. *Review of the River Plate*, 23 January 1948, 6; Chambers, "Some Factors in the Deterioration," 42-47; DiTella and Zymelman, *Las etapas del desarrollo*, 497.

6. DiTella and Zymelman, *Desarrollo económico argentino*, 122-134; Colin Lewis, "Anglo-Argentine Trade, 1945-1965," *Latin America in the 1940s* ed. Rock, 121; E. Louise Peffer, "Less Beef in the Plate?" *Inter-American Economic Affairs* XI (Summer 57), 27-30; Rock, *Argentina*, 296-298.

assumption that a third world war between the Soviet Union and the United States would occur before 1950. This war, they believed, would economically isolate Argentina as the last two had, cutting off industrial imports. Therefore, there was no reason for Perón to hoard reserves that soon would be useless anyway when he could utilize them instead for the purchase of machinery and capital goods. So while Miranda was willing to pay exorbitant prices for imports, IAPI was unable to refill the coffers as expected. Jorge Fodor pointed out how *peronistas* had been forced to lend widely and offer massive credits to Europe so that war torn nations could even purchase Argentine goods. Although Europe owed considerable debts to Argentina by 1948, this did not translate into the foreign exchange that Argentine desperately needed. Still, if the "economic czar" had any concern about draining Argentine coffers so rapidly, he did not allow his trepidation to affect his spending.[7]

As early as mid-1947, the strain of these policies was beginning to show. The nationalizations of ITT and other facilities, although popular, had been costly. Military expenditures, such as the British jet purchase, did nothing to improve Argentina's exchange position, and the Five-Year Plan also carried a high price tag. Projects such as the steel mill, gas pipeline, and hydroelectric program were constant drains on government revenue. Furthermore, it was becoming clear that rather than bringing technocratic expertise, IAPI was rife with corruption and hampered by a haphazard purchasing and distribution system. In one famous example, rows of imported automobiles, tractors, and trucks sat on the docks of Buenos Aires rusting and forgotten, thanks to bureaucratic red tape and bottlenecks.[8] Moreover, IAPI cloaked

---

7. Fodor, "Argentine Nationalism: Myth or Reality?"

8. Despite the well-documented inefficiency of IAPI, Miranda defended the organization to the end. When asked about this particular case, he opted instead to discuss the new trucks that IAPI had gotten into circulation. The port of Buenos Aires had only been shipping out 450,000 tons of goods per month in mid-1947. By December, however, it was dispatching over 1 million tons, thanks to IAPI's purchases. *Review of the River Plate*, 6 February 1948, 7; *Review of the River Plate*, 5 March 1948, 8; see also Easum, "Justicialismo in Retrospect," 38-41.

the drain of foreign exchange. Because the organization did not release its records, Perón could lie about the nation's finances and paint quite a rosy picture for Argentines. "We have the Central Bank full of gold," he proclaimed, "and we do not know where to put more." Since almost the only way that Miranda could raise the money to purchase goods in the United States was by selling his gold reserves, he was doing so at a breakneck pace. Much more was leaving the Central Bank than entering it, but Peronists nonetheless pressed forward, confident that austerity was not yet a necessary step.[9]

However, the British soon fired what turned out to be the first shot in a barrage that eventually collapsed the Peronist economy. Although pledged to allow the convertibility of sterling by the Miranda-Eady agreement, in August 1947, Whitehall unilaterally reversed its position and no longer would Miranda be able to convert his sterling into dollars. Since the English were unable to export large quantities of goods, nations had been selling to Britain and using the proceeds to make purchases in the dollar area. The British deemed the resultant drain on their dollar reserves to be a major threat to their own recovery, but for Argentines, the solution was a crippling one.[10]

Inconvertibility effectively ended the lucrative triangular trade that had been so profitable for Argentina over the decades. The United States, because of the "sanitary embargo" on South American meat and its own agro-pastoral surpluses, imported little from Argentina. Therefore, Perón and Miranda, like their predecessors, had little choice but to continue to sell to the English market. However, the British were unable or unwilling to sell the capital goods, machinery, and industrial raw materials that the Peronists desperately sought. Still, so long as the Argentines could convert sterling to dollars, the Argentine trade deficit with the United States was generally countered by a similar surplus with

---

9. Burrows, "Agrarian Unrest in Argentina," 11 April 1947, RG 59, 835.61; Apodaca, "Current Economic Review," 20 April 1949, RG 59, 835.50.

10. Escudé, *Gran Bretaña, Estados Unidos*, 316-319; John Fforde, *The Bank of England and Public Policy, 1941-1958* (Cambridge, 1992), 88-90.

England, as meat exports to Great Britain were easily translated into vitally needed U.S. products. In the months after the treaty's signing, Miranda had converted almost $170 million to help cover his purchases in the United States. Although the British claimed that nations like Argentina had precipitated this crisis by converting so aggressively, Perón and Miranda were quick to respond to the betrayal.[11]

Not surprisingly, the Argentines repudiated the Miranda-Eady pact immediately, and Miranda announced that he was stopping corned beef shipments to England unless the British paid in gold or dollars. The British business community in Buenos Aires fearfully forecasted that Miranda might even go so far as to suspend all food exports to England and seek out alternative markets.[12] Perón's emissaries did turn to Venezuela, offering to barter thousands of tons of meat for petroleum. Whitehall perceived this to be a dual threat, for not only would vitally-needed meat be sent to Venezuela, but the British oil companies in Argentina, which were responsible for importing most of the nation's petroleum, would be hurt badly by the deal. Despite the offer's initial promise, it fell through when the Venezuelan Minister of Agriculture threatened to resign over the prospect of importing beef exposed to *aftosa*. More importantly, it was highly unlikely that the Venezuelan population had any need for the quantities of meat that Miranda sought to export. With this initiative rebuffed, Whitehall could rest assured that "Britain's position as virtually the only fresh meat market remains unassailed at this point."[13]

In this atmosphere of mutual hostility and suspicion, Miranda and his English counterparts sat down to negotiate an end to this "cold meat war" in December. Miranda once again believed

---

11. Escudé, *Gran Bretaña, Estados Unidos*, 318; Fforde, *The Bank of England*, 88-90; Fodor, "Perón's Policies for Agricultural Exports," 135-161; Paz and Ferrari, *Política Exterior Argentina*, 160-161.

12. *Review of the River Plate*, 26 September 1947, 7-9; *Review of the River Plate*, 5 September 1947, 6; see also *Review of the River Plate*, 19 September 1947, 9-10.

13. *Review of the River Plate*, 2 January 1948, 11-12.

he held all of the cards and was determined to press for a restoration of convertibility of not only recently acquired sterling, but the remaining wartime balances of 140 million pounds ($560 million). Because the British had already proven themselves to be unreliable, he pressed to have all Anglo-Argentine transactions conducted in dollars. In addition, he demanded a fifty percent increase in meat prices and asserted that he would be justified in asking for a four hundred percent increase, as oil and coal prices had risen by that amount since 1939. If the British would not pay for Argentine goods, then Miranda was also amenable to a straight barter for oil, coal, and other vital minerals.[14]

The English position seemed decidedly weaker. Although they acknowledged their "*de facto* abrogation" of Miranda-Eady, restoring convertibility was simply not an option. Other nations held balances far larger than Argentina's, and any relaxation might lead to another catastrophic run on sterling. The solution to the question of the debt to Argentina, Whitehall believed, still rested in the sale of the railroads to Perón's government. Yet again, English officials were going to try to persuade the Argentines to take the dilapidated lines off their hands. But to keep food shipments flowing, Whitehall at last was willing to barter quantities of oil, coal, and other "essential" products. It hoped to keep this to a minimum, however, and to convince Miranda to relax import restrictions on "fripperies" like whiskey and cosmetics. Naturally, the British also hoped to keep their food prices low, but it was unclear how Sir Clive Ballieu and Ambassador Leeper were going to persuade Miranda to continue to sell beef for less than half of the Chicago price.[15]

---

14. Gallman to Secretary of State, 10 January 1948, RG 59, 635.4131; Bruce to Secretary of State, 30 January 1948, RG 59, 635.4131; Lewis, *Crisis of Argentine Capitalism*, 192-193.

15. Gallman to Secretary of State, 10 January 1948, RG 59, 635.4131; see also Memorandum of Conversation, Tewksbury, Atwood, Percival, 19 January 1948, RG 59, 635.4131; MacDonald, "The United States, Britain, and Argentina," 188-191; Fforde, *The Bank of England*, 88-89; Jorge Fodor and Arturo O'Connell, "La Argentina y la economía atlántica en la primera mitad del siglo," *Desarrollo Económico* 49 (Abril-Junio 1973), 3-66.

Like the Miranda-Eady negotiations, this new round of talks stalled from the onset as Miranda steadfastly refused to exchange his sterling balances for the railroads. Similarly, Ballieu would budge neither on the issue of convertibility nor the price of meat. If the British were forced to pay more for Argentine beef, the Canadians and Australians could well demand more for their produce as well. Miranda dismissed this complaint, bluntly asserting that this was not his concern. Ballieu countered by pledging that if Argentines insisted on raising the prices anyway, his government would simply buy less, even if it meant lowering meat rations in England. Although Ballieu was able to offer one million tons of coal for barter, he appeared to have little else with which to bargain. Faced with yet another stalemate, both sides tried to apply pressure.[16]

The British announced in early January 1948 that they had just consummated a major grain deal with Australia that would bring over two million tons of wheat to the British Isles. The threat to Argentina was implicit—other food suppliers around the globe were willing to be "reasonable" regarding prices. The Australians had accepted the equivalent of 33.55 pesos per quintal of wheat, whereas Miranda was demanding sixty. Alongside this subtle pressure, rumors were leaking out of London that HMG was on the verge of devaluing the pound. If this occurred, Argentina's sterling balances would have been drastically reduced with a stroke of the pen.[17] Miranda's counter, however, was even more dramatic. On January 25, apparently "without knowledge [of] either Perón [or] Bramulgia," Miranda announced that the Central Bank would no longer honor sterling drafts. As Bruce reported to Washington, "This means stoppage [of] all food shipments [to] England, including some [to] France for whom British are also purchasing." Frustrated with the impasse, Miranda was intent upon drawing the British to the bargaining table in earnest.

---

16. Bruce to Secretary of State, 31 January 1948, RG 59, 835.6131.

17. *Review of the River Plate*, 2 January 1948, 3-4; see also Lewis, *Crisis of Argentine Capitalism*, 192.

On the other hand, Miranda's gambit had the unforeseen consequence of drawing the State Department into the fray. Leeper and Ballieu, who was an old friend of Bruce's, met with the ambassador and informed him that there was "no alternative except [to] withdraw [the] trade mission." Bruce suggested to his superiors that they should "authorize me [to] intimate informally to Perón" the "great importance" of these negotiations to the United States, as Messersmith had done the year before.[18] Marshall, "greatly disturbed" by these developments, responded immediately, warning that Miranda's callous declarations and arbitrary acts might well jeopardize Argentina's relationship with the United States, as "this Argentine action might permit [the] institution of strict US rationing to ensure fulfillment of feeding programs." A United States that had been inconvenienced in this fashion would be "seriously prejudiced" against Argentina for some time to come. He instructed Bruce to inform Perón of this and to notify him "that this government views with alarm the breaking of current Brit[ish] negotiations."[19]

Bruce agreed "one hundred percent" and promised to "operate accordingly." Bruce and Ray met with Bramulgia and relayed Marshall's warnings in the hopes that he might persuade Perón to rein in Miranda. They believed that their visit was "very successful" in persuading Bramulgia, and then they approached the president himself. Bruce "pointed out to President Perón that it was scarcely fair" or "even particularly smart" to put the British "over a barrel in this way." Ironically, Bruce, whose faith in capitalism was his defining characteristic, argued that it was "unfair" for Argentines to try to get a good price when the British "so desperately needed the commodities." Perón called Miranda into his office, and in Bruce's presence, told the "economic czar" to lower his demands.[20]

---

18. Bruce to Secretary of State, 26 January 1948, RG 59, 635.4131.

19. Marshall to Bruce, 26 January 1948, RG 59, 635.4131.

20. Bruce to Secretary of State, 28 January 1948, RG 59, 635.4131; Bruce to Secretary of State, 31 January 1948, RG 59, 611.3531; Bruce, *Memoirs*, 261-262.

But the State Department was not done yet and opted to "show as little disposition as possible to supply dollars" to Argentina until the British food supply had been secured. In early 1948, a U.S. Army purchasing mission had gone to Buenos Aires to procure several hundred thousand tons of wheat for occupied Germany. Because this purchase promised to bring millions of dollars to Argentina, Peronists had very high hopes. If the U.S. Army took greater responsibility for feeding Europe and entered the bidding for Argentine food products on a large scale, then Miranda could become even more intransigent. To avoid this, Bruce urged his superiors to withdraw the mission to give England a "fighting chance."[21] Unwilling to take this radical step, the State Department did make it clear to Perón that the Army purchases would not compete with the British, and the Army even seems to have stalled its negotiations until the British completed theirs.

Although it is impossible to assert firmly that Bruce's conversations with Bramulgia and Perón, Marshall's warnings, and the Army mission's stalling broke the deadlock, Miranda and Ballieu signed the first Andes Agreement just two weeks later. Much of the deal was a classic bilateral barter. Argentina promised to ship 420,000 tons of meat and more than 1.3 million metric tons of grain to England. For their part, the British agreed to part with 2.5 million cubic meters of petroleum, one million tons of coal, seventy-seven thousand tons of steel, fifty-four thousand tons of tinplate, and various chemicals. The most significant feature of the deal, however, was the surprise sale of the British railroads, as Miranda suddenly opted to use the proceeds of 1948 meat sales and most of his remaining sterling balances to nationalize the rail lines. The terms of the purchase are somewhat puzzling. Argentina was obligated to pay nearly 2.7 billion pesos (£150 million) to gain the title to the railroads and pay off their debts. Miranda knew well that the decaying lines were worth no more than one billion pesos

---

21. Acting Secretary of State to Embassy Buenos Aires, 7 February 1948, RG 59, 635.4131; Bruce to Secretary of State, 11 February 1948, RG 59, 635.4131; see also Bruce to Secretary of State, 8 April 1948, RG 59, 835.61315; Memorandum of Conversation, Tewksbury, Atwood, and Percival, RG 59, 635.4131.

at best and recognized that the Argentine government would be forced to invest another billion to even make them profitable. Although Miranda had serious misgivings about the sale, Ballieu's team jubilantly proclaimed, "We got it!" as Leeper thanked Bruce for his "discussions with Bramulgia" that "certainly" had a considerable impact on the outcome.[22]

There can be little doubt that once again the British had managed to translate a weaker bargaining position into victory with the assistance of a U.S. ambassador. Although they were forced to sell "essential" industrial raw materials, they averted a serious increase in meat and grain prices. Just as significantly, however, they had unloaded the railroads and virtually erased Argentina's sterling balances with a stroke of the pen. Why Miranda relented remains something of a mystery. The British knew well that Miranda reacted to the mere mention of the railroads as bull to a "red rag." Ray credited Bramulgia with having changed Perón's mind, tacitly reinforcing the idea the U.S. embassy had played a key role in convincing the foreign minister.[23]

Certainly. the threat that the United States would not help Argentina solve its dollar shortage must have weighed heavily upon Perón, but more important, in all likelihood, was the threat of British devaluation. The British did, as Paul Lewis pointed out, devalue sterling shortly thereafter, so Peronists could claim to have made the best of a bad situation in this regard. Had they not purchased the railroads, their sterling balances would have evaporated, with little to show for them. Miranda had always argued there was no good reason to purchase this "old iron," and his sudden reversal strongly suggests that England, the United States, and Perón himself had conspired to give him no alternative.[24]

---

22. Lewis, *Crisis of Argentine Capitalism*, 193-194; Leeper to Bruce, 1 March 1948, Bruce Papers, Series 1; see also Ray to Secretary of State, 18 February 1948, RG 59, 835.50; MacDonald, "The United States, Britain, and Argentina," 193.

23. Fforde, *The Bank of England*, 105; see also Ray to Dearborn, 12 April 1948, RG 59, 735.41.

24. Lewis, *Crisis of Argentine Capitalism*, 194-195.

Although Perón may have accepted the English terms unwillingly, he claimed complete victory nonetheless, once again turning a necessity into a virtue. He advertised the purchase as the glorious culmination of his efforts to drive foreigners from Argentina. *Peronistas* took to the streets to celebrate, and Argentine newspapers jubilantly proclaimed, "Now they are ours!" and "Now they are in the hands of the people!" Nationalists called for him to complete the "recuperation" of the nation, some clamoring for the nationalization of the *frigorificos* next, while others looked for him to expropriate the oil facilities. Even if it made little financial sense, the railroad nationalization was effective politically. If there was any suspicion that Perón was abandoning his nationalist and revolutionary credentials to move into alliance with the *Yanqui* capitalists, the Andes Agreement reaffirmed his position with the masses, if nothing else.[25]

Despite Ballieu's early exuberance toward his victory, not all of his countrymen shared his enthusiasm. The *Daily Express*, angry over the sale of badly needed coal, called the Andes Agreement the "worst commercial defeat Britain has ever suffered." There was also criticism in Parliament. One critic argued that, in essence, the English were eating the railroads by trading them for meat and asked what part of the empire they would be forced to consume next year. However, the *Review of the River Plate* best articulated the British loss. The editors of the Buenos Aires commercial journal called the sale of the railroads "the end of an epoch" characterized by Anglo-Argentine partnership. The elimination of this major British investment in Argentina symbolically cut the ties that had made Argentina an informal dominion of the British empire.[26] Britain would never again be Argentina's great power patron, and hereafter, Perón would have no choice but to turn to the United States for assistance. Even if

---

25. *El Trabajador de Carne*, Febrero 1948, BBAA, FSR; *El Trabajador de Carne*, Marzo 1948, BBAA, FSR; see also Escudé, *Gran Bretaña, Estados Unidos*, 320-322.

26. *Review of the River Plate*, 20 February 1948, 4; *Review of the River Plate*, 27 February 1948, 3, 8; see also MacDonald, "The Unites States, Britain, and Argentina," 188-191.

the British had gotten the better of Perón this time, it was in the long run a Pyrrhic victory.

## III

With no hope of translating their sterling reserves into dollars, Perón's and Miranda's last real hope of sustaining their economic program rested in the European Recovery Program or, as it was popularly known, the Marshall Plan. Although Clayton had announced in 1945 that Latin America could not expect U.S. financial assistance until Europe was on its feet, U.S. efforts to reconstruct Europe nonetheless promised peripheral benefits for South America. The technocrats of the ECA would be allocating Marshall Plan dollars to European nations to be spent in the Western Hemisphere through offshore procurement, and Latin Americans would be able to earn desperately needed dollars to restimulate the triangular trade. Marshall estimated that the nations of the Western Hemisphere might be able to earn $10 billion through offshore procurement.[27]

Because no Latin American nation seemed to be in as strong a position as Argentina to capitalize upon the ERP, Perón and Miranda had reason for optimism. The International Emergency Food Commission (IEFC) reported that the world's grain needs exceeded available surpluses by over ten million tons in 1948. For Argentines, the combination of global food shortages and the opportunity to earn dollars appeared to offer nothing short of salvation. "It is scarcely an exaggeration," the *Journal of Commerce* opined, to say that the "Marshall Plan, as originally and at present conceived, would be rendered impractical by an Argentine decision to remain outside it." The *Journal* predicted that Argentina could count upon selling $168 million of meat, $730 million of grain, and more that $400 million of other goods in the first fifteen months. Miranda shared in the optimism, asserting that even though "the U.S. has all the marbles," the ERP would soon

---

27. *Review of the River Plate*, 14 November 1947, 12.

change that, as he announced that he would have $1.5 billion worth of goods ready to be sent once the ERP went into effect.[28]

Unbeknownst to the Argentines, however, the "Wall Street wolves" of the ECA had other ideas. The ECA had been created to allocate resources for Europe, bring down trade barriers, and economically integrate the continent. In short, its function was to promote multilateralism, U.S.-style privatist corporatism, and liberal capitalism, while "discourag[ing] totalitarianism and highly centralized governments." Regarding bilateralism and statism as nothing short of malevolent, the men who staffed the ECA saw no reason to reward Perón's Argentina for enacting policies so clearly antithetical to their ideals. Perón's domestic opponents concurred, warning that "buying from IAPI, [the United States] will strengthen that monopolistic system of simultaneous exploitation of the world and the Argentine people, of progressive strangulation of the system of free trade, and disruption of the Argentine market and other markets."[29] U.S. policymakers understood that "organizations like IAPI can only exist in highly centralized governments and, if we are unable to take advantage of this situation to reduce IAPI's activities, it will vitally affect the course of American business." "Not only in Argentina" would U.S. interests suffer, "but probably in neighboring countries who may be tempted to follow Argentina's example."[30]

More concretely, ECA officials believed that Argentina was not "doing its bit" to assist in European recovery. Miranda and IAPI appeared to be withholding food to exacerbate shortages and selfishly exploiting the world food crisis. Certain officials in the ECA viewed their position as an opportunity to exact some justice by punishing the Argentines. As D. A. FitzGerald, the ECA administrator largely responsible for procurement in Argentina,

---

28. *Review of the River Plate*, 6 February 1948, 6; *Journal of Commerce* statistics cited in *Review of the River Plate*, 9 April 1948, 9-11; Miranda quoted in *Review of the River Plate*, 4 June 1948, 3-4.

29. Hogan, *The Marshall Plan*, 138; Pinedo to Armour, 20 May 1948, RG 59, 835.50.

30. Embassy Buenos Aires to Tewksbury, 29 April 1948, RG 59, 611.3531.

noted, it was a "good time to beat the Argentine to its knees." Thus, in May 1948, ECA officials, apparently with at least the tacit cooperation of their chief, Paul Hoffman, began an independent campaign to derail the Peronist economic experiment.[31]

Bruce concurred with the ECA's position. Recognizing that the Argentines desperately needed dollars and that "the United States is the lifeline to the Argentine," he urged Marshall Planners to monitor expenditures in Argentina very carefully. "If the United States extended vast credits to Europe and permitted a certain percentage of these dollar credits to be used in Argentina for purchases without any conditions attached," he argued, "we would have no ammunition for trading purposes." He recommended "strongly that no action should be taken with regard to purchases from Argentina" unless he was consulted and went so far as to urge his superiors to "have the Marshall Plan set up" in such a way that the U.S. government could use "discretion in permitting Argentina to benefit."

Moreover, he understood that the question of whether "Miranda stays on or not will depend largely on how serious Argentina's financial and economic crisis becomes and whether Miranda is able to convince the President that he is doing anything constructive."[32] "It begins to look more and more as if Miranda's political position is in the balance," State Department functionary Rollin Atwood reminded his superiors, "so now Miranda has to produce US dollars" further linking the "economic czar's" job with both the Marshall Plan and the Argentine economy. Bruce understood that if Argentina recovered, or even made significant headway toward recovery, Miranda might claim victory and remain in power. Nonetheless, he urged that this be done quietly, warning that "it will antagonize even the Argentines who are our friends if we appear to gloat over Argentina's present discomfiture," and

---

31. Department Memorandum, "Instances of Apparent Discrimination by ECA Against Argentina," 25 January 1949, PSF, Foreign Affairs, Argentina, HST.

32. Bruce to Secretary of State, 24 December 1947, RG 59, 635.4131; Dearborn to Atwood and Martin, 21 October 1947, RG 59, MRIC, Argentina; Bruce to Secretary of State, 26 December 1947, RG 59, 835.4131; Bruce to Secretary of State, 6 October 1947, RG 59, 835.50.

made it clear that the policy of economic subversion had to be conducted quietly and without "indiscriminate advance publicity." Ray concluded that "Argentina's dollar situation is deteriorating rapidly, and things will come to a head within the next few weeks in such a way that it will be easier for us to deal" with Perón, provided the ERP did not inadvertently rescue him.[33]

Despite all predictions, the ECA had a unique opportunity to do just that. The U.S. wheat crop was the second largest ever, Canada also had a bumper crop, and French food production was up by twenty-five percent in 1948. When ECA and IEFC experts analyzed the data in the summer, they discovered that Argentina did not hold a whip hand over the Marshall Plan after all. In fact, it might even be possible to meet continental Europe's food needs without any Argentine contribution at all. Peronists who had assumed that Marshall Planners would be forced to come begging to IAPI soon learned that the ECA was quite content to ignore them altogether.[34]

The ECA had to be careful, however. Critics of the Marshall Plan had already started to attack it as a selfish program to help U.S. exporters sell to dollar-starved Europe. The ECA could feasibly give preferential treatment to U.S. goods and guarantee that the dollars spent for Europe returned to the United States. To undercut this criticism, Paul Hoffman had pledged to purchase from the supplier who offered the lowest prices, regardless of national origin, ensuring that U.S. taxpayers' dollars would be spent as prudently as possible. This policy turned out to be the long-sought weapon against Perón, as IAPI's pricing policies served admirably as a justification to withhold offshore procurement dollars and hoist Miranda by his own petard.

Although ECA officers argued that they were merely following the Congressional mandates for frugality, there can be no

---

33. Atwood to Tewksbury and Woodward, 1 October 1947, RG 59, MRIC; Bruce to Secretary of State, 2 July 1948, RG 59, 835.50; Ray to Lyon, 17 November 1947, RG 59, 835.50.

34. *Review of the River Plate*, 18 June 1948, 10; "Instances of Apparent Discrimination," PSF, Foreign Affairs, Argentina, HST.

doubt that the ECA's policies were deliberately aimed at punishing Perón. Richard M. Bissell, ECA Assistant Deputy Administrator, told the Senate Appropriations Committee that "no exports whatever are contemplated in the near future in Argentina, and none whatever will be made so far as we control them." The ECA informed the U.S. embassy in Copenhagen that its policy was simply "not to approve procurement authorizations for materials from Argentina." Similarly, it told an Italian delegation that there was not enough wheat available to meet their nation's needs—ignoring the Argentine surplus. The Greeks were told in July that the "prohibition" against "Argentina continues." The ECA was even willing to break its own rules to punish Perón. In August, FitzGerald authorized a purchase of Mexican beef, acknowledging that Argentine meat was cheaper, and gave instructions that meat was to be purchased from other nations, "no matter how much higher the price might be." The ECA defended this policy by asserting that it would not allocate dollars for Argentine meat until its grain prices had become "more reasonable."[35]

The ECA assumed that IAPI was going to continue to charge exorbitant rates for its grains. Therefore, it enforced the "prohibition" upon the Argentines alone "because they have not as yet demonstrated a willingness to sell to [ERP] participants at reasonable prices." As the U.S. embassy pointed out, however, Miranda repeatedly asserted that he was willing and even quite desperate to bring his grain prices down to the U.S. or world levels. Miranda's "*volte face* on grain prices," Ray noted, was not "evidence of his sympathy for starving Europe" but a realistic decision calculated to earn dollars. Although Bruce had informed Marshall and Truman of this development, the ECA had "adopted from its inception a policy of withholding all procurement from Argentina pending the negotiation of a satisfactory price agreement." To complete the Catch-22, the ECA refused to open such negotiations.[36]

---

35. "Instances of Apparent Discrimination," 25 January 1949, PSF, Foreign Affairs, Argentina, HST; Bruce to Truman, 15 November 1948, RG 59, 711.35.

36. Ray to Lyon, 17 November 1947, RG 59, 835.50; Bruce to Secretary of State, 31 January 1948, RG 59, 611.3531; Bruce to Secretary of State, 3

The ECA did dispatch Struve Hensel to Buenos Aires in June, and Argentines rejoiced as his visit seemed to herald the arrival of ERP dollars. But Hensel made it clear that he did not come to negotiate but to inform Perón that the ECA was fully prepared to reconstruct Europe without Argentine assistance. "Why should we pour dollars down here for something we can buy cheaper elsewhere?" Hensel inquired of Argentines, before informing them that they needed to sell their goods below U.S. or world levels to attract the Marshall planners and European purchasing missions. He concluded by making it clear that the ECA was not "intended to be a rescue agency for the Argentine economy" and that Perón was going to have to make dramatic changes in his national economy to lure ERP dollars.[37] In spite of his apparent candor, Hensel was not entirely forthright. He assured Perón that while the ECA would refuse to allocate dollars for Argentina, it would not interfere with direct Argentine dealings with Western European nations. In theory, IAPI could continue to negotiate with the Europeans, but the transactions would not involve Marshall Plan dollars. Nonetheless, throughout 1948, the ECA did "supervise" a number of European transactions that were conducted in other soft currencies.

In August, ECA liaisons offered to allocate dollars to Italy for U.S. wheat to weaken Miranda's bargaining position and drive down the price of Argentine wheat, lard, and corn. The French were given the same offer later that month. On other occasions, the ECA offered dollar expenditures for purchases in other Latin American nations or the United States to replace Argentine sales in other currencies. Although this practice defied congressional mandates to conserve ERP dollars for purchases that could not be made in other currencies, the ECA justified it by asserting that it was part of a larger effort to bring Argentine prices down and thereby stretch European purchasing power. Throughout 1948, the

---

November 1948, enclosure 1, Memorandum of Conversation, Bruce and Miranda, RG 59, 611.3531.

37. "Instances of Apparent Discrimination," 25 January 1949, PSF, Foreign Affairs, Argentina, HST.

ECA financed a meager $1.1 million of purchases in Argentina, while Canada, Australia, and other food-producing nations had been granted $360 million in sales. Even if the ECA was not responsible for Argentina's deepening economic crisis, it was impeding recovery, and as Escudé illustrated, doing lasting damage to Argentina. In short, the agency was making good on FitzGerald's pledge to "beat the Argentine to its knees."[38]

Unfortunately for the Truman Administration, FitzGerald, Edward Kunze, and other ECA functionaries were not content with their backroom efforts and boasted to reporters of their anti-Argentine endeavors.[39] When the *Journal of Commerce* published their remarks in late 1948, it violently rekindled anti-U.S. nationalism in Argentina. Mobs "carrying scaffolds and nooses" met in front of the U.S. embassy in Buenos Aires and put on what Bruce called "a first class anti-United States demonstration."

The ECA's indiscretions could not have come at a worse time. In late September, Argentine police had arrested the old labor chief, Cipriano Reyes, for plotting to assassinate the Peróns. Reyes was apparently entrapped by *peronista* military officers who tricked him into joining into a conspiracy. They linked him with Braden's old friend, John Griffiths, who had been Nazi-hunting and intriguing with the anti-Peronist opposition. Griffiths had convinced Supreme Court Justice Robert L. Jackson that he was close to uncovering war criminals such as Martin Bormann and had been given FBI assistance in his search. For the Peronist police, the link between Reyes, Griffiths, and the FBI was both clear and damning. Perón used this revelation to resurrect the specter of Braden and stir up anti-U.S. nationalism once again. After a speech before the Plaza de Mayo in which he blamed Washington for the abortive attempt on his life, *peronistas* "menaced" the U.S. embassy. Combined

---

38. State Department Memorandum, "Instances of Apparent Discrimination," 25 January 1949, PSF, Foreign Affairs, Argentina, HST; see also Bruce to Secretary of State, 31 January 1948, RG 59, 611.3531; Escudé, *Gran Bretaña, Estados Unidos*, 323-328.

39. *La Prensa*, 11 Noviembre 1948, 4; *La Prensa*, 19 Noviembre 1948, 3.

with the ECA revelations, the Reyes episode threatened the rapprochement that Bruce was working to build.[40]

Bruce himself was placed in a very sensitive position. Since his cousin Howard Bruce was the Deputy Administrator of the ECA, the ambassador was a natural target for resentment. Still, this did not seem to impair his ability to handle the crisis and restore the "harmonious arrangement" that the State Department had been working to build.[41] After returning from Washington, where he had been coordinating Truman's reelection campaign, and infuriated after spending three hours in the Casa Rosada "listening to Argentine complaints," he fired off letters to Truman and Marshall, protesting the ECA's "latest atrocities." Professing "no particular sympathy" with Perón's government or its policies, he argued that there was still no reason that Argentina should be "crucified" by "every jackass minor official who happens to hold a clerkship." He singled out FitzGerald, Kunze, and a dozen of their "collaborators" as the major culprits, and reminded the president that FitzGerald, a "disloyal" naturalized Canadian, had actively worked for the Republican Party during the 1948 election. Bruce conceded to Truman that "I'm sure I'm not as tough as you are," but nonetheless urged him to:

> . . . bring out the big stick on those boys and give them hell, and if you haven't got time to do that, just eliminate them from any future part in your party. What ECA needs is a tough Democrat to go into that flock of long-haired boys who haven't yet learned that you're the only person who knows how to run your own show, and tell him to cull out the herd, and the quicker he can hit them over the head the sooner you'll be able to get your administration identified with officials of your choice instead of inferior and worthless showoffs.

---

40. Giacalone, "From Bad Neighbors," 173-176; Crassweller, *Perón and the Enigmas of Argentina*, 192-3; Embassy Buenos Aires to Secretary of State, 20 October 1948, RG 59, 711.35.

41. Bruce to Marshall, 19 November 1948, RG 59, 711.35; Bruce to Truman, 13 November 1948, RG 59, 711.35.

Although he had the "highest regard for Mr. Hoffman," he asked that the ECA administrator discipline FitzGerald and the other "third and fourth rate bureaucrats" who were "using their governmental positions to vent personal prejudices against the Argentine."[42]

The vehemence of Bruce's outburst underscores the danger the ECA's stance posed. State Department officers recognized all too well that "if an economic bust comes," Perón would not "bear the brunt of the blame but instead will shift it to our shoulders." Moreover, Miranda would be able to preserve political support for his economic program by claiming that "he was being overwhelmed by Yankee imperialism" as he put up "a gallant fight for the poor Argentines."[43] By publicizing its intentions to punish Argentina, the ECA had needlessly triggered a nationalist backlash all too similar to the one Braden had provoked in 1946. Bruce did not protest the ECA's effort to deny dollars to Argentina—indeed, he had all but suggested it—but the failure of Peronism had to appear to be the result of the inherent flaws of statism, not another instance of "Yankee imperialism."

Bruce reassured Perón that he would "attempt to get the matter cured" himself and asked him "not to answer the ECA." He was successful for the time being and modestly reported to Truman that "we have kept everything quiet without blowing off the lid, and down here that is real diplomacy." He went even further to quell rumors of a rift between the two governments and absolve the U.S. government of any role in the Reyes plot by attending an opera at the famous Teatro Colon. Bruce suggested that he, General Matthew Ridgeway (who was "used to being shot at"), and their wives publicly join the Peróns in their box seats where the assassination was supposed to take place. "That way," Bruce claimed, "if anybody is going to be assassinated, we can all be

---

42. Bruce to Truman, 15 November 1948, RG 59, 711.35; Bruce to Marshall, 17 November 1948, RG 59, 711.35; see also Bruce Unreleased Press Statement, 11 November 1948, RG 59, 711.35.

43. Maleady to Secretary of State, 4 May 1949, RG 59, 711.35; Bruce to Secretary of State, 21 January 1949, RG 59, 711.35; see also MacDonald, "The Cold War and Perón," 410.

assassinated together." Truman recognized Bruce's achievements which had prevented "what might have become an unpleasant press campaign." Indeed, Perón had initially blasted the Truman Administration and the State Department for the ECA's policies but retracted his statements after conferring with Bruce. Bruce gave Perón a written statement exonerating the State Department that Perón read publicly almost verbatim. The president did not stop there, proclaiming "the gratitude of the Argentine Government and people for his efforts on behalf of the consolidation and improvement of relations with the United States" and lauding his "truly American spirit, as evidenced by his eagerness, above all, to serve harmony between the two American nations."[44]

The ambassador may not have realized the full significance of his actions at the time, but he had launched what British journalists came to call the "Bruce Plan." His vocal efforts on behalf of the Argentines, "charming blandishments" to Perón, and seemingly "sincere protests" against the ECA furthered his efforts to win the president's gratitude and trust. It appeared that the ambassador had acted boldly and defiantly to assist Argentina against his own countrymen, and even his own family.[45] Put simply, Peronists misinterpreted Bruce's protests, failing to understand that his goal was not to assist them in any meaningful way, but to convince the ECA to "lay off putting anti-Argentine propaganda in the press." Perón later claimed that the Marshall Plan had been an act of "economic aggression" but failed to see Bruce's part in it.[46]

---

44. Bruce to Truman, 15 November 1948, RG 59, 711.35; Statement Issued by Perón, 28 October 1948, Bruce Papers, Series 1; Bruce, *Memoirs*, 294-7; see also Truman to Bruce, 9 December 1948, PSF, Foreign Affairs, Argentina, HST.

45. Stanton Griffis, *Lying in State* (Garden City, 1952), 260; Luna, *Perón y su tiempo*, 208; Memorandum of Conversation, Miller, Griffis, Mallory, Perón, Cereijo, Ares, et al, 20 February 1950, RG 59, Records of the Assistant Secretary of State for Latin American Affairs, 1949-1953, Argentina (RASS).

46. Bruce to Secretary of State, 17 November 1948, RG 59, 711.35; Paz and Ferrari, *Política Exterior Argentina*, 154; see also Descartes, "Economic Cooperation," in Pool to Department of State, 20 April 1951, RG 59, 635.00; *Primera Plana*, 30 Agosto 1966, 38-39.

At the same time Bruce blamed the economic crisis "solely and entirely to the Argentines' own stupidity," Perón hailed Bruce's supposed efforts to "facilitate [Argentine] industrialization," "enable Argentina to occupy a more favorable position," and "make daily closer our traditional bonds of friendship." While Argentines had correctly ascertained that earlier bureaucratic disputes within the U.S. government had only concerned the proper "method or procedure to attain the same end," they failed to discern that Bruce's feud with the ECA was much the same. Both the ECA and the State Department were striving to build a global, liberal capitalist order, but the ECA's staff had not understood the importance of keeping these efforts "underground" when trying to preserve the veneer of non-intervention in a "Good Neighborhood."[47]

On the surface, the "Bruce Plan" involved little more than giving Argentines the impression that State Department was earnestly working to help Argentina out of its financial difficulties. While ECA officials worked to crush Perón, Bruce was able to convince Argentines that he was looking for some way the "Argentine dollar situation can be saved." Toward this end, he returned to Washington in August to plead the Argentine case before his superiors, accompanied by Orlando Maroglio, new head of the Central Bank. Bruce's journey showed Argentines that he was actively seeking a solution to their problems, so nationalists would find it difficult to blame the United States for their country's misfortunes. In addition, it was an opportunity for Bruce to inform Hoffman firsthand of what harm his underlings were doing and possibly change the ECA's policies for the better.[48]

---

47. Bruce to Acheson, 12 August 1949, Bruce Papers, Series 1; Statement Issued by Perón, 28 October 1948, Bruce Papers, Series 1; Luti to Cooke, 30 Enero 1946, AMREC, BA, EEUU, 1946, Política Exterior, 8, 2; Escudé, "La Traición a los derechos humanos, 1950-1955," *La política exterior argentina y sus protagonistas, 1880-1995*, ed. Silvia Ruth Jalabe (Buenos Aires, 1996), 81; *Gran Bretaña, Estados Unidos*, 215.

48. Bruce to Secretary of State, 22 June 1948, RG 59, 835.50; *Review of the River Plate*, 15 October 1048, 6.

The stated goal of Bruce's visit—to bring ERP dollars to Argentina—was one guaranteed to be popular in Buenos Aires. Although he was unsuccessful in effecting a notable change in the ECA policy, his efforts did not go unnoticed, as he attempted to convince his superiors to purchase over $200 million of canned meat from Argentina. British observers commented that the "indefatigable" Bruce had become almost an Argentine ambassador in Washington. Although he returned to Buenos Aires without having changed ECA policies or achieved any easing of the "sanitary embargo," he told Marshall that "the whole matter turned out very well, and I am sure that you will be pleased with the excellent publicity that the State Department has received." In the meantime, others in the Department took up his attack on the ECA.[49]

In January 1949, officials in the State Department's Office of River Plate Affairs, at Bruce's behest, released a comprehensive list of more than thirty specific occasions when the ECA had openly or covertly "discriminated" against Argentina. Some of the most damaging evidence came from the ECA's Robert Strange, who had examined his agency's Argentine policy in August. "Although Argentina had quoted U.S. or lower prices in every known dollar transaction during recent months," Strange reported, "ECA questioned that Argentina was willing to sell her exports at or below U.S. prices." The ECA had acted under the presumption that Argentina was impeding European recovery and had informed Perón that he should simply grant the Europeans credits for Argentine goods, even though this would do nothing to solve their own dollar shortage. In truth, Argentina, in the past three years, had lent ERP nations between $500 million and $1.5 billion, much of it, Strange concluded, through "extension of credits and the acceptance of blocked soft currencies." Indeed, even the *Review of the River Plate*, which was rarely sympathetic to Perón and

---

49. *Review of the River Plate*, 3 September 1948, 3-4; *Review of the River Plate*, 24 September 1948, 3-4; Bruce to Marshall, 19 November 1948, RG 59, 711.35.

Miranda, had to conclude that Argentina had indeed "done its bit" to assist in European recovery.[50]

Private businessmen also argued convincingly that the ECA's policies were wrongheaded and counter to the U.S. national interest. Unable to make dollar purchases, Argentina was turning back to Europe, favoring European firms that would conduct their transactions in other currencies. Rather than purchase Standard's oil, for example, Miranda announced in December that he would try to meet Argentina's needs exclusively from the sterling area in an effort to find some use for his excess sterling and conserve his precious dollars. Indeed, the Andes Agreement was already replacing many other U.S. exports with British substitutes. Robert Harrison, an engineer who had been contracted by the Argentine government, wrote Tewksbury with his concerns. He was being retained by the Peronists to make purchases of $80 million of heavy machinery from England—purchases "which rightfully belong in the U.S.A." Although he admitted that he should be satisfied with his "engineering fee and not give a damn where the machinery comes from," he was also a "pretty enthusiastic citizen of the United States." Harrison recommended that ECA should "buy beef for the British and insist that the Argentines earmark the dollars for U.S. machinery." Although Harrison considered himself to be nothing more than a "simple" engineer, he clearly articulated yet another of the ECA's failings.[51]

Stripped of pretense, the ECA's position became indefensible. Marshall, Acting Secretary of State Robert Lovett, and Henry Labouisse threw their weight behind Bruce's appeals and worked to convince Truman to end ECA "discrimination." Because some rationing measures were still in place for U.S. food consumption, the Marshall planners would have been hard-pressed to explain why Argentine surpluses were not being utilized. Thus,

---

50. "Instances of Apparent Discrimination," 25 January 1948, PSF, Foreign Affairs, Argentina, HST; *Review of the River Plate*, 10 September 1948, 8; see also Watrous to Secretary of State, 4 February 1948, RG 59, 835.50; Laura Randall, *Essays on the Economic History of Argentina* (New York, 1978), 230.

51. Harrison to Tewksbury, 24 September 1948, RG 59, 611.3531; see also Bruce to Secretary of State, 23 December 1948, RG 59, 835.50.

Truman and Hoffman announced that they "would now welcome ECA purchases in Argentina as elsewhere," as Howard Bruce told Bramulgia that Argentina might receive "several hundred million dollars" of offshore procurement "in the near future." Lovett "suggested that the figure should be regarded as more or less $100,000,000." He later recanted this pledge, but Miranda and Perón had good reason to think that ECA dollars were finally forthcoming, and that James Bruce's efforts had been the reason.[52]

## IV

At first glance, it may seem that Bruce and the State Department had suddenly become apologists for or defenders of Perón. Indeed, Bruce feared that some could reach the conclusion that he was "putting the stamp of approval too strongly on the existing regime."[53] But this was hardly the case. The Department had been hoping for years that Argentina would bankrupt itself, and the ECA's policies were certainly promoting that development. After years of experience with Perón, however, the State Department recognized that the ECA's vocal approach, like Braden's, was counterproductive. In all likelihood, had the ECA quietly and unobtrusively hamstrung Argentine exports, Bruce would have had no complaints. Indeed, he advocated such a policy himself, encouraged the ECA to drive for a *quid pro quo* that might spell the end of IAPI. He even characterized Hensel's performance in Buenos Aires as "perfectly splendid." Only when ECA officials made inflammatory public statements that ignited Argentine nationalism did the ambassador started firing off letters to Truman and Marshall. "This discrimination has made it more difficult to maintain friendly relations with the Argentine Government," he

---

52. Memorandum of Conversation, Tewksbury, Atwood, Martin, Meade, and Marten, 14 March 1949, RG 59, 835.4131; Daniels to Secretary of State, 22 March 1949, RG 59, 835.50; see also Lovett to Clifford, 7 January 1948, PSF, Foreign Affairs, Argentina, HST.

53. Bruce to Merz, 17 December 1948, Bruce Papers, Series 1.

noted, "and led it to believe that the U.S. was pursuing a vacillating policy,"[54]

One of the primary purposes of bankrupting Perón was from the onset to force him to make "sweeping changes" toward liberal capitalism, or possibly even see him overthrown by "moderates" such as General Sosa Molina. However, if Argentines perceived that Perón and their nation were being assailed once again by *yanqui* imperialism, the odds of such a change occurring dwindled. Ray had explained to his superiors that the embassy's approach was to quietly "whittl[e] away" at the worst features of Peronism without "provoking a violent disagreement which would be inevitable if we insisted on an immediate showdown." The ECA had risked just that.[55]

Both the ECA and the State Department strove to drive Argentina toward liberal capitalism and away from his state corporatism, but the ECA's amateurish methods had already been tested and found wanting. On the other hand, "Perón understands that he needs the help and cooperation of the United States and if we can offer them to him in a manner which Argentina can find acceptable," Ray noted early in 1949, "we could possibly write our own ticket, especially in view of Argentina's present precarious financial and economic situation."[56] Within months, Ray's prediction came true as Perón informed the State Department that it could indeed "write its own ticket."

---

54. Bruce to McCoy, 19 July 1948, Bruce Papers, Series 1.

55. Ray to Dearborn, 7 October 1947, RG 59, 835.50.

56. Ray to Secretary of State, 4 January 1949, RG 59, 611.3531.

# CHAPTER 9

## PERONISMO PENITENT:
## JANUARY-DECEMBER 1949

> At some point Perón will have to clean out Miranda and the other crooks associated with him or else the Army will probably clean out Perón. At the moment we do not know which way the cat is going to jump, but when it does the chances are that we will land with it on a better spot than the one we left.
>
> James Bruce, 2 July 1948[1]

## I

In January 1949, the State Department's policies finally bore fruit as the economic crisis that had afflicted Peronist Argentina finally drove Perón to his knees. In the process, *peronismo* lost the dynamic maverick nationalism that had characterized the movement. By the end of the year, Peronism was barely recognizable, as Perón became much more compliant with U.S. desires and finally fell into line with U.S. principles of liberal capitalism to some extent. The first U.S. victory was the firing of "economic czar" Miguel Miranda, the driving force behind the Peronist economic program. As the leading proponent of statism, bilateral barter, and independent internationalism, Miranda had long been a thorn in the side of the "Inter-American system." In January, his rivals joined together to oust him and bring a fundamental change to Argentine foreign and domestic economic policy. As Miranda had been running the Argentine economy almost single-handedly since 1946, he naturally bore the responsibility when that economy collapsed. Nevertheless, the State Department played an important role in his fall. A number of

---

1. Bruce to Secretary of State, 2 July 1948, RG 59, 835.50.

powerful *peronistas* had sought counsel from U.S. officials and had been told that Miranda, his state corporatist approach, and his brainchild—IAPI—were the primary impediments to true rapprochement between the U.S. and Argentina. By hinting further that Perón could expect U.S. aid once these roadblocks were cleared, U.S. policymakers privately but proudly took some credit for Miranda's ouster.

The impact of Miranda's absence was felt almost immediately, as Argentina once again opened negotiations with the British. Where once Miranda had been able to forcefully dictate terms to the British, the Argentines were now driven to accept Whitehall's dictates. The State Department also smelled blood in the water. With Perón sitting atop an empty treasury, in desperate need of U.S. aid, and apparently willing to renounce the radical alternative that he had put forward during the war, the Truman Administration pressed its advantage to roll back Peronism. Perón never completely abandoned his state corporatist vision, and therefore never became a perfect ally for the United States, but the Argentina that pleaded for U.S. loans in 1949 and 1950 was far removed from the one that had emerged from World War II boldly challenging U.S. hemispheric dominance.

## II

In January 1949, Perón took his first major step toward genuine rapprochement with the United States by relieving Miranda of his position as the Chairman of the National Economic Council. The commonly accepted rationale for this move is that Eva Perón had denounced him as a thief. According to Bruce, Miranda, in the course of looting the national finances, had ordered wool exporters to leave three percent of their profits on his desk as the price of doing business. When one of them questioned this practice, the "economic czar" responded that "he had to do this because he was collecting for the account of Sra. Perón." The exporter reported it to her, "whereupon the Sra. practically hit the ceiling and said she had never received a cent from Miranda in her life" and that "she did not intend to have her name bantered around in that fashion by a crook like Miranda." Bruce reported that she gave her husband an ultimatum—if Miranda "did not go, she was going to leave the country herself and go and live in Biarritz." Perón tried to placate her and "told her to be a calm little girl," to no avail. She persisted in pressuring him and, Bruce chortled, "Miranda's goose was cooked."[2]

After a stormy cabinet meeting the next week in which her supporters attacked the "economic czar," he resigned his position but remained associated with Perón briefly as a "technical advisor" before leaving government for good. This story, if true, should be seen as the straw that broke the camel's back, rather than the sole reason for his dismissal. Miranda, given almost complete control over the Argentine economy, had accepted credit for the economic boom after the war and had to shoulder the blame for the collapse of 1948-1949. Indeed, a closer examination of the events surrounding the fall of Miranda make it clear that his days were numbered even before Eva Perón turned her guns on him.

Miranda's position within the Perón Administration, although seemingly unassailable, had been deteriorating steadily for a year. The Amer-Ind episode in 1947 almost cost him his job and turned the Army irrevocably against him. Almost as important, however, were the opinions of his civilian peers. Bramulgia, the leader of the "moderate" wing of *peronismo*, resented his interference in foreign affairs and was an intractable foe whose star seemed to be rising. It had been Bramulgia who had elicited Howard Bruce and Robert Lovett's "pledge" that Argentina would receive upward of $100 million in ECA sales. Furthermore, heading a team representing six neutrals, he had earned considerable international acclaim for his skillful mediation of the Berlin crisis.[3] Although Bramulgia had long been hostile toward Miranda, the ranks of the "economic czar's" enemies swelled dramatically throughout 1948.

Foremost among these was his one-time protégé Orlando Maroglio. Maroglio, put in charge of the Central Bank and IAPI

---

2. Bruce to Secretary of State, 21 January 1949, RG 59, 711.35.

3. *Primera Plana*, 6 Junio 1966, 37-38; Ray to Secretary of State, 4 January 1949, RG 59, 611.3531; Ciria, *Política y cultura popular*, 113.

after Miranda was promoted to head the National Economic Council, had long been regarded as a loyal "tool of Miranda." Still, there were periodic "rumors" that he was "asserting himself."[4] By 1948, it was clear that there was some truth to the rumors, as Maroglio reevaluated Miranda's economic program—a reassessment facilitated by Bruce, who invited and accompanied the banker to Washington in September. Bruce introduced him to officials such as William Martin of the Export-Import Bank, Thomas Blaisdell of the Commerce Department, Thomas McCabe of the Federal Reserve, ECA chief Paul Hoffman, and Secretary of the Treasury John Snyder. Although Miranda believed that Maroglio was only "making a fool out of himself" by seeking U.S. assistance, these high-level discussions did have an impact.[5]

Maroglio may have come to the United States to clarify Argentina's position regarding the ERP offshore procurements and to request a credit that might salvage Argentina's precarious dollar situation but instead he received numerous sermons on the virtues of free trade and limited government intervention in the economy and browbeatings on the many failings of IAPI. U.S. officials predictably linked the prospect of assistance with the removal of the economic "restrictions imposed by IAPI." After being barraged repeatedly along these lines, Maroglio pleaded, "don't let's ever mention IAPI again" but was told that it was "pretty difficult to get on to any discussion of Argentine trade without touching on IAPI." His ardor for state trading was starting to cool when he arrived in Washington but by the time he departed, he had been convinced that wholesale changes were in order.[6]

---

4. Memorandum of Conversation, Torry, Carlstein, Tewksbury, Atwood, 24 November 1947, RG 59, 835.77.

5. Fforde, *The Bank of England*, 267; see also Tewksbury to Greenup, 29 September 1948, RG 59, 835.50; Giacalone, "From Bad Neighbors to Reluctant Partners," 189-191.

6. Tewksbury to Greenup, 29 September 1948, RG 59, 835.50; see also Tewksbury, "Visits of Orlando Maroglio," 30 September 1948, RG 59, 611.3531; Greenup to Secretary of State, 22 November 1948, RG 59, 611.3531.

Miranda, of course, was furious and informed Bruce that "we're just waiting for him to get back and we will fire him right away." Eva Perón concurred, apparently calling Maroglio a "son of a bitch," but Bruce warned against hasty action, suggesting that U.S. financial and governmental representatives would not be pleased. Instead he suggested that Miranda wait sixty days to fire him and, according to Bruce, "on the sixtieth day they fired him." Bruce, who privately believed that Maroglio was "simple" and "had only ten percent of Miranda's brains," had nonetheless bought two months for the man who, strangely enough, was nominally both the head of IAPI and Bruce's ally. They were months that Maroglio put to good use.[7]

Upon his return to Buenos Aires, Maroglio presented the cabinet with a report "supporting the thesis that Argentina should relax such control measures such as retard or prevent practical trade and financial operations." Apparently, Maroglio suggested something akin to the "elimination [of] IAPI," touching off a "terrific squabble" in Perón's inner circle. Naturally, Miranda asserted that Maroglio's report should "be consigned to the waste basket," as the feud intensified. By mid-December, Miranda was openly referring to his subordinate as a "dead duck." On January 12, according to two businessmen, a cabinet meeting almost degenerated into a brawl over IAPI and the dollar crisis, when "Mr. Miranda called Mr. Maroglio a liar and Maroglio called Miranda a clown."[8]

The U.S. embassy in Buenos Aires considered the discord in the *peronista* cabinet to be most "beneficial," as it served to "familiarize the Argentine officials with useful facts and afford repeated opportunities for exchanging viewpoints." Key Argentine officials were now discussing sweeping economic changes and their nation's posture toward the United States.[9] Maroglio's was not the

---

7. Bruce, *Memoirs*, 251-252.

8. Greenup to Secretary of State, 12 January 1949, RG 59, 835.6363; Ray to Secretary of State, 21 September 1948, RG 59, 835.5034; Greenup to Secretary of State, 22 November 1948, RG 59, 611.3531; Greenup to Secretary of State, 28 December 1948, RG 59, 835.50.

9. Greenup to Secretary of State, 22 November 1948, RG 59, 611.3531.

only defection from Miranda's camp. Dr. Oscar Ivanissevich, the former ambassador to the United States, underwent a similar transformation. Perón had dispatched Ivanissevich to study the U.S. educational system. When he arrived in the U.S., he had been, according to Bruce, "very prejudiced against us." By the time he returned to Argentina after conversations with Truman, Vandenberg, Connally, and other officials, however, he too started to argue for moderation and conciliation. Because he lived with and was trusted by the Peróns, his views carried some weight. Bruce reported that Ivanissevich had even converted Eva Perón to a "wholeheartedly pro-U.S." position, but this is somewhat suspect.[10] Although her criticisms of the U.S. as a bastion of privilege and exploitation did slack off for a time, she was regularly blasted in U.S. publications like *Time*, and could never be considered an admirer of the United States. Regardless of the reason, when she turned against Miranda, she brought her followers with her, including former *mirandistas* such as José Barro and Ramón Cereijo. Almost overnight, Miranda's position in the Perón administration collapsed completely.

Miranda did try to save himself with a desperate but familiar eleventh-hour ploy. The day he left office he told friends that "the reason he had resigned was that he could not withstand the pressure that had been put on him by Sra. Perón and the U.S. Ambassador." Bruce denied that he had done anything to weaken Miranda and dismissed the accusation as a rather feeble effort to "get us into a battle with him." Perón had used this maneuver in the past to good effect, but Miranda was unable to carry it off. Although Bruce denied that he had anything to do with the immediate decision to purge the "economic czar," he nonetheless took considerable pleasure from Miranda's ousting. "Anyway, the results were what we have been hoping for over a period of many months," he cheerily noted, adding that "it looks now as if there is at least a chance of getting this economy on a reasonably sound basis."[11]

---

10. Bruce to Secretary of State, 21 January 1949, RG 59, 711.35; see also *Primera Plana*, 14 Junio 1966, 40; Gambini, *La primera presidencia de Perón* 61-63.

11. Bruce to Secretary of State, 21 January 1949, RG 59, 711.35.

Miranda's departure had become almost a *sine qua non* of true rapprochement, and the State Department viewed it as a very significant "step in the right direction." While it would have undoubtedly preferred to see Maroglio elevated to Miranda's old posts, it was to be disappointed as Maroglio stepped down from his posts, claiming chronic illness. Nonetheless, Perón did tap two "Bramulgia men," Roberto Ares and Alfredo Gómez Morales, to replace Miranda and Maroglio, suggesting to the State Department that "Perón is accepting the views of Bramulgia as opposed to Miranda on international relations." The embassy reported that "the appearance of new directing figures on the scene appears to presage a fundamental reorganization" of the Argentine economic system, as the Peronists were clearly being driven toward conciliation with the United States.[12]

This impulse must be seen as the major reason for the removal of Miranda, for *peronistas* knew well that U.S. officials despised the "economic czar" and that he was a constant irritant to the State Department. Moreover, he habitually made decisions under the assumption that the United States would never consciously assist Perón. Miranda had long argued for an independent course, asserting that:

> ... we needn't waste time trying to get more dollars out of the United States. I as a trader know that. Nobody buys what he does not need ... what must our policy be? Forsake the dollar area so far as we possibly can.[13]

If Argentina was going to emerge from its economic crisis, Miranda argued that it would have to do so through tighter trade restrictions, even harder bargaining, and bilateralism. This attitude put him at odds with other *peronistas* who had been in growing

---

12. Memorandum of Conversation, Scarpati and Tewksbury, 9 February 1949, RG 59, 835.50; *Current Economic Developments*, 31 January 1949, 187, HST; Embassy Buenos Aires to Secretary of State, 24 January 1949, RG 59, 835.50; see also MacDonald, "The United States, Britain, and Argentina," 194-195; Paso *Del golpe de estado de 1943*, 137.

13. *Review of the River Plate*, 5 December 1949, 9.

contact with State Department and the ECA. Miranda was going to try to solve the financial crisis by using a more forceful application of the same tactics that had created it. However, the severity of the crisis and extravagant U.S. promises had persuaded the rest of the *peronistas* that significant changes had to be made.[14]

José Figuerola, another "extremist," and in many ways the intellectual architect of Peronism, soon followed Miranda into retirement. Figuerola's enemies set upon him in late 1948, as he was drafting the new Argentine Constitution. The traditional explanation for Figuerola's removal is that, like Miranda, he had earned Eva Perón's hostility. Regardless, the new Constitution—ultimately finished by other authors—prohibited foreigners from holding cabinet positions, and the Spaniard was summarily removed from office. With the departure of Miranda, Figuerola, and Maroglio, the men who had directed the Argentine economy for the first three years of Perón's presidency were suddenly gone.[15]

### III

The removal of Miranda from his lofty perch therefore must be seen as a sign that the *peronista* economic program had failed in its basic objectives and that the Argentines were becoming desperate. This manifested itself in negotiations with the British, as the Andes Agreement came up for its first annual amendment. Although Miranda had always been able to negotiate from strength—only to have the rug pulled out from under him at crucial moments by Bramulgia and his U.S. allies—the Argentines entered into the second Andes Agreement from a decidedly weaker position and paid a price for it. The British sensed that Argentina's economic problems would give them new leverage. Not only was Miranda gone, but Ares, Cereijo, Gómez Morales, and the rest of

---

14. Ordway to Secretary of State, 29 November 1948, RG 59, 835.50; Bruce to Secretary of State, 3 November 1948, Enclosure 1, Memorandum of Conversation, Bruce and Perón, RG 59, 611.3531; Greenup to Secretary of State, 22 November 1948, RG 59, 611.3531; Horowicz, *Los cuatros peronismos*, 123.

15. Page, *Perón*, 201-204.

the Argentine negotiators were relatively untested. Instead of a simple one-year barter renewal, this time the British requested a five-year comprehensive deal by which the weakened Argentines might be locked into England's orbit once again. At the very least, the British team believed that it could secure excellent meat prices—perhaps as low as pre-war levels. Charles Meade of the British embassy in Washington reported to the State Department that his government was in a better position than it had ever been, as "the British negotiators could pack up and go home this time if the Argentines were too unreasonable whereas they could not have done so before."[16]

Despite the strength of their position, the British sought further advantage as Meade and his colleagues called upon the State Department. They urged U.S. officials to stop purchasing Argentine meat and leading the Argentines to believe that there might be a $200 million market for canned meat in the U.S. The U.S. Army was following up its 1948 grain purchases for occupied Germany with similar efforts to acquire Argentine pork and beef. Meade and other British officials protested and urged the Truman Administration to buy the meat from any other Latin American nation but Argentina. The U.S. Army had paid more than thirty cents per pound of beef, which apparently led Peronists to rethink the 12.8 cents per pound that the British were accustomed to paying. The British feared that if the Army continued to make purchases, "it is inevitable that [the Argentine government] should be tempted to treat the United Kingdom as a mere residuary and ship to the United Kingdom only that meat which it is unable to dispose of more advantageously." Although it appears that the Whitehall was overstating the threat, considering its confidence that its diplomats could easily walk away from the negotiating table if they had to, Washington acceded to the request.[17]

---

16. Memorandum of Conversation, Meade, Tewksbury, Dearborn, 1 February 1949, RG 59, 635.4131; see also Paz and Ferrari, *Política Exterior Argentina*, 161-164.

17. British Embassy Aide Memoire, 16 February 1949, RG 59, 635.4131; Memorandum of Conversation, Meade, Tewksbury, Dearborn, 1 February 1949, RG 59, 635.4131; Memorandum of Conversation, Marten, Meade, Atwood, Dearborn, Martin, 25 April 1949, RG 59, 635.4131.

With no alternative but the British market, Perón and his new economic team had little choice but to give in to the English demands. Argentine negotiators still pressed for dollars in exchange for the meat, but the British refused to grant convertibility. Tewksbury had informed Meade and F. W. Marten that England could request ECA dollars to make the meat purchases that would help the Argentines immeasurably and facilitate the negotiations. Marten responded that ECA policy throughout 1948 had been to refuse procurement requests for Argentina, so there was no point in making them. Tewksbury countered that this policy had been changed, and the Marshall planners "would now welcome ECA purchases in Argentina as elsewhere." Marten and Meade did not respond. Because "the only opportunity now apparent for Argentina to acquire a considerable quantity of ECA dollars lies in the prospective meat purchase," this was one of the few opportunities to reward the Argentines for their recent policy reversals.[18] But as Perón and the State Department would learn soon, the British had another agenda.

Simply put, the British had no intention of helping the Peronists solve their dollar crisis. Instead, they sought to tie Argentina into the sterling web for the next five years. Anything that weakened Argentine dependence on England or strengthened U.S.-Argentine ties had no place in the British plan. Bruce suggested to Ambassador Jeronimo Remorino that the British had $79 million ECA dollars earmarked for meat purchases in Latin America, and in May, the Department sent an aide memoire to Buenos Aires formally articulating ECA's willingness to finance purchases in Argentina. Remorino asked Sir John Lomax, head of the British negotiating team, about the possibility of using ECA dollars for meat purchases. Lomax replied that "no consideration had been given to such a proposal and none would be." He explained to the Argentines that the "British Government is itself begging from the United States and hence could not well say, 'We have a friend who wants a lift—can you give him a hand-out also?'"

---

18. Memorandum of Conversation, Meade, Marten, Tewksbury, Atwood, Martin, 14 March 1949, RG 59, 835.4131; Martin to RPA, 15 March 1949, RG 59, 635.4131.

Lomax, using this "beggar story," was telling Argentines that the ECA would not allocate funds, at the same time that the State Department was urging him to at least make a request for ERP funding.[19]

But Lomax was not through yet. He came to the U.S. embassy in Buenos Aires with another interesting request. He told the embassy staff that the British, in their efforts to drive the price of Argentine meat down, had been stonewalled by the U.S.-owned *frigorificos* in Argentina. The British were offering to buy beef at the "reasonable" price of .60 pesos per kilo of meat, and the British-owned *frigorificos* had found this price acceptable. The U.S. meatpackers asserted that they would be unable to make a profit for any price less than .75 pesos per kilo. Lomax wondered if the embassy might "recommend" to its countrymen that they sell for the English price. If the U.S. packers did not come around, he warned, then the bulk of the meat sales could be diverted to British firms, "which might conceivably be unfavorable for the Americans." U.S. officials replied that this "smacked of a squeeze on the American packers which is incompatible with our program of assistance to Britain" and refused outright. When U.S. officials approached the owners of the *frigorificos*, both English and U.S. companies denied having had any discussions with Lomax at all. "Mr. Lomax, they agreed, was trying to enlist the assistance of the Embassy, and through it the American packers, in the British effort to hold down the price of meat."[20]

As the negotiations neared completion in May, the State Department started to express concern over the proposed treaty. Despite all Argentine efforts to commit the British to supply dollars, Whitehall managed to have all transactions conducted in inconvertible sterling. Lomax had deflected Argentine demands for convertibility by magnanimously offering to buy Argentine meat at

---

19. Embassy Buenos Aires to Secretary of State, 10 May 1949, RG 59, 835.50; see also Martin to RPA, 15 March 1949, RG 59, 635.4131; Memorandum of Conversation, Marten, Christelow, and Ranney, 7 May 1949, RG 59, 635.4131; Memorandum of Conversation, Remorino, Scarpati, Bruce, and Dearborn, 8 March 1949, RG 59, 835.50; Atwood to Bruce, 28 July 1949, RG 59, 635.4131.

20. Embassy Buenos Aires to Secretary of State, 10 May 1949, RG 59, 835.50.

17.3 cents per pound—his first offer that was greater than the packers' stated cost of production. Furthermore, the Argentines had to agree that twenty percent of their imports from England would be "inessential" items, such as whiskey and cosmetics. Ironically, at the time that Argentina desperately needed industrial imports and dollar exchange, they were being coerced into a deal that denied them both. Whitehall, "convinced that it was unlikely that Argentina would permit a break in negotiations," was pressing its advantage deftly.[21]

Still, all of these provisions were at least tolerable for Washington. Problems arose when it became known that the British were pressing to turn this treaty into a strict bilateral barter, based mainly upon an exchange of Argentine beef for British oil, steel, textiles, automobiles, and other products. Regarding petroleum, the British were proposing that the Shell corporation supply all of Argentina's oil imports for the next five years, supplanting Standard and the other firms that traditionally supplied much of Argentina's petroleum. This caused great consternation in both ECA and the Commerce Department. Thomas Blaisdell met with State Department officers to express his objections to the proposed treaties and to impress them with the "urgency" of the matter. "To continue with bilateralism which forced diversion of trade to the detriment of American trade in its traditional markets," he noted, "would seem to be in direct opposition to [the] objectives" of U.S. policy.[22]

The U.S. oil companies were not the only victims. The U.S.-owned *frigorificos* were going to be pressured to sell beef for less than a quarter of U.S. domestic prices, and half of the generally accepted world prices. Although some in the State Department had been suspicious of the British throughout the course of the negotiations, by May the British intentions had become very transparent. Shell, in all likelihood, would be unable to supply the Argentine requirements of 5.7 million tons of petroleum per year

---

21. Memorandum of Conversation, Marten and Atwood, 19 May 1949, RG 59, 635.4131; Douglas to Secretary of State, 26 April 1949, RG 59, 635.4131.

22. Randall to Martin, 13 May 1949, RG 59, 635.4131.

from the sterling area. Therefore, the English planned to spend dollars to purchase oil in Venezuela in order to sell it in Argentina. Rather than simply supply dollars to Argentina, which might help bail the Peronists out of their financial crisis, the British found it more useful to send dollars to Venezuela. Simply put, U.S. exporters would be excluded from large sectors of the Argentine market, while British exports would regain the privileged position they had occupied in the 1930s.[23]

The State and Commerce Departments mobilized to protest the proposed accord before it was finalized. Acting Secretary of State James E. Webb cornered Sir Derek Hoyar-Miller, protesting that U.S. products were being "squeezed" out of traditional markets by means of "discrimination." This reflected a "very deep-rooted problem" relating to "the economic shape of trade" in the post-war world. "If the British could expand exports by the means of fair and competitive methods," Webb posited, "it would be difficult for us to object—even though some American exporters might lose markets." However, he had to object to this occurring as a result of prejudicial trade agreements, which was a "very different thing." Since the United States had given the British a massive loan in 1946, not to mention Marshall Plan aid, in order to promote multilateral, non-prejudicial exchange, Washington had some cause for concern that Whitehall was so blatantly contravening U.S. policy.[24]

Webb's protest came too late. Hoyar-Miller innocently informed the Department that the agreement would be signed shortly, if it had not already been, and that it was no longer possible to make changes. Officials in Washington were furious. With State Department backing, Blaisdell pressed "very strongly" for Webb to tell the British to "stop making bilateral agreements with L[atin] A[merican] countries." He enlisted Secretary of Commerce Charles Sawyer to his cause and was "delighted" to learn that the State

---

23. Eakens to Brown, 13 May 1949, RG 59, 635.3531.

24. Webb to Secretary of Commerce, 7 June 1949, RG 59, 635.4131; see also Labouisse to Brown, 13 May 1949, RG 59, 635.4131; Labouisse to Thorp, 26 May 1949, RG 59, 635.4131.

Department was planning to continue with its protests to both Argentina and Britain, lest the British succeed in presenting them with a *fait accompli*.[25]

Protests to Perón were futile. The deal was so unfavorable to Argentina that there could be little doubt that the British had been the driving force behind the accord. Minister of Economy Ares openly "lamented" the necessity of "turning to England." Remorino took "the position that his government did not desire such an agreement" but "because of the dollar shortage and pressure from the United Kingdom, Argentina was forced into [it]." He claimed that the "only remedy" for the problem was for "the United States to intercede with the British" or otherwise alleviate "the Argentine dollar shortage." Remorino asserted that the State Department had an obligation to help Argentina extricate itself from the deal, as the U.S. itself bore no small part of the blame for it. He explained that at the same time the State and Commerce Departments had been expressing their support for Argentina, the ECA had continued to undercut the Argentines.[26]

As the negotiations proceeded, ECA officials had "instructed" the Greek government to "avoid any purchases from Argentina during the present UK-Argentine negotiations" which might hurt the British bargaining position. More significantly, on April 29, the ECA dropped a "bombshell" by suddenly announcing that it had authorized $21 million for British pork purchases in the United States at prices significantly higher than those prevailing in Argentina. Interestingly, this pork was the first meat sale—except for some horse meat—that the ECA had ever authorized in the United States. Paul Hoffman explained that "we bought that pork

---

25. Labouisse to Brown, 13 May 1949, RG 59, 635.4131; Nitze to WGB, 18 May 1949, RG 59, 635.4131; see also Martin to Brown, 13 May 1949, RG 59, 635.4131; Corse to Brown, 13 May 1949, RG 59, 635.4131; Juan Archibaldo Lanús, *De Chapultepec a Beagle: Política exterior Argentina, 1945-1980* (Buenos Aires, 1984), 32-33.

26. Bruce to Secretary of State, 10 June 1949, RG 59, 635.4131; Webb to Secretary of Commerce, 7 June 1949, RG 59, 635.4131; see also Memorandum of Conversation, Remorino, Scarpati, Daniels, Atwood, Daniels, 10 May 1949, RG 59, 711.35; Ray Memorandum, 2 June 1949, RG 59, 835.50.

because pork was getting in long supply" in the United States. On the same day, the ECA authorized a $7 million British purchase of canned beef from Mexico. Twenty-eight million dollars of meat sales, as well as a moral victory and a ray of hope, were denied to Perón's new team at a crucial point in its negotiations.[27]

Eleven days after this revelation, the ECA had added an even more devastating insult to the injury. Howard Bruce and Acting Secretary of State Lovett, in their efforts to undo the damage of the ECA's 1948 discrimination, had led Bramulgia to believe that Argentina would be able to earn approximately $100 million through ERP offshore procurements in 1949. Now, Howard Bruce informed the State Department that "no commitment of any kind nor indication as to probable purchases had been made."[28] Apparently, they had only been speculating, not promising. Nonetheless, Bramulgia had left Lovett's office "optimistic," and had returned to Buenos Aires convinced that Argentina might make substantial dollar sales. Although he had known in February that it would be "impossible to purchase more than five to eight million dollars in commodities from Argentina this year," Howard Bruce had allowed this misperception to persist for months.[29]

The ECA, it seemed, was still bent upon punishing Perón, despite the recent reforms and Truman's public orders to end the discrimination. Bruce echoed Remorino's complaints, hoping to ensure that his superiors understood that the "Anglo-Argentine agreement [was] engineered by junior staff ECA who used US taxpayer's dollars in attempt [to] force down Argentine meat prices and engineered pork purchase from US at much higher price."[30]

---

27. Atwood to Bruce, 28 July 1949, RG 59, 635.4131; Labouisse to Brown, 21 June 1949, RG 59, 635.4131.

28. Daniels to Secretary of State, 22 March 1949, RG 59, 835.50.

29. Pawley to Connally, 28 February 1949, Office File, HST; Memorandum of Conversation, Bramulgia, Remorino, Lovett, Pawley, Tewksbury, 11 December 1948, RG 59, 711.35.

30. Bruce to Secretary of State, 10 June 1949, RG 59, 635.4131.

Bruce supported the Department's protests aimed toward the British but was "afraid it's a case of locking the stable door after ECA let the horse be stolen." There could be little doubt that the Argentines had been forced into the agreement when the most "ardent nationalist" remaining in Perón's revamped cabinet asked, "Who would swap US Ford for British Austin?" if given a choice.[31]

When the State and Commerce Department turned their guns on Whitehall, the British naturally feigned injured surprise. British embassy officers claimed that they had informed American Republics Affairs chief Paul Daniels of their intentions months earlier and had encountered no resistance. This was to some extent true. Daniels and Acheson knew as early as March that there would be "problems related to American oil company operations."[32] Still, U.S. economic specialists railed against the British disingenuity. "Britain has long known our viewpoint *vis-à-vis* the use of bilateralism," and there had been no U.S. comment earlier because the State Department had been given only "limited concrete information" about the treaty. The British offered no explanation for their willingness to use dollars for Venezuelan oil rather than Argentine meat, except that they "considered it more economic to spend dollars for oil than to spend dollars on meat." The State Department concluded that the British explanation was far more of a "rationalization" than a "reasonable justification."[33]

Unimpressed, the Truman Administration started hinting at forceful action in June. State Department commercial specialists openly conjectured that the treaty, if implemented, "could conceivably threaten the entire ERP." Congress approved the use of taxpayer dollars to expand multilateral trade, but as one senator

---

31. Bruce to Secretary of State, 10 June 1949, RG 59, 635.4131; Ray Memorandum, 2 June 1949, RG 59, 835.50.

32. Daniels to Brown, 15 April 1949, RG 59, 635.4131; Memorandum of Conversation, Thorp, Labouisse, Vernon, Burns, Taylor, and Christelow, 17 June 1949, RG 59, 635.4131; Acheson to Embassy Buenos Aires, 18 March 1949, RG 59, 835.6363.

33. Corse to Brown, 13 May 1949, RG 59, 635.4131; Douglas to Secretary of State, 15 June 1949, RG 59, 635.4131.

queried, "what hope can the American people have" that "we are doing anything more than handing out our own supplies to others to build them up so that they will be stronger and more able to continue a throttling trade barrier practice in the years to come?" ECA chieftain Paul Hoffman told the Senate that the ECA "would cancel the aid program if it was felt that it was justified in view" of this second Andes Agreement. "In so far as we can bring pressure to bear," he added, "I assure you that it will be brought to bear."[34]

In their testimony before Congress, Hoffman and FitzGerald neglected to mention that ECA activities had directly influenced the pact, and it would have been interesting to see whether Hoffman would have made good on his pledge. At the same time Hoffman was making his statements in Congress, ECA officials, apparently hoping to hide their involvement, were urging Bruce and the State Department to drop their protests. In a matter of weeks, however, the point became moot, as the U.S. government suddenly and somewhat surprisingly abandoned all opposition to the pact.[35]

The more that the State Department learned about the Andes Agreement, the more it came to realize that it was not nearly as offensive as had originally been thought. Either Great Britain or Argentina could unilaterally cancel the deal every year, so Washington had little reason to fear that it was a long-term, binding agreement. The British were obligated to meet Argentina's petroleum needs, but the Argentines were not obligated to purchase all that was offered, leaving some freedom for U.S. producers. Similarly, the British were not forced to purchase all meat that was offered by the Argentines, so the deal was not a binding one that would hurt U.S. interests for years. As Ernest Cross explained with reference to a different barter, "since access to the market on a competitive basis is not affected, the element of discrimination against United States purchasers does not appear to be involved."[36]

---

34. Labouisse to Brown, 21 June 1949, RG 59, 635.4131.

35. Atwood to Bruce, 28 July 1949, RG 59, 635.4131.

36. Cross to Saltonsall, 22 July 1949, RG 59, 635.4131.

Furthermore, Standard Oil and Shell were working out an arrangement whereby they could coordinate sales and purchases for Argentina to minimize any damage to their operations. Officials in ARA still had objections to the treaty, and Atwood considered it the "most serious blow to American business interests in Argentina" since the Roca-Runciman Agreement of 1933. Nonetheless, Winthrop Brown, Director of the State Department's Office of International Trade Policy, and Undersecretary of State for Economic Affairs Willard Thorp informed the British embassy that they were "gratified" to learn that the pact had "substantially larger elements of flexibility" than had been thought.[37]

Therefore, they withdrew the Department's objections to the accord and asked that the British offer a perfunctory statement supporting the ideal of multilateral trade. The British obliged, and on June 27, the State Department issued a press release regretting the need for "emergency" measures such as this pact, but nonetheless expressing appreciation for the British commitment to multilateralism. At the signing ceremony in Buenos Aires, the British ambassador stressed that the treaty represented a departure from the triangular trade—a departure that the British viewed with "regret and reluctance." Whitehall further characterized the treaty as one in which the "the evil practice" of having "ulterior motives" was never "the object or any consideration."[38] The economic team that sat across the bargaining table from the British in 1949 clearly occupied a far different position than Miranda had in the previous two negotiations and paid for it. Regardless of Whitehall's "ulterior motives," the U.S. "economic boycott" had clearly been an almost complete success.

## IV

37. Atwood to Bruce, 28 July 1949, RG 59, 635.4131; Memorandum of Conversation, Brown and Burns, 24 June 1949, RG 59, 635.4131; Brown to Taylor, 24 June 1949, RG 59, 635.4131.

38. State Department Press Release, 27 June 1949, RG 59, 635.4131; Franklin to Secretary of State, 28 June 1949, RG 59, 635.4131; United Kingdom Press Release on Anglo-Argentine Trade Agreement, 10 June 1949, RG 59, 635.4131.

If the Argentine acquiescence to the British was one good indication of the critical economic problems Perón faced in early 1949, his new approach to the U.S. was an even clearer one. Perón informed ITT executive Sosthenes Behn in May that the U.S. government could "'write its own ticket' in return for whatever aid it might be able to afford to Argentina." Remorino echoed his president, telling State Department functionaries that "he had fought hard to have Miranda ousted and, now that Miranda was out, his government was asking: what now?"[39] Bramulgia tried similar direct appeals to Assistant Secretary of State William Pawley, requesting "assistance in finding a solution for Argentine present economic difficulties." He even unofficially sent his own nephew to Washington to "enlist the 'moral' support of General Marshall." In short, the *peronistas* had disposed of Miranda, as the State Department had encouraged them to do for years, and the new economic team expected some reward.[40]

Overthrowing Miranda was but one of the accomplishments that Bramulgia could present to the U.S. as evidence of Argentina's willingness to cooperate as the new economic team also worked steadily to bring IAPI to rein. Remorino informed Daniels that "IAPI in the future would not market products which Argentina exported to the United States." By eliminating IAPI's tax on items such as corned beef, Remorino hoped to open the U.S. market and perhaps circumvent the "sanitary embargo." Furthermore, Perón promised to use twenty to thirty percent of his dollar receipts to pay off the nearly $300 million dollar debt Argentina now owed to U.S. banks and exporters. In the course of the conversation, Daniels described IAPI's operations as "inefficient," and Remorino could

---

39. Memorandum of Conversation, Behn, Blake, Daniels, and Martin, 20 May 1949, RG 59, 835.50; Memorandum of Conversation, Remorino, Quirós, Hensel, Bruce, and Dearborn, 25 February 1949, RG 59, 835.50.

40. Memorandum of Conversation, Solar del Campo, Bruce, and Tewksbury, 11 March 1949, RG 59, 835.50; see also Remorino to Bramulgia, 13 Junio 1949, AMREC, BA, EEUU 1949, 19, 7; Remorino a Paz, 9 Enero 1949, AMREC, BA, EEUU 1949, 19, 7.

only commend his "diplomacy" for choosing that particular adjective.[41]

He nonetheless warned that IAPI could not be dismantled overnight and asked that the State Department accept his promises that the organization was being eliminated as swiftly as possible. Since Miranda had kept few records, it was particularly difficult for his relatively untested successors to sort out IAPI's far-flung empire and ease out state trading. Dr. Juan Scarpati of the Argentine embassy in Washington augmented Remorino's pledges by promising that the new team would "completely reorient economic and financial policies" and "gradually" join international relief organizations. Scarpati, who would be one of Perón's primary emissaries in Washington for the next year, bluntly repudiated the fundamental premise of Peronism, asserting that "Argentina should not attempt to become an industrial nation. Its wealth is in exporting agricultural products."[42]

While no small part of the new economic team's attitude can be attributed to the complete failure of Miranda's regime of state trade, it also clearly reflected an attempt to gain vital U.S. assistance. Bruce and his superiors certainly had given it reason to expect that aid might be forthcoming. Bruce had informed Bramulgia, Maroglio, and others that Argentina might be able to sell up to $500 million worth of goods in the U.S. market annually "as soon as restrictions" like IAPI "were removed." Although the Department of Agriculture's "sanitary embargo" remained in full force against Argentine meat, he worked to convince Remorino and Scarpati that there was a $250 million market for Argentine meat products in the U.S.[43] Incidentally, Bruce, a dairy executive, was

---

41. Memorandum of Conversation, Remorino, Scarpati, Daniels, Atwood, and Dearborn, 10 May 1949, RG 59, 711.35.

42. Memorandum of Conversation, Scarpati, Tewksbury, and Dearborn, 9 February 1949, RG 59, 835.50; Memorandum of Conversation, Remorino, Scarpati, Daniels, Atwood, and Dearborn, 10 May 1949, RG 59, 711.35; see also Ordway to Secretary of State, 17 May 1949, RG 59, 835.60.

43. Memorandum of Conversation, Remorino, Scarpati, Bruce, and Dearborn, 8 March 1949, RG 59, 835.50.

doing little if anything to ease the restraints on Argentine beef importation, and his staff ignored an Argentine request to discuss the matter. U.S. policymakers believed that a "display" of "mutual interest" in the discussion of *aftosa* might be "constructive," but rehashing old arguments and reminding Argentines of the restrictions would probably result in little more than "unfavorable publicity" for the United States.[44]

Some of Bruce's other ideas were as intriguing to the Argentines as they were implausible. He informed Remorino and Scarpati that as soon as they canceled "all decrees, laws, and regulations setting up restrictions on trade," they would be able to sell $150 million of wool to the United States. How this would occur, given the highly protective nature of the U.S. cotton and textiles industry, remained unclear. The ambassador went from the extremely unlikely to the absurd when he suggested that the Argentines should examine the possibility that they could market "new kinds of soup" to the United States. Bruce, still trying to encourage the Peronists, cheerily forecasted that "with the removal of restrictions on trade, Argentina would be back on its feet in ninety days" and that U.S. capital would pour in once government intervention ceased. Although U.S. policymakers offered many fantastic but vague opportunities by which Argentina could save itself from financial ruin, all were based upon the elimination of government intervention in the economy and allowing the invisible hand of market forces to end the crisis. In short, Bruce persisted in his argument that "Perón seems caught in a vise of intense corruption from which he cannot or does not want to extricate himself" and that "the present corruption could not possibly exist if there was not a controlled economy."[45]

Naturally, Peronists were seeking something more concrete to allow them to preserve the vestiges of the state-guided industrial

---

44. Boonstra to Secretary of State, 12 July 1949, RG 59, 611.3556.

45. Memorandum of Conversation, Remorino, Scarpati, Bruce, and Dearborn, 8 March 1949, RG 59, 835.50; Bruce to Merz, 17 December 1948, Bruce Papers, Series 1; see also Memorandum of Conversation, Remorino, Quirós, Bruce, Hensel, and Dearborn, 25 February 1949, RG 59, 835.50.

program. Ares, Cereijo, and Gómez Morales approached Bruce in June, seeking direct financial assistance. Although Miranda had claimed that he would cut off his hands before he allowed them to accept a loan from foreigners (and Perón had said much the same thing), the new team reversed course.[46] Cereijo, after cataloging the steps they had taken to stabilize the economy, finally suggested to Bruce that the U.S. government or the Export-Import bank establish a $500 million revolving credit for Argentina. The United States would be able to purchase huge amounts of heretofore unmarketable Argentine surpluses and rest assured that the money would be returned to the United States through Argentine imports. U.S. businesses would be able to make sales that had been impossible because of the dollar drain, and the Peronists could repay their debts, loosen the British stranglehold, and take further steps to ease the state out of the private sphere.

According to Ray, Cereijo and his peers "seem to feel that if we wanted to, it would be a very simple matter for us to buy a half a billion of Argentina's products and with a stroke of the pen settle all of Argentina's dollar difficulties." Ray dismissed this type of thinking, bluntly asserting that "Santa Claus doesn't live here any more." When a State Department functionary told César Bunge of the Argentine embassy that the U.S. was "very interested" in seeing U.S.-Argentine commercial difficulties settled quickly, Bunge, who had already proclaimed that failure to receive financial assistance from the United States would be "enough to cause a collapse the present government," commented that "you are interested but to us it is a matter of life and death."[47]

Clearly unwilling to consider any constructive efforts yet, the State Department continued to press Perón for further changes. Ray, "in a purely informal way," submitted to Bramulgia fourteen

---

46. Ray to Secretary of State, 4 January 1949, RG 59, 611.3531.

47. Ray to Secretary of State, 4 January 1949, RG 59, 611.3531; Memorandum of Conversation, Bunge and Woolf, 9 November 1949, RG 59, 835.6131; see also Memorandum of Conversation, Scarpati and Tewksbury, 9 February 1949, RG 59, 835.50; Giacalone, "From Bad Neighbors," 215; Mario Rapoport and Claudio Spiguel, *Estados Unidos y el peronismo: La política norteamericana en la Argentina, 1949-1955*, (Buenos Aires, 1994), 65.

points that "would facilitate mutual understanding" between the two governments in March 1949. In essence, Ray was presenting Bramulgia and Perón with even more conditions for U.S. aid. Most of these fourteen points concerned the operations of U.S. businesses in Argentina and the omnipresent fear of expropriation. Ray sought guarantees for U.S. investment and an end to the practice of "expropriation by attrition." Although he was on firm ground with some of these requests, which were familiar enough, others toed the line of intervention in Argentine internal affairs. The first of these was a suggestion that Argentina should lower the prices of agricultural exports, even if this meant changing exchange rates. The second was a thinly veiled attack on IAPI, calling for the Peronists to permit exports through "recognized, established trade channels."[48] Perón had said that Washington could "write its own ticket," and Ray was doing just that.

Perón made some genuine efforts to comply with Ray's fourteen points. The most notable involved Article 40 of the new Argentine constitution. The new document predictably embodied much of the economic nationalism that had characterized *peronismo*, and Article 40 was the most disturbing manifestation. Simply put, it stated that vital public services and industries were the property of the state and obligated the government to expropriate them from foreigners. Although the original owners were to be paid for their property, the profits they had reaped from their investments would be subtracted from their compensation, so businessmen might conceivably owe the government money after the expropriation of their properties.[49]

Perón tried to assuage the United States. When Behn warned him that this article would scare off potential investors, he asked what could be done to alleviate this fear. Behn worked with the president to draft legislation to alter the provisions and wrote a

---

48. Ray to Secretary of State, 29 March 1949, RG 59, 835.50; "Argentine Response to US 14 Points," 13 May 1949, RG 59, 711.35.

49. Perón, *La tercera posición, la Constitución de 1949, breviario justicialista*, (Buenos Aires, 1973), 67-115; Page, *Perón*, 203-205; Rapoport and Spiguel, *Estados Unidos y el peronismo*, 43-53.

brief statement supporting foreign investment that Perón integrated almost verbatim into his State of the Union address.[50] Perón also gave his interpretation of the offending article, asserting that only those businesses with direct concessions from the government would be expropriated, and they would be compensated as well as ITT had been in 1947. Finally, he pledged never to use the article against U.S. investments and urged his followers to eliminate the article from the draft constitution. They declined of course, further illustrating how difficult a path Perón was treading between his own movement and the United States.[51]

Perón may indeed have made an earnest effort to remove Article 40, but for the State Department, the Argentina that approved such a provision was not one with a favorable climate for investment or an attitude conducive either to cooperation with foreigners or liberal capitalism. Nationalism would be an inherent characteristic of Peronism until Perón made sweeping changes, and so long as such nationalism manifested itself, it was clear that the Peronists were not making the hard choices that Washington demanded. Article 40 was little more than an irritant, but it was one of the many that U.S. policymakers, who "were able to afford a policy of righteous indignation," would not be inclined to overlook.[52] Indeed, Perón had made a career of publicly issuing fierce anti-U.S. rhetoric that fueled anti-foreign nationalism at the same time he called for capitalist investment behind closed doors. To the State Department, at least, it appeared that once again Perón was attempting to have his cake and eat it, too.

In other words, Perón's public diplomacy still had not changed despite his private assurances and pleas for aid. Perón's propaganda continued to assail Yankee imperialism and the vices of

---

50. Memorandum of Conversation, Behn, Blake, Daniels, and Martin, 20 May 1949, RG 59, 835.50.

51. Memorandum of Conversation, Remorino, Scarpati, Dearborn, Atwood, and Daniels, 10 May 1949, RG 59, 711.35.

52. Memorandum of Conversation, Lyon and Magowan, 5 May 1947, RG 59, 635.4131; see also Potash, *Arms and Politics in Argentina: Perón to Frondizi*, 100-101; Page, *Perón*, 202-205; Paso, *Del golpe de estado de 1943* 117-172.

capitalism in a vain attempt to preserve his position as the standardbearer of the "Third Position." Although he was clearly reorienting his administration, bringing it into line with U.S. demands for a more privatist capitalism, in so doing, he jeopardized the revolutionary and populist stance that had thrust him into power. Speeches and declarations that made "the imperialist United States a whipping boy" were a cheap and easy way to affirm his nationalist credentials, at the same time his envoys worked to smooth over any fallout in Washington.

He urged U.S. officials to ignore his public proclamations, privately telling Bruce's successor, Stanton Griffis, "damn it, can't people realize that certain things are said for domestic consumption?" He added that when he attacked "capitalism," he referred to the "old extreme capitalism" that the United States had not practiced since the election of Franklin Roosevelt. Likening himself to Roosevelt as a practitioner of a middle way, Perón tried again to pose as a defender of capitalism and a moderate reformer. Needless to say, this sort of "clarification" rarely found its way into his public rhetoric and only appeared in his subsequent private apologies to U.S. officials.[53]

For the State Department, which still had little appreciation for Perón's attitude that "it is sometimes politically wise and necessary to give the foreigners in general a small kick," no true rapprochement could occur before Perón abandoned the "polysyllabic fence-sitting" of the Third Position. Assistant Secretary of State Edward G. Miller pronounced that "frankly, this sort of mouthing by Perón, if continued, is going to make it impossible for us to continue upon the course on which we have embarked." "The U.S. was almost childishly eager to improve business and all other relations with Argentina," Griffis proclaimed, but U.S. leaders were "constantly embittered by being kicked in the rear when they weren't looking."[54] Why, Miller asked, would

---

53. Embassy Buenos Aires to Department of State, 1 March 1950, RG 59, RASS; Griffis to Miller, 1 August 1950, RG 59, RASS; see also Miller to Griffis, 5 August 1950, RG 59, RASS; Dearborn Memorandum, 29 December 1950, RG 59, RASS.

54. Griffis to Miller, 31 August 1950, RG 59, RASS; Miller to Griffis, 5

private capital venture to Argentina where "something different from capitalism" was being practiced?

Furthermore, any attack upon capitalism only lent strength to communist propaganda which was unarguably hostile to the United States. Eva Perón added fuel to this particular fire by announcing in early 1950 that she and her followers would "without any hesitation throw in their lot with the Communists" if "it ever appeared likely that [the Peróns] were to be defeated by the oligarchy." While Perón worked toward entente with the United States in private, public denunciations did little to encourage amity. In other words, "it is all well and good for [Perón] to send me letters assuring me of his undying devotion to the cause of the United States (marked 'confidential'), but these are of small comfort to me when his public statements are inconsistent with his private protestations."[55] While Griffis and Miller predictably saw little point in rewarding a government philosophically opposed to liberal capitalism and vocal in that opposition, it soon became clear that this too had to be rethought.

## V

The crisis that stimulated yet another State Department policy shift involved the fallout of Miranda's removal. As U.S. officials celebrated the cabinet shake-up that had started with Miranda's firing and had seemed to end in the triumph of the "Bramulgia men," Bramulgia himself fell. In August, after it had become clear that the ECA would be undertaking no significant purchases in Argentina, Perón suddenly demanded Bramulgia's resignation. Ambassador Remorino, probably coveting the Foreign Ministry post, had confronted Bramulgia earlier that month. According to Remorino, Bramulgia had been suppressing his reports from Washington and misinforming Perón. As a result of one such deception, Perón had "made a bitter attack on the United

---

August 1950, RG 59 RASS; Griffis to Miller, 1 August 1950, RG 59, RASS; Miller to Griffis, 5 August 1950, RG 59, RASS.

55. Maleady to Secretary of State, 3 March 1950, RG 59, 735.11; Miller to Griffis, 5 August 1950, RG 59, RASS.

States." After hearing Remorino's explanation, Perón, insisting that that "there is no use trying to save face," instructed him to "tell them up there that I apologize; that I made a terrible mistake, but it was because I was misled." Remorino informed Miller that "he and the President both feel that Argentina's future lies with the United States," as he proceeded to vilify Bramulgia. The approach seems to have been successful. Miller was "profoundly impressed by this decisive demonstration of friendship" and considered Remorino's and Perón's admissions to be of "transcendental importance" in "showing the good faith of the Argentine Government." The other outgrowth was Bramulgia's firing soon thereafter.[56]

In all likelihood, Bramulgia was the victim of Remorino's ambitions. Aside from their personal differences, Remorino may have resented the widespread perception that Bramulgia was the *peronista* who could best deal with the United States. Bramulgia's removal did create a tremendous vacuum in the Argentine foreign policymaking apparatus that Remorino undoubtedly hoped to fill. When Perón appointed relatively obscure Hipólito Paz to Bramulgia's post, Remorino did become the dominant force in the Foreign Ministry.[57] Nonetheless, the episode is significant, and indicative of the new direction Peronism was taking. *Peronistas*, no longer concerned with "economic independence," were now competing for Perón's favor on the basis of whom could cooperate most effectively with the United States.

Still, for U.S. policymakers, Bramulgia's removal was as disturbing as Miranda's had been pleasing. Bruce had warned in February that if the ECA did not make sizeable purchases in Argentina, "it very likely that Foreign Minister Bramulgia will be completely discredited and dropped from the Cabinet"—a

---

56. According to Remorino, Bramulgia had gone so far as to insult Miller personally in order to preserve his own position. Remorino dutifully repeated the alleged insults to Miller. Miller to Mallory, 12 August 1949, RG 59, RASS; Miller to Mallory, 12 August 1949, RG 59, RASS.

57. An alternative theory that Eva Perón, holding an old grudge against Bramulgia since October 17, 1945, finally engineered his removal is refuted by Rita Giacalone. Giacalone, *From Bad Neighbors to Reluctant Partners*, 209-212.

development that would cause "irreparable damage" to U.S.-Argentine relations. Bramulgia had compromised his position on several occasions to promote U.S.-Argentine amity, and each instance had led to an Argentine retreat. At best, Bramulgia appeared to be ineffectual, at worst, a quisling. He had argued to Perón all along that cooperation with the U.S. would bring rewards and had apparently gambled on being vindicated by U.S. aid. Bramulgia informed the embassy that "the ostensible reason for his resignation was failure to arrange adequately pending matters with the US," but that "internal politics and intrigues" were the deeper cause.[58]

Indeed, Peronists like Remorino, Cereijo, and Scarpati, who sought rapprochement on U.S. terms, were treading a very tenuous path. The State Department believed that unless they "received some encouragement," they "will be in a very difficult position to put over their point of view as against those" who "are in favor or a more nationalistic policy." Failure to provide some assistance might result in the collapse of this "new and hopeful trend—or possible trend." Indeed, Miller informed Griffis that it would be "extremely helpful" if he could mention to Perón what a "high opinion we have" of his new team. Even without Miranda, U.S. leaders knew well that "Evita's hatchet" remained "very sharp these days" and that her influence was growing by the day.[59]

Not only did U.S. policymakers have to fear nationalist pressure but infighting within the group that had once been labeled "Bramulgia men." Remorino, Argentine sources reported to Miller, "feels very put out over the fact that Cereijo is getting all of the publicity in connection with current negotiations and all the credit." Still. Cereijo's difficulties ran much deeper, as he apparently had become a target for nationalists who were quite disturbed by his continuing negotiations in Washington. His enemies may have included even Eva Perón herself. Although embassy sources gave

---

58. Pawley to Connally, 28 February 1949, Office File, HST; *Current Economic Developments* 218, 6 September 1949.

59. Miller to Griffis, 28 December 1949. RG 59, RASS; Miller to Griffis, 8 December 1949, RG 59, RASS; Mallory to Miller, 3 June 1950, RG 59, RASS.

Cereijo "at least even chance" of continuing in office, U.S. officials stressed that "it would be disastrous from the standpoint of Argentina and our 'era of cooperation' if one of the principal authors of the new scheme of things should be thrown out." Griffis met with Perón and sang Cereijo's praises at every opportunity, emphasizing the "excellent work" he had done to build on the "fine foundation work begun by Ambassador Remorino." Internecine conflicts had been in no small part responsible for Argentina's turnabout, and U.S. diplomats were not above using such "indirect methods to keep things on the rails a little" and guarantee that the "new economic team" was not dismantled in the same fashion as Miranda's old one had been.[60]

Perhaps spurred by the bureaucratic infighting that threatened the "era of cooperation" and knowing full well that "Dr. Cereijo and his government expected financial assistance from the US in return for their cooperation," Miller and his superiors finally started to consider giving the Peronists both. Toward the end of 1949, Cereijo petitioned the Export-Import bank for financial aid. The bankers, acting in accordance with what they believed U.S. policy to be, rejected the application out of hand. But to take "the best advantage of the constructive attitude" in Argentina, Miller went to representatives of the Export-Import Bank, asking that Argentina's situation be reviewed. He met with Chairman Herbert Gaston in December and informed him that the State Department now had "no political objection to financial assistance to Argentina." In short, Miller was trying to "[start] the ball rolling in an effort to have the application given at least proper consideration."[61]

---

60. Miller to Griffis, 5 April 1950, RG 59, RASS; Miller to Malloy, 17 May 1950, RG 59, RASS; Mallory to Miller, 23 May 1950, RG 59, RASS; Mallory to Miller, 3 June 1950, RG 59, RASS; Memorandum of Conversation, Griffis and Perón, 21 April 1950, RG 59, 735.00; Mallory to Miller, 23 May 1950, RG 59, RASS.

61. Memorandum on Argentina, 14 July 1950, RG 59, RASS; Miller to Griffis, 8 December 1949, RG 59, RASS; Memorandum of Conversation, Gaston, Miller, Nufer, Malenbaum, et al., 2 December 1949, RG 59, RASS; Miller to Griffis, 10 January 1950, RG 59, RASS.

"Obviously provoked," Gaston "launched into a spirited criticism" of the State Department. Because State Department representatives had been holding out the tantalizing lure of an Export-Import Bank loan to Argentina for over a year, Gaston feared that it "was now coming over to the bank with a *fait accompli*." Furthermore, Gaston expressed some confusion over Miller's apparently contradictory policies. One year earlier, a State Department representative had reported to him that there were "'no political objections' to loans to Argentina" but had "winked his right eye." Was "it the same 'with a wink of your left eye this time?'" Gaston queried, harkening back to the days when the ECA pledged that it had no objections to purchases in Argentina. Miller responded that there truly were "no political objections" any longer and convinced Gaston to commence a study of Argentine proposals. After Miller had overcome the Bank's "latent hostility," Perón received a $125 million credit in May 1950 that Argentine banks would be able to use to settle their debts with U.S. creditors.[62]

Although Miller conceded that the credit represented a "new departure in our policy with respect to Argentina," it was hardly a magnanimous gesture.[63] First and foremost, the specific conditions of the credit guaranteed that the Argentines would not be able to utilize the funds for any new statist projects. Just as important, conciliatory Argentines such as Remorino and Cereijo would be able to return triumphantly to Argentina with *yanqui* aid and hopefully avoid Bramulgia's fate. Since Peronists preaching conciliation had not won any real victories in four years, this alone was significant. It could also be considered a reward to Perón himself, who was, at the time, ratifying the Rio Pact and offering his support for the United Nations' action in Korea. The State Department and the Export-Import Bank thus cooperated to lend

---

62. Memorandum of Conversation, Gaston, Miller, Nufer, Malenbaum, et al., 2 December 1949, RG 59, RASS; Miller to Griffis, 8 December 1949, RG 59, RASS; see also Gaston to Miller, 24 May 1950, Miller Papers, Assistant Secretary of State, Correspondence File.

63. Miller to Griffis, 8 December 1949, RG 59, RASS.

concrete assistance to those Peronists who sought rapprochement and favored Argentine readmittance into the "Inter-American system."

Furthermore, the structure of the aid package made it clear that it was little more than a loan. This was significant simply because the Peronists had sought any alternative to a loan. After being rebuffed by the ECA, they had requested that the U.S. government simply purchase some of Argentina's "blocked holdings of Spanish pesetas and French francs in exchange for dollars." Naturally, Miller refused to consider this alternative.[64] Perón had boasted endlessly that his alternative was achieving "economic independence" from the United States and Europe and had repatriated the national debt and nationalized key industries to keep this promise. By accepting the Export-Import Bank credit, he was tacitly conceding that his program had failed. In essence, Perón had accepted a Yankee loan—albeit one with a "political appellation suitable to his internal situation." This made it impossible for him to pose credibly as the standardbearer for anti-U.S. nationalists and cost him any pretense to genuine "anti-imperialist leadership." After four years of *peronismo*, Argentina was again indebted to foreigners and retreating toward economic orthodoxy, as Peronists abandoned "the belligerent position that we had to take with the United States."[65]

As Miller explained to Jacob Potofsky and other U.S. labor leaders who were horrified by the prospect of U.S. aid to Perón, "our present policy toward [Argentina] has not been arrived at haphazardly."[66] Miller understood well that the fundamental goal of U.S. policy was not to eliminate Perón, but to discredit his alternative and draw Argentina back into the "Inter-American system." The credit was aimed specifically at achieving these dual

---

64. Miller to Griffis, 8 December 1949, RG 59, RASS.

65. Mallory to Department of State, 1 March 1950, RG 59, RASS; Paz, "La Tercera Posición," 62; see also *Primera Plana*, 21 Junio 1966, 38.

66. Miller to Potofsky, 4 May 1950, RG 59, RASS; see also Potofsky to Miller, 2 May 1950, RG 59, RASS; Miller to Romualdi, 9 January 1950, RG 59, RASS.

goals. By strengthening the hands of those Peronists who accepted U.S. hegemony and were willing to accommodate themselves to the old order, it had helped keep Perón on the "correct" path. The credit alone would not be sufficient to draw Argentina out of its financial crisis, and *peronistas* would be encouraged to persist in their *volte face*. As Perón himself conceded, "after all, the Import-Export Credit merely bails out U.S. business interests." Finally, the credit eroded Perón's international standing and illustrated that he truly did not represent a new and independent alternative to the "Inter-American system." Although the Export-Import credit was in some ways a dramatic policy reversal for the Truman Administration and a far cry from Braden's "economic boycott," it should be seen as a final and decisive stage in the evolution of U.S. efforts to "contain" Peronism.[67]

## VI

Although some had believed that Bramulgia's removal would prompt a return to "extremism" and an end to the days when Washington could "write its own ticket," this was not the case. A spirit of "moderation" and defeat had taken control over Perón's cabinet, and Bramulgia's presence was no longer necessary to prevent a return to Miranda's disgraced alternative. Perón's acceptance of the Export-Import Bank credit was the symbolic end of Peronism as an independent, dynamic force, as a number of contemporaries and historians noted.[68] Peronism had failed in its efforts to transform Argentina into a prosperous, socially just, industrial nirvana, and Perón had crawled back into the "Inter-American system."

---

67. Griffis to Miller, 31 August 1950, RG 59, RASS; Miller to Thorp, 25 November 1949, RG 59, RASS; see also MacDonald, "The United States, Britain, and Argentina, 196-197; and "The US, the Cold War, and Perón, 409-410; Escudé goes even further, claiming that with the credit, Washington sought to "buy the ratification" of the Inter-American Defense Pact by Perón's government. This may well have been true. Escudé, "La Traición a los derechos humanos," 84-86.

68. For example, see MacDonald, "The United States, Britain, and Argentina;" Giacalone, "From Good Neighbors to Reluctant Partners;" Vannucci, "U.S.-Argentine Relations."

The firing of Miranda marked the true turning point in both U.S.-Argentine relations and *peronismo* itself. Miranda had been the driving force behind the economic policies that Washington had feared and detested, and, for a time, the most formidable man in Perón's retinue. As Bruce remarked later, "somehow, a great many of my problems, great and small, seemed to involve" the "economic czar." Although his economic programs had driven the nation to financial ruin, Perón later tried to rekindle the old defiant spirit of *peronismo* by reminding the nation of Miranda's efforts toward industrialization and social justice. "The true pioneer," he asserted, "was Miguel Miranda."[69]

By 1950, Peronism was clearly in a stage of transition, and few of the old guard remained. Luis Gay and Cipriano Reyes had been purged from the labor movement. Miranda, Bramulgia, Figuerola, Maroglio, and Ivanissevich had all been removed from the government, replaced by "more malleable technicians."[70] With the help of these "technicians," Perón turned away from his populist corporatism and most of the redistributive policies associated with them as he became a much more "traditional" Latin American authoritarian. Not coincidentally, his relations with Washington improved with each subsequent step he took in this direction. In time, the new economic team did manage to undo some of the damage that statist corporatism and the U.S. response to it had done, but never again did Peronism mount a serious challenge to the United States, and never again was Perón taken seriously as a threat to the hemispheric order.

---

69. Bruce, *Memoirs*, 269; Prológo del Gen. J. D. Perón, in Jorge Antonio, *Y ahora que?* (Buenos Aires, 1970).

70. Ciria, *Política y cultura popular*, 31.

# CHAPTER 10

## CONCLUSION

Fear of an organization of regional groups in the Americas has for years played an important role in our policy in the Western Hemisphere. The threat which gives us the worst case of cold shivers is that of a southern bloc dominated by Argentina.

Guy Ray, 5 January 1948[1]

There is no hope that the great majority of Latin American countries can, in the foreseeable future, achieve anything like the level of the U.S. standard of living, yet we must convince those countries that our system of free enterprise offers the best prospect for economic betterment.

Policy Planning Staff, 18 October 1948[2]

### I

This study ends in 1950 when the nature of the Peronist threat to the hemispheric order, and U.S. hegemony over it, changed dramatically. The firing of Miranda, the rollback of IAPI, and the acceptance of an Export-Import Bank loan all demonstrated clearly that Perón's economic program had failed and failed completely. With Miranda gone, the new team that replaced him could move freely toward economic orthodoxy and were of course encouraged strongly to do so rapidly by U.S. officials. The reduction of IAPI's role was a natural outgrowth of this, and an

---

1. Ray to Secretary of State, 5 January 1948, RG 59, 711.35.

2. Policy Planning Staff Report, "The American Republics," 18 October 1948, RG 59, PPS.

explicit repudiation of state-directed commerce and industrialization. Finally, by accepting a loan from the United States, Perón and his supporters were forced to admit that their efforts to modernize Argentina, and the alternative corporatism they had embraced, had failed. Still, as Mario Rapoport and Claudio Spiguel pointed out, Perón did not reverse his course completely or ever become a genuine partner in the "Inter-American system."[3]

Rapoport and Spiguel illustrated that there was little difference between the Peronism of the 1940s and that of the 1950s. They made this argument by pointing out that after 1949, Perón retained his "Third Position" by persisting in his efforts to integrate South American economies, strengthening economic ties with the Warsaw Pact nations, and remaining aloof from the Korean War. These arguments have a great deal of merit. Perón never did completely abandon the rhetorical "Third Position" or totally accept liberal capitalist economic orthodoxy, but the magnitude of the threat he posed to the "Inter-American system" had dwindled to next to nothing.[4]

The 1950s did, on the surface, seem to present a better opportunity for Perón to cultivate allies in South America. His friend, Carlos Ibañez, won the Chilean presidency; Getulio Vargas, embracing a new brand of populism, returned to power in Brazil; Víctor Paz Estenssoro and the MNR won the National Revolution in Bolivia; and Perón's ally, Manuel Odría, dominated Peru with a program that initially bore some resemblance to that of the *peronistas*. Not surprisingly, Perón did endeavor to cultivate their governments, with varying degrees of success.

In 1953, he finally managed to cement a customs union with Ibañez' Chile with the Act of Santiago and worked to integrate other nations into the framework. Although little came of the Act of Santiago, Perón pressed onward, still proclaiming that the year 2000 would see Latin America either united or conquered. The

---

3. Rapoport and Spiguel, *Estados Unidos y el peronismo*.

4. Rapoport and Spiguel, *Estados Unidos y peronismo*; MacDonald, "The Cold War and Perón," 411-412.

United States offered only token resistance to these efforts. Claude Bowers, still U.S. Ambassador to Chile in 1952, tried to sound the alarm that "Peronism is sweeping the continent," but few, if any, took it seriously and with good reason. Estenssoro's Bolivia was eventually embraced by Washington and showed little interest in an Argentina that could offer it little except for difficulties with the United States. Odría went even further, inviting a team of U.S. businessmen to plan his economy and offering to turn control of the Peruvian navy over to U.S. naval officers. Although these developments might well be partially attributable to the heating up of the Cold War, the decline of Perón's Argentina made his efforts to finally forge a "southern bloc" a minor nuisance in the 1950s.[5]

Similarly, Perón's efforts to stir up labor discontent with the AFL's and CIO's hemispheric organizations were but a shadow of the danger they had represented in the 1940s. In the 1950s, he launched ATLAS, a vehicle to extend the CGT's influence throughout the hemisphere and undercut AFL and CIO efforts to do the same. Although on paper ATLAS was a far more coherent, serious attempt to disseminate *peronismo* than his ill-fated efforts during the 1940s, Perón again had difficulty getting the attention of U.S. policymakers. Peronism, as a disgraced alternative economic and organizational pattern, could not truly compete against better funded and more reputable AFL and CIO initiatives.[6]

He did also straddle the fence during the Cold War, which under other circumstances, might have constituted an almost unpardonable sin for Washington in the 1950s. Perón, fearing that he would never receive substantial U.S. aid, promulgated a series of bilateral barters with the Soviet Union and the communist bloc. Although this could be viewed as maverick policymaking as Perón was opting out of the Cold War and the "Inter-American system," there is very little evidence that the United States ever took these

---

5. Bowers to Miller, 15 August 1952, PSF, Foreign Affairs, Chile, HST; Rapoport and Spiguel, *Estados Unidos y el peronismo*, 119-124; Perón, *Doctrina Universal* and *Política y Estrategia*; see also *Nuestros vecinos argentinos*, 65-78.

6. John T. Deiner, "ATLAS: A Labor Instrument of Argentine Expansionism under Perón." (Unpublished Ph.D. dissertation, Rutgers University, 1969).

flirtations very seriously or gave them much attention. There was no new *Blue Book*, no CIA intervention such as that occurred in Guatemala, and no major call to arms. Indeed, throughout the late 1940s, Washington engaged in a systematic effort to destabilize an avowedly anti-communist regime, which is a telling commentary. Although the State Department was irritated by Perón's unwillingness to commit to the Korean War, it did little to punish Argentina or any other Latin American nation for it. Perón was starting to make his overtures to the Soviet bloc at the height of McCarthyism and the Cold War, but U.S. policymakers were strikingly unconcerned over these developments. Put simply, Perón had faded to obscurity and was almost forgotten by U.S. policymakers, who now could treat him as a simple dictator. In 1954, Perón had fallen, in the words of Paz and Ferrari, into the "shadow of [Guatemalan President Jacobo] Arbenz." During the 1940s, Peronist Argentina had cast its own shadow.[7]

Indeed, one need only examine Perón's own comments to see the collapse of his movement. In January 1951, George Messersmith returned to Buenos Aires as a semi-private citizen. Assistant Secretary of State Miller had asked the ex-ambassador to talk with Perón and attempt to convince the Argentine once again to mend his ways. Messersmith agreed and, at Perón's request, made a list of suggestions that might assist in the Argentine recovery. After Messersmith had given him a lecture lasting a half-hour, Perón, his head in his hands, lamented that "it is too late." His experiments in state corporatism had failed utterly and left the nation in shambles. Even worse, Perón's movement had lost the truly revolutionary flavor that had distinguished Perón from other authoritarian leaders in Latin America. He could try to resurrect that spirit by attacking U.S. racism or imperialism, and did so regularly, but to little noticeable effect. That Miller actually made the effort to recruit Messersmith demonstrates that the Argentine situation was not entirely to Washington's liking, but as it was the extent of his efforts, also suggests that the State Department had

---

7. Rapoport and Spiguel, *Estados Unidos y peronismo*. esp. 284-288; Rapoport, *Política y diplomacia*; Seipe, Llairo, and Gale, *Perón y las relaciones con el Este*.

little to fear from the renovated Peronism that emerged in the 1950s.[8]

IAPI's role in the new Peronist state was a clear indication of the new direction of *peronismo*. Recognizing the damage that IAPI had done to the *pampas*, in 1951 Perón started utilizing it to subsidize farmers, purchasing grain at above world prices, and focusing imports on farm equipment. Argentina's strength had always been the agro-pastoral produce of the *pampas*, and Perón returned to it, tacitly accepting that industrialization and economic diversification would have to wait. Whereas he had tried to achieve industrial self-sufficiency in 1946, in the end he fell back on the traditional order—tacitly accepting Argentina's role as a food exporter.[9]

At the same time that IAPI's role as a redistributive device was curtailed, Perón reversed his stand toward his labor constituency. He decreed a wage freeze and permitted inflation to outstrip the gains made by the workers. One of the key components of his economic program, freezing rents, was sacrificed soon thereafter, as he made significant strides toward economic orthodoxy in a very short time. Just as these measures infuriated the working classes, and to some extent validated Romualdi's predictions that Perón would eventually turn on them, they did give a boost to the manufacturers. Although this Second Five-Year Plan was advertised as a sequel to the first, in many ways it was a complete turnabout. By 1953, he was actively recruiting foreign investment and doing everything in his power to create a favorable climate for the *extraneros*. Even though the *peronista* Constitution of 1949 seemed to be a nationalist document, providing for further expropriation of foreign-owned properties, Perón was moving in a different direction. The repudiation of nationalism was completed in 1954 when he granted Standard Oil a major concession to drill in Patagonia.[10]

---

8. Messersmith Memoirs, n.d., Messersmith Papers, 2010.

9. Cafiero, *Cinco años después*, 320-335; Wynia, *Argentina in the Post-War Period*. 71-80.

10. Gerchunoff, Pablo, "Peronist Economic Policies, 1946-1955," *The Political*

Predictably, these endeavors tore open rifts within the Peronist movement. Although labor naturally protested the moves toward austerity at its expense, Perón's colleagues in the Army supported his move toward the United States and orthodoxy. When Perón tried to nominate his wife for the vice presidency in 1951, he met with fierce resistance from the Army, which was able to essentially veto the selection. Sra. Perón, as well, recognized the schism. In 1951 she turned her attention toward eliminating the control that the military held over her husband, by arranging for the purchase of large quantities of automatic weapons—to be distributed to the masses and the unions in order to protect Perón from the Army. Perón instead turned the weapons over to the Army. So although Perón handily won the 1951 election, he was no longer able to command either the authority or the popular backing that he had been able to muster in the salad days of his first Presidency.

The reversal of the 1950s must not be overstated, as Rapoport and Spiguel demonstrate well, but there was a clear transformation of Peronism. It never achieved liberal capitalist orthodoxy, but it had made significant movement in that direction. Shorn of its revolutionary substance, Perón had to turn to public spectacles and repression to perpetuate his regime. In a widely denounced move, *La Prensa*, the esteemed if overrated anti-*peronista* newspaper, was closed down in 1949 as Perón tightened restrictions on the press. Peronists eventually resorted to arson, simply torching the bastion of the elite, the Jockey Club, and other symbolic buildings.

Eva Perón's death in July 1952 deprived Perón of his most loyal ally and valuable asset. Griffis considered the president and his wife to be a "two-cylindered machine" and forecasted that without her, Perón would have serious problems. Rather than treat "Evita's" death as a defeat, Peronists sought advantage from the tragedy. Instead of simply burying her body, Perón entrusted Dr. Pedro Ara to preserve it forever. Ara essentially mummified the

---

*Economy of Argentina, 1946-1955*, eds. DiTella and Dornbusch, 71-83; Harris G. Warren, "Diplomatic Relations Between the United States and Argentina," *Inter-American Economic Affairs* VIII (Winter 1954), 63-82.

corpse and coated it with plastic for public display. Although her cadaver disappeared after Perón's fall in 1955, when it was rediscovered in 1971, it was still almost perfectly preserved. Peronism had always relied upon grand spectacles and a certain amount of repression (or more commonly, the threat of repression); the violence and drama in these moves bespoke the tragicomic desperation that was gripping Perón as the 1950s progressed. In other words, after the economic collapse of 1949, Perón had to devote all of his efforts merely to hold together the fraying cords of his coalition and preserve his grip on power. Whereas U.S. ambassadors had once feared and, in Messersmith's case, respected him, Griffis was comfortable enough to ridicule Perón and refer to him as "old President Eczema." Miller, who refused to view Argentina as a rival (and had little reason to do so after 1949), similarly took a joking tone when referring to Argentine developments. Argentina had fallen very far down the line of U.S. priorities and concerns very quickly.[11]

## II

Although Perón would remain in the Casa Rosada until 1955, the remainder of his time in office was spent dismantling the corporate state that he had erected in the 1940s and simply hanging onto power. The end of his aggressive state-sponsored economic development program naturally brought improved relations with the United States. True to the predictions of Messersmith, Bruce, and Cabot, Perón without his state corporatism was at least palatable to U.S. policymakers. By abandoning his economic and ideological offensive, he had tacitly moved Argentina into the "Inter-American

---

11. For example, Miller, assessing presents he had received, wrote that "none of these compare to the gift conferred upon me by your close friend J. D. Perón which consists of a .45 caliber automatic pistol. I have not yet taken the hint." 20 October 1950, Miller Papers, Assistant Secretary, Correspondence File, HST; Griffis to Truman, 1 March 1950, PSF, Foreign Affairs, Argentina, HST; Griffis to Miller, 11 April 1951, Assistant Secretary, Miller Papers, Correspondence File, HST; Fraser and Navarro, *Eva Perón*, 168-191; Bohlin, "United States-Latin American Relations," 74-77.

system," even if his public pronouncements still exuded nationalism and defiance.

In essence, by repudiating radical state corporatism, Perón had forsaken a path by which Argentina might have escaped dependency and the Third World. Unable to finance his drive to transform Argentina into a producer and major exporter of finished goods, he had shifted the focus of his administration to the agropastoral exporting sector that had always been Argentina's natural niche in the "world system." The Peronists had recognized very early on that agropastoral exporting was a trap and that Argentina had been securely snared in it much earlier in its history. Despite their efforts, it had been unable to escape through state-driven growth in the short span of four years.

They had predicted that after the immediate crisis of World War II and the post-war period, food prices would drop, leaving Argentina with the same problems that it had faced during the 1930s. True to these estimates, by 1948 European agriculture was starting to recover, U.S., Canadian, and Australian farmers were increasing their outputs dramatically, and modern agricultural methods were promising bumper crops across the world. Technology and new innovations were further threatening other traditional Argentine exports. Linseed oil, one of Argentina's most lucrative exports, provides an excellent example of this trend. In the post-war period, U.S. farmers increased linseed production four hundred percent, while foreign manufacturers discovered that soybean oil and Nigerian conopher oil could replace linseed oil. If Argentine linseed exports survived at all, they would be at a dramatically lower value than before when facing this competition. Perón had come to power anticipating problems such as these and dedicated himself to solving them through state corporatism but had ultimately failed.[12]

Because Perón's state corporatism had served the goals of economic nationalism, the State Department had reason to be pleased by his reversal after 1949. U.S. policymakers had perceived Peronism to be a fascist variant transplanted from Europe and dealt with Perón as if he were a Latin American Mussolini or,

---

12. *Review of the River Plate*, 23 July 1948, 3-4.

in Braden's words, an "Al Capone with Nazi tendencies." The United States had entered World War II to defeat and discredit the German, Japanese, and Italian challenges to liberal capitalism and were not about to allow Perón to "keep the old pirate flag afloat." Historians and social scientists can write extensive tomes on whether Perón was a "true" fascist in the European context, but for purposes of this study, that issue has little significance.[13] What matters is that U.S. policymakers believed that Perón was a fascist and acted accordingly. Just like the fascists, Perón utilized authoritarianism, intense nationalism, and state corporatism to challenge the status quo. So although Perón may not have perfectly fit textbook definitions of European fascism, his state corporatism bore enough of a resemblance in key areas that many U.S. policymakers did not perceive a significant difference. Even those who did see the distinctions still feared and worked to ameliorate the statist leanings of *Peronismo*. By advocating state corporatism as a solution to the problems of society, like the fascists he was an easily discernable threat to the U.S. hegemony, if only on a regional level.

So when Hull and later anti-Peronists labeled him a fascist, they were not simply looking for a pretext to persecute a Latin American nationalist or bring down the one nation that had "dared to brave their lightning." Braden had been supremely confident that his actions were no less heroic than those of U.S. soldiers liberating Europe, as he shattered Roosevelt's hallowed non-intervention pledge. Although historians and contemporaries assigned great significance to this "dismantling" of the Good Neighbor policy, viewing Braden's intervention from this narrow hemispheric perspective is somewhat misleading.[14] Non-intervention was, in and of itself, little more than a specific tactic calculated to best serve the goal of preserving U.S. hegemony and economic principles in Latin America. By violating the non-intervention pledge, Braden and his superiors had abandoned a policy that, they

---

13. Buchrucker, *Nacionalismo y peronismo*; see also José Enrique Miguens, *Los neofascismos en la Argentina* (Buenos Aires, 1983).

14. Wood, *The Dismantling of the Good Neighbor Policy*, 96.

believed, had been rendered ineffective by the emergence of a Peronist "fascist menace"—a rival political and economic system more dangerous than the simple economic nationalism that the Good Neighbor had been designed to counter. In other words, Braden's campaign was a local manifestation of a global effort to preserve liberal capitalism and permanently end the threat of fascist totalitarianism. The issue of interventionism, then, was a peripheral one to U.S. policymakers concerned with deeper issues and greater threats.

Neither can it be claimed that U.S. policy suffered entirely from a "syndrome of irrelevance of rationality," as Escudé argued. U.S. policymakers clearly engaged in an "economic boycott" and practiced "moral imperialism," as he illustrated magnificently. Hull and Braden's campaigns certainly bore little resemblance to "rational" policymaking. Still, Peronist Argentina did pose a significant threat to the United States and its hegemony over the Western Hemisphere, one that even Braden's most ardent critics recognized well. That the tactics U.S. statesmen employed had a catastrophic impact on long-term Argentine development cannot be denied, but for Washington, the elimination of the Peronist threat justified this price. Had the Argentine challenge been less formidable or fundamental, there is little chance that U.S. labor, Wall Street, the Democratic and Republican parties, and the U.S. Army would have set aside their differences to all contribute to the Argentine decline.[15]

So in some respects, Perón was a transition between World War II and the Cold War. World War II had gone a considerable distance toward discrediting European fascism as an alternative political and economic system. Still, Perón and others believed that authoritarian state corporatism melded to classic Latin American nationalism could be useful as a developmental model. Perón's failure, as the State Department had hoped, "proved" that such a

---

15. Escudé, *Estados Unidos, Gran Bretaña*, and "La historia, la cultura política, los errores y las lecciones en las relaciones argentino-norteamericanas," *Argentina y Estados Unidos: Fundamentos de una nueva alianza*, eds. Felipe A. M. de Balze and Eduardo A. Roca (Buenos Aires, 1997), 199-206; and *Estados Unidos, Gran Bretaña*.

model was not viable in Latin America. Leaders like Ibañez and Odría would emulate aspects of Peronism but stopped far short of offering any challenge to the "Inter-American system." The remaining alternative to U.S.-style corporate capitalism was revolutionary Marxism, which like Peronism, was a state-based redistributive ideology with mass appeal.

The U.S. policymakers who had formulated the Good Neighbor policy in the 1930s had assumed that the regimes that would threaten U.S. hegemony would be dictatorships that repudiated liberal capitalism. When confronted by populist leaders such as Perón, and later Arbenz and Castro, who were dedicated to overturning the economic order, naturally they had difficulty in formulating a fitting response to this relatively new phenomenon. But through their experience with Perón, men such as Thomas Mann, who would play a major role in Eisenhower and Kennedy's crusade against Castro, learned important lessons that they would employ when confronted with new brands of populism.[16]

The basic premise behind the Good Neighbor policy—that the U.S. could not afford to intervene often or arbitrarily—remained, but this only meant that the State Department, and later the CIA, had to take their efforts underground to deal with the challenge offered by Latin American nationalism. U.S. dealings with Perón are a microcosm of this shift. Hull and Braden's ill-fated early, public campaigns against Argentine "fascism" boomeranged, leading U.S statesmen to do their work behind closed doors. Behind those doors, Messersmith worked to persuade Perón, while the State Department made a concerted effort to repulse Perón's overtures to his neighbors. After it had become apparent that Perón would not be simply convinced to

---

16. Mann maintained that "a series of closed Latin American nationalist blocs, exemplified by Peronism and spread like contagion by anti-Yankeeism" could easily "wreck the possibilities of market economies, U.S. investment, and Latin American development on North American terms," as he continued to believe that Peronism was a greater threat than communism into the early 1950s. Walter LaFeber, "Thomas C. Mann and the Devolution of Latin American Policy: From Good Neighbor to Military Intervention," *Behind the Throne: Servants of Power to Imperial Presidents, 1898-1968*, eds. Thomas McCormick and Walter LaFeber (Madison, 1993), 170-173.

abandon his program without good reason, Bruce worked to secure a rift in the *peronista* movement itself. Although the State Department was ill-equipped to do much more than this, the CIA's later covert activities can easily be seen as an outgrowth of this basic approach.

## III

The value of studying Perón's New Argentina and its dealings with the United States rests in the gambles—wild gambles, it turns out—that *peronistas* took to escape the problems of underdevelopment that have become very familiar to scholars of a later generation. It is not enough to view these relations within a Cold War context, for Braden's crusade started while Stalin was still amicably regarded as "Uncle Joe" in U.S. newspapers. Bureaucratic approaches similarly break down, for even though conflagrations such as Hull-Welles, Messersmith-Braden, ECA-State Department seemed epic to the participants, they generally boiled down to procedural questions, not fundamental goals—as the Argentines, at least, understood. Viewing these relations in isolation, without the larger contexts and implications, risks missing the true significance of the clash between Perón and the United States.

Although this work has addressed these issues, the role of the British has been downplayed considerably. Although the British were clearly a factor in this contest, they were in actuality peripheral to the outcome of what was essentially, to use Gary Frank's words, a "struggle for hegemony" in Latin America that the British had neither the resources nor the inclination to fight in earnest.[17] Great Britain's influence in the Western Hemisphere, as Leeper, Eady, and Lomax understood well, was fading quickly. The British could still make a major impact, as they did when they declared sterling inconvertible, but the contest was between the Truman Administration and Perón, and both sides knew it. One is struck by how easily Perón conceded to U.S. desires during the negotiations of the Eady-Miranda pact and first Andes Agreement.

---

17. Frank, *Struggle for Hegemony in South America.*

At the same time, *peronistas* had no qualms about directly challenging U.S. economic hegemony in their bilateral negotiations with Chile, Bolivia, Peru, and other hemispheric nations. That the United States opposed these accords was an open secret, but Perón rolled the dice nonetheless. The stakes were the "Inter-American System," and while the British and the Soviets might have periodically entered the game, it was one that the United States and Argentina had to play to its end.

In essence, Perón's post-war challenge may well have been the most serious homegrown one that the United States faced in Latin America prior to Fidel Castro's ascension. Even so, one need look no further than Castro to see that Perón was no simple dictator or that *peronismo* was a revolutionary ideology in some respects. As a young revolutionary in the late 1940s, Castro joined with Peronist delegations and agitators in Cuba under the banner of "anti-imperialism." Castro's early travels around the Caribbean were, in part, funded by *peronista* money. Castro may have viewed *peronismo* as but one step along the way to "true revolution," but throughout his career he supported Perón, despite the ex-president's well-documented anti-communism. Indeed, once in power, Castro invited the exiled Perón to Cuba. The early connection between Castro and Perón's agent provocateurs in the Caribbean is a telling commentary on Perón's foreign policy. Perón envisioned himself as the leader of a broad coalition of revolutionary opponents of U.S. hegemony and was sufficiently credible to attract leftists such as Castro.[18] In this context, it is possible to view Perón as an ideological steppingstone between the determined nationalism of the Mexican Revolution, and the ideologically charged next generation of Marxists such as Castro. U.S. policymakers understood the threat to their interests inherent in all of these movements and acted predictably against each.

Only by viewing Peronism in this fashion can the U.S.-Argentine clash of the late 1940s be fully understood. The threat of the "southern bloc" gave U.S. policymakers who dealt with Latin America "the worst case of cold shivers" in a day when there was little chance of communist penetration. Perón's state corporatism

---

18. Tad Szulc, *Fidel: A Critical Portrait* (New York, 1986), 168-170, 338.

and anti-*yanqui* "Third Position" in both foreign and domestic affairs were blows at the weakest links in the "Inter-American System" and dangerous alternatives to U.S. hegemony and liberal capitalism. The United States had not faced such a fundamental challenge on so many different levels in Latin America before and was in many ways unprepared for it initially. However, U.S. policymakers quickly adapted to the ideological challenge that Peronist statism posed. Perón had set out to "pluck the eagle's feathers" in 1946 and had succeeded, but only for a time.

# BIBLIOGRAPHY

## I. Unpublished Government Records

**Argentina**

   Archivo del Ministerio de Relaciones Exteriores y Culto, Buenos Aires
     Departamento Económico
     Departamento Político

**Peru**

   Archivo del Ministerio de Relaciones Exteriores, Lima
     Entrada
     Salida
     Entrada (Confidential)
     Salida (Confidential)

**United States of America**

   Harry S. Truman Library, Independence, Missouri
     Dean G. Acheson Papers
     Assistant Secretary of State for Economic Affairs
       Office Files
       *Current Economic Developments*
     Merwin Bohan Papers
     John M. Cabot Papers (on microfilm)
     William L. Clayton Papers
     Stanton Griffis Papers
     Edward G. Miller Papers
     John W. Snyder Papers
     Harry S. Truman Papers
     Columbia Oral History Project
       Oral History Interview with Merwin Bohan
       Oral History Interview with John Cabot
       Oral History Interview with Paul Daniels
       Oral History Interview with D.A. FitzGerald
       Oral History Interview with Thomas Mann
   National Archives of the United States, Washington DC
     Record Group 59, Department of State
       Decimal Files
         Records of the Assistant Secretary of State for Latin American Affairs
         Records of the Deputy Assistant Secretaries of State for Inter-American Affairs, 1945-1956

Records of the Office of American Republics Affairs, its Predecessors, and
      its Successors
      Records of the Office of Intelligence and Research
      Records of the Policy Planning Staff
Record Group 84
   Post Files, U.S. Embassy Buenos Aires
   Post Files, U.S. Embassy La Paz
   Post Files, U.S. Embassy Lima
   Post Files, U.S. Embassy Santiago
Record Group 319
   Records of the Investigative Records Department
Record Group 353
   Records of the Interdepartmental and Intradepartmental Committees
      Records of the Argentina Committee
      Records of the State-War-Navy Coordinating Committee

## II. Manuscript Collections, Non-Governmental Archives and Personal Papers

Archives for Urban and Labor History, Detroit, Michigan
   Records of the Congress of Industrial Organizations
      Executive Board Minutes
      James Carey Papers
M. P. Catherwood Library, Cornell University, Ithaca, New York
   Records of the International Ladies Garment Workers Union
      David Dubinsky Papers
      Jacob Potofsky Papers
      Serafino Romualdi Papers
Clemson University Library, Clemson, South Carolina
   James S. Byrnes Papers
Fundación Simón Rodríguez Archivo de Historia del Movimiento Obrero
   *Periodico Seminal de la C.G.T*
   *El Trabajador del Carne*
Lilly Library, Bloomington, Indiana
   Claude Bowers Papers
University of Delaware Library, Newark, Delaware
   George S. Messersmith Papers
University of Maryland Library, College Park, Maryland
   James Bruce Papers

## III. Published Papers and Government Publications

Acheson, Dean G. *Present at the Creation: My Years in the State Department*. New York: Norton, 1954.

Alexander, Robert J. *The ABC Presidents: Conversations and Correspondence with Presidents of Argentina, Brazil, and Chile*. Westport: Praeger, 1992.

_____. *The Bolivaran Presidents: Conversations with Presidents of Bolivia, Peru, Ecuador, Columbia, and Venezuela*. Westport: Praeger, 1994.

Andrade, Victor. *La revolución boliviana y los EE.UU*. La Paz: Gisbest, 1979.

Antonio, Jorge. *Y ahora que?*. Buenos Aires: Colleción, 1970.

Bissell, Richard M. *Reflections of a Cold Warrior*. New Haven: Yale University Press, 1996.

Bowers, Claude. *Chile Through Embassy Windows, 1939-1953*. New York: Simon and Schuster, 1958.

Braden, Spruille. *Diplomats and Demagogues*. New Rochelle: Arlington, 1971.

Bruce, James. *Memoirs*. Baltimore: Gateway, 1997.

_____. *Those Perplexing Argentines*. New York: Longmans Green, 1954.

Cabot, John Moors. *Toward our Common American Destiny*. Medford: Metcalf, 1955.

Cafiero, Antonio. *Cinco años después*. Buenos Aires: n.p., 1961.

_____. *La política exterior Peronista, 1946-1955: sobre la falacia del "mito aislacionista."* Buenos Aires: Corregidor, 1997.

Descartes (Juan Domingo Perón). *Política y estrategia*. Buenos Aires: Editorial Pleamar, 1973.

Dobney, Frederick J. ed. *Selected Papers of Will Clayton*. Baltimore: Johns Hopkins, 1978.

Duggan, Laurence. *The Americas: The Search for Hemispheric Security*. New York: Henry Holt, 1949.

Griffis, Stanton. *Lying in State*. Garden City: Doubleday, 1953.

Hull, Cordell. *Memoirs of Cordell Hull*. 2 vols. New York: Macmillan, 1948.

Instituto Argentino para la Promoción del Intercambio. *Memoria Anual*. Ejercicio 1949. Buenos Aires: Ministerio de Economía de la Nación, 1950.

Kelly, Sir David. *The Ruling Few*. London: Hollis and Carter, 1953.

Perón, Eva. *La razon de mi vida*. Buenos Aires: Ediciones Peuser, 1953.

Perón, Juan Domingo. *La comunidad organizada*. Buenos Aires: Ediciones Cepe, 1964.

_____. *Doctrina universal: continentalismo, ecología, universalismo*. Buenos Aires: Ministerio de Cultura y Educación, 1975.

_____. *Libro azul y blanco: respuesta al libro azul del Departamento de Estado de Estados Unidos*. Buenos Aires: Editorial Freeland, 1946.

_____. *La fuerza es el derecho de las bestias*. Santiago: Empresa Grafica, 1956.

_____. *La tercera posición, la Constitución de 1949, breviario justicialista*. Buenos Aires: Ediciones Argentina, 1973.

Romualdi, Serafino. *Presidents and Peons: Recollections of a Labor Ambassador*. New York: Funk and Wagnalls, 1970.

Solari, Juan Antonio. *Doce años de opobrio: Itinerario de la dictadura*. Buenos Aires: Bases Editorial, 1956.

Truman, Harry S. *Memoirs*. 2 vols. Garden City: Doubleday, 1955.

United States Congress, "Hearings Before the Committee of Agriculture, House of Representatives, 80th Congress, First Session, 1947."

United States Department of State. *Consultation among the American Republics with Regard to the Argentine Situation*. Washington: GPO, 1946.

_____. *Bulletin*. Washington: GPO, 1946-1950.

_____. *Foreign Relations of the United States of America: Diplomatic Papers, 1945*. Vol. IX. Washington: GPO, 1969.

_____. *Foreign Relations of the United States of America: Diplomatic Papers, 1946*. Vol. XI. Washington: GPO, 1969.

_____. *Foreign Relations of the United States of America: Diplomatic Papers, 1947*. Vol. VII. Washington: GPO, 1969.

_____. *Foreign Relations of the United States of America: Diplomatic Papers, 1948*. Vol. IX. Washington: GPO, 1969.

_____. *Foreign Relations of the United States of America: Diplomatic Papers, 1949*. Vol. VII. Washington: GPO, 1969.

Welles, Sumner. *Where Are We Heading?* New York: Harper, 1946.

## IV. Select Books

Abel, Christopher and Colin Lewis. eds. *Economic Imperialism and the State: The Political Economy of the External Connection from Independence to the Present*. London: Athalone, 1985.

Alexander, Robert J. *Organized Labor in Latin America*. New York: Free Press, 1985.

_____. *The Perón Era*. New York: Columbia University Press, 1960.

_____. *Prophets of the Revolution: Profiles of Latin American Leaders*. New York: Macmillan, 1962.

Baily, Samuel L. *The Durability of Peronism*. Buffalo: CIS, 1975.

_____. *Labor, Nationalism, and Politics in Argentina*. New Brunswick: Rutgers University Press, 1967.

_____. *The United States and the Development of Latin America*. New York: New Viewpoints, 1976.

Barager, Joseph R. *Why Perón Came to Power: The Background to Peronism in Argentina*. New York: Knopf, 1968.

Berkowitz, Edward D. and Kim McQuaid, *Creating the Welfare State: The Political Economy of Twentieth Century Reform*. Lawrence: University of Kansas Press, 1980.

Bernstein, Barton J. ed. *Politics and Policies of the Truman Administration*. Chicago: Quadrangle, 1970.

Bernstein, Irving. *The Turbulent Years: A History of the American Worker, 1931-1941*. Boston: Houghton Mifflin, 1970.

Blaisier, Cole. *The Hovering Giant: U.S. Responses to Revolutionary Change in Latin America*. Pittsburgh: University of Pittsburgh Press, 1976.

Blanksten, George. *Perón's Argentina*. Chicago: University of Chicago Press, 1958.

Borden, William S. *The Pacific Alliance: United States Economic Policy and Japanese Trade Recovery. 1947-1955*. Madison: University of Wisconsin Press, 1984.

Braeman, John, Robert H. Bremner, and David Brody. eds. *The New Deal: The National Level*. Columbus: Ohio State University Press, 1975.

Brody, David. *Workers in Industrial America: Essays on the Twentieth Century Struggle*. New York: Oxford University Press, 1980.

Buchrucker, Cristián. *Nacionalismo y peronismo: La Argentina en la crisis ideológico mundial*. Buenos Aires: Editorial Sudamericana, 1987.

Cardoso, Fernando Henrique and Enzo Faletto. *Dependencia y desarrollo en América Latina*. Mexico DF: Siglo XXI, 1969.

Carmen Anguiera, Maria del and Alicia del Carmen Tonini. *Capitalismo del Estado, 1927-1956*. Buenos Aires: CEAL, 1986.

Chávez, Fermín. *Perón y el justicialismo*. Buenos Aires: CEAL, 1984.

Child, John. *Unequal Alliance: The Inter-American Military System: 1938-1978*. Boulder: Westview, 1980.

Chumbita, Hugo. *El enigma peronista*. Buenos Aires: Puntosur, 1989.

Ciria, Alberto. *Partidos y poder en la Argentina moderna*. Buenos Aires: Alvarez, 1960.

_____. *Perón y el justicialismo*. Buenos Aires: Siglo XXI, 1971.

_____. *Política y cultura popular: la Argentina peronista, 1946-1955*. Buenos Aires:
Ediciones de la Flor, 1983.

_____. *Los Estados Unidos nos mira*. Buenos Aires: La Bastilla, 1973.

Cirigliano, Antonio Angel. *Federico Pinedo: teoría y práctica de un liberal*. Buenos Aires: CEAL, 1986.

Cobbs, Elizabeth Anne. *The Rich Neighbor Policy: Rockefeller and Kaiser in Brazil*. New Haven: Yale University Press, 1992.

Collier, David. ed. *The New Authoritarianism in Latin America*. Princeton: Princeton University Press, 1979.

Collins, Robert M. *The Business Response to Keynes, 1929-1964*. New York: Columbia University Press, 1984.

Conil Paz, Alberto and Gustavo E. Ferrari. *Política exterior argentina, 1930-1962*. Buenos Aires: Huemul, 1966.

Conklin, Paul. *The New Deal*. Arlington Heights: Harlan Davidson, 1975.

Cotler, Julio and Patrick Fagen. eds. *Latin America and the United States: The Changing Political Relations*. Stanford: Stanford University Press, 1984.

Crassweller, Robert. *Perón and the Enigmas of Argentina*. New York: Norton, 1987.

Daniels, Walter M. ed. *Latin America in the Cold War*. New York: Wilson, 1952.

Dean, Warren. *Brazil and the Struggle for Rubber: a Study in Environmental History*. Cambridge: Cambridge University Press, 1987.

de Balze, Felipe A.M. and Eduardo A. Roca. eds. *Argentina y Estados Unidos: Fundamentos de una nueva alianza*. Buenos Aires, Consejo Argentino para las Relaciones Internacionales, 1997).

del Campo, Hugo. *Sindicalismo y peronismo: los comienzos de un vínculo perdurable.*
  Buenos Aires: CLACSO, 1982.
Demitrópulos, Libertad. *Eva Perón.* Buenos Aires: CEAL, 1984.
Diaz Alejandro, Carlos. *Essays on the Economic History of the Argentine Republic.*
  New Haven: Yale University Press, 1970.
DiTella, Guido and Rudiger Dornbusch. eds. *The Political Economy of Argentina, 1946-1983.* Pittsburgh: University of Pittsburgh Press, 1989.
DiTella, Guido and D. C. M. Platt. eds. *The Political Economy of Argentina, 1880-1946.*
  New York: St. Martins Press, 1986.
DiTella, Guido and D. Cameron Watt. eds. *Argentina Between the Great Powers, 1939-1946.* Pittsburgh: University of Pittsburgh Press, 1990.
DiTella, Guido and Manuel Zymelman. *Las etapas del desarrollo económico argentino.*
  Buenos Aires: EUDEPA, 1967.
DiTella, Torcuato. ed. *Argentina-Chile: Desarrollos paralelos.* Buenos Aires: ISEN, 2000.
_____. *Latin American Politics: A Theoretical Framework.* Austin: University of Texas Press, 1990.
_____. *Sociología de los procesos politicos.* Buenos Aires: Grupo Editor Latinoamericano, 1985.
Drosdoff, Daniel. *El gobierno de las vacas, 1933-1936: Tratado Roca-Runciman.*
  Buenos Aires: La Bastilla, 1972.
Dubofsky, Melvin and Warren Van Tine. eds. *Labor Leaders in America.* Urbana: University of Illinois Press, 1984.
Escudé, Carlos. *Estados Unidos, Gran Bretaña, y la declinación argentina, 1942-1949.*
  Buenos Aires: Editorial Belgrano, 1983.
Falcoff, Mark and Ronald H. Dolkart. eds. *Prologue to Perón: Argentina in Depression and War.* Berkeley: University of California Press, 1975.
Fayt, Carlos. *Naturaleza de peronismo.* Buenos Aires: Edición Argentina, 1967.
Ferns, H. S. *Britain and Argentina in the Ninteenth Century.* Oxford: Clarendon, 1960.
Ferrer, Aldo. *The Argentine Economy.* Berkeley: University of California Press, 1967.
Fforde, John. *The Bank of England and Public Policy, 1941-1958.* Cambridge: Cambridge University Press, 1992.
Fossedal, Gregory. *Our Finest Hour: Will Clayton, the Marshall Plan and the Triumph of Democracy.* Stanford: Stanford University Press, 1994.
Francis, Michael J. *Limits of Hegemony: United States Relations with Argentina and Chile during World War II.* Notre Dame: University of Notre Dame Press, 1977.
Frank, Gary. *Juan Perón vs. Spruille Braden: The Story Behind the Blue Book.* Lanham: University Press of America, 1980.
_____. *Struggle for Hegemony in South America: Argentina, Brazil, and the United States During the Second World War.* Miami: University of Miami Center for Advanced International Studies, 1979.
Fraser, Nicholas and Marysa Navarro. *Eva Perón.* New York: Norton, 1980.

Frye, Alton. *Nazi Germany and the American Hemisphere, 1931-1941*. New Haven: Yale University Press, 1967.

Gambini, Hugo. *Historia del peronismo: el poder total*. Buenos Aires: Editorial Planeta, 1999.

_____. *La primera presidencia de Perón: testimonios y documentos*. Buenos Aires: CEAL, 1983.

Gardner, Lloyd C. *Economic Aspects of New Deal Diplomacy*. Boston: Beacon, 1971.

Gellman, Irwin F. *Good Neighbor Diplomacy: United States Policies in Latin America, 1933-1945*. Baltimore: Johns Hopkins, 1979.

Goñi, Uki. *La auténtica Odessa: la fuga nazi a la Argentina de Perón*. Buenos Aires: Paidós, 2002.

_____. *Perón y los alemanes: la verdad sobre el espionaje nazi y los fugitivos del Reich*. Buenos Aires: Editorial Sudamericana, 1998.

Green, David. *The Containment of Latin America: Myths and Realities of the Good Neighbor Policy*. Chicago: Quadrangle, 1971.

Grow, Michael. *The Good Neighbor Policy and Authoritarianism in Paraguay: United States Economic Expansion and Great-Power Rivalry in Latin America during World War II*. Lawrence: The Regents Press of Kansas, 1981.

Gugliamelli, Juan Enrique. *Geopolitica del cono sur*. Buenos Aires: Tierra Nueva, 1976.

Halperin Donghi, Tulio. *Argentina en el callejon*. Buenos Aires: Editorial ARCA, 1964.

Hawley, Ellis. *The New Deal and the Problem of Monopoly*. Princeton: Princeton University Press, 1966.

Hearden, Patrick. *Roosevelt Confronts Hitler: America's Entry to World War II*. DeKalb: Northern Illinois University Press, 1987.

Hoff-Wilson, Joan. *American Business and Foreign Policy, 1920-1933*. Lexington: University Press of Kentucky, 1971.

Hogan, Michael J. *Informal Entente: The Private Structure of Cooperation in Anglo-American Diplomacy*. Columbia: University of Missouri Press, 1977.

_____. *The Marshall Plan: America, Britain, and the Reconstruction of Western Europe, 1947-1952*. Cambridge: Cambridge University Press, 1988.

Hogan, Michael J. and Thomas Patterson. eds. *Explaining the History of American Foreign Relations*. Cambridge: Cambridge University Press, 1991.

Horowicz, Alejandro. *Los cuatros peronismos*. Buenos Aires: Hyspamerica, 1985.

Horowitz, Joel. *Argentine Unions, the State, and the Rise of Perón, 1930-1945*. Berkeley: Institute of International Studies, 1990.

Jalabe, Silvia Ruth. ed. *La política exterior argentina y sus protagonistas, 1880-1995*. Buenos Aires: CARI, 1996, 71-87.

Justo, Liborio. *Argentina y Brasil en la integración continental*. Buenos Aires: CEAL, 1983.

Knudson, Jerry K. *Bolivia: Press and Revolution, 1932-1964*. Lanham, University Press of America, 1988.

Lanús, Juan Archibaldo. *De Chapultepec a Beagle: Política exterior Argentina, 1945-1980*. Buenos Aires: EMECE, 1984.

Lewis, Paul. *The Crisis of Argentine Capitalism*. Chapel Hill, University of North Carolina Press, 1990.
Lieuwen, Edwin. *Arms and Politics in Latin America*. New York: Praeger, 1961.
Loveman, Brian. *Chile: The Legacy of Hispanic Capitalism*. New York: Oxford, 1988.
Lucchini, Cristina. *Apoyo Empresarial dn los orígenes del peronismo*. Buenos Aires: CEAL, 1990.
Luna Felix. *El 45: Cronica de un año decisivo*. Buenos Aires: J.Alvarez, 1973.
_____. *Perón y su tiempo*. 3 vol. Buenos Aires: Editorial Sudamericana, 1984.
Machado, Manuel A. *Aftosa: A Historical Survey of Foot-and-Mouth Disease and Inter-American Relations*. Albany: SUNY Press, 1969.
MacKinnon, Moira. *Los años formativos del partido peronista, 1946-1955*. Buenos Aires: Siglo XXI, 2002.
Magnet, Alejandro. *Nuestros vecinos argentinos*. Santiago: Editorial del Pacifico, 1956.
Maier, Charles S. *Recasting Bourgeois Europe: Stabilization in France, Germany and Italy in the Decade after World War II*. Princeton: Princeton University Press, 1975.
Malloy, James. *Bolivia: the Uncompleted Revolution*. New York: Oxford University Press, 1970.
_____. ed. *Authoritarianism and Corporatism in Latin America*. Pittsburgh: University of Pittsburgh Press, 1977.
McCann, Frank D. *The Brazilian-American Alliance, 1937-1945*. Princeton: Princeton University Press, 1973.
McCormick, Thomas J. *America's Half-Century: United States Foreign Policy and the Cold War*. Baltimore: Johns Hopkins University Press, 1991.
McCormick, Thomas J. and Walter LaFeber. eds. *Behind the Throne: Servants to Power to Imperial Presidents, 1898-1968*. Madison: University of Wisconsin Press, 1993.
McGann, Thomas. *Argentina, the United States, and the Inter-American System*. Cambridge: Harvard University Press, 1957.
McQuaid, Kim. *Big Business and Corporate Power, from FDR to Reagan*. New York: Morrow, 1982.
Miguens, José Enrique. *Los neofascismos en la Argentina*. Buenos Aires: Editorial Belgrano, 1983.
Miguens, José Enrique and Frederick C. Turner. eds. *Juan Perón and the Reshaping of Argentina*. Pittsburgh: University of Pittsburgh Press, 1983.
_____. *Racionalidad del peronismo*. Buenos Aires: Grupo Editorial Planeta, 1988.
Mimsburg, Naúm. *Capitales extraneros y grupos dominantes argentinos*. 2 vols. Buenos
Aires: CEAL, 1987.
Moneta, Carlos. ed. *Geopolítica y politica en el atlantico sur*. Buenos Aires: Editorial Pleamar, 1983.
Muñoz, Heraldo and Carlos Portales. *Una amistad esquiva: Las relaciones de Estados Unidos y Chile*. Santiago: Pehuén, 1987.
Needler, Martin. *The Problem of Democracy in Latin America*. Lexington: DC Heath, 1987.

Newton, Ronald. *The 'Nazi Menace' in Argentina, 1931-1947*. Stanford: Stanford University Press, 1992.

O'Donnell, Guillermo. *Modernization and Bureaucratic Authoritarianism: Studies in South American Politics*. Berkeley: University of California Press, 1973.

Page, Joseph. *Perón: A Biography*. New York: Random House, 1983.

Parkinson, Francis. *Latin America, the Cold War, and the World Powers: A Study in Diplomatic History*. Beverly Hills: Sage, 1978.

Parrini, Carl. *Heir to Empire: United States Economic Policy, 1916-1923*. Pittsburgh: University of Pittsburgh Press, 1969.

Paso, Leonardo. *Del golpe de estado de 1943 al de 1955*. 2 vols. Buenos Aires: Biblioteca Política Argentina, 1987.

Peterson, Harold F. *Argentina and the United States, 1810-1960*. New York: State University of New York Press, 1964.

Plotkin, Mariano. *Mañana es San Perón: Propaganda, rituales políticos, y educación en

el régimen peronista, 1946-1955*. Buenos Aires: Ariel, 1994.

Potash, Robert. *Arms and Politics in Argentina: Perón to Frondizi*. Stanford: Stanford University Press, 1980.

_____. *Arms and Politics in Argentina: Yrigoyen to Perón*. Stanford: Stanford University Press, 1969.

_____. *Perón y el G.O.U.: Los documentos de una logia secreta*. Buenos Aires: Editorial Sudamericana, 1984.

Radosh, Ronald. *American Labor and United States Foreign Policy*. New York: Random
House, 1969.

Randall, Laura. *Essays on the Economic History of Argentina*. New York: Columbia University Press, 1978,

Rapoport, Mario. *Gran Bretaña, Estados Unidos, y las clases dirigentes argentinos, 1940-1945*. Buenos Aires: Editorial Belgrano, 1980.

_____. *Política y diplomacia en la Argentina: Las relaciones con EE.UU. y la URSS*.
Buenos Aires: Editorial Tesis, 1986.

Rapoport, Mario and Claudio Spiguel. *Estados Unidos y el peronismo: La política norteamericana en la Argentina, 1949-1955*. Buenos Aires: Grupo Editor Latinamericano, 1994.

Rapp, Fred, ed. *Gustav Stern Conference on Foot and Mouth Disease*. New York: Gustav Stern, 1969.

Rock, David, *Argentina, 1519-1982*. Berkeley: University of California Press, 1985.

_____. *Authoritarian Argentina: The Nationalist Movement, Its History, and Its Impact*. Berkeley: University of California Press, 1994.

_____. ed. *Argentina in the Twentieth Century*. London: Duckworth, 1985.

_____. ed. *Latin America in the 1940s: War and Postwar Transitions*. Berkeley: University of California Press, 1994.

Rodríguez, Carlos J. *La idea peronista: Contenido ideológico del justicialismo*. Buenos Aires: Libra Editorial, 1994.

Romning, C. Neale and Albert P. Vannucci. eds. *Ambassadors in Foreign Policy: The Influence of Individuals in U.S.-Latin American Foreign Policy*. New York: Praeger, 1987.

Rouquié, Alain. *Poder militar y sociedad política en la Argentina*. Buenos Aires: Emecé, 1983.

Sabado, Hilda. *Agrarian Capitalism and the World Market: Buenos Aires in the Pastoral Age, 1840-1890*. Albuquerque: University of New Mexico Press, 1990.

Schaller, Michael. *The American Occupation of Japan: The Origins of the Cold War in Japan*. New York: Oxford, 1984.

Schonberger, Howard. *Aftermath of War: Americans and the Remaking of Japan, 1945-1952*. Kent: Kent State University Press, 1984.

Scott, Jack. *Yankee Unions Go Home: How the AFL Helped the U.S. Build an Empire in Latin America*. Vancouver: New Star, 1978.

Sebreli, Juan José. *Los deseos imaginarios del peronismo*. Madrid: Legasa, 1983.

Seipe, R. Monserrat Llairo and N. Gale. *Perón y los relaciones con el Este*. Buenos Aires: Biblioteca Política Argentina, 1994.

Smith, Peter H. *Politics and Beef in Argentina: Patterns of Conflict*. New York: Columbia University Press, 1960.

Stiller, Jesse. *George S. Messersmith: Diplomat for Democracy*. Chapel Hill: University of North Carolina Press, 1987.

Szulc, Tad. *Fidel: A Critical Portrait*. New York: Morrow, 1986.

Taylor, J.M. *Eva Perón: The Myths of a Woman*. Chicago: University of Chicago Press, 1981.

Torre, Juan Carlos. *La vieja guardia sindical y Perón: Sobre las orígenes del peronismo*. Buenos Aires: Editorial Sudamericana, 1990.

Tulchin, Joseph. *Argentina and the United States: A Conflicted Relationship*. Boston: Twayne, 1990.

Van Tine, Warren R. *The Making of a Labor Bureaucrat: Union Leadership in the United States, 1870-1920*. Amherst: University of Massachusetts Press, 1973.

Waldmann, Peter. *El peronismo, 1943-1955*. Buenos Aires: Hyspamerica, 1986.

Wiarda, Howard J. *Corporatism and National Development in Latin America*. Boulder: Westview, 1980.

Windmuller, John P. *American Labor and the International Labor Movement, 1940-1953*. Ithaca: Institute of International Industrial and Labor Relations, 1954.

Wood, Bryce. *The Dismantling of the Good Neighbor Policy*. Austin: University of Texas Press, 1985.

Woods, Randall Bennett. *The Roosevelt Foreign-Policy Establishment and the "Good Neighbor."* Lawrence, Kansas University Press, 1979.

Wright, Winthrop R. *British-Owned Railroads in Argentina: Their Effect on Economic Nationalism*. Austin: University of Texas Press, 1974.

Wynia, Gary. *Argentina in the Post-War Period: Politics and Economic Policymaking in*
> *a Divided Society*. Albuquerque: University of New Mexico Press, 1978.

Zeigler, Robert H. *American Workers, American Unions*. Baltimore: Johns Hopkins, 1986.

## V. Select Articles

Ashby, Joe C. "Labor and the Philosophy of the Argentine Revolution." *Inter-American Economic Affairs* V (Summer 1951): 71-96.

Beals, Carleton. "Chile, Copper, and Communism." Walter M. Daniels. ed. *Latin America in the Cold War*. New York: Wilson, 1952: 130-153.

Bowen, Nicholas St. Francis. "The End of British Economic Hegemony in Argentina: Messersmith and the Eady-Miranda Agreement." *Inter-American Economic Affairs* 28 (Spring 1975): 3-24.

Brody, David, "The New Deal and World War II." John Braeman, Robert Bremner, and David Brody. eds. *The New Deal: The National Level*. Columbus: Ohio State University Press, 1975: 267-309.

Callis, J.J. "Foot-and-Mouth Disease." Fred Rapp. ed. *Gustav Stern Conference on Foot-and-Mouth Disease*. New York: Gustav Stern, 1969.

Cardoso, Fernando Henrique. "On the Characterization of Authoritarian Regimes in Latin America." David Collier. ed. *The New Authoritarianism in Latin America*. Berkeley: IIS, 1979: 33-60.

Chalmers, Douglas A. "The Politicized State in Latin America. James Malloy. ed. *Authoritarianism and Corporatism in Latin America*. Pittsburgh: University of Pittsburgh Press, 1977: 23-45.

Chambers, Edward J. "Some Factors in the Deterioration of Argentina's External Position." *Inter-American Economic Affairs* VIII (Winter 1954), 27-62.

Collier, David. "Overview of the Bureaucratic Authoritarian Model." David Collier. ed. *The New Authoritarianism in Latin America*. Berkeley: IIS, 1979: 3-22.

Dubofsky, Melvin and Warren Van Tine, "John L. Lewis and the Triumph of Mass Production Unionism." Melvin Dubofsky and Warren Van Tine. eds. *Labor Leaders in America* Urbana: University of Illinois Press, 1987: 185-207.

Escudé, Carlos. "Argentine Territorial Nationalism." *Journal of Latin American Studies* 20: 139-165.

_____. "La historia, la cultura política, los errores y las lecciones en las relaciones argentino-norteamericanas." Felipe A. M. de Balze and Eduardo A. Roca. eds. *Argentina y Estados Unidos: Fundamentos de una nueva alianza*. Buenos Aires, Consejo Argentino para las Relaciones Internacionales, 1997, 199-206.

_____. "La Traición a los derechos humanos, 1950-1955." ed. Silvia Ruth Jalabe. *La política exterior argentina y sus protagonistas, 1880-1995*. Buenos Aires: CARI, 1996, 71-87.

_____. "US Political Destabilization and the Economic Boycott of Argentina during the 1940s." Guido DiTella and D. Cameron Watt. eds. *Argentina Between the Great Powers*. Pittsburgh: University of Pittsburgh Press, 1990: 56-76.

Falcoff, Mark and Ronald H. Dolkart. "Political Developments." Mark Falcoff and Ronald Dolkart. eds. *Prologue to Perón: Argentina in Depression and War*. Berkeley: University of California Press, 1975: 31-56.

Ferguson, Thomas. "From Normalcy to New Deal: Industrial Structure, Party Competition, and American Public Policy in the Great Depression." *International Organization*, 38 (Winter 1984): 41-98.

Fodor, Jorge. "Argentina's Nationalism: Myth or Reality?" Guido DiTella and Rudiger Dornbusch. eds. *The Political Economy of Argentina, 1946-1983*. Pittsburgh: University of Pittsburgh Press, 1989, 31-53.

_____. "The Origins of Argentina's Sterling Balances, 1939-1943." Guido DiTella and D. C. M. Platt. eds. *The Political Economy of Argentina, 1880-1946*. New York: St. Martins Press, 1986: 155-179.

_____. "Perón's Policies for Agricultural Exports: Dogmatism or Commonsense?" David Rock. ed. *Argentina in the Twentieth Century*. London: Duckworth, 1985: 66-87.

Fodor, Jorge and Arturo O'Connell. "La Argentina y la economía atlántica en la primera mitad del siglo." *Desarrollo Económico* 49 (Abril-Junio 1973), 3-66.

Garcia Heras, Raul. "World War II and the Frustrated Nationalization of the British-Owned Railroads in Argentina." *Journal of Latin American Studies* 17: 135-155.

Gerchunoff, Pablo. "Peronist Economic Policies, 1946-1955. Guido DiTella and Rudiger Dornbusch. eds. *The Political Economy of Argentina, 1946-1983*. Pittsburgh: University of Pittsburgh Press, 1989: 58-85.

Gilderhus, Mark T. "An Emerging Synthesis? U.S.-Latin American Relations Since the Second World War." *Diplomatic History* 16 (Summer 1992): 429-452.

Godson, Roy. "The AFL Foreign Policymaking from the End of World War II to the Merger." *Labor History* 16 (1975), 325-337.

Green, David. "The Cold War Comes to Latin America." Barton Bernstein. ed. *Politics and Policies of the Truman Administration*. New York: Quadrangle, 1970: 149-195.

Haines, Gerald K. "Under the Eagle's Wing: The Franklin Roosevelt Administration Forges an American Hemisphere." *Diplomatic History* 1 (Fall 1977): 370-388.

Hilton, Stanley E. "The Argentine Factor in Twentieth-Century Brazilian Foreign Policy Strategy." *Political Science Quarterly* (Spring 1985): 27-51.

_____. "Las relaciones Argentino-Brasileña: el punto de vista de Brasil." Carlos Moneta. ed. *Geopolítica y política en el atlantico sur*." Buenos Aires: Editorial Pleamar, 1983: 29-39.

Holmes, Olive. "'Greater Argentina' Dream." Walter Daniels. ed. *Latin America in the Cold War*. New York: Wilson, 1952: 126-129.

Horowitz, Joel. "The Impact of Pre-1943 Labor Traditions on Peronism." *Journal of Latin American Studies* 15: 101-116.

_____. "Industrialists and the Rise of Perón." *The Americas* 48 (October 1990): 199-217.

Kimball, Warren F. "'The Juggler': Franklin D. Roosevelt and Anglo-American Competition in Latin America." Guido DiTella and D. Cameron Watt. eds. *Argentina Between the Great Powers* Pittsburgh: University of Pittsburgh Press, 1990: 18-33.

Koistenen, Paul. "Mobilizing the World War II Economy: Labor and the Military-Industrial Complex." *Pacific History Review* 42 (1973): 443-478.

LaFeber, Walter. "Thomas C. Mann and the Devolution of Latin American Policy."
Thomas McCormick and Walter LaFeber. eds. *Behind the Throne: Servants of Power to Imperial Presidents, 1898-1968*. Madison: University of Wisconsin Press, 1993: 166-203.

Lewis, Colin. "Anglo-Argentine Trade, 1945-1965." David Rock. ed. *Argentina in the Twentieth Century* London: Duckworth, 1985: 114-134.

Lewis, Daniel. "Internal and External Convergence: The Collapse of Argentine Grain Farming." David Rock. ed. *Latin America in the 1940s: War and Postwar Transitions*. Berkeley: University of California Press, 1994.

Lichtenstein, Nelson. "Walter Reuther and the Rise of Labor Liberalism." Melvin Dubofsky and Warren Van Tine. eds. *Labor Leaders in America*. Urbana: University of Illinois Press, 1987: 290-300.

Little, Walter. "Popular Origins of Peronism." David Rock. ed. *Argentina in the Twentieth Century*. London: Duckworth, 1985: 160-182.

Lopez, Ernesto. "El peronismo en el gobierno y los militares." José Enrique Miguens and
Frederick C. Turner. eds. *Racionalidad del peronismo*. Buenos Aires: Editorial Planeta, 1988: 83-99.

Lopez-Alves, Fernando. "Why Not Corporatism? Redemocratization and Regime Formation in Uruguay." David Rock. ed. *Latin America in the 1940s: War and Postwar Transitions*. Berkeley: University of California Press, 1994: 187-209.

MacDonald, Callum A. "The Braden Campaign and Anglo- American Relations in
Argentina, 1945-1946." Guido DiTella and D. Cameron Watt. eds. *Argentina Between the Great Powers, 1939-1946*. Pittsburgh: University of Pittsburgh Press, 1990: 137-153.

_____. "The Politics of Intervention: The United States and Argentina, 1941-1946." *Journal of Latin American Studies* 12: 365-396.

_____. "The U.S., Britain, and Argentina in the Post-War Period." Guido DiTella and
D. C. M. Platt. eds. *The Political Economy of Argentina, 1880-1946*. New York: St. Martins Press, 1986: 183-199.

_____. "The U.S., the Cold War, and Perón." Christopher Abel and Colin Lewis. eds. *Economic Imperialism and the State: The Political Economy of the*

*External Connection from Independence to the Present*. London: Athalone, 1985: 405-414.

Machinandiarena de Devoto. Leonor and Carlos Escudé. "Las relaciones Argentino-Chilenas, 1946-1953, y las ilusiones expansionistas del peronismo." *Argentina-Chile: Desarrollos paralelos*. ed. Torcuato DiTella. Buenos Aires: ISEN, 2000: 181-200.

Maier, Charles. "The Politics of Productivity: Foundations of American International Economic Policy after World War II." *International Organization* 31 (August 1977), 707-633.

Malloy, James M. "Authoritarianism and Corporatism in Latin America: The Modal Pattern." James M. Malloy. ed. *Authoritarianism and Corporatism in Latin America*. Pittsburgh: University of Pittsburgh Press, 1977: 3-19.

May, Ernest R. "The Bureaucratic-Politics Approach: U.S.-Argentine Relations, 1942-1947." Julio Cotler and Patrick Fagen. eds. *Latin America and the United States: The Changing Political Relations*. Stanford: Stanford University Press, 1984: 130-164.

Navarro, Marysa. "Evita and Peronism." José Enrique Miguens and Frederick C. Turner. eds. *Juan Perón and the Reshaping of Argentina*. Pittsburgh: University of Pittsburgh Press, 1983: 14-33.

Newton, Ronald. "Disorderly Succession: Great Britain, the United States and the 'Nazi Menace' in Argentina." Guido DiTella and D. Cameron Watt. eds. *Argentina Between the Great Powers, 1939-1946*. Pittsburgh: University of Pittsburgh Press, 1990: 111-134.

O'Donnell, Guillermo A. "Corporatism and the Question of the State." James M. Malloy. ed. *Authoritarianism and Corporatism in Latin America*. Pittsburgh: University of Pittsburgh Press, 1977: 48-87.

Pach, Chester. "The Containment of U.S. Military Aid to Latin America, 1944-1947." *Diplomatic History* 6 (Summer 1982): 225-243.

Peffer, E. Louise. "Less Beef in the Plate?" *Inter-American Economic Affairs* IX (Summer 1957): 3-35.

Rabe, Stephen G. "The Elusive Conference: United States Relations with Latin America, 1945-1952." *Diplomatic History* 2 (Summer 1978): 279-294.

Rapoport, Mario. "Foreign and Domestic Policy in Argentina: The Traditional Political Parties and the Military Regime, 1943-1945." Guido DiTella and D. Cameron Watt. eds. *Argentina Between the Great Powers, 1939-1946*. Pittsburgh: University of Pittsburgh Press, 1990: 77-101.

Schatz, Ronald W. "Phillip Murray and the Subordination of the Industrial Unions to the

U.S. Government." Melvin Dubofsky and Warren Van Tine. eds. *Labor Leaders in America*. Urbana: University of Illinois Press, 1987: 234-256.

Trask, Roger R. "The Impact of the Cold War on United States-Latin American Relations, 1945-1949." *Diplomatic History* 1 (Summer 1977): 271-285.

_____. "George Messersmith vs. Spruille Braden: World War II, the Cold War, and Argentine Policy, 1945-1947." *Journal of Inter-American Studies and World Affairs* 26 (February 1984), 69-95.

Tulchin, Joseph. La relación Argentino-Brasileña: punto de vista Argentina." Carlos Moneta. ed. *Geopolítica y política en el atlantico sur*. Buenos Aires: Editorial Pleamar, 1983: 43-57.

Vannucci, Albert P. "Elected by Providence: Spruille Braden in Argentina in 1945." C. Neale Romning and Albert P. Vannucci, eds. *Ambassadors in Foreign Policy: The Influence of Individuals in U.S.-Latin American Foreign Policy*. New York: Praeger, 1987: 49-67.

_____. "The Influence of Latin American Governments on the Shaping of United States Foreign Policy: The Case of Argentina, 1943-1948." *Journal of Latin American Studies* 16: 355-382.

Villaneuva, Javier. "Economic Developments." Mark Falcoff and Ronald H. Dolkart. eds. *Prologue to Perón: Argentina in Depression and War*. Berkeley: University of California Press, 1975: 57-82.

Warren, Harris G. "Diplomatic Relations Between the United States and Argentina." *Inter-American Economic Affairs* VIII (Winter 1954): 63-82.

Weil, Felix J. "Can Peron Be Bought?" *Inter-American Economic Affairs* VI (Summer 1950): 27-36.

Wood, Bryce. "The Department of State and the Non-National Interest." *Inter-American Economic Affairs* (Autumn 1961): 5-24.

## VI. Dissertations and Theses

Bohlin, Thomas G. "United States-Latin American Relations and the Cold War." Unpublished Ph.D. dissertation, Notre Dame University, 1985.

Deiner, John T. "ATLAS: A Labor Instrument of Argentine Expansionism under Perón." Unpublished Ph.D. dissertation, Rutgers University, 1969.

Giacalone, Rita. "From Bad Neighbors to Reluctant Partners: Argentina and the United States, 1946-1950." Unpublished Ph.D. dissertation, Indiana University, 1977.

Machinandiarena de Devoto, Leonor A. "La influencia del justicialismo en Chile, 1946-1952." Tesis de Doctorado, Universidad de Buenos Aires, 1995.

Vannucci, Albert P. "United States-Argentine Relations, 1943-1948: A Case-Study in Confused Policy Making." Unpublished Ph.D. dissertation, New School for Social Research, 1979.

## VI. Periodicals

Argentina
- *Boletin Interamericana de la C.G.T. Argentina*
- *Epoca*
- *La Nación*
- *Periodico Seminal del C.G.T.*
- *La Prensa*
- *Primera Plana*
- *Review of the River Plate*
- *El Trabajador de Carne*

Bolivia
- *El Diario*

Chile
- *La Hora*
- *El Mercurio*
- *La Nación*
- *El Siglo*
- *Zig-Zag*

Peru
- *El Comercio*

United States of America
- *Journal of Commerce*
- *New York Times*
- *Time*

# INDEX

Acheson, Dean 8-10, 45, 78, 90, 92, 205, 209-210, 217, 280
Adam, Hector 73-74
Aftosa 107-111, 242, 285
Aldunate, Fernando 174
Allende, Salvador 175
American Federation of Labor (AFL) 83, 128, 137, 140-146, 150-152
Andes Agreement 246-249, 272
Apodaca, Joseph 206
Arbenz, Jacobo 302
Ares, Roberto 271, 273, 278, 286
Arnold, Bill 121
Avalos, Eduardo 47-48

Baldwin, Joseph 86
Ballieu, Clive 243-248
Banco Central 61-63, 67, 237, 241, 259
Barro, José 229, 270
Batlle Berres, José 102
Behn, Sosthenes 121, 283, 288
Belgium 90, 228
Belmonte Pabón, Elías 73, 189
Benítez Vera, Victoriano 75
Berle, Adolph 43, 74-75
Berretta, Tomás 71-72
Betancourt, Romulo 200-201
Bissell, Richard 253
Blaisdell, Thomas 276-278
Blue Book 54-57, 82, 84, 97, 146, 157, 208, 216
Bohan, Merwin 36, 217
Bolivia 32, 45-46, 72-74, 102-104, 162, 182-192, 194
Borlenghi, Angel 34, 70, 139
Bormann, Martin 255
Bowers, Claude 49, 81-82, 98, 164, 166-182, 301
Braden, Spruille 38-47, 49-50, 53-57, 78-83, 89, 91-94, 97-98, 100, 104, 145, 151, 159, 164, 167, 203-218, 233, 255
Bramulgia, Juan 34, 70, 116-118, 142, 184, 221, 229, 244-247, 261, 267, 271, 279, 283, 285, 287, 290-292

Brazil 30, 44-45, 74-75, 101-102, 187
Brown, Winthrop 282
Bruce, Howard 256, 261, 267, 279
Bruce, James 180, 204, 218, 221-233, 235-236, 245, 251, 256-263, 265, 266, 268-271, 280, 285-286

Buitrago, Mariano 183, 188, 190, 192
Bunge, César 286
Bustamante i Rivero, José 193-196
Byrnes, James 46-47, 53-55, 78, 86-89, 92, 98, 100, 145, 158, 173-174, 205, 208-209

Cabot, John Moors 25, 48, 50-57, 59-60, 74, 78, 83-86, 88, 94, 98
Carey, James 152-155
Carías, Tiburcio 201
Castillo, Ramón 27-29
Castro, Fidel 22, 311
Cellar, Emmanuel 110
Cereijo, Ramón 270, 273, 286, 292-295
Chapultepec Accords 38, 40, 77, 79, 85, 97, 106-107, 133, 210
Chile 26, 28, 102, 162-182
Clayton, William 8-10, 78-79, 97, 100, 105-106, 110-111, 118, 121, 162, 173, 198-199, 210-211
Combined Food Board 65, 90
Confederación General de Profesiones (CGP) 18
Confederación General de Trabajadores (CGT) 18, 34-36, 128, 138-146, 150-159, 221-222
Confederación General de Universidades (CGU) 18
Congress of Industrial Organizations (CIO) 83, 142, 152-159
Connally, Tom 41, 88, 215, 217, 270
Cooper, Prentice 196
Correa, Javier 195
Cripps, Stanford 118
Crittenberger, Willis 230
Cross, Ernest 282
Cruz Coke, Eduardo 175

Czechoslovakia 215, 223

Daniels, Paul 263, 280
Devries, Carlos 186
Doerge, Heinrich 70, 107
Drago, Martin 82
Duran, Gustavo 215-216
Dutra, Enrico 102

Eady, Wilfred 114-117
Economic Cooperation Administration

236, 250-263, 274-281
Eisenhower, Dwight 90
Espy, Carlos 185
Export-Import Bank 175, 178, 286, 294-296

Fabricaciones Militares 90, 169, 224-225
Falange 35
Farrell, Edelmiro 31, 38, 43-46, 48, 61,
71
Figuerola y Tressols, José 34, 69, 128, 206, 272
FitzGerald, D.A. 250-251, 253, 255-256, 281
Five-Year Plan 69, 128-134, 212-213, 239
Flack, Joseph 98, 102-104, 183-185, 188-190
Flannigan, Henry 133
Forrestal, James 224
Franco, Francisco 76, 98, 212
Freude, Ludwig 70, 107
Freude, Rodolfo 70
Frigorificos 76-77, 122-124, 165, 248, 275-277

Gaston, Herbert 294
Gay, Luis 34, 139-146, 236
General Agreement on Tariffs and Trade (GATT) 9
Germany 6, 13, 26-27, 30-32, 37, 80, 97, 132, 167, 207, 246
Gómez Morales, Alfredo 270, 273, 286
Gompers, Samuel 138
González Videla, Gabriel 102, 163, 166-182
Good Neighbor Policy 10-15, 78-79

GOU 31- 33, 162
Great Britain 18, 26-27, 29, 37, 42, 87,
89-90, 112-120, 133, 211, 214, 241-249, 272-283, 310-311
Green, William 142, 144, 152
Griffis, Stanton 1, 289-290, 292-293, 304
Griffiths, John 69, 255

Hall, James 185
Harrison, Robert 261
Hellmuth, Oscar 33, 89
Hemingway, Ernest 53
Hensel, Struve 254, 262-263
Hernandez, Aurelio 146, 151
Herrera, Luis Alberto 71-72
Hertzog, Enrique 183-192
Hillman, Sidney 138, 216
Hoffman, Paul 10, 152. 251-252, 257, 261, 268, 279, 281
Hoover, Herbert 5, 50, 76
Hoover, J. Edgar 34
Hoyar-Miller, Derek 277
Hull, Cordell 5-9, 28-32, 36-37, 89, 108, 153

Ibañez del Campo, Carlos 22, 300, 309
Instituto Argentino para la Promoción del Intercambio
(IAPI) 17-18, 63-67, 131-132, 138, 186, 219-220, 226, 238-240, 250, 268-269, 284, 303
International Emergency Food Commission (IEFC) 249
International Trade Organization (ITO) 9, 168, 174
Irigoyen, Hipólito 25
Italy 13, 26-27
Ivanissevich, Oscar 142, 217, 270

Jackson, Robert 255
Japan 10, 28
Junta de Vigilancia 107
Justicialismo 15, 21

Kaiser, Henry 14
Kennan, George 214
Korean War 300
Kunze, Edward 255-256

Labouisse, Henry 261
Larraín Moreno, Jaime 164, 173-174
Ledgard, C.E.B. 156, 194-195
Leeper, Reginald 114-119, 243
Lend-Lease 27, 30, 89
Lewis, John L. 137, 143, 158
Ley Mitre 113, 115, 117
Lomax, John 275-276
Lombardo Toledano, Vicente 141, 216
López Muñiz, Julio 162
Lord, Royal 133
Lovett, Robert 221, 261, 267
Luti, Luis 203

Magowan, John 214
Malbran-Eady Treaty 112-113
Mann, Thomas 90
María Eva Duarte de Perón Foundation
 148, 227
Maroglio, Orlando 259, 268-271, 285
Marshall, George 213-217, 245, 261,
 263, 283

Marshall Plan 9-10,213, 236, 249-263,
 274-281
Martin, William 268
McCabe, Thomas 268
McCarthy, Joseph 215.
Meade, Charles 273-274
Meany, George 83
Messersmith, George 79, 88, 92-93,
 96-97, 108-127, 142, 169-170, 184,
 199, 203-218, 302
Mexico 98, 204-205
Michanowski, George 83, 142, 154,
 157
Miller, Edward 231, 290-296, 302
Miranda, Miguel 1, 17, 20, 61, 65, 68-
 69, 113-119, 123-124, 164, 170-172,
 182, 185, 188, 191-192, 194-196,
 206, 212, 219-221, 223-226, 229,
 237, 239, 241-246, 249, 251-254,
 261, 265-272, 297
Miranda-Eady Treaty 117-119, 211,
 241
Moley, Raymond 5
Morgenthau, Henry 83
Morinigo, Higinio 75, 91, 102

Movimiento Nacionalista Revolutionario (MNR) 32, 103-104,
 188-189
Murray, Philip 136-137, 155
Mussolini, Benito 26, 132

National Industrial Recovery Act
 (NIRA) 5
National Labor Relations Board
 (NLRB) 135-136
Neal, Jack 52,
New Deal 5-7, 105, 135-138

Oakley, A. Kenneth 207-208
Oderigo, Hugo 193-196
Odría, Manuel 22, 197-198, 300-301,
 309
O'Konski, Alvin 215-217
Ortiz, Roberto 26-27

Paraguay 75, 102, 162
Patrón Costas, Ramon 29-30
Pawley, William 50, 283
Paz, Hipólito 291
Paz Estenssoro, Víctor 32, 72-74, 102-
 104, 183, 188-189, 300-301
Pearl Harbor 28
Peek, George 5
Perez Jimenez, Manuel 22
Perón, Eva 47-48, 70, 147-150, 220,
 222-223, 266-267, 269-270, 272,
 290, 293, 304-305
Perón, Juan Domingo 1-4, 15-19, 39-
 45, 111-112, 121-122, 123-127, 129,
 218, 286-289, 291, 295
 Army 25-26, 31, 222-231, 257, 304
 Economic Policy 65-67, 237-242,
 245, 303-304, 306
 Election 47-49, 52-58, 84-84
 Foreign Policy 19-22, 71-79, 100-
 104, 115-118, 161-201
 Labor 33-36, 138-146
Peru 193-198
Pinedo, Federico 27, 63
Potofsky, Jacob 83, 142, 154, 216,
 233, 296
Potsdam Conference 80
Prebisch, Raúl 27
Prestes, Luis 81
Prewitt, Virginia 167

Quijano, Hortensio 164

Ramírez, Pedro 30-31, 33
Rawson, Arturo 30
Ray, Guy 218-220, 227, 230, 247, 263,
   286-287, 299
Remorino, Jeronimo 274, 278, 284, 291-293, 295
Repetto, Nicolás 145.
Reuther, Walter 136-137
Reyes, Cipriano 34, 140, 236, 255
Ridgeway, Matthew 258
Roca-Runciman Treaty 112-113, 282
Rockefeller, Nelson 14, 37-38, 152
Rodríguez Larreta, Alberto 71
Roman Catholic Church 16-17
Romualdi, Serafino 70, 83, 128, 140-146, 150-152, 296
Roosevelt, Franklin 5-7, 36, 38-39, 105, 289
Roosevelt, Theodore 10
Rubber Development Corporation (RDC) 42-44
Ruiz-Guiñazú, Enrique 28

Savio, Manuel 224-225
Sawyer, Charles 278
Scarpati, Juan 284-285, 292
Schacht, Hjalmar 6, 66
Schaetzel, Robert 111
Silva, René 175
Smith, Gerald 207
Smoot-Hawley Tariff 108
Snyder, John 268
Sociedad de Beneficencia 149
Sociedades de Economía Mixta 61-62, 120, 130
Somoza, Anastasio 201
Sosa Molina, Humberto 223-231
"Southern Bloc" 18-22, 71-76, 101-04,
   208, 212
Soviet Union 80, 98-101, 178, 210-211, 215-217
Spaak, Paul-Henri 90
Stalin, Jozef 80, 132, 301
Stettinius, Edward 38
Storni, Segundo 30-31
Strange, Robert 260

Taft-Hartley Act 137-138, 143

Tamayo, Ernesto 73
Tamborini, José 49, 55, 57, 60, 80, 146
Tewksbury, Howard 206, 261, 274
Thorp, Willard 282
Tittmann, Harold 196-198
Trujillo, Rafael 82, 91, 200
Truman, Harry 78, 80, 98, 110, 137, 152, 155, 204-205, 208-209, 217, 256, 261, 263, 270

Unión Demócratica 49, 55-57, 60
Unión Industrial Argentina 67-68
Unión Telefónica 120-122, 130
United States
   Army 90-92, 208, 214-215, 246, 273
   Embargo 42-47, 89-92
Uruguay 51, 71-72, 102, 104

Vandenberg, Arthur 41, 88, 110, 215, 217, 270
Vargas, Getulio 74-75, 80, 101, 300
Venezuela 242, 277
Vergara, Roberto 173
Villarroel, Gualberto 32, 72-74, 102-104, 183, 194
Von Der Becke, Carlos 90

Wallace, Henry 83, 110-111, 233
Webb, James 277
Welles, Sumner 28-29, 41, 108
Western Hemisphere Defense Program (WHDP) 91-92
Woll, Matthew 151

Yacimientos Petrolíferos Fiscales (YPF) 229